MORALITY AND SOVEREIGNTY IN THE PHILOSOPHY OF HOBBES

Also by George Shelton

DEAN TUCKER:
Eighteenth-Century Economic and Political Thought

Morality and Sovereignty in the Philosophy of Hobbes

GEORGE SHELTON

St. Martin's Press　　New York

© George Shelton 1992

All rights reserved. For information, write:
Scholarly and Reference Division,
St. Martin's Press, Inc., 175 Fifth Avenue,
New York, N.Y. 10010

First published in the United States of America in 1992

Printed in Hong Kong

ISBN 0–312–08094–8

Library of Congress Cataloging-in-Publication Data
Shelton, George, 1927–
Morality and sovereignty in the philosophy of Hobbes / George Shelton.
p. cm.
Includes bibliographical references and index.
ISBN 0–312–08094–8
1. Hobbes, Thomas, 1588–1679.   I. Title.
B1248 . E7S54   1992
171 ' . 2—dc20   92–6301
                                                                        CIP

Which when Anacharsis understood, he laughed at it to see that Solon imagined with written laws to bridle men's covetousness and injustice. For such laws, said he, do rightly resemble the spider's cobwebs, because they take hold of little flies and gnats which fall into them, but the rich and mighty will break and run through them at their will. Solon answered him that men do justly keep all their covenants and bargains which one make with another, because it is to the hindrance of either party to break them, and even so he did so temper his laws that he made citizens know it was more for their profit to obey law and justice than to break it.

Plutarch, *Solon* (Thomas North translation)

For Mary
Who kept the home fires burning

Contents

Preface		viii
Note on References		x
1	Human Nature	1
2	The State of Nature and Natural Law	18
3	The Laws of Nature and Morality	41
4	Morality as Reciprocity	67
5	The Social Contract and the Golden Rule in Practice	85
6	Morality and Objectivity	98
7	The Nature of Hobbesian Morality	119
8	Hobbes and Kant	144
9	Contract Theory Today	165
10	Reason and Moral Relativity	184
11	Contract and the Commonwealth	205
12	Sovereign and Subject	226
13	Democracy and the Right of Revolution	246
14	The Nature of Sovereignty	272
15	Sovereignty and Constitutional Rights	294
Notes		310
Index		316

Preface

It is probably safe to say that the two most controversial areas in the philosophy of Hobbes are his theory of morality and his theory of sovereignty. Regarding the former, many critics do not think that he has such a theory, at least in the commonly accepted sense of the word. Those scholars who do, often attempt to give it a religious basis which the others reject as contrary to his whole outlook. The thesis I am putting forward is that Hobbes's originality lies not in his moral beliefs, which turn out to be quite traditional, but in the way he attempts to justify them. His method is to derive them by elementary logic from a couple of premises about human nature. Thus, if one accepts his premises and also the rules of logic, one is able to re-erect morality on a firmer foundation, without supernatural assistance. As I, myself, find his argument quite convincing, I believe it can be used just as effectively today as it was when he proposed it. Accordingly, I go on to test his theory against a number of modern alternatives, as well as the still influential moral philosophy of Kant.

In the case of sovereignty, it is my aim to demonstrate that because his theory works as well for sovereignty of the people as it does for the sovereignty of a monarch, it is incorrect to see in him a supporter of absolutism rather than of absolute sovereignty. However, since the concept of sovereignty itself is looked upon with suspicion by many critics, I try to defend it by using historical examples drawn mostly from American experience.

One of the main challenges in dealing with Hobbes is to extract from his words the meaning he intended them to have. As a result, I follow his text quite closely in those chapters where I am attempting to explicate what I believe his ideas actually are. One has to be constantly on guard against a number of problems: his tendency to exaggerate for the sake of effect, his occasional use of one word in two different senses, and possible changes in the meaning of words since the seventeenth century. Paying attention to context is extremely important if one hopes to avoid common misunderstandings. As he himself said in *Leviathan*:

> For it is not the bare words, but the scope of the writer, that giveth

the true light, by which any writing is to be interpreted; and they that insist upon single texts, without the main design, can derive nothing from them clearly . . . (602, 626)

Note on References

In order to avoid the unnecessary multiplication of footnotes, I have adopted the following procedures:

For works by authors other than Hobbes I give the first reference in a footnote and after that the page number in parentheses following the quotation. Where there is more than one title I add the name of the work.

For *Leviathan*, my quotations are from Volume III of *The English Work of Thomas Hobbes* edited by Sir William Molesworth (London, 1839). However, for the convenience of readers I have also provided the page number from the more accessible Penguin Classics paperback edition, edited by C. B. Macpherson (London, 1985). Thus all references from *Leviathan* appear as two numbers in parentheses after the passage quote as, for example, (72, 149).

Since the other Hobbes works which I have used are divided into sections, I have used the following forms:

The Elements of Law: (EL,II,7,4)
De Cive: (DC,3,16)
De Homine: (DH,I,3)

For works not included here, the volume number of Molesworth's edition is used after the reference as follows: (*English Works*, I,223).

1
Human Nature

Since any theory of morality rests on certain presuppositions about human nature, it is necessary to be clear as to what these are in any study of such a theory. In the case of Hobbes, the picture of man he presents has been subject to a certain amount of misunderstanding. Much of this, admittedly, is at least partially due to his language, the colourfulness and force of which can give the wrong impression. In order to see whether Hobbesian man is really all that different from ordinary human beings, I would like to take a fresh look at what he says on the subject, with the aim of clearing away possible misconceptions. As the controversial bits are scattered throughout the early chapters of the relevant works, I shall survey them briefly before moving on to his moral theory itself. Any study of Hobbesian morality which rests on a mistaken picture of his view of human nature risks being seriously flawed.

In *De Cive*'s Preface to the Reader, Hobbes states that as a result of his interest in philosophy, he had projected a study of its first elements in three parts. This plan was later fully realized but not in its logical order. *De Corpore*, which should have been first, appeared in 1655 and *De Homine*, which was intended to follow it, in 1658. However, the final part, *De Cive* itself, had already appeared in 1642, with a revised version in 1647. As is well known, the reason for its publication at that time was the Civil War raging in England. 'Therefore it happens that what was last in order, is yet come forth in time, and the rather, because I saw that grounded on its own principles sufficiently known in experience it would not stand in need of the former sections' (DC,Pref.). This passage is significant because Hobbes is such a system builder that there is a natural tendency to assume the later parts of it are derived from the earlier ones and to be critical if this connection appears not to hold up. The quotation shows quite clearly that he regarded his moral and political philosophy as a free-standing structure.

Nevertheless, it does rest on assumptions about human nature and these are developed at greater length in some of his other works. *The Elements of Law*, originally circulated privately in 1640, appeared, presumably without the author's participation, in two parts, *Human Nature* and *De Corpore Politico* shortly before Hobbes's return to England in 1651, as did a translation of *De Cive*, entitled *Philosophical Rudiments concerning Government and Society*, and *Leviathan* itself. Thus English readers had all three versions of his political thought available at more or less the same time. I have chosen to follow the text in *Leviathan*, adding references to the other works when appropriate. Although each of these books differs somewhat in emphasis and in the audience for which it was intended, I do not feel that the differences are significant for my purposes.

While the discussions concerning human nature in *Leviathan*, and the first thirteen chapters of *The Elements of Law*, as well as in the later *De Homine* are not absolutely essential, they are certainly helpful for the understanding of his moral and political theory. The same, unfortunately, cannot be said about the materialistic foundations of his system. There is the usual gap between the motions which originate in an object and eventually reach the brain via the sense organs on the one hand and the actual colours, sounds, etc., which are perceived on the other. The various forms of materialism, from the atomism of Democritus to the corpuscular vortices of Descartes, bring with them some form of what is often called the subjectivity of secondary qualities. This idea had great appeal in the seventeenth century and it became the basis of Lockean empiricism. But it was something of a Trojan Horse since it led also to the subjective idealism of Berkeley and the scepticism of Hume. Recent physicalists, knowing far more about the workings of the body than Hobbes did, have attempted to reduce mental activity completely to electro-chemical activity in the brain. No one doubts that there is a connection but it is just as difficult to understand today as it was for Descartes. That the colour yellow is produced by light of a certain wave length is an interesting fact. However, it is of little help in explaining the unique character of the colour as we individually perceive it. Other phenomena of the mind or heart such as pain and love are even more resistant to explanation. The most common response of physicalists to this problem has been to ignore it, on the ground that science will eventually solve it.

Hobbes seems unaware that there is a problem. Having established to his own satisfaction that reality is matter in motion, he attempts to show how this can account for more complex phenomena such as perception, memory, imagination and emotion. In this process he quickly and effortlessly slips over into a mentalistic vocabulary which implicitly accepts the existence of mind, together with its various operations, and proceeds from there. Thus his mechanistic materialism is, in the end, really no more than a personal opinion about the nature of the external world and it has very little relevance to his ideas about human nature. Its principal effect in practice has been to leave his moral philosophy open to attack by those for whom materialism has pejorative implications.

Hobbes's materialism also does not point him towards the most compatible type of psychology: some form of what was later to be known as behaviourism. Instead we find him defending, without embarrassment, the use of introspection. In *Leviathan*, after referring to the fashionable saying 'that *wisdom* is acquired, not by reading of *books*, but of *men*', he says that a better one is '*nosce teipsum, read thyself*'.

> [This is meant] to teach us, that for the similitude of the thoughts and passions of one man, to the thoughts and passions of another, whoever looketh into himself, and considereth what he doth, when he does *think, opine, reason, hope, fear*, etc. and upon what grounds; he shall thereby read and know, what are the thoughts and passions of all other men upon the like occasions. (xi, 82)

Furthermore, he actually rejects observation, by itself, as a satisfactory method of understanding human beings because we cannot see through their dissembling and misleading behaviour to what is in their hearts. 'And though by men's actions we do discover their design sometimes; yet to do it without comparing them with our own, and distinguishing all circumstances, by which the case may come to be altered, is to decipher without a key . . . ' One man can hope to do this only with the relatively few people he knows but 'he that is to govern a whole nation, must read in himself, not this or that particular man; but mankind'. Although this is not easy to do, Hobbes has set down his own reading in an orderly manner, so that 'the pains left another, will be only to consider, if he also find not the same in himself' (xii, 83). In other words, any generalizations he makes about human nature are drawn from a comparison of the behaviour of others with what he finds within himself. His moral and political theory thus originates in an unflinching examination of what goes on inside Thomas Hobbes and he asks only that his readers adopt the same method with themselves. Judging by their reactions over the years most of them are not prepared to follow him that far.

Despite the importance of introspection, Hobbes uses the idea of motion again to explain the origin of human passions which he does after a discussion of the senses, imagination, speech and reason – topics I shall set aside for the moment. There are in animals two sorts of motions: the vital motions such as the circulation of the blood, and motions, such as those of the limbs, which unlike the others, are 'first fancied in our minds'. If an animal motion is towards something, it is called appetite or desire, and in the other direction, aversion. We are said to love what we desire and hate that for which we have an aversion. This leads up to an extremely important definition: 'But whatsoever is the object of any man's appetite or desire, that is it which he for his part calleth *good*: and the object of his hate and aversion, *evil*' (41, 120). The terms are used here in what is clearly an individualistic sense. Hobbes does refer to the more traditional usage in *De Homine*, where he says that 'Aristotle hath well defined *good* as that which all men desire.' However, he adds that 'since different men desire and shun different things, there must be many things that are *good* to some and *evil* to others; so that what is *good* to us is *evil* to our enemies'. At the same time he admits that a common good is possible and 'it can rightfully be said of something, *it is commonly a good*, that is, useful to many, or good for the state' (DH,XI,4).

In *Leviathan* he amplifies his definitions of good and evil by referring to Latin words whose meaning is similar. 'So that of good there be three kinds: good in the promise, that is *pulchrum* [fair or attractive in some way]; good in effect, as the end desired, which is called *jucundum, delightful*; and good as the means which is called *utile, profitable*; and as many of evil . . . ' (41, 121). *Bonum* and *malum* are not mentioned because, as the Latin version confirms, these are the equivalents of the words he is defining. He concludes: '*Pleasure* therefore, or *delight*, is the appearance, or sense of good; and *molestation*, or *displeasure*, the appearance, or sense of evil' (42, 122). However, one should not jump to the conclusion that Hobbes is an ethical hedonist. Definitions of 'good', after all, take up no less than five pages of the *Oxford English Dictionary* and many of them are not obviously ethical. The roots of the word lie in the notions of fitting, suitable or pleasing. It expresses a value, but often a non-moral one, as when I say chocolate is good because eating it gives me pleasure. It is important to remember that 'good' has non-moral meanings since if one always treats Hobbes's use of it as ethical, one can end up with a very distorted idea of his moral theory.

The problem is that almost at once Hobbes raises doubts about this interpretation. The fact that 'these words of good, evil and contemptible, are ever used with relation to the person that useth them: there being nothing simply and absolutely so' need not disturb us since they simply reflect the reality that my taste is not the same as yours. But then, he adds in the same sentence, 'nor any common rule of good or evil, to be taken from the nature of the objects themselves; but from the person of the man, where there is no commonwealth; or in a commonwealth, from the person that representeth it; or from the arbitrator or judge, when one disagreeing shall by consent set up, and make his sentences the rule thereof' (41, 120). This seems strange on the face of it. If my good is something pleasing, delightful or profitable to me, and your good is the same for you, what need is there for anyone to enforce a common standard? Since a similar passage does not appear in the corresponding section of *The Elements of Law* (I,7), perhaps Hobbes had come to the conclusion that it was prudent to add an advance warning of the effect that the covenant would have on such an individualistic interpretation. Whatever his reason for doing so, he succeeded in giving the words a somewhat different meaning from what they had before. He is obviously thinking of situations in which one acts on the basis of one's own idea of good in a way that conflicts with that of another. If I like eating chocolate I call that good and if I enjoy hurting people, that also is, for me, good. However, since other people do not like being hurt, from the viewpoint of society the latter action is bad, not good. But this is obviously a deviation from the meaning he has been using and is out of place in a chapter devoted, not to the imperatives of conduct in a community, but to the passions, and its introduction here can easily lead to confusion.

Hobbes goes on to distinguish between the pleasures of sense and those of the mind which 'arise from the expectation that proceeds from foresight of the end, or consequence of things'. The latter is usually called joy and its opposite, grief. From these and the other so-called 'simple passions' – appetite, aversion, love, hate, etc., he derives a whole series of more complex passions, starting with hope, which he defines as 'an appetite, with an opinion of attaining'

(43, 122). An examination of these indicates that the Hobbesian conception of man is not all that different from the traditional one. For example, we have: 'Desire of good to another, BENEVOLENCE, GOOD WILL, CHARITY. If to man generally, GOOD NATURE' (43, 123) and *'Love* of persons for society, KINDNESS' (44, 123). Less satisfactory in the eyes of some critics is the following: *'Grief,* for the calamity of another, is PITY; and ariseth from the imagination that the like calamity may befall himself; and therefore is called COMPASSION' (47, 126). They object that he tries to give a selfish motive for a genuinely altruistic emotion. It was the slightly sharper version of this passage in *The Elements of Law* which called forth Bishop Butler's famous 'refutation'. What Hobbes really meant, on the basis of what he said later concerning the golden rule, is better expressed in *De Homine.*

> To grieve because of another's evil, that is, to feel another's pain and to suffer with him, that is, to imagine that another's evil could happen to oneself, is called compassion. And so those who have become accustomed to similar evils are more compassionate; and conversely. For evil that hath been less experienced one fears less. (DH,XII,10)

Since this raises one of the key questions concerning Hobbes's approach to ethics, it will be more fully considered later. However, it is worth quoting Alasdair MacIntyre on this subject since his response is not atypical:

> Aubrey has a story of how, outside St. Paul's Cathedral, an Anglican clergyman who had seen Hobbes give alms to a poor man tried to improve the occasion by asking of Hobbes (who was reputedly impious and atheistic) if he would have given the alms, had not Christ commanded it. Hobbes's reply was that he gave the alms because not only did it please the old man, but it pleased him to see the poor man pleased. Thus Hobbes tries to exhibit his own behavior as consistent with his theory of motives, namely that human desires are such that they are self-interested. The kind of lie told by Hobbes according to this anecdote is a kind of lie indulged in more often by philosophers than by other men, a lie told in the interests of saving the face of a theory. It remains a lie and a culpable lie, although one that Hobbes needed to tell.[1]

It seems to me that Hobbes was very much telling the truth when he said that he gave the alms because the action not only pleased the old man but pleased himself. He was merely stating the mixed motives behind feelings of compassion which, as we shall see, led Kant to deny its moral worth.

Another definition which has been found objectionable is the following: '*Contempt*, or little sense of the calamity of others, is that which men call CRUELTY; proceeding from the security of their own fortune. For, that any man should take pleasure in other men's great harms, without other end of his own, I do not conceive it possible' (47, 126). This has been used to show that just as Hobbes has no sense of disinterested good, he also has no comprehension of the possibility of disinterested evil, or sadistic behaviour for its own sake. However, his usage of the word 'cruelty' is not the common one of today: for him it was the opposite of pity, i.e. indifference to another's suffering, rather than a deliberate effort to cause suffering. Its origin in the same root as the word 'crude' is here evident. The equivalent passage in *The Elements of Law* is clearer: 'The contrary of pity is *Hardness* of heart proceeding either from slowness of imagination, or from extreme good opinion of their own exemption of the like calamity, or from hatred of all, or most men' (EL,I,9,10).

Hobbes has also been frowned upon for his apparently insensitive approach to laughter. In order to understand it one must first look at several other definitions.

> *Joy*, arising from imagination of a man's own power and ability, is that exultation of the mind which is called GLORYING: which if grounded upon the experience of his own former actions, is the same with *confidence*: but if grounded upon flattery of others; or only supposed by himself, for the delight in the consequences of it, is called VAIN-GLORY . . . *Sudden glory*, is the passion which maketh those *grimaces* called LAUGHTER; and it is caused either by some sudden act of their own, that pleaseth them; or by the apprehension of some deformed thing in another, by comparison whereof they suddenly applaud themselves. (45, 124)

This certainly presents an unflattering portrait of human beings and by itself, would support the judgement that Hobbes holds a 'base' view of them. But, as he immediately makes clear, not only is this just one type of laughter but also it is one of which he disapproves.

And it is incident most to them, that are conscious of the fewest abilities in themselves; who are forced to keep themselves in their own favour, by observing the imperfections of other men. And therefore much laughter at the defects of others, is a sign of pusillanimity. For of great minds, one of the proper works is, to help and free others from scorn; and compare themselves only with the most able. (46, 125)

He broadens his definition further in *The Elements* where, after noting that 'men take it heinously to be laughed at or derided', goes on to say: 'Laughter without offence, must be at absurdities and infirmities abstracted from persons, and where all the company may laugh together' (EL,I,9,13). Thus the well-known difference between laughing *at* and laughing *with* some one is fully recognized by Hobbes. The fact that he is ready to take note of our less attractive characteristics does not mean that he approves of them.

Having discussed the various emotions or forces within us which lead to action, Hobbes now has to consider the struggle which takes place among them before a decision to act in one way rather than another occurs. This is called deliberation according to him 'because it is a putting an end to the *liberty* we had of doing, or omitting, according to our own appetite, or aversion' (48, 127). His etymology is, of course, fanciful, as the word is actually derived from *librare*, to balance or weigh. This also makes more sense from his viewpoint since the liberty of 'doing or omitting' continues through the process of deliberation and only comes to an end when deliberation itself ceases and one alternative is chosen over another. '*Will* therefore *is the last appetite in deliberating*' (49, 128).

There has been considerable criticism of this formulation and it would, perhaps, have been more acceptable if he had chosen a word other than appetite. However, it is obvious from what he says elsewhere that he includes aversion, especially fear, and in general any form of motivation which is involved in making the final decision, including those which run counter to our immediate desires. The inclination which is found to have the most weight after the comparison which takes place in deliberation will tip the scale and decide the nature of the action which is initiated. The vexed question of free will versus determinism was explored at length by Hobbes in his exchanges with Bishop Bramhall. At this point I shall merely note his exasperation with what he regarded as the confusion in traditional attitudes as expressed in an earlier work.

Appetites, fear, hope, and the rest of the passions are not called voluntary; for they proceed not from but are the will; and the will is not voluntary. For a man can no more say that he will will, than he will will will, and so make an infinite repetition of the word will, which is absurd, and insignificant. (EL,I,12,5)

The language of passion and reason are not identical, but are similar. Hobbes states that 'all passions may be expressed *indicatively*; as I *love*, I *fear*' etc., whereas deliberation 'is expressed *subjunctively*; which is a speech proper to signify suppositions, with their consequences; as *if this be done, then this will follow* . . . ' (49, 128). The only difference is that the language of reasoning is general whereas that of deliberation is about particulars. This is quite significant since if deliberation is a form of reasoning, Hobbes has introduced reason into a process where its presence as an active agent has often been doubted. In fact, Hobbes's definition of will as the 'last appetite in deliberation', if taken literally, might appear to put him in the same camp as Hume who thought of reason as the slave of the passions. Hume's quite valid point is that reason should not be seen as a faculty which can be used to override desires and emotions rather than merely as a means of choosing between them. Hobbes had earlier gone into the origins of the word in the mundane art of bookkeeping.

> The Latins called accounts of money *rationes*, and accounting *ratiocinatio*; and that which we in bills or books of account call *items*, they call *nomina*, that is *names*; and thence it seems to proceed, that they extended the word *ratio* to the faculty of reckoning in all things. (25, 106)

Thus reason would have an important part to play in deliberation because the most likely outcome of various actions has to be calculated before a choice can be made. Reason would better be called a servant, not of the passions but of the man himself since it helps him to decide which of his motivations should be given the most weight. If he is moved to action by an emotion so powerful that it bypasses this process, he often lives to regret his 'thoughtlessness'.

In deliberation, then, we try to foresee 'the good and evil consequences, and sequels of the action whereof we deliberate', which depends on the 'foresight of a long chain of consequences, of which very seldom any man is able to see the end' (50, 129). We aim at the 'apparent or seeming good' and the extent to which we are successful in fulfilling our expectations will govern the degree to which we enjoy that 'continual prospering' he calls felicity. Thus the groundwork has been laid for an understanding of human behaviour. Everything we do or refrain from doing stems from a calculation of the likely effects on our well-being but, unfortunately, the ultimate goal of felicity is an ever-receding one, not attainable in this life. As he puts it in *De Homine*:

> For if the end be final, there would be nothing to long for, nothing to desire; whence it follows not only that nothing would itself be a good from that time on, but also that man would not even feel. For all sense is conjoined with some appetite or aversion; and not to feel is not to live. For of goods, the greatest is always progressing towards even further ends with the least hindrance. (DH,XI,15)

Hobbes's treatment of 'discourse', or the quest for knowledge, is similar to that he adopted for the passions.

> And that which is alternate appetite, in deliberating concerning good and evil; the same is alternate opinion, in the enquiry of the truth of *past*, and *future*. And as the last appetite in deliberation, is called the *will*; so the last opinion in search of the truth of past, and future, is called the JUDGMENT, or *resolute* and *final sentence* of him that *discourseth*. (52, 130)

As the sequence of alternating appetite is called deliberation, so the sequence of alternating opinions is called, by him, doubt.

> No discourse whatsoever, can end in absolute knowledge of fact, past, or to come. For, as for the knowledge of fact, it is originally, sense; or ever after, memory. And for the knowledge of consequence, which I have said before is called science, it is not absolute, but conditional. (52, 131)

Man cannot know absolutely i.e. that this is or has been; he can only know that if this is, that is, etc. The conditional nature of discourse parallels the subjunctive mood in which deliberation is expressed. Although he does not put it this way, he is obviously differentiating what is often called practical reason from theoretical or speculative reason.

We have still not touched more than the fringes of morality in its strictest sense but the title of the next chapter is encouraging since it includes the word 'virtues'.

> VIRTUE generally, in all sorts of subjects, is somewhat that is valued for eminence: and consisteth in comparison. For if all things were equal in all men, nothing would be prized. And by *virtues intellectual*, are always understood such abilities of the mind, as men praise, value and desire should be in themselves; and go commonly under the name of a *good wit* . . . (56, 134)

Thus we seem again to be dealing with a term which often has a specifically ethical content but here means simply excellence, merit or distinction. There are two kinds of wit. 'Natural wit' is what we would probably call intelligence but used broadly so as to include a fertile imagination, good judgment and discretion. 'As for *acquired wit*, I mean acquired by method and instruction, there is none but reason . . . ' (61, 138).

A concept which is important for our purposes and is one of the traditional virtues, is discussed in this chapter as well as elsewhere.

> When the thoughts of a man, that has a design in hand, running over a multitude of things, observes how they conduce to that design; or what design they may conduce unto; if his observations be such as are not easy, or usual, this wit of his is called PRUDENCE; and depends on much experience, and memory of like things, and their consequences heretofore. (60, 137)

He had already introduced the subject in Chapter III, where he said: 'Sometimes a man desires to know the event of an action; and then he thinketh of some like action past, and the events thereof one after another; supposing like events will follow like actions'. This is called *'foresight*, and *prudence*, or *providence'* (14, 97). The more experience he has had, the more prudent he will usually be. Since, however, the future is unknown or a 'fiction', as he calls it, even the most experienced can have no certainty and prudence could just as well be called presumption. In *The Elements of Law* he puts it another way.

> The remembrance of the succession of one thing to another, that is, of what was antecedent, and what was consequent, and what

> concomitant is called an experiment . . . To have had many experiments, is that we call EXPERIENCE, which is nothing else but remembrance of what antecedents have been followed with what consequents . . . (I,4,6) Experience concludeth nothing universally . . . And PRUDENCE is nothing else but conjecture from experience, or taking signs from experience warily . . . (I,4,10)

Experience is, of course, the key factor in deliberation. The more experience one has had in the past, the more likely one's judgment about the possible impact of one's potential actions will be correct and the more likely the action embarked upon after deliberation will turn out to have been the most prudent choice.

The cause of the difference in 'wits' between individuals is the passions, especially 'the more or less desire of power, of riches, of knowledge, and of honour', the last three of which are merely other forms of power.

> And therefore, a man who has no great passion for any of these things; but is, as men term it, indifferent; though he may be so far a good man, as to be free from giving offence; yet he cannot possibly have either a great fancy, or much judgment. For the thoughts are to the desires, as scouts and spies, to range abroad, and find the way to the things desired: all steadiness of the mind's motion, and all quickness of the same, proceeding from thence: for as to have no desire, is to be dead, so to have weak passions, is dullness . . . (61, 139)

Two important points are made in this passage. One is that not all men feel the desire for power equally. This disposes of the notion, which Hobbes seems to encourage elsewhere and which has been advanced by some critics, that all men are alike in their endless and insatiable quest for power. In addition to those dull persons who suffer from weak passions, others have passions indifferently for every thing, which he calls 'giddiness', or an excessive passion for one thing, which he regards as madness. The other point is his use of the word 'good' in a more ethical sense than heretofore, as applied to a person who does not give offence.

In Chapter X, 'Of Power, Worth, Dignity, Honour, and Worthiness', Hobbes moves from the desire for power to its content. Natural power consists of the qualities of body and mind which give us eminency over others, and instrumental power which flows from the natural and takes the form of riches, reputation, friends and good fortune generally. Significantly, he says: 'The greatest of human powers, is that which is compounded of the powers of most men, united by consent, in one person, natural, or civil, that has the use of all their powers depending on his will; such as is the power of a commonwealth: or depending on the wills of each particular; such as is the power of a faction or of divers factions leagued' (74, 150). He thus puts his finger on the key to political organization: one person can multiply his power by acquiring friends, servants, followers and consenting subjects.

In his treatment of worth occurs a passage used by C. B. Macpherson to defend his thesis[2] that Hobbes is an exponent of a bourgeois ideology: 'The *value*, or WORTH of a man, is as of all other things, his price ... And as in other things, so in men, not the seller, but the buyer determines the price' (76, 151). The idea that there is something specifically bourgeois about references to money equivalents is a tempting over-simplification but it is important to note that since the invention of money, practically everything has had its price, including human beings in slave-owning societies. Furthermore, it is especially hard to see how a Marxist interpretation is helpful in this particular context since the illustrations given are of a general being worth more in time of war than peace, and an uncorrupt judge in peace than in war. When he goes on to say that the 'manifestation of the value we set on one another, is that commonly called honouring, and dishonouring', we are being prepared for a long discussion of coats of arms and aristocratic titles, which are much more relevant to a feudal than a bourgeois society.

Another example of the sort of statement which can lead to misunderstanding, if taken out of context, is the following: 'Covetousness of great riches, and ambition of great honours, are honourable; as signs of the power to obtain them. Covetousness, and ambition, of little gains, or preferments, is dishonourable' (80, 156). This sounds as if Hobbes is expressing his personal moral judgement but he is merely describing the mores of his own society. Just as in the past the adulteries of Zeus and the thefts of Hermes were praised by Homer, so in his day private duels were honourable despite their illegality, and would remain so 'till such time as there shall be honour ordained for them that refuse, and ignominy for them that make the challenge' (81, 157).

When he talks about worthiness as fitness or aptitude, we are given a foretaste of things to come.

> Again, a man may be worthy of riches, office, and employment, that nevertheless, can plead no right to have it before another; and therefore cannot be said to merit or deserve it. For merit presupposeth a right, and that the thing deserved is due by promise: of which I shall say more hereafter, when I shall speak of contracts. (84, 160)

Since there has been considerable controversy over Hobbes's use of the word 'right', this passage is quite helpful. It makes clear that for him a claim to have a right is not enough. What is necessary to justify a right is a previous promise, usually in the form of a contract.

Under the seemingly innocuous title, 'Of the Differences of Manners', Chapter XI introduces a number of quite important questions.

> By MANNERS, I mean not here, decency of behaviour; as how one should salute another, or how a man should wash his mouth, or pick his teeth before company, and such other points of the *small morals*; but those qualities of mankind, that concern their living together in peace, and unity. (85, 160)

Thus he differentiates morality proper from mere etiquette. But instead of going on to discuss the content of morality, he goes back to psychology, beginning with felicity. Given the nature of man there can be no *finis ultimus* or *summum bonum*, since the pursuit of felicity leads to 'a perpetual and restless desire for power after power, that ceaseth only in death' (85, 161). This he calls a 'general inclination of all mankind' but, since he has already said that some people have a much weaker desire for power than others and has just finished referring to 'the diversity of passions, in divers men', it is clear that this 'general inclination of all mankind' occurs in varying degrees and is not an absolute. Furthermore, the contention caused by this desire for power is opposed by another characteristic of man.

> Desire of ease, and sensual delight, disposeth men to obey a common power: because by such desires, a man doth abandon

the protection that might be hoped for from his own industry, and labour. Fear of death, and wounds, disposeth to the same; and for the same reason. On the contrary, needy men, and hardy, not contented with their present condition; as also, all men that are ambitious of military command, are inclined to continue the causes of war; and to stir up trouble and sedition: for there is no honour military but by war; nor any such hope to mend an ill game, as by causing a new shuffle. (86, 161)

Two important qualifications to Hobbes's general theory as familiar from later passages in the book emerge here. One is that although most men are prepared to submit to a common authority for various reasons, *some* men are not, and prefer to face the risks of the 'state of nature'. The argument has been used against Hobbes that not everyone may want to participate in the formation of a commonwealth. In this part of *Leviathan*, at least, Hobbes agrees. He also offers here a reason why some men are prepared to risk everything in sedition: the reshuffling of the deck caused by a breakdown in law and order might create new opportunities for them.

The second qualification is revealing. Among the motives that incline a man to obey a common power, Hobbes offers first a desire for ease and protection for the products of his industry. Only then does that fear of death, which is emphasized so much later on, appear. Desire for knowledge and for leisure round out the list. Fear of death takes up a single sentence and is given no prominence whatsoever: it is merely one of a number of reasons people covenant together.

However, this should not be seen as an inconsistency threatening the structural simplicity of his contract theory. He is speaking here of factors which incline people to obey an already established power. Civil society provides many benefits in addition to that of basic security, and their value is discussed again later in the book. However, as far as his own theory is concerned, he is required to be a minimalist.

Hobbes then touches on another kind of behaviour which does not fit easily into the self-preservation stereotype. Desire for praise can lead to laudable actions which please those whose judgment we value. This applies to our wish for fame after death. By then our ultimate fate renders it insignificant, 'yet is not such fame vain; because men have a present delight therein, from the foresight of it, and of the benefit that may redound thereby to their posterity; which though they now see not, yet they imagine; and any thing that is pleasure to the sense, the same also is pleasure in the imagination' (87, 162). Thus our present pleasure can be extended into the future through the imagination. This opens the door for all kinds of actions, including self-sacrifice, which may cause present pain or even death, yet can still be fitted into an apparently hedonistic scheme because of our capacity for mental enjoyment in the present based on anticipation of the future. This is important because it is another refutation of those critics who believe he places too much emphasis on immediate gratification of the senses. Hobbes's desire for theoretical simplicity does not mean he is simple-minded. He is more aware than most people of the variety and complexity of human nature.

A fault shared by many of us is ignorance 'of the causes and original constitution of right, equity, law, and justice . . . ' This inclines us to take for right or wrong what is commonly considered such by custom, 'or, as the lawyers which only use this false measure of justice barbarously call it, a precedent . . . ' We behave like children who 'have no other rule of good and evil manners, but the correction they receive from their parents and masters' except that men do not even follow that rule but, 'appeal from custom to reason, and from reason to custom, as it serves their turn . . . which is the cause, that the doctrine of right and wrong, is perpetually disputed, both by the pen and the sword: whereas the doctrine of lines and figures, is not so; because men care not, in that subject, what be truth, as a thing which crosses no man's ambition, profit or lust' (91, 165). If a theorem of geometry adversely affected some men's interests, Hobbes had no doubt that attempts would be made to suppress it.

For the first time we find words being used in a context which looks unquestionably ethical. The assumption is that there *are* fixed standards of right and wrong but that in practice people either unthinkingly follow the mores of society as embodied in custom or the legal system, or they unscrupulously utilize whatever means come to hand, whether these be based on custom or reason, to justify their actions. His reference to geometry implies that until people are convinced that the truths of morality are as demonstrable as those of Euclid, it will continue to be a prey to man's 'ambition, profit or lust'.

This brief survey of Hobbes's conception of man, if looked at impartially, indicates that his ethical standards are not essentially different from those of the average person. The contention that they are base or inferior rests heavily on what has been regarded as his cynicism. I am sure he believed he was merely being realistic. He does not claim that people act only from selfish motives and he does not deny the possibility of altruism. But he does view us as we are and not as we would like to see ourselves. Wishful thinking is a poor foundation for an effective ethical theory. Hobbes describes what he sees, bluntly and without sentimentality. If that is a fault then we would have to jettison some of our favourite novels, since the comedy of manners is based on mankind's foibles and pretentions. If we do not condemn Jane Austen for her ability to 'see through' people and create characters who are amusing precisely because she makes clear the self-serving motivation behind their actions, why should we criticize Hobbes for being equally clear-eyed?

It was not in Hobbes's interest to describe human beings as egocentric monsters. In order to justify obedience to the sovereign he had to start with people as they are. If they were, in reality, much better than that, he would not have had to work so hard. Furthermore, he did not believe that all people are alike; there are similarities but there also are differences. An important difference is that some are nicer than others. But a system of morality designed with only them in mind would hardly be feasible. Such a system must take into consideration the bad as well as the good. Finally, much stress has been placed on what is supposed to be Hobbes's radical individualism. In fact, as we have seen, his people live in an intensely social setting, full of the clash of competing interests. Wealth is important but so are status and reputation. We need others to recognize our wealth and our influence in order to make them worthwhile. Nevertheless we are individuals, individual centres of pleasure and pain, of joy and sorrow. For theoretical purposes the individual must be abstracted from the group; he or she must be studied as a person in order for us to better understand society. And that is what Hobbes has tried to do.

2
The State of Nature and Natural Law

Having set the stage, Hobbes now starts moving towards the heart of his thesis in Chapter XIII, 'Of the Natural Condition of Mankind as Concerning Their Felicity, and Misery'. He regards men as equal by nature, at least in the sense of physical vulnerability, since it is not difficult for even a relatively weak person to kill someone else no matter how strong or clever. 'From this equality of ability, ariseth equality of hope in the attaining of our ends.' The result is that 'if one plant, sow, build, or possess a convenient seat, others may probably be expected to come prepared with forces united, to dispossess, and deprive him, not only of the fruit of his labour, but also of his life, or liberty'. Since the invader is liable to the same fate, the circumstances breed fear and 'diffidence'. In such a situation 'there is no way for any man to secure himself, so reasonable, as anticipation; that is, by force or wiles, to master the persons of all men he can, so long, till he see no other power great enough to endanger him . . . ' (111, 184). This is essentially a state of war; although fighting may not be continuous, the disposition to fight is always there. It is under these inhospitable conditions that life can be described as 'solitary, poor, nasty, brutish and short' (113, 186).

Now since it is so easy to oversimplify and misunderstand Hobbes, it is necessary to note carefully what he actually said. Invaders *'may probably be expected'* to seize the property of others and thus there is nothing 'so *reasonable*, as anticipation' [emphasis added]. Not all individuals necessarily want to behave in a hostile fashion, but as long as some of them might, it is only rational to expect the worst and take appropriate action. If those who 'otherwise would be glad to be at ease within modest bounds, should not by invasion increase their power' (112, 185), they would not long survive. As he puts it in *De Cive*, 'for though the wicked were fewer than the righteous, yet because we cannot distinguish them, there is a necessity of suspecting, heeding, anticipating, subjugating, self-defending, ever incident to the most honest and fairest conditioned' (DC,Pref.). Thus aggression becomes, perforce, the norm. It is clear, that he does not see *all* men as jungle animals; the fact that *some* are, is sufficient to create the conditions he describes.

Hobbes admits that all this is inference based on his analysis of the passions, but for someone who wants confirmation from experience, Hobbes suggests he has only to look at his own behaviour. Even though he knows there are laws and officers to protect him, does he not bolt his doors at night and lock away his valuables? Does he not accuse mankind as much by his actions as Hobbes does by his words? But, the philosopher hastens to add, neither of them accuses man's nature. 'The desires, and other actions of man, are in themselves no sin. No more are the actions, that proceed from these passions, till they know a law that forbids them . . . ' (114, 187).

Although Hobbes generally emphasizes fear or diffidence in outlining man's motivation under such conditions, it is important, again, to note what he actually says. 'So that in the nature of man, we find three principal causes of quarrel. First, competition; secondly, diffidence; thirdly, glory. The first maketh men invade for gain; the second, for safety; and the third, for reputation.' The first two fit in with what was said above: there are those who want to take what is not theirs and those who have to defend themselves by adopting much the same behaviour. However, his third factor is a little different. The idea that we are driven by a need for 'trifles, as a word, a smile, a different opinion' (112, 185) implies an ordered society already in existence: much like that in which Hobbes lived. Concern for reputation would appear to be a luxury one could not afford in the harsh world of isolated individuals he is describing, whereas it seems quite natural within a social structure which provides rewards and punishments through a hierarchy of status. All three motives function within such a society but it is difficult to see how 'glory' could be relevant outside it.

Even though Hobbes has not so far in *Leviathan* used the phrase 'state of nature', (it is used at the end of Chapter I of *De Cive* as equivalent to the state of war) that is obviously what he is talking about; and in order to clarify such puzzles as the above it is necessary to make a distinction that Hobbes himself does not make. Like most political philosophers who use this idea, he talks sometimes as if it is historical and other times as if it is merely a useful fiction. Thus, in order to eliminate a potential source of confusion I want to make explicit what is only implicit in his discussion: he is really discussing two different states of nature, one of which is the *real* state of nature and the other, the *hypothetical* state of nature.

The first must be defined very broadly since it covers so many actual or possible situations. If we start with political life as it exists in the present, then those who are 'without a common power to keep them all in awe' (113, 185), are in a real state of nature. Hobbes gives three examples: sovereigns in relation to one another, subjects of a sovereign who has lost the power to protect them due to civil war, and primitive people, like those in America, who have no government beyond that of the family. One could easily expand this concept to include much of what goes on within a commonwealth. Since all our actions are not regulated, it is possible for us to be extremely unpleasant to each other without breaking the law. Hobbes recognizes this later on when he distinguishes between sin and crime. To the extent that the authorities do not intervene at this level it can be claimed that we are living in a state of nature all the time.

Although the government can punish crime, it cannot always prevent it, no matter how efficient the policing. If we accept that small children, the mentally handicapped and the mentally ill are not always fully responsible for their actions, they remain to some extent in a state of nature. Furthermore, since even those who may have entered freely into a political body, and are good citizens, retain the right of self-defense if their lives or physical freedom are threatened, it can be seen how pervasive the real state of nature is, partially or potentially, even in an ideal polity. It is, of course, only the extreme case, resulting from complete breakdown of law and order, that Hobbes wants to, and indeed can, do something about.

However, the state of nature which Hobbes needs for his theoretical purposes is entirely different. The distinction is blurred because he uses examples of the real state of nature to illustrate what the hypothetical one would be like. It is important to understand, because there has been so much confusion on this point, that the hypothetical state of nature not only has *never* occurred historically, but it also *cannot* occur. The reason for this is that man is imagined to be living in a condition which is impossible in reality. As Hobbes puts it in *De Cive*: 'Let us return again to the state of nature, and consider men as if but even now sprung out of the earth, and suddenly (like mushrooms) come to full maturity, without all kind of engagement to each other' (DC,VIII,1). Earlier, in the Preface, he had said that he would treat civil governments 'as if they were dissolved'. The 'as if' in both passages tells us that the state of nature here is purely hypothetical. He is abstracting the individual not only from state and society but even from his parental family, without whom he could not be present in the first place. Hobbes is trying to do what Galileo did when he calculated the trajectory of a projectile in an airless environment. Just as a real cannon ball does not travel through a physical vacuum, so a real human being does not live in a social vacuum.

Because the ebb and flow of history had cast up many different types of social and political organizations, it was difficult to draw from the real world the kind of obligation that Hobbes required to support the strong form of government which he felt was so desperately needed. He thus had to derive such obligation from the imperatives of human nature by performing a sort of mental experiment. How would a man have to behave if he woke up one morning to find that all political structures had vanished during the night? Hobbes used this idea explicitly in his *De Corpore*, (English Works, I, 92), where he has a man imagine that the physical world has been annihilated. The closest example of this situation one could find in real life would probably be a group of shipwreck survivors who, after landing on their desert island, would have to create some kind of political structure almost immediately. However, since they presumably came from the same ship and were already parts of a pre-existing social structure, they would not be the completely isolated individuals his theory requires. Robinson Crusoe and Friday would be closer, but a two-person society has limited possibilities. Better examples of what is involved would be clubs, companies and other voluntary organizations, which are set up by persons with common interests. These require some form of constitution which lays down the rules governing the relationships of the members. Such corporations, however, are usually found only within an established commonwealth and do not possess the power over life and death which is characteristic of the state.

Hobbes unfortunately does not keep the theoretical state of nature, completely abstract as it is, distinct from the real states of nature which he had to use for purposes of exposition. As a result, he falls easily into contradictions, such as those illustrated in the following passage from *De Cive*.

The foundation therefore which I have laid standing firm, I demonstrate in the first place, that the state of men *without* civil society (which state we may properly call the state of nature) is nothing else but a mere war of all against all; and in that war all men have equal right unto all things; next, that all men as soon as they arrive to understanding of this hateful condition, *do desire* (even nature itself compelling them) to be freed from this misery. But that this cannot be done except by compact, they all quit that right they have to all things. Furthermore I declare, and confirm what the nature of compact is; how and by what means the right of one *might be transferred* unto another to make their compacts valid; also what rights, and to whom they *must necessarily be granted* for the establishing of peace . . . (DC,Preface; emphasis added.)

The last two of the phrases which I have italicized, 'might be transferred' and 'must necessarily be granted', indicate that the transactions described are conditional in some way. On the other hand, when he writes '*do* desire to be freed' instead of 'would' or 'must desire to be freed', he has moved from the hypothetical to the real. As a result of this tendency to slip back and forth between the two states of nature, Hobbes has to be read very carefully in order to avoid misunderstanding.

The first italicized word in the above quotation exposes another area of potential trouble. Hobbes talks of 'the state of men *without* civil society', which is correct in the hypothetical context. However, he was not always so scrupulous. For example, again in *De Cive*, he says: 'Nature hath given every one a right to all; that is, it *was* lawful for every man in the bare state of nature, or *before* such time as men had engaged themselves by an covenants or bonds, to do what he would . . . ' (DC,I,10; emphasis added). The italicized words imply that these events have actually occurred. Hobbes has slipped from logical priority to temporal priority. That he ran into this difficulty is not surprising since it is almost impossible to handle an imaginary situation which has such close parallels to real ones without doing the same.

This distinction can be extremely useful in understanding many of the apparent contradictions that arise in his writings. One of these appears in Chapter XIII of *Leviathan*, which we have been discussing. When describing man's natural condition as one of war in which force and fraud are the cardinal virtues, Hobbes says: 'The notions of right and wrong, justice and injustice have there no place. They are qualities that relate to men in society, not in solitude' (115, 188). Yet in the next chapter he makes such statements as: 'Covenants entered into by fear, in the condition of mere nature, are obligatory' i.e. it would be wrong to break them (126, 198).

As far as the words justice and injustice are concerned, one can easily make a case that they are intimately linked to law, which requires a legislator. To say that in the absence of a legislator and a body of law, there is no justice or injustice is not controversial at all, so long as the words are used in a technical sense. But the same certainly cannot be said of right and wrong. A solution to this problem can be found by differentiating between the two states of nature. In the hypothetical one men exist in solitude, even though they are surrounded by other men, because lack of mutual trust keeps them apart. Although there is a collection of individuals, they remain solitaries until they have consented to form a society. Few would object to the idea that moral obligations only arise when two or more people are found in a context which is genuinely social. A hermit may abuse his body by excessive drinking, and some might consider that wrong as Hobbes concedes elsewhere, but it is obviously a special use of the word since it hurts no one but himself. Thus when Hobbes contends that right and wrong are qualities that 'relate to men in society, not in solitude', he is merely saying that outside of society morality has, at the very least, a different meaning than it does inside.

When, in the following chapter, Hobbes goes on at some length about what is permissible in the state of nature, my suggestion is that he has now slipped over into a real state of nature, which if it has not actually existed, *could* have existed. All this would be clearer if he had admitted a theoretical distinction between the large and relatively sophisticated commonwealth in which he was interested, and smaller social and political units. For the purposes of his argument, all that was necessary was the hypothetical state of nature and the seventeenth-century kingdom, which appeared to be its only practicable alternative at the time. However, he could not avoid talking about other types of social organization along the way because he had to defend his position by referring to the behaviour of people in actual rather than imaginary situations. Nevertheless, he did so reluctantly, since an examination of the historical evolution of the state from more primitive entities might not help and, indeed, might hinder his case for the absolute sovereignty which he thought was required.

Getting back to the argument of *Leviathan*, we find that having delineated in the starkest terms the horrors of a condition in which 'every man is enemy to every man' Hobbes is prepared to show us the way out. 'The passions that incline men to peace, are fear of death; desire of such things as are necessary for commodious living; and a hope by their industry to obtain them.' Although fear of death is first on the list this time, it is still just one of three reasons for abandoning the state of nature. Since, in the previous paragraph he had noted that in such a situation, 'there can be no propriety [property], no dominion, no *mine* and *thine* distinct', the need for laws to establish and preserve property rights is a major factor in making this decision. Thus we are driven by our passions to seek peace and 'reason suggesteth convenient articles of peace' (116, 188). These are the laws of nature.

Hobbes starts with definitions:

> The RIGHT OF NATURE, which writers commonly call *jus naturale*, is the liberty each man hath, to use his own power, as he will himself, for the preservation of his own nature; . . . A LAW OF NATURE, *lex naturalis*, is a precept or general rule, found out by reason, by which man is forbidden to do that which is destructive of his life. . . . For though they that speak of this subject, use to confound *jus*, and *lex*, *right* and *law*: yet they ought to be distinguished. (116,189)

The distinction Hobbes makes here between *jus naturale* and *lex naturalis* is another one of his attempts to clarify a question of terminology which had become somewhat murky over the centuries. As usual, his solution was not widely accepted. The majority opinion is probably that he either twisted the traditional idea of natural law out of all recognition, or else that it was extraneous to the thrust of his argument and should have been dispensed with altogether. To take the last point first, I think that natural law was so much a part of the political vocabulary of the time that he had little choice but to use it; Grotius before him and Locke after him did so and the fact that it remained current until at least the end of the eighteenth century is surely a testament to its continuing power of persuasion. As for his relationship to the natural law tradition – before that can be assessed one must take a sharper look at it than do most of his critics.

First of all, it is necessary to do what Hobbes did, and differentiate between *lex* and *ius* (or *jus*). A problem for those who speak English has always been that where there are two words in Latin and most other languages, one word usually serves in English. That word, 'law', leads to confusion because it blurs or obliterates the difference that does exist between these two words. This is not to deny that a degree of ambiguity is present in the other languages as well. Since law to quote Salmond, 'arises from the union of justice and force, of right and might',[1] there is bound to be disagreement about the exact proportion of each present in any statements on the subject.

In Roman times, the word *lex* was used for an enacted law and is often distinguished from other forms by calling it a statute. The rule of the road is the usual modern example of law as regulation. *Ius*, on the other hand, has a broader meaning, since it referred to law in general as in *ius civile*. The word for justice, *iustitia*, indicates that there was always a moral aspect in *ius*, which is largely lacking in *lex*. This rather protean word could thus include a number of related meanings including what is right and also *a* right, although in Roman private law a right was attached to its reciprocal obligation so closely that its separate existence was not emphasized. In any case, *ius* carried within itself a moral as well as a legal element, whereas in the case of *lex*, any moral significance is conferred from outside by the authority which promulgated it, whether human or divine. It is thus possible to imagine a *lex* or statute which is unjust but less easy to so do with *ius*, since justice is implicit in the concept. One way of putting it which often occurs in books on the subject is that *lex* is right because it is law and *ius* is law because it is right.

When we move from law as such to natural law, there are further complications. Although the idea of a universal law lying behind the man-made rules of individual states was put forward in Greece long before the time of the Stoics, it was their version which passed into Roman thought through the writings of Cicero. In his *De Re Publica* (III,22) he says: 'There is in fact a true law [*lex*] namely, right reason – which is in accordance with nature, applies to all men, and is unchangeable and eternal . . . [It is] binding at all times upon all people; and there will be, as it were, one common master and ruler of men, namely God, who is the author of this law, its interpreter and its sponsor.' (Sabine trans.) In the *De Legibus* (I,6) he adds that 'the origin of justice [*iuris*] is to be found in law [*lex*], for law is a natural force; it is . . . the standard by which Justice and Injustice are measured' (Keyes trans.). Cicero thus derives justice or right from a superior law for which he uses the word *lex*. If the code of a state violates this law, its precepts 'no more deserve to be called laws than the rules a band of robbers might pass in their assembly' (*De Leg.*, II,5). Although this notion had revolutionary implications with which Hobbes later had to contend, in Cicero's case it was largely rhetorical since he had no argument with the status quo.

However, the emphasis was somewhat different, as one might expect, when the idea was utilized by the jurists responsible for the opinions collected in the *Digest* and *Institutes* of the *Corpus Iuris Civilis* published by Justinian in 533 AD The earliest reference to natural law is found in the *Institutes* of Gaius (161 AD) where it appears as *ius* rather than *lex*, and where his *ius naturale* is not distinguished from *ius gentium*, the law of nations. This points up the fact that the concept of natural law really combines two ideas: what all legal systems had in common, as opposed to their differences, and the belief that these similarities represented a higher or divine law. Because the latter was not as significant for the jurists as it was for Cicero they found the distinction between the two difficult to maintain. As A. J. Carlyle puts it: 'Cicero is thinking of [natural law] as a part of the eternal law of God, while Gaius is only thinking of law in relation to this world'.[2]

A distinction was later made by Ulpian and several other jurists, but their version of natural law was different again. It accepted slavery as part of the *ius gentium* but not of the *ius naturale*. Originally all men were free but with the advent of warfare came slavery, a condition which was recognized by the law of all nations. Here *ius naturale* is associated with a golden age in the past, but although, contrary to Aristotle, slavery was no longer considered 'natural', it was accepted as legitimate in the contemporary world. For example, just a few pages after Ulpian (referring to slaves) says: 'All of which originated from the *ius gentium*, since, of course, everyone would be born free by the natural law . . . ' (*Dig*, I.1.4), we find Tryphoninus discussing a testamentary disposition whereby a female slave was to be freed if she bore three children: 'She bore one child at the first birth but triplets at the second. The question is whether any and if so which of the triplets is free' (*Dig*, I.5.15). The problem arose because the status of the child was determined by that of its mother and she would be emancipated during the delivery. The answer was that as triplets do not emerge from the womb all at once but in sequence, the first two would be slaves and the last one free. This example gives the flavour of the *Digest* much better than the few references to *ius naturale*. However, the latter was technically useful when indicating something that is normally outside the jurisdiction of civil law.

'By the law of nature [*naturali jure*] these things are common to mankind – the air, running water, the sea, and consequently the shores of the sea. No one, therefore, is forbidden to approach the seashore, provided that he respects habitations, monuments, and buildings, which are not, like the sea, subject only to the law of nations [*iuris gentium*]' (*Inst.*, II,1,1). Note the casually expressed equivalence of the law of nature and the law of nations. A different usage is seen in a distinction made between the treatment of adopted and natural children, which is considered 'very proper, for the civil law cannot destroy natural rights; children cannot cease to be sons or daughters, grandsons or granddaughters, by ceasing to be *sui heredes*' (*Inst.*, III,1,11). As often happens, the same word – *iura* – is here translated once as law and once as rights.

When we move from the lawyers to the Church fathers, we find a return to the terminology of Cicero. In Romans II,1,15, St. Paul had said that 'when Gentiles which have no law do by nature the things of the law, these, having no law are a law unto themselves; in that they show the work of the law written in their hearts . . . ' This law '*scriptum in cordibus suis*' was equated with natural law as defined by Cicero and his predecessors. As a result St. Ambrose and St. Augustine, among others, referred to it as *lex naturalis*. This usage predominated among the scholastics except where the context is specifically legal. In the *Summa Theologica* of St. Thomas, for example, we find: 'natural law [*lex naturalis*] is nothing else than the participation of the eternal law [*legis aeternae*] in rational creatures' (I–II, qu.91, art.2). Through the use of our reason we can determine what is right or wrong according to the divinely ordained moral law.

Although the distinction between *lex naturalis* and *ius naturale* is easy to blur, both in original usage and in English translation, it is a meaningful one. As we have seen, there was a legal tradition which favoured *ius* and a theological one which preferred *lex*. If natural law is perceived as the equivalent of an ordinance or command at the human level than *lex* is the obvious word to use. In that case morality flows from the will of God, as it did with Cicero. If, on the other hand, it was interpreted as what was naturally right or just, such as the power of a parent over a child or the right to take or use that which belonged to no one, then *ius* was the more appropriate term. In the latter case, *ius naturale* is thought of in relation to civil law and the law of nations, whereas in the former *lex naturalis* is associated with divine or eternal law. Since the massive summaries of medieval philosophers touched on many subjects, including jurisprudence, we find that both traditions may be incorporated in their work, but usually the terminology remains quite distinct.

The moral and legal questions raised by Spain's relations with the people who inhabited the territory conquered by her in the new world led to a revival of interest in natural law, which paved the way for modern international law. These issues were discussed by a number of Spanish theologians in the sixteenth century. Probably the greatest of these late scholastics was Francisco Suarez. His *Treatise on Laws and God the Lawgiver* (1612)[3] is an exhaustive study of law in all its aspects, which begins with a useful attempt to clarify the terminology. The title of Chapter 1 of the first book is 'The Meaning of the Term "law" (*Lex*)' and that of the second chapter is 'What IUS means and How it is to be Compared with LEX'. Biblical, classical, patristic sources as well as both civil and canon law are ransacked for citations representing the various points of view.

Suarez recognizes the major difficulty at the beginning of Chapter 2 when he notes that *ius* is sometimes used as a synonym for *lex*. 'Accordingly, it is necessary to explain the word *ius* and to compare it with *lex*' (27). In order to do this he looks into the etymology of the word and selects the two most widely accepted. One derived it from *iubere* (to command) and the other, associated with Ulpian, from *iustitia*. Modern scholarship traces *ius* back to an Indo-European word meaning 'binding', as in an oath. Suarez knew nothing of this but he was aware that some felt that *ius* was the root of *iustitia* rather than vice versa, a possibility he rejected.

In any case, *ius* is intimately connected with justice both in the general sense of a virtue in the abstract – 'Whatever is fair and in harmony with reason' and in a stricter sense, when it is 'bestowed upon a certain moral power which every man has, either over his own property or with respect to that which is due him'. The 'owner of a thing is said to have a right (*ius*) in that thing, and the labourer is said to have that right to his wages by reason of which he is declared worthy of his hire' (30). Here the English translation 'right' is, of course, far more appropriate than 'law'.

Suarez goes on to say: However, 'according to the other etymology, which derives *ius* from *iubendum* (ordering), the true meaning of *ius* would seem to be *lex*. For *lex* is based upon ordering (*iussio*) or command' (31). This is the connotation Suarez has in mind when he concludes a detailed discussion of the subject by saying that it 'will become synonymous with *lex*, in so far as we shall be speaking of *lex*, too, in its general aspect' (36). Since the Latin title of his book is *De Legibus, Ac Deo Legislatore*, it is clear that he has chosen *lex* to represent law as the command of God, the lawgiver, and thus it is used throughout for natural law except, again, when he is talking about it in relation to *ius gentium* and *ius civile*.

When we turn to Hugo Grotius, a Dutch Protestant, credited with the founding of modern international law, we find that the Latin title of his famous work, *The Law of War and Peace* (1625)[4] is *De Jure belli ac Pacis* and the subtitle uses *ius naturae et gentium* for the law of nature and of nations. Since Grotius was a lawyer it was only natural that he should use the terminology of the legal tradition. The subject was now out of the hands of theologians, and the successors of Grotius on the continent used similar titles, such as *De Jure Naturae et Gentium* (1672) of Samuel Pufendorf, *Fundamenta Iuris Naturae et Gentium* (1705) of Christian Thomasius and *Institutiones Juris Naturae et Gentium* (1750) of J. C. Wolff.

Grotius used *ius* almost exclusively in his book. He explains its name as follows: 'In giving to our treatise the title "The Law of War", we mean first of all, as already stated, to inquire whether any war can be just, and then, what is just in war. For law [*ius*] in our use of the term here means nothing else than what is just, and that too, rather in a negative than in an affirmative sense, that being lawful which is not unjust' (34). He goes on to say: 'There is another meaning of law [*iuris*] viewed as a body of rights, different from the one just defined but growing out of it, which has reference to the person. In this sense a right [*ius*] becomes a moral quality of a person making it possible to have or to do something lawfully [*iuste*] . . . A legal right (*facultas*) is called by the jurists the right to one's own (*suum*); after this we shall call it a legal right [*ius*] properly or strictly so-called' (35). I have added the Latin in square brackets to that provided in parentheses by the translator. This makes it apparent that he uses 'legal right' for *facultas* as well as *ius*, which he usually translates as law. Under what is called legal right, Grotius lists 'power, now over oneself, which is called freedom [*libertas*], now over others, as that of the father (*patria potestas*) and that of the master over slaves; ownership [*dominium*], either absolute, or less than absolute, as usufruct and the right of pledge; and contractual rights [*creditum*], to which on the opposite side contractual obligations [*debitum*] correspond' (35-36). In connection with this topic we find in the *Digest* (1,5,4): 'Freedom [*libertas*] is one's natural power [*facultas*] of doing what one pleases, save insofar as it is ruled out either by coercion or by law [*iure*].' In this instance *facultas* is translated not as 'legal right' but as 'power', which is one of the meanings listed under *facultas* by Grotius. What we have here is the usual second meaning of *ius*, and it is the one adopted by Hobbes since it combines the notions of a legitimate right and the freedom to act as one sees fit.

What little Grotius has to say about *lex* is found in the following:

> There is a third meaning of the word law [*ius*] which has the same force as statute [*lex*] whenever this word is taken in the broadest sense as a rule of moral actions imposing obligation to what is right [*rectum*]. We have need of an obligation; for counsels and instructions of every sort, which enjoin what is honourable indeed but do not impose an obligation, do not come under the term statute [*lex*] or law [*ius*]. (38)

No indication is given in the English version that it is *lex* which is being translated as statute, so the reader is not aware that it has made an appearance, albeit a very brief one, since Grotius uses *ius* from then on for all the various meanings he has distinguished. So fond is he of the word that when he quotes a passage from Cicero's *Tusculanae Disputationes* (I,xiii,30) he unwittingly substitutes it for *lex*.[5] It is easy to see why an English speaker, like Hobbes, would become impatient with this rather unnecessary blurring and opt for *lex* as a perfectly satisfactory term for law in its statute or command sense.

This is made even more evident when Grotius goes on to define the law of nature: 'The law of nature [*ius naturale*] is a dictate of right reason, which points out that an act, according as it is or is not in conformity with rational nature, has in it a quality of moral baseness or moral necessity; and that, in consequence, such an act is either forbidden or enjoined by the author of nature, God' (38-39). Since the idea of command is undeniably involved, *lex*, by his own definition of it, could have been utilized for greater clarity. It was precisely this tendency to use an ambiguous word when a more specific one was available, that Hobbes criticized. The possibility for confusion is especially evident in English. The eighteenth-century translator of the Barbeyrac edition of the Grotius work called it *The Rights of War and Peace*, and 'right' is used instead of 'law' extensively throughout.[6] Further blurring occurs because it means what is right in some places and *a* right in others. The concept of a right is complex enough in positive law; when it is extended to natural law it is capable of meaning almost anything. This ambiguity of both *ius* and right made them ideal for political purposes. The shift from the rather neutral 'law of nature' to the revolutionary and inflammatory 'rights of man' speeded up in the eighteenth century as the groundwork was laid for the American and French Revolutions. This is ironic since it is Hobbes who is credited with the introduction of natural right into political discourse, at least in English. However, in his own thought, the concept was immediately deprived of its radical potential by the nature of the covenant. With respect to his use of *lex* for 'law', this appears to have already been an English preference. Bracton's famous work was entitled *De Legibus et Consuetudinibus Angliae* (c. 1250) and Sir John Fortescue was the author of *De Natura Legis Naturae* (c. 1463) and *De Laudibus Legum Angliae* (c. 1470).

Hobbes was more vulnerable when he attempted to equate *ius* with a right. Passerin d'Entrèves, for example, says:

The different meanings of the word *ius* had of course long been familiar to the lawyers who had been brought up in the study of Roman law. They had carefully distinguished between 'objective' and 'subjective right', between the *norma agendi* (the rule of action) and the *facultas agendi* (the right to act) which can both be indicated by the same name of *ius*, and which are indicated in English by the different names of law and right. But they had never overlooked the fact which Hobbes seems either to ignore or implicitly deny, that the two meanings of *ius* are not antithetic but correlative. . . . There is a right inasmuch as there is a law.

The distinction is capital if we are to understand the full implication of the modern theory of natural law. The great majority of natural law writers in the seventeenth century would not have accepted Hobbes' anarchical conception of 'natural right' as opposed to 'natural law'. To them 'natural law' was a presupposition of 'natural right'.[7]

The first point to be made here is that one has to distinguish between legal terminology and the borrowing of that terminology by philosophers. For example, the law of contract can be used to remedy the right of a creditor created under it. The relationship to which Passerin d'Entrèves refer is clear in that case. But 'law' and 'right' are really only metaphors when used outside the context of a sovereign state with its power of enforcing its own particular legal code. Thus when we say 'natural law' we are using law in the sense of moral rules which obligate because they seem to us naturally right and fair. Only if we see them as commands of God, who will punish disobedience in this world or the next, can they be perceived as analogous to the law of the state. But since this position rests on faith, it is not strictly comparable to secular law with its visible machinery of enforcement.

The second point is that when Hobbes equates *ius naturale* with natural right he is admittedly using only one of the two most important meanings of *ius*, but his intention is to restore some order to a subject which badly needed it. For example, the 'modern theory of natural law', to which Passerin d'Entrèves refers, could just as easily and probably more truly be called the 'modern theory of natural rights', since we are dealing not with one idea but with two different ideas which are joined together in the word *ius*. Before the situation can be clarified we must firmly unbundle the two ideas and differentiate them, as Hobbes did. And if we are going to talk about natural law at all, we must recognize the difference between positive law and legal rights on the one hand and their 'natural' versions on the other. We must also recognize that there is no predetermined relationship between the latter as there is between the former. A child has a legal right to a free education in many countries because there are laws in place which provide the schools and teachers necessary to implement this right. But the legislation usually owes its existence to a strong popular feeling that a future citizen of the country should not be deprived of an education because his or her parents do not have the money to pay for one. This feeling can be defended on several grounds, one of which is that it is a moral right. In the latter case the natural right is seen as preceding the law which makes its realization possible. When it is a question of morality rather than legality one can start with rights or with laws, as one chooses. In Hobbes's case it was to be rights or, more specifically, one right: the right of nature.

If we accept that this is a legitimate procedure, the next question is

The State of Nature and Natural Law

whether the particular right he has chosen is a convincing one. Here is the relevant passage, this time quoted in full:

> The RIGHT OF NATURE, which writers commonly call *ius naturale*, is the liberty each man hath, to use his own power, as he will himself, for the preservation of his own nature; that is to say, of his own life; and consequently, of doing any thing, which in his own judgment, and reason, he shall conceive to be the aptest means thereunto.
>
> By LIBERTY, is understood, according to the proper signification of the word, the absence of external impediments: which impediments, may oft take away part of a man's power to do what he would; but cannot hinder him from using the power left him, according as his judgment, and reason shall dictate to him. (116, 189)

In *The Elements of Law*, where he discusses natural right at greater length before moving on to natural law, Hobbes notes that it is not against nature for a man to do what is necessary to preserve himself.

> And that which is not against reason, men call RIGHT, or *jus*, or blameless liberty of using our own natural power and ability. It is therefore a *right of nature*: that every man may preserve his own life and limbs, with all the power he hath. (EL,I,14,6)

Calling it a 'blameless liberty' is probably the best way to characterize his conception of the right of nature. Because no blame can be attached to the actions required for self-preservation, in what is essentially a state of war, everyone is morally free to do them and accordingly possesses a natural liberty-right to that end.

There has been some dispute as to how far this right goes. Some commentators see Hobbes taking an extreme position in *The Elements of Law* and then drawing back from it in the two later works, but any changes can also be interpreted merely as an attempt to clarify what he had in mind all along, in order to avoid misunderstanding. In any case his theory can only justify actions which the individual honestly feels are required for the purpose of survival and not gratuitous cruelty or other excesses. Nevertheless, the notion that we have a right to do *anything*, no matter how base or barbarous in order to survive, has been found deeply offensive by Hobbes's critics and is, of course, a major reason for his unenviable reputation. However, this should not be allowed to obscure the fact that self-preservation, in itself, has been considered a respectable objective by most philosophers and theologians. It is not necessary to go back to the Greeks who, with their generally naturalistic approach to ethics, could be expected to agree with Hobbes. We can instead refer to the biblical injunction to 'love thy neighbour as thyself' which assumes self-love to be the model for all other kinds of love and therefore nothing of which to be ashamed.[8] In the natural law tradition we need look no further than St. Thomas, who wrote:

> The order of the precepts of the natural law corresponds to the order of our natural inclinations. For there is in man a natural initial inclination to good which he has in common with all substances; in so far as every substance seeks its own preservation according to its own nature. Corresponding to this inclination, the natural law contains all that makes for the preservation of human life, and all that is opposed to its dissolution. (*Summa theologica*, II, 1 Q 94 art. 2)

After survival come the other instincts shared with animals such as sexual relationships and the rearing of children, and only then man's 'natural inclination to know the truth about God and to live in society' (ibid.). This is a recognition of what seems obvious to most of us, namely that regardless of any ultimate purpose, life is meant to be lived. Not only do we normally *want* to continue living but it is often considered an obligation to do so. Christianity places great emphasis on the sanctity of life and regards suicide as a sin. Without the gift of life there would be no controversy about how we should live it, or about anything else for that matter. Above all, one cannot do good unless one first exists. In the language of rights we can safely say that if anything is entitled to be called a natural right, it would have to be the right to continue living. Or to put it negatively, in terms of 'blameless liberty', we cannot be condemned (again under normal circumstances) for taking any steps which are necessary for survival. There is nothing more 'natural' than the urge to remain alive, since the Latin word *natura* itself originates in the idea of being born. The adoption by Hobbes of self-preservation as his first principle, then, does not seem as indefensible on further examination as it might at first glance.

What about his conception of natural law?

> A LAW OF NATURE, *lex naturalis*, is a precept or general rule, found out by reason, by which a man is forbidden to do that, which is destructive of his life, or taketh away the means of preserving the same; and to omit that, by which he thinketh it may be best preserved. For though they that speak of this subject, use to confound *jus*, and *lex*, *right* and *law*: yet they ought to be distinguished; because RIGHT, consisteth in liberty to do, or to forbear: whereas LAW, determineth, and bindeth to one of them; so that law, and right differ as much, as obligation, and liberty; which in one and the same matter are inconsistent. (116, 189)

The legitimacy of this step has been questioned by many critics, of whom Samuel Mintz can be taken as representative.

> What then becomes of the doctrine of natural law, of an eternal and immutable morality antecedent to political institutions and implanted by God in the hearts of men? Hobbes retained the name of this doctrine, but little else; whereas for Hooker, whose views carried immense authority in the seventeenth century, the laws of nature are the laws eternal originating 'in the bosom of God', self-evident and hence known to all reasonable men, and providing the foundation upon which all positive civil law rests, for Hobbes the laws of nature are not really laws at all; rather are they theorems of conduct for the ordering of men's lives in a commonwealth so as to ensure civil peace. They are a *method*, suggested to men by reason, and deduced from human, not divine nature . . . They are secular and utilitarian articles of peace which reason suggests and reasonable men will follow; but they do not coerce except as they are assimilated into positive law . . . The sovereign is not obliged to lay down civil law on the basis of these 'natural laws' . . . And so they are not really the traditional 'laws of nature', not really, that is to say, moral laws which exist prior to positive law and oblige even in the absence of positive law, and which draw their authority from the will of God.[9]

Mintz admits that his description strips away 'a great many of the subtleties and refinements, as well as a number of equivocations and inconsistencies, with which [Hobbes] has surrounded it', but he thinks it is fair and he does not agree with Strauss, Lamprecht, Warrender and others who argue that 'Hobbes's natural law theory depends upon a doctrine of absolute morality'. He believes, with Oakeshott, that any obligations involved are rational and not moral. 'They are "natural" laws only because they follow naturally from a man's natural consideration of his own self-interest; and they are "laws" only in the sense that they are precepts or principles of conduct' (27, fn. 1).

Whether or not this is a fair assessment of Hobbes's position, the question can certainly be asked: is the concept of natural law against which Hobbes is being measured, an accurate one. If the previous discussion of the history of natural law theory has shown anything it is that more than one meaning had been attached to it. A secular as well as a religious interpretation had always been available and even the latter did not have to be specifically Christian. Furthermore there was a split in the Christian tradition. Voluntarists like William of Ockham believed that what is right or wrong is so because God willed or commanded it, thus making it quite possible for the Creator, in his omnipotence to reverse the Ten Commandments, for example, and make right what had previously been wrong. The alternative view, that what is right is intrinsically so, with even God unable to make it otherwise, was not usually stated so starkly but often allowed for God's omnipotence while at the same time insisting, as Suarez did, that God would always will the good. Given this variety of opinions about natural law, Hobbes had just as much right to utilize the term as did his seventeenth-century critics.

As to whether Hobbes's 'law of nature' is truly law, we have already noted that the word is borrowed from jurisprudence and cannot be expected to have exactly the same meaning in a context other than that of positive law. When Mintz says that Hobbes's laws are 'mere precepts', he is using the very word that St. Thomas used in the passage quoted above as equivalent to law. The only situation in which the law of God can be considered as identical to or at least very similar to human positive law is that which prevailed when God made a covenant with Moses and provided a set of laws for the governance of the Hebrew people. As 'divine positive law' it is differentiated from natural law which applies to all people and although the latter can be called divine it is also directly accessible through reason.

However, if one confines the meaning of natural law specifically to that which Mintz characterizes as carrying immense authority in the seventeenth century, it is quite true that Hobbes's conception of it certainly looks different. But it is fair to ask whether the version accepted as dogma by most of his contemporaries was satisfactory as it stood. If natural law is truly 'self-evident and hence known to all reasonable man', why was there any disagreement about it? In fact, it was precisely because of this uncertainty that Hobbes tried to place the whole matter on a firmer foundation.

At the beginning of his *Decretum* (1139) the Canonist Gratian says: 'natural law is what is contained in the Old and New Testaments, which commands every man to do unto another what he would have done unto himself and forbids him to do unto another what he would not have done unto himself'.[10] He thus identifies natural law with the golden rule, just as Hobbes was to do. Generally natural law was considered also to include moral precepts contained in the Bible such as the injunctions against killing, theft, adultery, etc. Once one moves from a small core of fundamental principles, however, one faces potential conflict. Slavery was generally considered contrary to natural law but Augustine, along with many others, found it to be more or less natural in man's fallen state. Many of the church fathers felt that private property was contrary to natural law. St. Thomas lumped usury and homosexuality together with murder and theft as contrary to nature although he thought, as did Hobbes, that the theft of food might be justified in the case of a starving man. Neither social nor political equality were for him, part of natural law. Men may have originally been naturally equal but Aquinas accepted the right of the superior few to rule the many. Differences of opinion as to what was contrary to natural law and what was not, continued up to Hobbes's time and beyond. Although now usually put in terms of rights rather than laws, they are still around today over such questions as contraception, abortion and capital punishment, as well as over what role government should play in our lives.

Just before Hobbes began writing, Grotius had popularized the use of natural law as a touchstone but, although he agreed with others that it was what was reasonable, self-evident and so on, he had a tendency to include in it that which had his personal approval, while diverting into *ius gentium* what others might consider natural law but which he did not. It was only too easy for people to elevate their particular prejudices into natural law. Hobbes was aware of these difficulties and he penned a critique of the concept as it was interpreted at that time, certainly by Grotius, in *The Elements of Law* and *De Cive*, although not in *Leviathan*. Here is what he says in *De Cive*:

> All authors agree not concerning the definition of the natural law, who notwithstanding do very often make use of this term in their writings. The method therefore, wherein we begin from definitions and exclusion of all equivocation, is only proper to them who leave no place for contrary disputes. For the rest, if any man say, that somewhat is done against the law of nature, one proves it hence, because it was done against the general agreement of all the most wise and learned nations: but this declares not who shall be the judge of the wisdom and learning of all nations. Another hence, that it was done against the general consent of all mankind; which definition is by no means to be admitted. For then it were impossible for any but children and fools, to offend against such a law; for sure, under the notion of mankind, they comprehend all men actually endued with reason. These therefore either do nought against it, or if they do aught, it is without their joint accord, and therefore ought to be excused. But to receive the laws of nature from the consents of them, who oftener break, than observe them, is in truth unreasonable. Besides, men condemn the same thing in others, which they approve in themselves; on the other side, they publicly commend what they privately condemn; and they deliver their opinions more by hearsay, than any speculation of their own; and they accord more through hatred of some object, through fear, hope, love, or some other perturbation of mind, than true reason. And therefore it comes to pass, that whole bodies of people often do those things by general accord, or contention, which those writers most willingly acknowledge to be against the law of nature. (DC,II,1)

It is evident that Hobbes is thinking in terms of the secular tradition which is closer to the idea of *ius gentium* than of divine law. If neither the agreement of the wisest nations nor the consent of all mankind is a suitable basis for natural law, what then is? Hobbes turns to another strand in the traditional fabric:

> But since all do grant that is done by right, which is not done against reason, we ought to judge those actions only wrong,

which are repugnant to right reason, that is, which contradict some certain truth collected by right reasoning from true principles. But that wrong which is done, we say it is done against some law. Therefore true reason is a certain law, which (since it is no less a part of human nature, than any other faculty, or affection of the mind) is also termed natural.

He goes on to define the law as 'the dictate of right reason'. This phrase which, as *recta rationis* goes back at least to Cicero, Grotius had used in his definition: 'The law of nature is a dictate of right reason, which points out that an act, according as it is or is not in conformity with rational nature, has in it a quality of moral baseness or moral necessity . . .'[11] Hobbes does not introduce morality with all its potential for disagreement at this stage. His definition in full is as follows:

> Therefore the law of nature . . . is the dictate of right reason, conversant about those things which are either to be done or omitted for the conservation of life and members, as much as in us lies. (DC,II,2)

This shift from morality to self-preservation might seem scandalous to the conventionally minded but it is only temporary, since what Hobbes wants to do is build a firm foundation for morality first. His argument is sketched out in a footnote to the word 'reason' in this passage:

> By right reason in the natural state of men, I understand not, as many do, an infallible faculty, but the act of reasoning, that is, the peculiar and true ratiocination of every man concerning those actions of his which may either redound to the damage or benefit of his neighbours . . . I call it true, that is, concluding from true principles rightly framed, because that the whole breach of the laws of nature consists in the false reasoning, or rather folly of those men who see not those duties they are necessarily to perform towards others in order to their own conservation. (DC,II,1,fn.)

He wants to get away from Reason, capitalized as a faculty, to the kind of calculation in which we regularly engage prior to acting. For Hobbes, reasoning should not be transformed into something remote from everyday life but must be recognized as a process which is an intimate part of that life. It is a means to an end, and no end makes more sense, at least in the first instance, than personal survival. Mintz is quite right when he says that 'as he uses the term "right reason", it is shorn of its divine afflatus; it is no more correct reasoning applied to the theory of the passions, and as it yields knowledge which is rooted in sense-experience and in language, it can never attain to a knowledge of God' (35). Hobbes certainly did want to exclude any idea of reason as 'divine afflatus' and he just as obviously believed that it yielded knowledge rooted in sense-experience. Whether it could attain to a knowledge of God would have to depend on one's conception of God.

If we define natural law as a moral law which is above positive law, immutable and eternal, then Hobbes was within the natural law tradition. However, if on the other hand, it is interpreted as granting the individual the right to disobey civil laws which he regarded as contrary to natural law or the right to rebel against the authority that enacted them, then Hobbes was not. However, the natural law tradition was, in general, a conservative one and for that reason Hobbes's position was as orthodox as that of most of his predecessors. It was the relentless logic with which he pursued the implications of traditional ideas which disturbed his critics.

3
The Laws of Nature and Morality

Although a case can be made that Hobbes had a legitimate right to use natural law concepts, it is true, as Mintz says, that his interpretation appears not to be typical of the seventeenth century. The difference can be seen without quoting his more religious critics. We need only refer again to Grotius who, after including 'a quality of moral baseness or moral necessity' in his definition added: 'and that, in consequence, such an act is either forbidden or enjoined by the author of nature, God' (38–39). Allusions to morality and to God would be a normal part of any contemporary view of natural law but they are missing in Hobbes's definition. A law of nature is, to quote *Leviathan* again, 'a precept or general rule, found out by reason, by which a man is forbidden to do that which is destructive of his life, or taketh away the means of preserving the same; and to omit that, by which he thinketh it may best be preserved' (116, 189).

The use of the term 'forbidden' may lead to difficulties which could be avoided by remembering that self-preservation can be seen in different ways. The *ius naturale* gives us the right or liberty to do what is necessary for self-preservation without incurring any moral disapproval which he calls 'blameless liberty' in *The Elements of Law*. Hobbes assumes that in addition to the right, we have the desire to preserve ourselves. Since we *want* to continue living, we look to our reason to tell us what it is necessary for us to do or not to do in order to attain that end. The obligation to do what is required to survive is therefore a rational one. Whether or not it is also a moral one will be considered. But although it sounds like a moral prohibition, 'forbidden' is often used to avoid threatening situations, such as putting one's head out a train window or climbing a pole carrying high voltage electricity.

Actually Hobbes was not as far from his critics as might appear from the emphasis on self-preservation in his definition. However his method, with its stark phraseology, tended to alienate many of his readers right at the beginning, with the result that they just did not believe that he was being sincere when he later spoke in a quite unexceptionable way. The words might be familiar ones but Hobbes's right to use them was called into question. His credibility had been undermined early on by his reckless challenge to conventional wisdom so that in many cases his critics turned a blind eye to the development of his argument. Mintz, for example, says that Hobbes stripped his laws 'of their absolute moral character; but he chose nevertheless, out of a fine sense of irony, to retain their traditional name, and to describe them in traditional language' (35). This is why in his own description of Hobbes's doctrine he felt obliged to 'shear away a great many of the subtleties or refinements, as well as a number of equivocations and inconsistencies, with which he has surrounded it' (27, fn. 1). What he calls 'subtleties' and 'equivocations' may, however, be a vital part of Hobbes's thought and ought not to be 'sheared away' before they have been fairly examined.

Here is what Hobbes has to say at the end of his discussion of natural law: 'The laws of nature are immutable and eternal; for injustice, ingratitude, pride, iniquity . . . and the rest, can never be made lawful . . .   And the science of them, is the true and only moral philosophy'. Thus he does not exclude morality although, as we shall see, his path to it is not the orthodox one. Neither does he exclude God: 'These dictates of reason, men used to call by the name of laws, but improperly: for they are but conclusions, or theorems concerning what conduceth to the conservation and defence of themselves; whereas law, properly, is the word of him, that by right hath command over others. But yet if we consider the same theorems, as delivered in the word of God, that by right commandeth all things; then are they properly called laws' (147, 216).

This passage has led to considerable controversy. To quote Mintz again: 'for Hobbes the laws of nature are not really laws at all; rather they are theorems for the ordering of men's lives in a commonwealth so as to ensure civil peace' (26). This is quite true since Hobbes says the same thing in the first sentence quoted above, but he then qualifies his statement by adding that if they are considered as God's commands then 'they are properly called laws'. Obviously he means to say that they are theorems or laws, depending on how you look at them.

There are others such as Howard Warrender[1] who take the latter part of the quotation more seriously than the former and see Hobbes as a traditional natural (or more properly divine) law theorist because he invokes God's command as his ultimate authority. This viewpoint has been much criticized, and is certainly difficult to defend in light of the kinds of arguments habitually used by Hobbes. Furthermore, it should be noted that the last sentence is conditional: *if* we consider them as God's command they can then be called laws. Since Hobbes has just limited the legitimate use of the word 'law' to the command of a rightful authority, if one wants to use it in this case one has to call upon the only being who 'by right commandeth all things,' and that is God. This option is certainly open to us if we prefer, but so is that of referring to them as theorems or dictates of reason. The matter is perhaps clarified somewhat if we look at what he had to say in *The Elements of Law*:

> The laws mentioned in the former chapters, as they are called the laws of nature, for that they are the dictates of natural reason; and also moral laws, because they concern men's manners and conversation one towards another; so are they also divine laws in respect of the author thereof, God Almighty; and ought therefore to agree, or at least, not to be repugnant to the word of God revealed in Holy Scripture. In this chapter therefore I shall produce such places of Scripture as appear to be most consonant to the said laws. (EL,I,18,1)

According to this passage, these 'theorems' can be called natural, moral or divine laws as one pleases. The specific question of whether the word 'law' is appropriate is raised here also, as it is in *De Cive*. 'And forasmuch as law (to speak properly) is a command, and these dictates, as they proceed from nature, are not commands; they are not therefore called laws in respect of nature, but in respect of the author of nature, God Almighty' (EL,I,17,12). It is as if Hobbes is replying to a critic who has asked: 'How can you call these theorems "laws", if, as you believe, a law must be issued by an authority with the right to command?' Bringing in God as the ultimate lawgiver allows Hobbes to retain the word 'law' for these precepts. He could have dropped the word and used something like 'rules' throughout, but he obviously preferred to retain it because of its traditional connotations. However, it does not follow necessarily, and this is where I disagree with Warrender, as I understand him, that these rules are binding *only* because they are commands of God. They are dictates of reason, which to Hobbes is the primary meaning of natural law, and they are also moral obligations. The fact that his laws of nature can also be found in the Bible is used to confirm and support what he had originally arrived at by reason. The priority of reason is underlined by a revealing passage in *The Elements of Law*:

> Finally, there is no law of natural reason, that can be against the law divine; for God Almighty hath given reason to a man to be a light unto him. And I hope it is no impiety to think, that God Almighty will require a strict account thereof, at the day of judgment, as of the instructions which we were to follow in our peregrination here; notwithstanding the opposition and affronts of supernaturalists now-a-days to rational and moral conversation. (EL,I,18,12)

The disagreement over what Hobbes meant is due largely, to his use of the word 'law'. When he chose *lex* as his Latin equivalent, he opted for the statute model, of which the usual example is the rule of the road. The law commands us to drive on the left or the right side of the road and punishes those who choose the alternative. We do not question it, because the authority which enacts and enforces it is regarded by us as possessing the rightful power to do so. This kind of law is very familiar to inhabitants of modern states who are subject to a continuous flow of legislation regulating their lives in all areas. However, for most of Hobbes's contemporaries the matter was not so simple. As we have seen, *ius* contains moral connotations lacking in *lex*. It speaks to us of justice, equity, and what is right, as well as of rights. However, difficulties of interpretation are not eliminated by using *ius*, as Grotius did. After defining natural law as a dictate of right reason establishing the right and the wrong, he says 'that in consequence, such an act is either forbidden or enjoined by the author of nature, God'. But he adds a famous qualification shortly thereafter:

> The law of nature, again, is unchangeable – even in the sense that it cannot be changed by God. Measureless as is the power of God, nevertheless it can be said that there are certain things over which that power does not extend . . . Just as even God, then, cannot cause that two times two should not make four, so He cannot cause that which is intrinsically evil be not evil. (39)

Thus, Grotius sees the good as something that God commands because it is good rather than being good because God commands it. The latter is, of course, the voluntarist position of Ockham and others. Was it also that of Hobbes? Many of his critics seemed to think so. Like Grotius, they felt that the moral law was binding on all agents including the sovereign and even God. This was going a little further than the traditional natural law theory of, for example, Suarez, who said that God *would* not command evil, rather than that he *could* not. The difference seems excessively subtle since we are hardly privy to God's innermost thoughts. But it does reflect a genuine theological conundrum. Is God omnipotent or is he not? One alternative is to say that God created a world governed by certain laws and that once these were in effect even God was bound by them. On the other hand, if God were genuinely all-powerful, there was nothing to stop him from changing his own laws if he so wished. The first possibility made God resemble a constitutional monarch; the second led him to look more like a Hobbesian sovereign. These political parallels, of course, were not lost on the disputants.

The belief that even God could not change the moral law, that it was somehow primary in its immutability, seems the best choice for a number of reasons. However, there was one serious stumbling block: some of God's actions in the Old Testament. When he ordered Abraham to slay Isaac, Hosea to take up with a harlot, and the children of Israel to despoil the Egyptians, he was asking them to violate his own sixth, seventh and eighth commandments. In order to defend him from charges of inconsistency and even immorality, the voluntarists argued that what he commanded then was not wrong although it would be so now, because in the interim he had changed the rules. The traditionalists, like Suarez, did not think that it was necessary to go this far; they felt that God could act in a specific instance without being under the necessity of altering his own laws. This was not completely satisfactory since it made God into a monarch somewhat like Henry VIII, who generally ruled according to the law but was not above bending it in his own case when a wife got in the way. A liberal Christian of today would probably not feel the need of elaborate justification since he would regard God's actions in the earlier part of the Old Testament as reflecting a stage in the evolution of the religion rather than as having actually occurred.

However, a real problem remains. The stories of the Old Testament, like the myths of other religions, are at least an attempt to understand why bad things happen to good people or, as Hobbes puts it, 'why evil men often prosper, and good men suffer adversity' (346, 398). There is a natural tendency on the part of individuals to cope with disaster by using whatever soothing balm comes to hand. If one survives an accident, it is because God has answered one's prayers; if one does not, it is because God has called one to his bosom. The fact that these are somewhat contradictory is of little account when human beings seek consolation. However, another possible explanation is the sheer capriciousness of God or the gods. The dilemma is faced squarely in that part of the Bible which so influenced Hobbes: the book of Job. A good man who had been visited with many misfortunes, Job laments his lot and asks God what he has done to deserve such a harsh fate. God's reply is to ask some telling questions of his own:

> Where were you when I laid the foundation of the earth? . . . Have you commanded the morning since your days began . . . ? Can you bind the chains of the Pleiades, or loose the cords of Orion? . . . Can you send forth lightnings, that they may go and say to you, 'Here we are'? (Job 38)

As evidence of his power, God reminds Job that it was he who created Behemoth, the hippopotamus: 'Behold, his strength in his loins, and his power in the muscles of his belly'. But it is above all Leviathan, the crocodile, who receives the most enthusiastic attention. In the long concluding passage God celebrates the strength and invulnerability of this awesome creature. He emphasizes Job's impotence by asking more ironic questions:

> Can you draw out Leviathan with a fishhook or press down his tongue with a cord? . . . Will he make supplications to you? Will he speak to you in soft words? Will he make a covenant with you to take him for your servant forever? Will you play with him as with a bird, or will you put him on leash for your maidens? Who can penetrate his double coat of mail?

God's final words are these: 'Upon earth there is not his like, a creature without fear. He beholds everything that is high: he is king over all the sons of pride' (Job 41).

In addition to providing Hobbes with his metaphor for the

omnipotent state, God has used Leviathan as a symbol for his own unlimited power. Hobbes could do little else but abase himself, like Job did, before God's irresistible will. Whatever his specific religious beliefs may have been, there is little doubt that Hobbes was deeply impressed by the image of God to be found in this book. Omnipotence does not have to explain or justify itself or make excuses for appearing to be unfair. In the Biblical story the Lord forgives Job for his insolence and gives him twice what he had before, but the message is clear. Like an absolute monarch, whether he is kind or cruel, he does not have to answer to anyone for his behaviour. If a mere human, like Job, has the audacity to question it, all God has to say is 'Where were you when I laid the foundation of the earth?'

However, the God of Job was of little use to natural law theorists, since proclaiming his own omnipotence was no substitute for some specific guidance on what he wanted. The Old Testament deity had provided regulations for the Jewish people in the past, but in more recent times there had been no direct unequivocal expression of his will, although there was never a shortage of those who were prepared to speak on his behalf. The obvious solution in the face of confusion and uncertainty, was to see what reason could come up with, and this had been customary approach for Christian and non-Christian moralists alike. The only way in which Hobbes differed from them was that he attempted to apply a more rigorous logic to a less sentimental view of human nature than his predecessors. In this way he was able to arrive at theorems which could also be regarded as dictates of reason and therefore the command model of law could be retained even when the power of God was not invoked. However, since rationality can be seen as a gift of God, the laws of nature could also be looked upon as divine commands. Beyond this he is not required to go, but he does so because he feels it is necessary to demonstrate that his laws are at least 'not repugnant to the word of God revealed in Holy Scripture'.

To sum up: the right of nature is man's blameless liberty to do whatever is necessary to preserve himself, and the rules or precepts which reason tells him he must obey if he wants to survive are the laws of nature. Hobbes does not himself use the conditional because he assumes that human beings normally want to survive, but it is implicit in the structure of his argument. The right to do something does not include the desire to do it. Motivation must be present in the first place for a right to have any significance. If it is true that we want to survive, is it then permissible for us to do whatever is necessary to avoid an untimely end? Yes, says Hobbes: permission is granted by the right of nature. I emphasize this in order to avoid the confusion that ensues when it is contended that we are under a moral obligation to preserve ourselves. To the extent that an obligation is involved, it is the rational obligation referred to by Oakeshott in the Introduction to his edition of *Leviathan*. We have a right, not an obligation, to preserve ourselves but in order to do so we must follow the rules dictated by reason and in that sense they are obligations.

At this early stage in his exposition, then, Hobbes is relying only on prudence as motivation for obeying the laws of nature. But he has so far merely defined the latter; he must now specify what they are. Since the unlimited right of nature – that every man has a right to every thing, even to another's body – applies not just to me but to every one else, it follows that there is no security for any of us in the state of nature.

> And consequently, it is a precept, or general rule of reason, *that every man, ought to endeavour peace, as far as he has hope of obtaining it; and when he cannot obtain it, that he may seek, and use, all helps, and advantages of war.* The first branch of which rule, containeth the first, and fundamental law of nature; which is, *to seek peace, and follow it.* The second, the sum of the right of nature; which is, *by all means we can, to defend ourselves.* (117, 190)

Given the situation that prevails in the state of nature, there are two options available to the individual who wants to survive: to get out of it by seeking peace or if that is not possible, to go on fighting. The situation is mirrored in the real world when two nations are at war. Peace can be *sought* by one of the belligerents but it cannot be *achieved* by one side only, so that if there is no agreement the peace-seeking nation must go on fighting or succumb. Unilateral disarmament in the middle of a war would be suicidal. In the case of the individual, the first law of nature thus directs him to do everything in his power to end the hostilities of the state of nature by making a treaty of peace with his fellows.

One point should be made before proceeding. When Hobbes says that every man *ought* to seek peace, he is using the word in a sense which does not require morality but merely prudence. Given the dangers of the state of nature, it is only reasonable for a man to wish to escape from it. If he wishes to bring this life-threatening situation to an end, he ought to endeavour peace in the same way that he ought to see a doctor if he is in a great deal of pain. Something stronger than prudence might appear to be indicated in the next paragraph, where Hobbes derives his second law from the first one, 'by which we are *commanded* to endeavour peace' [emphasis added]. However, this can be interpreted as simply a more emphatic way of restating what he has just said. Reason commands us to do what we ought, in our own interest, to do. It is similar in effect to his use of 'forbidden' in the original definition of a law of nature.

The second law of nature provides the mechanism by which the goal expressed in the first one, can be achieved. It is:

that a man be willing, when others are so too, as far-forth, as for peace, and defence of himself he shall think it necessary, to lay down this right to all things; and be contented with so much liberty against other men, as he would allow other men against himself. For as long as every man holdeth this right, of doing any thing he liketh; so long are all men in the condition of war. But if other men will not lay down their right, as well as he; then there is no reason for any one, to divest himself of his: for that were to expose himself to prey, which no man is bound to, rather than to dispose himself to peace. This is the law of the Gospel; *whatsoever you require that others should do to you, that do ye to them.* And that law of all men, *quod tibi fieri non vis, alteri ne feceris.* (118, 190)

As Hobbes's references to the golden rule indicate, his second law of nature is a version of that rule which, in essence, is the principle of reciprocity. The formation of any human group requires an understanding on this basis. It is the key to society and the key to Hobbesian political theory. More will be said about the golden rule later, but one point should be noted here. Hobbes attempts to disarm immediately a possible criticism: that since he suspends the golden rule if others are not prepared to be governed by it, he abandons it when it is most needed. By putting his argument in the context of the state of nature, he shows that unless the decision to live by it is mutual, anyone who does so merely offers himself as a victim to the others. In an international context it would have the same effect as unilateral disarmament in the midst of war. With respect to the individual, it would violate the whole purpose of a natural law which is to forbid a man from doing that 'which is destructive of his life'.

Since this law is derived from the first one, it too is a counsel of prudence. In order to bring about peace one has to be prepared to surrender one's unlimited natural right if others agree to do the same. A network of reciprocal arrangements will thus be established. Because it is contingent on the behaviour of others, this law is not absolute for any one person; it can only be fulfilled through cooperation. However, there is every reason for people to do so since the benefits are immediately apparent. 'To *lay down* a man's *right* to any thing, is to *divest* himself of the *liberty*, of hindering another of the benefit of his own right to the same' (118, 190). The outcome is that by giving up unlimited right I am able to enjoy the rights that remain, without the impediment of the unlimited rights of others to interfere with my enjoyment of them, such as is the case in the state of nature.

Although this law is prudential, once the necessary agreement has taken place the possibility of a genuinely moral situation has been created. For the moment I use the word 'moral' to describe behaviour that seems to go beyond considerations of immediate self-interest. After noting that rights can be either renounced or transferred, he continues:

> And when a man hath in either manner abandoned, or granted away his right; then he is said to be OBLIGED, or BOUND, not to hinder those, to whom such right is granted, or abandoned, from the benefit of it: and that he *ought*, and it is his DUTY, not to make void that voluntary act of his own: and that such hindrance is INJUSTICE, and INJURY, as being *sine jure*; the right being before renounced, or transferred. (119, 191)

What is noteworthy here is the number of undeniably ethical terms Hobbes has introduced, complete with italics and capitals. The reason these words can now appear is that Hobbes has laid the foundation for his system of morality. Men can only come in from the cold of the state of nature if they make a reciprocal arrangement such as that he has just described. The rewards are great, but the price is that all of them must fulfil the conditions of the agreement. Since each man has accepted the terms voluntarily, he is committed to carrying them out. Not to do so is likened to an absurdity or a self-contradiction. A comparison with logic has been found by some of Hobbes's critics to be singularly unconvincing but a case can be made for it which I shall put aside for the moment. What is of the greatest importance to note here is that Hobbes has defined what he means by 'obliged' in such a way as to detach it from immediate self-interest. The groundwork for genuine moral obligation has been laid.

The transfer or renunciation of rights is accomplished by a sign which may take the form of words or actions or both. 'And the same are the BONDS, by which men are bound, and obliged: bonds that have their strength, not from their own nature, for nothing is more easily broken than a man's word, but from fear of some evil consequence upon the rupture.' However, not all rights can be renounced or transferred. 'For it is a voluntary act: and of the voluntary acts of every man, the object is some *good to himself.*' Such is the case with his right to resist the taking of his life. 'The same may be said of wounds, and chains, and imprisonment . . . because a man cannot tell, when he seeth men proceed against him by violence, whether they intend his death or not.' Since the motivation for renouncing unlimited right is 'nothing else but the security of a man's person, in his life, and in the means of so preserving life, as not to be weary of it,' he must be allowed to retain these fundamental rights. If he appears willing to alienate his ultimate right of self-preservation, 'he is not to be understood as if he meant it, or that it was his will; but that he was ignorant of how such words and actions were to be interpreted' (120, 192).

The reason for this caveat is to protect the foundation of Hobbes's theory. Man's primary goal is self-preservation which is threatened by the anarchy of the state of nature. The motive for surrendering his unlimited right of nature in exchange for others doing the same is to enhance his chances of survival. Now if the rights he renounces include the right to defend himself against violence, he is undermining the purpose of the whole exercise. The point is made clear later when Hobbes says: 'A covenant not to defend myself from force, by force, is always void. For, as I have showed before, no man can transfer, or lay down his right to save himself from death, wounds, and imprisonment, *the avoiding whereof is the only end of laying down any right* [emphasis added] . . . For though a man may covenant thus, *unless I do so, or so, kill me;* he cannot covenant thus, *unless I do so, or so, I will not resist you, when you come to kill me*' (127, 199). Therefore it is essential that the theory retain for the individual his ultimate right of self-defense. This is of some significance, as we shall see, for his political philosophy.

The phrase: 'means of preserving life as not to be weary of it' is worth noting since it supports the notion that Hobbes did not believe life was worth continuing at all costs. Suffering of various kinds can make it unbearable. He makes this point elsewhere including *De Homine*: 'On the other hand, though death is the greatest of all evils (especially when accompanied by torture), the pains of life can be so great that, unless their quick end is foreseen, they may lead men to number death among the goods' (DH,XI,6). Despite his emphasis on survival, he obviously thought that quality of life was also significant. This is important because it is sometimes felt that when Hobbes says that someone who seems prepared to abandon this right is only acting on ignorance, he is depriving him of the freedom to do away with himself if life becomes a burden. It should be remembered that he is talking about abandoning the *right* to survive. As we said before, there is no obligation to continue living and one may take one's life if the circumstances warrant it. But nothing could ever justify the surrender of the right itself.

'The mutual transferring of right, is that which men call CONTRACT' (230, 192). With this sentence Hobbes introduces a subject vital to the understanding of what actually takes place when the second law of nature is observed. There are essentially three types of contracts: the transfer may take place for immediate benefit such as ready money; one party may deliver, trusting the other contractor to fulfil his part at a later time; or both sides may promise to perform in the future. The latter two variations, in which trust is involved, are called pacts or covenants. When a right is transferred by one party only, in the hope of gaining some service from the other, a reputation for charity or generosity, relief from the pain of compassion or a heavenly reward, it is not a contract but a free gift. 'Signs of contract are either *express*, or *by inference*.' A contract expressed in words pertaining to the future is a promise. 'Signs by inference, are sometimes the consequence of words; sometimes the consequence of silence; sometimes the consequence of actions; sometimes the consequence of forbearing an action: and generally a sign by inference, of any contract, is whatsoever sufficiently argues the will of the contractor' (121, 193). The fact that one can enter into a contract without either acting or speaking is very important to Hobbes's theory but he does not emphasize that here. In *The Elements of Law* he does lay a basis for tacit agreements when he says:

'Silence in them that think it will be so taken, is a sign of consent; for so little labour being required to say No, it is to be presumed, that in this case he that saith it not, consenteth' (EL,I,13,11).

Covenants of mutual trust are obligatory where there is a common power capable of compelling performance but they are void on reasonable suspicion in a state of nature. 'For he that performeth first, has no assurance the other will perform after . . . And therefore he which performeth first, does but betray himself to his enemy; contrary to the right, he can never abandon, of defending his life, and means of living' (124, 196). However, it should be noted that the cause of the fear, which initiates such a covenant must arise *after* the covenant is made; otherwise the covenant, even though made in the state of nature, is *not* void. 'For that which could not hinder a man from promising, ought not to be admitted as a hindrance of performing' (125, 196). This is one of numerous instances of something that many of Hobbes's commentators are not prepared to accept, which is that the law of nature is operative in a state of nature under the right circumstances. Another example follows shortly thereafter: 'Covenants entered into by fear, in the condition of mere nature, are obligatory' (126, 198). As he puts it in *The Elements*: 'For there appeareth no reason, why that which we do upon fear, should be less firm than that which we do for covetousness' (EL,I,15,13). And in *De Cive* he says that if they did not bind, 'it would follow, that these promises which reduced men to a civil life, and by which laws were made, might likewise be of none effect; (for it proceeds from fear of mutual slaughter, that one man submits himself to the dominion of another) . . . ' (DC,I,2,16). Such covenants may be void if forbidden by civil law, but not on grounds of fear.

Thus it appears that a covenant made in the state of nature in full knowledge that there are risks involved, is binding and therefore the grand covenant which establishes the body politic is not impossible by definition, as some have felt. This is all that it is necessary to demonstrate for the hypothetical state of nature, since any further details are irrelevant for a situation which is only imagined. However, they are important for a real state of nature, such as the relations between sovereign states. They are also of consequence for agreements which, although they occur in a commonwealth, are not legally enforceable. Sometimes an attempt is made to strengthen mere words by swearing an oath which invites the wrath of the deity if it is broken. But, notes Hobbes, this adds nothing to the obligation. 'For a covenant if lawful, binds in the sight of God, without the oath, as much as with it: if unlawful, bindeth not at all; though it be confirmed with an oath' (130, 201). The law referred to here is, of course, the law of nature.

This discussion has paved the way for the third law of nature, *'that men perform their covenants made*: without which, covenants are in vain, and but empty words; and the right of all men to all things remaining, we are still in the condition of war' (130, 201). It is only now that justice is possible since no action can be unjust prior to a covenant. 'But when a covenant is made, then to break it is *unjust*: and the definition of INJUSTICE, is no other than *the not performance of covenant*. And whatsoever is not unjust, is *just'* (130, 202). The various meanings of justice will be discussed later; for now I shall assume that there is no substantial difference between injustice as used here and moral wrongness.

In his two earlier works, Hobbes goes on at this point to talk about justice and injustice in general before continuing with his list of natural laws. In *Leviathan*, however, he pauses to emphasize the role of coercion which is not discussed in other books until he deals with the formation of the commonwealth.

> But because covenants of mutual trust, where there is a fear of not performance on either part, as hath been said in the former chapter, are invalid; though the original of justice be the making of covenants; yet injustice actually there can be none, till the cause of such fear be taken away; which while men are in the natural condition of war, cannot be done. Therefore before the names of just, and unjust can have place, there must be some coercive power, to compel men equally to the performance of their covenants, by the terror of some punishment, greater than the benefit they expect by the breach of their covenant; and to make good that propriety, which by mutual contract men acquire, in recompense of the universal right they abandon and such power there is none before the erection of a commonwealth. (131, 202)

This passage needs to be read very carefully since it, like others expressing the same idea, can easily lead to confusion. A few pages earlier, he had discussed certain types of contracts, such as those extorted by fear, which *are* binding in the state of nature. They are not affected by this statement, since it refers only to 'covenants of mutual trust, where there is a fear of not performance on either part'. If we assume that the covenant establishing the commonwealth is of this type, then we must also assume that the commonwealth comes into existence at the moment of agreement, so that any fear of non-performance would be allayed immediately. All this is only a problem if one is thinking about an actual event taking place in real time. If we start instead with a hypothetical state of nature, the problem disappears, since we would be looking at logical rather than chronological priority.

What Hobbes wants to convey here is simply that before it is safe to enter into the more formal types of contracts familiar to inhabitants of a commonwealth, a power must be in place that is capable of enforcing them. He refers specifically to property (propriety) in the above quotation and then adds that the schoolmen say that justice consists of giving to every man his own. 'And therefore where there is no *own*, that is no propriety, there is no injustice; and where there is no coercive power erected, that is, where there is no commonwealth, there is no propriety; all men having right to all things' (131, 202). Thus private property is a creature of the commonwealth: it could not exist in the state of nature. This is a very significant claim since if one accepts, with many natural rights theorists such as Locke, that property must be included along with life and liberty as fundamental rights retained from the state of nature, one limits the sovereignty of the state in a crucial area. The unrest that led to the Civil War was fuelled by the unwillingness of many Englishmen to pay certain taxes levied by the king. Obviously if private property did not depend on the institution of the commonwealth and was not an inalienable right already possessed by the individual in the state of nature, their case was much weakened. However, Hobbes does not develop the topic further at this point.

Unlike the first two laws of nature which can clearly be founded on the dictates of prudence, the third law, which requires men to keep their covenants, looks to be different in an important way. It is obviously in our interest to seek peace and to make an agreement which provides for it but when Hobbes goes on to say that we must do what we have said we would do, the rewards for such desirable behaviour are not as evident for many of us as the benefits that might accrue from *not* doing what we said we would do.

The probability that we are now in what would appear to be a moral rather than a prudential world seems to be indicated by the introduction of coercion. The necessity for this kind of reinforcement indicates that self-interest is not effective enough by itself. Only when the possibility of punishment is factored into our assessment of the results of our actions, can self-interest again be relied on to encourage us to keep our covenants. But does this reasserted primacy of self-interest mean that morality has been displaced as soon as it appears? I do not think that necessarily follows. Hobbes has said that to break a covenant is unjust and the fact that it is too dangerous to make certain kinds of covenants before coercive power is in place does not detract from the status of the original statement. The provision of some form of punishment for breaking a covenant may give the unscrupulous a reason for not doing so but that is not what makes the action unjust; it merely protects the individual who does not want to violate his contract because he agrees with Hobbes that it would be unjust to do so.

Another reason that Hobbes now appears to be talking about moral rather than prudential actions is that he immediately finds it necessary to defend his position against the amoral man.

> The fool hath said in his heart, there is no such thing as justice; and sometimes also with his tongue; seriously alleging, that every man's conservation, and contentment, being committed to his own care, there could be no reason, why every man might not do what he thought conduced thereunto: and therefore also to make, or not to make; keep, or not to keep covenants, was not against reason, when it conduced to one's benefit. He does not therein deny, that there be covenants; and that they are sometimes broken, sometimes kept; and that such breach of them may be called injustice, and the observance of them justice: but he questioneth, whether injustice, taking away the fear of God, for the same fool hath said in his heart there is no God, may not sometimes stand with that reason, which dictateth to every man his own good; and particularly then, when it conduceth to such a benefit, as shall put a man in a condition, to neglect not only the dispraise, and revilings, but also the power of other men. (132, 203)

In other words, if his reason tells a man that a certain action will redound to his benefit, why should he not do it regardless of whether other men call it just or unjust, so long as he thinks he can get away with it? This is an important question which goes back at least to Thrasymachus in Plato's *Republic* and is a fair question to ask of someone like Hobbes whose emphasis has been precisely on the rationality of seeking one's own good. His answer is that the reasoning behind this position is false. Before going into his argument I should just like to point out that the word 'justice' is used in two different ways within a couple of sentences here: the fool first says 'there is no such thing as justice' but then admits that the observance of covenants may be called justice. What he appears to be contending is not that there is no such thing as justice but that if it conflicts with one's self-interest it should be ignored. In this case justice in the first sense must have been intended to mean more than merely a name: it must represent an obligation that has priority over one's good. This is more than Hobbes himself has explicitly claimed for it up to this point. Despite any implications such a definition might have, his criticism of the fool's position rests firmly on prudential foundations.

He begins by saying that he is talking specifically about a situation 'either where one of the parties has performed already; or where there is a power to make him perform . . . ' The question is 'whether it be against reason, that is, against the benefit of the other to perform, or not' and his answer is that it is not against reason. (Note the clear identification of reason with benefit.) First of all it is not wise for a man to do something which 'notwithstanding any thing can be foreseen, and reckoned on, tendeth to his own destruction . . . ' (133, 204). Secondly, in a state of war there is no way in which a man can survive without the help of 'confederates,' who will expect his help in return.

> He therefore that breaketh his covenant, and consequently declareth that he thinks he may with reason do so, cannot be received into any society, that unite themselves for peace and defence, but by the error of them that receive him; nor when he is received, be retained in it, without seeing the danger of their error; which errors a man cannot reasonably reckon upon as the means of his security . . . (134, 205)

Since a man cannot count on such errors, he is putting his survival at risk, and that is not reasonable. Typically Hobbes uses rebellion as an example. It is a poor gamble because not only are the odds against succeeding high but even success has its dangers since it encourages others to do the same for themselves. 'Justice therefore, that is to say, keeping of covenant, is a rule of reason, by which we are forbidden to do anything destructive to our life; and consequently a law of nature' (134, 205).

The argument that Hobbes uses here does not seem consistent with his theoretical model of the state of nature. One of the covenants he has in mind, in which one party has already performed, apparently precedes the institution of a commonwealth; the other assumes the existence of 'a power to make him perform'. If we lump these together, as he has done, we seem to be in a twilight zone not at all characteristic of the hypothetical state of nature. The description he offers us of men seeking out 'confederates' to help in their battle for survival is obviously closer to the real world. Although he is still looking at the situation from the viewpoint of an individual who has to make his own choices, he is dealing not with other individuals as in the hypothetical state of nature but with a confederation that is already in existence. This could, of course, be a large political unit like England or France, but it could also be a smaller community such as an extended family or tribe. In fact it could be a group of any size, composed of people who are cooperating with each other to enhance their chances of survival in a hostile environment. Hobbes has more to say about this real world of human relations later on.

By including covenants made where there is a power to enforce them, Hobbes is admitting that coercion, of which he made so much in the previous section, is not in itself sufficient to ensure the performance of all covenants. It is a powerful inducement, of course, especially where the circumstances and legal remedies are clearly defined. But the mere fact that Hobbes feels obliged to consider the fool's arguments at all, indicates that opportunities for breach of covenant are plentiful even in the civil state. Where the agreements involved are not legally binding but are based on good faith alone, the need for additional motivation is even more pressing. The commonwealth does not provide for all our needs, by any means, and practically every one realizes the value of having friends who are prepared to trust him and assist him when he needs help. A willingness to give as well as receive is essential in maintaining such friendships. One can violate this rule for a time and take advantage of the good nature of others but once they realize what is happening, their friendship is lost and one has to face the unpleasant consequences. This is not the exact situation that Hobbes had in mind but it forms a small-scale model for the expulsion of an individual from a group – an event that could definitely be life-threatening under certain circumstances. What is significant is that we are dealing here with the pressure of public opinion, a form of social control which was given less weight in Hobbes's calculations that it deserves, although he was obviously aware of its importance.

Essentially Hobbes is arguing that although there may be short-term gains in violating covenants these are more than cancelled out by the long-term losses and therefore it is contrary to our goal of doing nothing that might be destructive to our life. The fool is taking a calculated risk that he can get away with unjust behaviour; Hobbes's reply is that a further calculation would show that the odds are not in his favour and that therefore his belief is unjustified and contrary to reason.

There is another argument the fool could have used which would have severely tested Hobbes's reply if it had not been hypothetical: the ring of Gyges story. Told by Glaucon in Plato's *Republic* (Book II, 359d–360d) it actually refers to a shepherd ancestor of Gyges of Lydia, who discovered a ring which, when twisted on his finger, could make him invisible. Using the advantage this gave him, he seduced the queen and with her help killed the king and took his place. What prudential argument could cope with this shield of invisibility behind which one could be as unjust as one wanted without anyone ever knowing? In his *De Officiis* (III, 38), Cicero retold the story to make the point that a wise man (presumably a Stoic sage) would behave no differently if he had the ring than if he did not. He was obviously annoyed at 'certain philosophers' who would not cooperate in a discussion of hypothetical situations. The editor of a recent edition of Cicero's work identifies these philosophers as Epicureans.

> They taught that men are not deterred from crime by an innate law but rather by the fear of being detected. Even a perfect crime would be known to the man who committed it and he could never be absolutely certain that he would never be detected. Without such absolute certainty, his happiness would constantly be disturbed. Therefore crime, for the Epicurean, was not advisable. As for Plato's fable, the Epicureans object to it because the ring of Gyges magically assures that absolute certainty of escaping detection which they claim can *never* come about, and that claim is crucial to their analysis of wrongdoing.[2]

In this they were at one with Hobbes, although he and his fool would probably not have considered the disturbance of a mild Epicurean happiness as a sufficient deterrent to wrongdoing.

In any case, the practice of justice no less than that of honesty, turns out to be the best policy. But this should not be taken as nothing more than another victory for prudence. To claim that it is in one's long-term self-interest to be just is not the same as saying that this is the only reason for being just. However, it is the only argument that is likely to convince the fool or anyone else who, in effect, asks why he should be just. This is why I do not think that in advancing prudence as a reason for acting morally, Hobbes is necessarily denying that morality can stand on its own. The fact that an equivalent passage does not exist in his two earlier works would seem to indicate that Hobbes was bringing a prudential argument in to shore up his moral one. Critics who rely heavily on the fool's argument to support the thesis that Hobbes has no genuine morality should take this possibility into consideration.

Hobbes goes on to deal with those for whom a law of nature does not 'conduce to the preservation of man's life on earth; but to the attaining of an eternal felicity after death; to which they think the breach of covenant may conduce' (135, 208). This religious belief could be used as a justification for rebelling against the sovereign power. However, Hobbes does not find such an argument convincing.

> But because there is no natural knowledge of man's estate after death; much less of the reward that is then to be given to breach of faith; but only a belief grounded upon other men's saying, that they knew it supernaturally, or that they knew those, that knew them, that knew others, that knew it supernaturally; breach of faith cannot be called a precept of reason, or nature. (135, 206)

This extension of prudence to the afterlife made good sense but the scepticism it reflected did not help Hobbes with his religious critics.

Hobbes also disagrees with those who, while they accept that keeping faith is a law of nature, are prepared to make an exception in special cases, such as heretics or those who in the past have not performed their covenants. 'For if any fault of a man, be sufficient to discharge our covenant made; the same ought in reason to have been sufficient to have hindered the making of it' (135, 206). In other words, we cannot escape the responsibility we have undertaken just because we think we have a good excuse to do so.

Hobbes now makes a distinction of paramount importance in understanding the true nature of his ethical theory. It occurs in his discussion of the difference between the justice of actions and that of men. 'A just man therefore, is he that taketh all the care he can, that his actions may be all just: and an unjust man, is he that neglecteth it.' Such men are more commonly called righteous or unrighteous. A just or righteous man who occasionally commits unjust actions in the heat of passion does not lose his right to the title, 'nor does an unrighteous man, lose his character, for such actions, as he does or forbears *to do, for fear: because his will is not framed by the justice, but by the apparent benefit of what he is to do*' (135, 206, emphasis added). The righteous man is not distinguished from the unrighteous simply because of a general tendency to act justly but also, judging from the italicized words, by his motivations.

It is highly significant that after having just finished providing the fool with prudential reasons for preferring justice, he now implies that acting from fear or apparent benefit is inferior to acting solely from a sense of justice. An act is either just or unjust whatever the motives of the actor, but his motives are important in deciding whether he is entitled to be called righteous. This distinction between mere prudence, and what appears to be genuinely moral behaviour is the subject of the next sentence. 'That which gives to human actions the relish of justice, is a certain nobleness or gallantness of courage, rarely found, by which a man scorns to be beholden for the contentment of his life, to fraud, or breach of promise' (136, 207). This is what is meant when justice is called a virtue. But it is noteworthy that he believes this quality is rarely found and it is doubtless for this reason that he places so much emphasis on prudential motivation. However, this does not alter the fact that intention is what makes an action moral. As he says in *De Cive*:

> But when the words [just and unjust] are applied to persons, to be just signifies as much as *to be delighted in just dealing*, to study how to do righteousness, or to endeavour in all things to do that which is just; and to be unjust is to neglect righteous dealing, or to think it is to be *measured not according to my contract, but some present benefit*. So as the justice or injustice of the mind, the *intention* . . . is one thing, that of an action or omission, another . . . [He] is properly said to be unjust, who

doth righteousness *for fear of punishment annexed unto the law*, and unrighteousness by reason of the *iniquity of his mind*. (DC, III, 5; emphasis added)

The italicized words are further proof that Hobbes's conception of morality is similar to that most commonly held. His insistence on non-prudential motivation is especially important as it is so often denied in his case.

Hobbes deals with the remainder of his laws of nature in fairly short order. The fourth is gratitude for benefit received by free gift. Without this 'there will be no beginning of benevolence, or trust, nor consequently of mutual help . . . ,' which are necessary to escape the state of war (138, 209). The fifth is complaisance or willingness to accommodate oneself to others. This is directed at those who strive to retain what is superfluous to themselves but necessary to someone else. Those who observe this law are called 'sociable' by Hobbes. He does not accept that all men are inherently sociable but it is a characteristic they must try to cultivate in the interests of peace. 'A sixth law of nature, is this, *that upon caution of the future time, a man ought to pardon the offences past of them that repenting, desire it*' (139, 210). The seventh law flows from this one, since it forbids us from inflicting punishment 'with any other design, than for the correction of the offender, or direction of others' (140, 210). Revenge following revenge will only lead back to the state of nature. Other laws are directed against contumely or showing contempt for another, pride or not acknowledging others as your equals, and arrogance or a desire for more than your share. The eleventh is the law of equity and the twelfth provides that those things that cannot be divided be shared in some equitable way. The later laws are mostly technical arrangements for settling disputes and generally smoothing the way for people to live peaceably together.

The fact that the lists provided by Hobbes in his three political works are slightly different is not important since he does not feel that it is necessary to specify them in detail. Most men 'are too busy in getting food, and the rest too negligent to understand'. However, pleading ignorance of the laws is no excuse since 'they have been contracted into one easy sum, intelligible even to the meanest capacity; and that is, *Do not that to another, which thou wouldst not have done to thyself*' (144, 214). In *The Elements of Law* he calls this 'an easy rule to know upon a sudden, whether the action I be to do, be against the law of nature or not' (EL,I,17,9).

The laws of nature oblige always in the court of conscience (*in foro interno*), 'that is to say they bind to a desire they should take place' but not always in action (*in foro externo*). 'For he that should be modest, and tractable, and perform all he promises, in such time, and place, where no man else should do so, should but make himself a prey to others, and procure his own certain ruin, contrary to the ground of all laws of nature, which tend to nature's preservation.' On the other hand, if he has sufficient security that others will observe the laws, he has no excuse for not observing them himself. The importance of motivation is again stressed when Hobbes adds that even when an action is in accord with the law of nature, if the intention was otherwise, the person concerned has committed a breach *in foro interno*. Although the laws of nature are eternal and immutable they are easy to observe because since 'they require nothing but endeavour, he that endeavoureth their performance, fulfilleth them; and he that fulfilleth the law, is just' (145, 215). Here too we find an emphasis on the mental state of the individual: it is the honest and unfeigned desire to observe the law that matters.

In my sequential treatment of the laws of nature above, I noted that morality did not begin until the third law since the first two could be justified on the basis of mere prudence. However, by introducing the notion of *in foro interno* obligation, Hobbes has provided a foundation for their moral status. In conscience they are as obligatory as the rest, but since they are prior to, or outside of, the covenant they are not obligatory *in foro externo*. The best way I know of putting this is that while it is morally desirable to seek peace and take the necessary steps to that end, it only becomes morally obligatory when others have agreed to do the same.

These natural laws comprise the sum and substance of moral philosophy, which he describes as 'nothing else but the science of what is *good* and *evil*, in the conversation, and society of mankind'. Hobbes refers again to his earlier definitions of good and evil as names signifying our appetites and aversions, 'which in different tempers, customs and doctrines of men, are different . . . ' Furthermore, the same man may differ in his opinion as to what is good from one day to the next. Because this leads to disputes and conflict, all men agree that peace is good, 'and therefore also the way or means of peace, which, as I have shewed before, are *justice, gratitude, modesty, equity, mercy*, and the rest of the laws of nature, are good; that is to say *moral virtues*; and their contrary *vices*, evil'. He concludes this section with a highly significant explanation as to why his science of vice and virtue is the *true* moral philosophy.

> But the writers of moral philosophy, though they acknowledge the same virtues and vices; yet not seeing wherein consisted their goodness; nor that they come to be praised, as the means of peaceable, sociable, and comfortable living, place them in a mediocrity of passions: as if not the cause, but the degree of daring, made fortitude; or not the cause, but the quantity of a gift, made liberality. (146, 216)

Hobbes is claiming that, whereas Aristotle's golden mean tells us only how much of a certain type of action must be exercised for it to be called virtuous, he has explained *why* it is called virtuous.

The exact status of Hobbes's Laws of Nature has been a matter of dispute. Warrender saw them as being 'validated' by the covenant but I think it is better to say that they are suspended although not invalidated in circumstances where it is too dangerous to follow them or, in other words, to practise the golden rule which expresses them in brief. This emphasizes the fact that since we live mostly in ordered communities, we are rarely, if ever, in a seriously threatening version of the state of nature and therefore are bound by these eternal laws most, if not all, of the time. Hobbes assumes that, given man's nature, the golden rule is the only guide to living in peace and therefore it always applies to the vast majority of people who want to do so. Only in time of war or when our lives are otherwise endangered by others, are we temporarily freed from its authority.

For this reason, his morality, as I have tried to show, does not differ substantially from the traditional one. He is even willing to accept the Laws of Nature as the commands of God for those who wish to consider them as such. Later, when talking about the power of rulers, he always emphasizes that although they can violate morality on earth they still face divine retribution, so he relies on the fear of God in that case although he does not invoke it much elsewhere in his writings. This raises the question of Hobbes's religious beliefs, which I would like to glance at briefly here.

Hobbes has been seen as everything from an atheist to someone for whom religion was vital, as for example, by F. C. Hood, in his book *The Divine Politics of Thomas Hobbes* (Oxford, 1964). The subject has aroused more interest recently but I feel the most sensible summary was made in 1865 by F. A. Lange.

> His real view of religion is so trenchantly expressed in a single sentence, that we cannot but be surprised at the unnecessary breath that has often been spent upon the theology of Hobbes. He lays down the following definition: *'Fear of power invisible, feigned by the mind or imagined from tales publicly allowed*, RELIGION: *not allowed*, SUPERSTITION.' When Hobbes, then, in the same book, with the utmost calmness mentions as simple facts the building of the tower of Babel, or the miracles worked by Moses in Egypt, we must nevertheless recall in astonishment his definition of religion. The man who compared the miracles to 'pills' which we must swallow down without chewing can, in fact, only not have held these miraculous stories for superstitions, because in England the authority of the Bible is established by the supreme political power. When, therefore, Hobbes is speaking upon religious subjects we must constantly distinguish these three cases. *Either* Hobbes speaks directly from his own system and then he views religion as only one form of superstition; *or* he is referring incidentally to some particular points, when he only practically applies a principle of his system – then he views the doctrines of religion as simple facts, with which however, science has nothing more to do; Hobbes is then sacrificing to Leviathan.
>
> The worst contradictions are thus, at least in form, explained away, and we have only the *third* case left – where Hobbes is offering to Leviathan, as it were *de lege ferenda*, respectful suggestions for the purification of religion and for the abolishing of the worst superstitions.

Lange goes on to give examples and then concludes:

> If we add to this the remarkable rudiments of a historico-critical treatment of the Bible, we easily see that the whole armoury of Rationalism is already to be found in Hobbes, and only needs to have its range of application extended.[3]

It could be pointed out that the sentence following the quoted passage is: 'And when the power imagined, is truly such as we imagine, TRUE RELIGION' (45, 124). This, of course, leaves open the question of whether there is a true religion or not. What is true is that Hobbes's system can work without the Christian God, although God can be fitted into it quite usefully. When he holds the threat of God's punishment over the head of a ruler who violates the Law of Nature, he does not require that God exist but only that a belief in him exist. Since the belief was widespread in his day this threat had a certain persuasive force.

4
Morality as Reciprocity

Hobbes's political theory has a tendency to swallow up his ethical theory in the works of most commentators. However, he does distinguish between them although not as clearly as would have been desirable. In *Leviathan*, morality is discussed in Part One, 'Of Man'; in *De Cive*, in Part One, entitled 'Liberty'; and in *The Elements of Law* in Part One, which was first published separately under the title of *Human Nature*. Political theory proper is to be found in the next section in each book, entitled respectively, 'Of Commonwealth', 'Dominion' and 'De Corpore Politico'. The reason I emphasize this is the little noted fact that Hobbes gives two versions of the social contract, one in each part of all three books. I have chosen to interpret this as meaning that it was his intention to found morality as well as the commonwealth on a social contract. He does not succeed in making this distinction clear, I believe, because it is difficult to think of them as separate, particularly if one's original interest is political. He has been accused of not differentiating between the state and society but I believe that this was what was in his mind when he provided two versions of the contract. The wording he gives for the first contract is applicable to a community of any size, from the family on up. He tends to think in terms of the large states, the stability of which he was trying to defend but his ideas apply to social entities of all types. He talks about the city in *De Cive* and he assumes the existence of smaller units when he refers to the need for confederates in the condition of mere nature. The key element in this first contract is the relinquishing of one's right to all things in exchange for others doing the same, which results in the establishment of a moral system. Some form of control is required because of those who would take advantage of this trust but it need not be something as elaborate as a state. Obviously smaller societies will rely more on public opinion than large states do, but within the latter, public opinion and social pressure still play a part when it comes to those areas of morality which are not covered by the legal system.

Since it is obviously not Hobbes's intention to paint a picture of how human societies evolved historically, but to justify the obedience of subjects or citizens to the authority of the states in which they live at the moment, his moral theory will only make sense if it is interpreted with that in mind. In the real world, an individual is born into a social system of some kind and is expected to follow its rules. He may object to the limitations this places on his freedom to do as he pleases, but if he asks why he should have to put up with such a situation, Hobbes, in effect, tells him to look at the alternative. He must imagine himself plunged into a state of nature, where on the one hand, he is free of all the constraints that society has imposed on him but on the other, he is also deprived of the protection provided by the imposition of those constraints on others. He is now on his own, competing with everyone else for survival in a war of all against all. Grotius, Locke, or Rousseau would object that life in the state of nature need not be so nasty and brutish: one can just as easily imagine a state of nature in which men are more benign and cooperate readily with one another. However, in such versions of the state of nature men have already taken steps towards forming a society. What Hobbes wants to show is why they have to take these steps in the first place and for that he needs a model completely devoid of any socialization – one of stark, unadulterated individualism. He is, after all, trying to give one individual person convincing reasons for belonging to a society, and for having to submit to rules which drastically curtail his liberty. This person is not alone, however. He has to share the world with other individuals who, like himself, want unlimited freedom of action. For a mental experiment like this to work, the number of assumptions must be as small as possible. Even if it is admitted that there are friendly people about, one cannot count on it. In fact, however, one must assume that other people are like the original questioner. He has asked why he should not do exactly as he pleases, which means that he wants to escape from those very restrictions that force him to pay attention to the wants of others. Such a person must be given a chance to see what would happen if everyone else were put in a situation where they could exercise their egoism to its limits as he wants to do. In other words Hobbesian man is a construct, deliberately designed to prove a point. Like Euclid's triangles, he may not exist in the real world but can still do the job for which he was designed.

Once this completely fictional scenario is accepted for what it is, one can move on to its implications. Faced with others who are prepared to be as unrestrained as he himself is, our questioner, like them, must indulge in behaviour that is completely immoral by the rules that he wants to jettison. I say 'must' because he no longer has any choice. Even if he is somewhat reluctant to do so, he has to assume the worst in others and take the necessary precautionary measures. Since offense is the best defence, he has to behave in a totally ruthless and aggressive manner if he wants to survive.

Because of the desperate situation he is in, the individual has to be prepared, as we have said, to do anything necessary for his survival, no matter how immoral. Can this be justified? Hobbes says 'yes' when he grants everyone the right of nature, which is the blameless liberty 'to use his own power . . . for the preservation of his own nature'. Neither the English word 'right' nor its Latin counterpart, '*ius*' can be used in this context without involving a moral judgment. Although Hobbes did not specifically say so, he is clearly assuming that life is the supreme value and that anything done to preserve it cannot be wrong. If we look upon life as a game, the greatest game of all, any discussion of its rules, such as that undertaken by a philosopher like Hobbes, is meaningless if no provision is made for players. In order to play the game one has to remain alive, and without the right to do that, all other moral judgments are irrelevant. The right of survival must take precedence over all other rights. Hobbes assumes that we want to go on living but, as noted earlier, this is not an obligation. Although we do not have to stay in the game, the urge to remain alive is, with rare exceptions, the strongest drive we have. Hobbes is surely right in counting on it as the most reliable foundation for a theory of human behaviour.

Given a desire for self-preservation, the obvious next question is how this can best be satisfied. Since there is no security in the state of nature, our questioner is strongly motivated to escape from it by endeavouring to make peace. The first law of nature is thus, 'to seek peace and follow it'. The means for achieving peace is spelled out in the second law of nature: the right to all things must be abandoned and he must content himself with as much liberty against others as he is willing to grant them. This is essentially an agreement to be bound by the golden rule. Hobbes casts this agreement in the form of a mutual transfer which, when trust is involved, as it is here, he refers to as a pact or covenant. The third law of nature, 'that men perform their covenants made' spells out the obligation which arises from this arrangement.

Hobbes's assumption is that anyone who asks why he cannot have unlimited freedom to do as he pleases can be led step by step to agree that the result of granting him, and everyone else, this liberty would be so unpleasant that he would be forced by the logic of the situation to place himself, of his own free will, under the constraints to which he originally objected. What he has had to do is to admit that he would have voluntarily submitted himself to the system of morality under which he already lives. At all stages of the argument he is free to object. He could deny that self-preservation is important to him, or that other people would want to act like himself in the state of nature, or that there is some way of making peace other than agreeing to treat others as he would want to be treated himself. Hobbes appears confident that such a person would not be able to produce convincing alternatives. These are rational choices based on human nature as Hobbes sees it, but the questioner always retains the option of behaving irrationally and acting against his own long-term interest by engaging in anti-social actions. Many individuals, unfortunately, do just that, which is why there must be a public authority empowered to impose a cost on such actions.

Since I am claiming that for Hobbes morality starts here, it is important to determine exactly wherein lies the transition from prudence. It occurs at the moment when an individual enters into a covenant. Although Hobbes declares certain types of covenants invalid under specified conditions, he never even contemplates the possibility of a valid covenant that does not carry with it an obligation of performance. How does the obligation arise? When a man enters into a contract by words or other signs, either he is lying and has no intention of fulfilling his promise, in which case it is not in his mind a real contract, but bogus from the start, or he is sincere and does intend to perform. In the latter case, if in the end he does not perform, he is contradicting himself, an action which in logic would be called an absurdity. This may not, at first sight, seem like a convincing analogy. Absurdity in argument does not usually have the dire consequences that injury does in the world, but the logical structure is parallel. When I enter into a contract, I do so voluntarily: Hobbes has emphasized this point several times. I have committed myself deliberately and in full knowledge of what I have done. Now if I make a habit of contradicting myself in scholarly disputes I shall quickly lose credibility and my reputation will be gone along with any right I have to be taken seriously. This is exactly what happens to someone who does not honour his contracts. Actually more is at stake in that situation as Hobbes points out in his argument with the fool. It is dangerous in both cases but that is not what makes it immoral when a covenant is involved. The reason it is immoral is very simple: that is how Hobbes defines immorality or injustice. As he puts it, 'and the definition of INJUSTICE, is no other than the *not performance of covenant*' (131, 202). He does not expect this to stop some people from violating their covenants if they think they can get away with it. Coercion is necessary to encourage these people to behave justly but whether or not they do so does not alter the fact that by going back on an agreement they entered into voluntarily they acted in a manner that was clearly wrong and immoral.

The key to his conception of morality is personal commitment. By committing myself directly or indirectly, I create an obligation. Later in *Leviathan*, Hobbes says that there is 'no obligation on any man, which ariseth not from some act of his own; for all men equally, are by nature free' (203, 268). A covenant is binding until it is discharged by performance or forgiveness because it represents a voluntary surrender of one's freedom to act otherwise. Someone who asks why he should have to keep his promises is unaware of the extent to which he is demeaning himself. Sayings like 'A man's word is his bond' and 'A man is only as good as his word' reflect the signal importance attached by society to promises. It is on this basis that one establishes a reputation by which one is judged by others but even more important, by oneself. The difference between prudence and morality may come down to whether I am more concerned about the opinion others have of me or *my* opinion of me, using the same standard I apply to everyone else. My self-esteem depends on the image I have of myself.

What differentiates the argument advanced above from that of Warrender is that it does not derive moral obligation from God's commands. As noted earlier, the laws of nature can stand on their own as dictates of reason. This, of course, does not justify their being treated as anything other than prudential but the same question arises if they are regarded as commands modelled after those of the sovereign. If a command, whether it is issued by the sovereign or by God, is obeyed because of the threat of punishment then it has to be treated as prudential. Certainly insofar as those of the sovereign are concerned, their force comes only from a previous agreement to be bound by them. 'For a covenant obligeth by promise of an action, or omission, especially named and limited; but a law bindeth by a promise of obedience in general' (EL,2,10,2). Behind the right of the sovereign to be obeyed lies the moral authority of the covenant freely agreed to. Although the threat of punishment has a role to play in both prudence and morality they are again differentiated, in this case by its source. In the latter it is the pangs of conscience which are to be feared rather than the external sanctions of the state.

There are several criticisms that can be made of any attempt to demonstrate that Hobbes introduced real moral obligation into his system. One is that if he genuinely believed he had done so he was mistaken, because it is contrary to the whole spirit of his work. In his criticism of Warrender, Thomas Nagel said:

> I shall attempt to show that genuine moral obligation plays no part in *Leviathan* at all, but that what Hobbes calls moral obligation is based exclusively on considerations of rational self-interest . . .
>
> One cannot miss the arguments in *Leviathan* based on self-interest. An egoistic theory of motivation permeates the entire book.[1]

Nagel believes that 'preserve yourself' rather than 'seek peace' is Hobbes's fundamental law of nature and that one cannot found moral obligation on such an appeal to self-interest. However, he confesses that he does not know what Hobbes intended by the passage in which he differentiated between the right of nature and a law of nature. Reasons have been given above for assuming that Hobbes meant what he said when he carefully distinguished between right as liberty and law as obligation. Nevertheless, self-interest is certainly prominent in his work and must be taken seriously. The problem is clearly presented when he says that laws of nature oblige *in foro interno* but not *in foro externo*, when one's life was at stake.

Two points can be made in answer to the criticism that this undermines his claim that they are real moral obligations. First of all, Hobbes says that the laws of nature are binding, except under certain circumstances, in the state of nature. Since the hypothetical state of nature exists only in one's mind, the laws of nature are never in question in a settled society. As to a real state of nature such as war, no sane person is going to expect a soldier to treat a declared enemy the way he would a next-door neighbour. The same applies to anyone whose life is threatened by a lawbreaker in a civil society. The second point is that self-interest must not be confused with self-preservation. Hobbes is not saying I can ignore the laws of nature any time it is convenient for me to do so. He is saying that since I have a legitimate right to preserve myself I cannot be bound by the rules of a civilized society when I am not in one and my life is endangered. As he emphasizes repeatedly, I agree to submit to these laws in order to secure my continued existence, not to put it at risk. No reputable philosopher from the ancient Greeks to his own time would have challenged Hobbes on this contention.

Of course the critic can say that we are still not dealing with true morality if our actions are ultimately governed by the needs of the self rather than those of others. This will be discussed later. For the moment it might be useful to take a harder look at the two concepts with which we are dealing: prudence and morality. When Hobbes says that 'Of the voluntary acts of every man, the object is some *good to himself*', I am sure he did not feel that he was being controversial, but was merely stating the obvious. The alternatives are 'harm to himself' which few would accept as reasonable, or 'good to someone else', which is certainly not true of many actions but is also not excluded by the generalization since there is no necessary contradiction between the two. In order to refute Hobbes one would have to show that there is a class of actions which is both good for others and harmful to oneself.

Obviously any dispute over this will hinge to a large extent on one's understanding of what 'good' means in a particular context. For example, when a heavy smoker, a prime candidate for lung cancer, lights up his fortieth cigarette of the day, few would claim that he was doing himself any good. If what Hobbes said is to hold, it must be applied very broadly; in this particular case 'good' must be taken to mean the satisfaction of a very intense need for a smoke. Anyone who tried to talk this man out of his action would argue that he is putting his life in jeopardy. Giving up a momentary pleasure is surely a small price to pay for a continuation of his existence. Two 'goods' are competing here: short-term pleasure and the long-term goal of survival. The outsider will always assume that an individual wants to live as long as possible and will be likely to condemn as imprudent any act which appears to undermine this objective. Behaviour which tends to preserve life will, on the other hand, be labelled prudent. Prudence, of course, applies also to the preservation of one's assets as well as one's life and in general to any long-term goal one has in mind. It implies careful calculation of the most probable consequences of one's actions in light of one's future objectives.

In discussions of Hobbes, prudence is often used as synonymous with selfishness, self-centredness, lack of regard for the welfare of others and so on. It has been used here in opposition to morality mostly for purposes of exposition but we must remember that it was one of the old cardinal virtues. The imprudent as well as the unfortunate are liable to become burdens on society and to that extent at least a prudent person is contributing to the welfare of others. It is the element of calculation which seems to give prudence a bad name: all the time spent on adding and subtracting the advantages and disadvantages of my actions to me seems to leave little for concern about others. However, this ignores the fact that my welfare in a family or community is inextricably tied to that of my relatives and neighbours. Furthermore, the exercise of prudence in my own affairs encourages the formation of habits of self-control and self-denial without which it would be difficult for me to act morally. If you find a man who has behaved in a prudent fashion throughout his life you will also, in most cases, find someone who had done much good and little harm, even though that may not have been his intention. He will certainly have brought about less suffering than a person who is prepared to sacrifice others as well as himself in the name of some great cause.

Why then do we contrast prudence unfavourably with morality? The answer undoubtedly lies in the different reactions we have to the same benevolent action performed by two different people, when one is clearly motivated by expectation of future benefit and the other by what appears to be sheer warm-heartedness. We naturally rate the latter action higher because it seems to be selfless and therefore moral rather than prudential. However, we can never be sure of why people do things and most of us have made wrong and sometimes disastrous judgments about motivation. Many a calculating individual has received credit for apparent virtue – it can be a function of acting ability – whereas the kindness of others is sometimes regarded with suspicion. If our real motivation is known to anyone it should be known to ourselves but even then we cannot always be certain.

However, as far as society is concerned, the reason for an action is not as important as the effect that action has on the well-being of other members of the society. In order for society to function there must be a reasonable degree of security, which means that the incidence of murder, assault and theft be kept as low as possible. The really vital parts of the moral code have to be prohibitions – 'thou shalt not's. Because of that, the most important moral behaviour takes the form of inaction rather than action. When I restrain myself from engaging in violence or taking someone else's property, I am acting morally even though I do nothing. However, I cannot expect constant expression of approval and gratitude from those around me for not indulging in a spree of murder or robbery. Whether I control myself out of prudence or selflessness is of little significance to the outsider since nothing has happened. Yet this kind of inaction is far more important to the continuance of a viable society than going out of my way to help others, nice as that is. The simple truth is that a society can survive if its members are selfish and unpleasant to each other but it cannot last if they take to killing each other indiscriminately.

This is not to say that a prudent man will content himself with mere obedience to prohibition. Social life provides many opportunities for earning gratitude and the possibility of future benefits by helping others. Unselfishness is not necessarily contrary to prudence. A society of really prudent people would be a better society than the ones with which most of us are familiar. The reason is that people in general are not prudent enough. Their long-term self-interest would be enhanced if they were less self-centred in their behaviour and willing to do more for others. The most intense struggle that takes place within us is not between egoism and altruism as such, but between the desire for immediate gratification and the promise of more lasting rewards in the future in exchange for self-denial in the present.

However, as we have noted, Hobbes does use genuinely moral language at times and was almost certainly under the impression that he had provided the underpinnings for a system of morality. Most commentators refer to his use of the golden rule but they do not attach much significance to it because it seems to be overshadowed by the principle of self-preservation. Nevertheless, I believe that if there is a key to his ethical thought, that key is the golden rule. In addition to the references in *Leviathan*, he quotes versions of it several times in *The Elements of Law* and *De Cive*. It is obviously of the greatest importance to him since he regards it as the guide to, and the summation of, the laws of nature. Furthermore, the second law of nature whereby each individual agrees to 'be contented with so much liberty against other men, as he would allow other men against himself', is itself a version of the golden rule.

Hobbes not only quotes the rule but offers an explanation of how and why it works. After his statement of it in *Leviathan*, he adds that anyone 'has no more to do in learning the laws of nature, but, when weighing the actions of other men with his own, they seem too heavy, to put them into the other part of the balance, and his own into their place, that his own passions, and self-love, may add nothing to their weight . . . ' (144, 214). In *De Cive* he says: 'When he doubts whether what he is now doing to another may be done by a law of nature or not, he conceives himself to be in the other's stead. Here instantly those perturbations which persuaded him to the fact, being now cast into the other scale, dissuade him as much' (DC,III,26). In *The Elements of Law* the 'easy rule' to decide if an action runs contrary to the law of nature is this: *'That a man imagine himself in the place of the party with whom he hath to do, and reciprocally him in his*; which is no more but a changing (as it were) of the scales. For every man's passion weigheth heavy on his own scale, but not in the scale of his neighbour' (EL,1,17,9). Mechanically, the golden rule operates as a scale or balance in which I exchange the weight of the other person's interests for my own; psychologically, it would be called empathy, a process whereby I change places imaginatively with the other person and act accordingly. Success is not guaranteed but, as we have noted before, it is the intention that counts since 'he that endeavoureth [the laws'] performance, fulfilleth them . . . ' (145, 215).

What is the current status of the golden rule? A glance at recent works in moral philosophy indicates that it has not attracted much attention and any reference to it are usually critical. However, after having been considered and rejected earlier in a book it may reappear later in a more sophisticated guise. Kant seems to have been a pioneer of this approach.

> Let no one think that here the trivial *quod tibi non vis fieri*, can serve as a standard or principle. For it is merely derivative from our principle [to treat other persons as ends, not just as means], although subject to various qualifications: it cannot be a universal law since it contains the ground neither of duties to oneself nor of duties of kindness to others (for many a man would readily agree that others should not help him if only he could be dispensed from affording help to them), nor finally of strict duties towards

others; for on this basis the criminal would be able to dispute with the judges who punish him, and so on.[2]

Kant's moral philosophy will be discussed later in more detail. Here I shall merely note that his own fundamental principle is: Act only on that maxim whereby you can at the same time will that it should become a universal law. This appears to be an intellectualized version of the basic notion behind the golden rule and, despite Kant's care in spelling it out, it has no more escaped criticism than has the golden rule. Furthermore, like more recent examples, it is too abstract to be readily accessible to the average man who, as Hobbes pointed out, needs a rule that is simple and easy to apply. The very simplicity of the rule requires, however, that a certain amount of common sense must be exercised in its application. Taken literally, it is open to the criticism levied against it by Bernard Shaw, who said: 'Do not do unto others as you would that they should do unto you. Their tastes may not be same'.[3] I think that an allowance for differences in taste is taken for granted in the usual wording but it can easily be made explicit by adding some such phrase as 'if you were in their shoes'. This was obviously in Hobbes's mind when he interpreted the rule in the quotations given above. In fact, the golden rule is as close to a universal moral principle as one is ever likely to find. Versions of it appear not only in the Bible (Matthew VII, 12) but in the Hindu epic, the *Mahabharata* and the writings of Zoroastrianism and Buddhism. Confucius reduced it to one word. 'Tsze-Kung asked, saying is there one word which may serve as a rule of practice for all one's life? The Master said, Is not RECIPROCITY such a word? What you do not want done to yourself, do not do to others' (*Analects*, XV, 23). Reciprocity is surely broad enough to eliminate much of the quibbling associated with the usual form. Thales, born about 640 BC almost a century before Confucius, when asked how men might live virtuously, is reported to have replied 'If we never do ourselves what we blame in others (Diogenes Laertius "Thales", VIII). According to a Talmudic anecdote, Rabbi Hillel, who lived shortly before Christ, when asked to tell the whole of the Torah while standing on one foot, said: 'What is hateful to yourself do not do to your fellow man. That is the whole of the Torah and the rest is but commentary' (*Shabbat*, 31, a). Finally, anthropologists have noted that something similar to a principle of reciprocity is found almost everywhere. We can thus see that Hobbes is in good company on this issue and that the golden rule deserves to be taken more seriously than it usually is by moral philosophers.

One point needs to be clarified here. In the examples mentioned above, the golden rule nearly always occurs in its negative form. The version in Matthew VII, 12 is positive but it is interesting that when St. Augustine quoted it in one of his works, he used the negative form, and the canon law version of Azo, *quod tibi fieri non vis, alteri ne feceris* mentioned by both Hobbes and Kant, is negative. Hobbes uses the negative formulation except when quoting from the Bible, and has been criticized for this. Many people seem to feel that the positive form has a higher moral value because it requires one to do good rather than just avoid evil. However, it has a grave defect which probably explains why it was not more popular: it is too open-ended to be workable as it stands. If I were to make a list of things that I would like others to do for me and that I would therefore have to do for them, it could be endless. No matter how bountiful my supply of benevolence, I cannot help everybody all the time. The positive version is open to the type of criticism made by Leibniz: 'We would wish for more than our share if we had our own way; so do we owe the others more than their share?' However, he quickly produces his own version: 'The true meaning of the rule is that the right way to judge more fairly is to adopt the point of view of the people', which manages to catch part of its essential meaning.[4]

Obviously the positive version can only be applied selectively and this need for the constant exercise of judgment undermines its usefulness as a practical rule. There is no doubt that the common moral opinion expects us to do more than the bare minimum for others but on the question of how much more, it is silent. In practice the amount will depend less on a conscious application of the rule than it will on the individual's character and upbringing. We know we should do as much good as we can but beyond that we enter into the general debate about the rights and wrongs of particular acts in particular situations which characterizes the moral life of a community. Only in those clear-cut cases where a person is in imminent danger if one does not act, can the positive form give the definite guidance which is desirable in a rule. But these cases can be covered easily by the negative form also. 'Do not leave an injured person unattended' means the same as 'Go to the aid of an injured person'.

Since avoiding harm has a much higher priority for human

beings than receiving benefits, the negative formulation of the golden rule is concerned with our most urgent needs. The fact that no community could exist if some of the acts it forbids were allowed to occur at will makes its value obvious. Furthermore, it is easier to apply since all it usually calls for is restraint. Because it is limited and quite precise in what it requires it is obviously more useful as a rule, a characteristic it shares with all negative prescriptions. Prohibitions are much more prominent in moral codes than injunctions and moral injunctions often conceal a prohibition. Both types have a part to play but they must be clearly distinguished in order to avoid confusion.

A frequently used example of a supposed weakness of the golden rule is sado-masochism, but it is actually quite ineffective. Although the sadist enjoys hurting other people, that does not mean that he likes to be hurt himself, so the rule applies. The masochist likes to be hurt and would only be a menace to others if he assumed, contrary to their protestations, that they wanted to be hurt. This is highly unlikely since his main interest is in finding someone to inflict pain on him rather than vice versa. In any case, however, the negative form is quite able to handle this situation as it requires him *not* to do something rather than to do it. Of course, even the positive form would apply if we add the unspoken proviso that I take into consideration the other person's differences from myself. A masochist is as much aware as anyone that all others are not like himself; as a member of a minority he is probably more aware.

Another example is the white supremacist who sincerely believes that all blacks should be slaves and would be prepared to be enslaved if he were a black, or the Nazi who sincerely believes that all Jews should be exterminated and would wish to be so treated if he were a Jew. I find these cases farfetched since I do not believe that anyone in his right mind would really want to be enslaved or exterminated. But, even if there were such people, the negative form would prevent them from making a moral rule out of their racism. Such a person is not being asked whether he would be willing to be enslaved if he were black, or exterminated if he were Jewish. In the first instance, he is being asked: Do you, as you are now, wish to be enslaved or exterminated? If not, do not do it to others.

More elaborate examples have been offered in criticism. Is the rich man, who can obtain the best possible health care by paying for it, not immoral when presumably following the golden rule, he votes against free medical treatment for the poor? I think this example would fail both the negative form and the similar treatment proviso but, regardless of that, it is not a fair test of the golden rule, which is intended to govern one's relations with other individuals on a personal basis. It is not designed to pass judgment on the morality of opposing political viewpoints. The world of politics with its multitude of conflicting interests is not a suitable arena for a rule which is intended to govern the relations of one individual with others. Furthermore, public and private morality often do not coincide. All too often someone who loves all mankind is indifferent to the welfare of those closest to him, whereas many a political reactionary makes an excellent husband, father or friend.

Another criticism which is based on an inappropriate use of the golden rule is that of Kant involving the judge and the criminal. Alan Gewirth also advances similar instances.

> Not only criminal punishment but the collection of money owed by recalcitrant borrowers, the payment of lesser wages for inferior work, the giving of lower grades to poorer students, and the infliction of many similar sorts of hardship would be prohibited by the Golden Rule whenever it could be shown that the respective agents would not themselves want to undergo such adverse treatment.[5]

The mistake here is to confuse official relationships with personal ones. The judge has to act in his capacity as a representative of the legal system regardless of his own feelings about the accused. In each case the agent is not acting in a moral context vis-à-vis the other party but in an institutional one where there are certain duties which he is under a prior obligation to fulfil.

Another example given by Gewirth in the same place is based on Henry Sidgwick's reservation that 'one might wish for another's cooperation in sin, and be willing to reciprocate it'.[6] His version is the case where one bribes a corrupt policeman to ignore a law violation. This would be a very effective criticism if one could ignore the presence of words like 'sin', 'bribe' and 'corrupt'. These indicate that previous commitments to the moral or legal system will be violated and such actions are therefore beside the point. The golden rule obviously cannot be utilized to undermine an obligation imposed by an earlier exercise of the principle of reciprocity. The arguments I have used against these objections may appear to make the golden rule more difficult for the average man to apply than Hobbes thought it was and therefore diminish its usefulness. However, the average man would immediately see them for what they are: legalistic trickery designed to get around the clear intent of the rule.

The golden rule is also found wanting by those who, like Kant, object that it does not contain the ground of our duties or tell us what we ought to do regardless of reciprocity. Although more general than the other criticisms, this one is potentially more serious. It is to be found also in Hans Kelsen's essay, 'What is Justice', where he says:

> If interpreted according to its intention, the golden rule cannot, as its wording pretends, establish a merely subjective criterion of the right behavior, the right behavior of the individual being the behavior that he wants to get from others; such criterion is incompatible with any social order. The golden rule must establish an objective criterion. Its true meaning is: 'Behave in relation to others as the others shall behave in relation to you'. But how shall they behave? This is the question of justice. The answer to this question is not given, but presupposed by the golden rule; it is given by an established social order – by any such order, whether just or unjust.[7]

Interestingly enough, Kelsen condemns Kant's approach on the same grounds. Referring to the categorical imperative he says:

> Its meaning is that one's acts should be determined only by principles that one shall wish to be binding on all men. But what are these principles . . . ? This is the decisive question of justice. To this question the categorical imperative, just as the golden rule – its model – is no answer. (18)

He says they are both empty because they can serve as the justification of any social order.

This criticism is strange coming from Kelsen since, after rejecting other possible answers to his question, he comes to the conclusion that absolute justice is an illusion and falls back on moral relativism. However it is not relativism as between different societies but as between different individuals. On what basis, however, can individuals decide? His answer is tolerance and what it implies.

'"My" justice, then is the justice of freedom, the justice of peace, the justice of democracy – the justice of tolerance' (24). This attempt to combine subjectivism with a defiant personal advocacy of the usual moral ideals is typical, as we shall see, of much modern ethical philosophy.

However, the question remains as to whether his criticism of the golden rule is valid. According to Hobbes, justice is only realizable after we have agreed to be bound by the golden rule; its definition is a social not an individual matter. But to say that the golden rule presupposes an established social order is not correct, at least in the case of Hobbes. And one cannot say, as Kelsen does, that apart from a particular society the golden rule is empty. It is essentially a formal principle and as such has no specific content, but it is used as the basis for deriving specific rules for governing various aspects of human behaviour. One can quickly arrive at prohibition of murder, assault, theft in its various forms and, to give some logical support to Kelsen's personal choice, intolerance. In other words, one can easily develop a moral code which not only looks quite familiar to us but also forms the core of the moral systems of most societies. The advantage of a supreme moral principle like the golden rule is that if accepted it gives us the reasoning behind other rules and commandments which may not make sense to us if we do not find religious, customary or other forms of justification convincing. It is an attempt to provide a logical foundation for those who find they cannot be satisfied with the traditional explanation.

There are two other reservations people may have about the golden rule. One applies solely to the negative form, which appears to leave out much of what has been included in traditional ethics, particularly acts of benevolence. However, my emphasis on it was never meant to eliminate observance of the positive version, which remains as a guide which we should follow as much as possible. This would certainly be the view of Hobbes, who uses both versions. It should be noted as well that the positive form can be very definite if it is seen as applying to situations where others have, in effect, requested our help. It is not necessary that they do so in words as when, for example, someone who is drowning calls out for help, but the circumstances may make the need obvious, as when a blind person waits for assistance in crossing the street. Similarly, although I cannot devote all my energies to the needs of the Third World, I can certainly respond to a request from Oxfam or some other agency. In these cases the alternatives are clear-cut as they are with the negative form. An important difference should not be forgotten, however. Society regards killing as far more culpable than letting someone die in circumstances where one could have saved the person's life. Violation of the negative golden rule can be a crime as well as wrongdoing, whereas violation of the positive form is subject usually only to social disapproval.

The other reservation is a certain distaste at the emphasis on self in the golden rule, which is often expressed indirectly. To base morality on a rule which refers back to one's self seems somehow contrary to the whole point of morality. It can be seen in C. D. Broad's comments on R. M. Hare's version of putting oneself in another's place as a test for wrongness.

> Mr. Hare says that A will be inclined to judge it to be *wrong* for him to treat B in a certain way, if, on imagining himself to be in a similar situation as *patient* instead of agent, he finds that he would *dislike* to be treated in that way. What is not clear to me is what Mr. Hare takes to be the relevance of this 'dislike' on A's part.
>
> It seems to me that all that is *logically* relevant is that A should judge that it would be *wrong* for another to treat him as he is proposing to treat B. Whether he would *dislike* or *like* being treated in that way seems logically irrelevant.[8]

This is an example of the type of question-begging which dogs any attempt to develop a coherent ethical theory. Introducing the word to be defined into a suggested definition certainly does not advance the cause. Furthermore, Broad ignores the fact that I may genuinely not know if my intended action is wrong and I should therefore not do it, until I have imaginatively put myself in the other person's place to see what its likely effect will be.

Brian Barry refers to this process as self-interested choice and quotes Broad's rejection of it with approval.[9] This is odd given what Barry says later, but it appears to be based on a misunderstanding. What has occurred can only indirectly be called a self-interested choice. The sequence of events is as follows: I have a strong desire to do something which impinges on the well-being of another. Before performing the action I imaginatively put myself in that person's place and discover that I would not like having done to myself what I intend to do to him. I conclude that the action is wrong and I refrain from doing it. In taking this decision I am actually behaving unselfishly; I am denying myself the pleasure of doing something I would have enjoyed doing. I would have been acting selfishly, on the other hand, if I had just gone ahead and done it. The point is that this kind of process does not result in a self-interested choice but in the exact opposite. The reason I said that Barry's comment was odd is that later on in his book, after associating Hobbes with justice as self-interested rather than justice as impartiality (which is his own position) he says: 'The essence of justice as impartiality is encapsulated in the Golden Rule; the efforts of Hobbes and Gauthier [a recent proposal of the self-interest justification] require hundreds of pages of subtle reasoning' (364). He thus seems not to see the link between putting oneself in another's place and the golden rule, as well as missing the vital role that the golden rule plays in Hobbesian morality.

I should perhaps make explicit what is obviously implicit in the golden rule, i.e. that its purpose is to avoid harming others. Since none of us normally wants to die or be subjected to pain, whether physical or mental, we must avoid activities which are likely to result in such harm. Because human beings are usually sensitive to pain and are certainly capable of inflicting it on each other, one has to assume that if we are to live together in groups we must be willing to exercise enough restraint so that a reasonable degree of peace and security is achieved. No one would be willing to belong to a collectivity if some norm of reciprocity were not accepted by the members. The golden rule merely helps us determine in particular situations which actions are likely to violate this agreement.

5
The Social Contract and the Golden Rule in Practice

So far we have dealt with the golden rule mainly as a brief way to summarize the laws of nature and therefore as a quick method of determining whether an action is right or wrong.

However, as we have seen, Hobbes has already utilized the rule as his second law of nature: *'that a man be willing, when others are so too . . . to lay down this right to all things; and be contented with so much liberty against other men, as he would allow other men against himself'* (118, 190). Although he refers to both the Gospel form and the negative Latin version at this point, it is the latter which correctly represents the second law of nature since it requires that we do *not* interfere with the liberty of the other person once the agreement has been made. We could never leave the state of nature, and society could not exist without this proviso since it is the social contract on which all human communities are based. Prior to this agreement the individual still has a choice, but once he has entered into it freely and of his own volition he has a commitment to observe it. The third law, *'that men perform their covenant made'*, is a codification of this responsibility and therefore 'the fountain and original of JUSTICE' (130, 202). Since the breaking of a covenant is what defines injustice, an individual can only act unjustly or immorally if he has entered into an agreement by promising to be bound by the terms of it and then breaks his promise.

As was noted earlier, Hobbes immediately complicates the situation by first claiming on the one hand that 'where there is no commonwealth, there nothing is unjust,' and then on the other that if one of the parties to a covenant has performed already, the other still has to perform, even though they are in a state of nature. The latter situation is found in his argument against the fool, and I presume he is referring to the state of nature because he differentiates it from circumstances where 'there is a power to make him perform,' which would indicate the presence of a civil state. This apparent conflict can be explained, I think, if we go back to our two states of nature. In his case against the fool he is thinking of a real state of nature, in which it is possible to make this kind of covenant. An agreement between feudal nobles in the Middle Ages would be one of many possible examples. With respect to the claim that there is no injustice outside the commonwealth, Hobbes was thinking specifically of property when he wrote that paragraph, as we noted before, and meaningful property rights are hard to imagine in a genuine state of nature. Furthermore, if we put this passage in the context of the hypothetical state of nature instead of the historical one, his emphasis on the commonwealth as the only alternative is understandable. It must be remembered again that the structure of his argument pits the anarchy of a completely individualistic state of nature, in which property rights are inconceivable, against the existing seventeenth-century state with all the safeguards it provided for property owners. Naturally, it was no contest.

The point of all this is that breaking a covenant freely made is unjust, wrong and immoral whether it is done in the state of nature or the commonwealth. Hobbes's detailed discussion of the various types of covenants and the conditions under which they are valid is genuinely significant for the real state of nature. Individuals as well as states are constantly making agreements which are not enforceable by law. These are governed by the rules which he has laid out, e.g., if you learn, after having made a contract, that the other party has no intention of performing, then you are, yourself, excused from performance. Any obligation created by a valid covenant, with the exceptions he notes, is morally binding because 'the definition of INJUSTICE, is no other than *the not performance of covenant*'.

The situation in the hypothetical state of nature is, however, not so clear. If such extreme conditions actually existed, it is hard to imagine that anyone would be willing to enter into a covenant, especially the kind that required one party to perform before the other. If one were made, in full knowledge of the dangers involved, it would, of course, be valid and therefore binding. However, there is only one covenant which really matters in the hypothetical state of nature and that is the mutual surrender of rights which is required to create a society. Is this covenant also hypothetical and, if so, is it binding? I agree with Gregory Kavka who, in his discussion of hypothetical consent says: 'Obligation, as Hobbes and others have understood it, is created only by actual consent [for Kavka this includes tacit consent], and people's actual consents (with their corresponding obligations to act as they have consented to act) play no role in hypothetical consent theory'.[1] However, I do not think we are dealing with hypothetical consent, as he defines it.

The hypothetical state of nature is so extreme that it could never actually exist. Since we are born into families, we are in a social setting from the beginning of our lives. Any situation which one can envision arising in the real world, in which individuals are completely on their own, would disappear almost immediately as they came together to form groups for mutual protection. This tendency merely confirms the logic of Hobbes's position but he has to hold these individuals apart imaginatively long enough to examine the implications of their plight and to work out the rationale behind their behaviour. Since he is trying to justify the existence of the political entities of his own day, the small groups which developed and gradually evolved into larger ones over historical time are essentially irrelevant to his political theory. But for his theory of moral obligation, social groups are extremely significant, regardless of size. What is important are the implications of the individual's decision to belong to a group rather than face the world alone. By running that imaginary transition from the state of nature to society in slow motion Hobbes is trying to get us to face up to the commitment we have undertaken when we accept the benefit of belonging.

To put it in terms of a covenant can, of course, be seen as rather an artificial way of handling it. But not to do so is to risk never really understanding what is involved, and falling back on non-explanations such as an instinct of sociability. When a ghetto youth, at the mercy of warring street gangs, decides to join one of them for protection, he has entered into a covenant even though he might not be familiar with the terminology. If you asked him what benefits he received from the membership and what he had to do in return, his answer would not differ in any material way from a Hobbesian agreement. This would be true whether or not he had gone through a formal initiation process. The details would not have to be spelled out in order for him to realize that he has undertaken a commitment in return for security. In this example we are dealing with a real state of nature – the modern urban jungle – but the principle involved is the same. If you were to ask that same youth some time after he had originally joined the gang why he continued to belong, he would have to reply in terms of his current situation as opposed not to his original circumstances prior to joining but to the conditions he would likely have to face now on the outside, i.e., a hypothetical alternative of the type we have been discussing. Whether you are born into a group, became a member long ago or became a member recently, the logical structure of the dilemma is the same: your real life situation now as a member of a group, versus the likely alternative outside the group, also as of now. Thus, although the imagined state of nature is hypothetical, your response to the question is not. When you choose your current membership in the group instead of the state of nature, with all its insecurities, you are, at the same time, choosing to be bound by the covenant without which that social group could not exist.

Of course people are rarely asked this kind of question and therefore are not put in the position of having to make a choice and commit themselves one way or the other. But as Hobbes says, concerning signs that a contract has been made: 'Signs by inference, are sometimes the consequence of words; sometimes the consequence of silence; sometimes the consequence of actions; sometimes the consequence of forbearing an action: and generally a sign by inference, of any contract, is whatsoever sufficiently argues the will of the contractor' (121, 193). Different evidence can be adduced to support the feeling that an implicit contract has been made but the most convincing, to me, is the way in which we expect to be treated by others within our group, and our outrage when one of them does not treat us that way. Since we behave as if he or she were breaking an agreement, and there is no overt agreement, we must be operating on the presumption that there is an implicit one to which we are committed by tacit consent. The nature of this covenant would be apparent to all because of the ineluctable logic of the social situation.

Hobbes has convincing grounds for equating the social contract with other contracts and therefore requiring it to be morally binding. We have been talking about it in the abstract but it is not, and could not be just any agreement. We can make agreements about anything we desire later on but first there must be the minimal arrangement necessary for the existence of a community of human beings, and that is his second natural law: the social contract, which is, at the same time, the golden rule. When we expect a fellow member of our group to behave in a certain way towards us it is because we are assuming that the principle of reciprocity will govern our relationship. We are upset when he does not obey it because we know that without its observance by most of us, we could not go on living together in peace.

Thus we have two factors involved. One is the principle of reciprocity (the second law of nature) without which peaceful coexistence with our fellows is not possible and the other is the obligation to keep to that principle once we have agreed to it. This flows from the general requirement to perform any valid covenant to which one is a party (the third law of nature). We can agree to follow the principle of reciprocity because it appears to be in our interest at the moment but that alone is not enough. We cannot remain in a situation in which we are able to change our minds when it seems to be in our short-term interest to do so. Morality arises from personal commitment. Hobbes knows that words are mere gossamer but, as we have seen, words are not necessary to create an obligation. By saying 'I do' in a marriage service, a man and woman solemnize the oldest contract known to human beings. But such a ceremony is not necessary to create mutual obligations. A couple cannot decide to live together or even 'go steady' without setting up a network of reciprocal ties and expectations. Once the relationship goes beyond casual friendship, it is usually understood that they will not go out with other members of the opposite sex, and as it develops further, looking after the welfare of each other becomes even more important. Should one of them betray this unwritten and unspoken agreement, the other will feel justified in complaining or even ending the affair. What we have here is the smallest possible version of the social contract. Since it usually occurs within a settled society, considerations of security are not primary although still important. But there are many advantages to both partners in this simplest and most basic of all social arrangements. These advantages flow from the mutual surrender of rights which Hobbes lays down in his second law of nature. The couple do not need Hobbes to tell them about this because he has merely crystallized out what is inherent in their relationship. When two people decide to become a couple the usual tensions that exist between any two normal self-centred individuals have to be resolved. This resolution *has* to take a certain form because of the logic behind the equation. That logic, which is the principle of reciprocity, applies to all groups, from the couple up to the nation-state. Hobbes has merely pointed this out and formalized it in his laws.

However, what I want to emphasize here is that although it is quite useful to model this agreement on a civil law contract, as Hobbes has done, it is not necessary that words be spoken or written. Once the two people have crossed a certain boundary line in their relationship, the covenant is there whether they would put it that way or not. Expectations and obligations emerge at that point and any words that may be uttered merely recognize a situation that already exists, and one that is commonly referred to as an 'understanding'. In law such arrangements are often recognized as 'quasi-contracts'.

Once an understanding is reached it continues to exist until it breaks down for one reason or another. But during the period of its existence, the parties are aware that it continues to function just as it did when it first came into being. It is as if the arrangement is constantly renewed from moment to moment. One does not have to look back to an original tacit agreement – once in operation the will to maintain it is what counts for everything. When that will is gone the agreement, with its benefits as well as its obligations, is terminated.

If all this is accepted, Hobbes's covenant can be seen as a useful way of expressing a fundamental truth about how human beings are able to live in groups, rather than as an unconvincing attempt to explain the rise of moral obligation. At any given moment in time, moral obligation exists. If people accept this unquestioningly, there is no reason to offer an explanation. But if someone does ask why he is under an obligation to behave morally, then Hobbes presents the hypothetical alternative to the current circumstances and attempts to demonstrate on the basis of logic and the known facts about human behaviour what is obvious to most people: that when the questioner chooses to remain in the group he automatically places himself under an obligation to act in a certain fashion towards his fellow members.

This is true of any collectivity of human beings organized for a specific purpose. The analogy of a game is often used, as Hobbes himself did. Whether it be a board game like chess, a card game like bridge, or a sport like tennis, there are rules which must be followed if a player is to remain in the game. One objective, of course, is to win if you can, but since not everyone can win, the other objective is merely to participate in the game: to enjoy the challenge to your intelligence and skills entailed in surmounting the obstacles placed in your way by the rules. To suspend the rules in your case so that you can always win would not only be unacceptable to the other players but would vitiate the whole point of the game, which is to try to win within the rules. They are there precisely to make the game difficult and therefore interesting.

Interesting, that is, for those who want to play it. Each game is fascinating for some and boring for others. Those who are not intrigued by the demands of the game, see no reason to play and therefore do not. Participation, except where it is a requirement for educational purposes, is voluntary. But once a person has freely decided to play, he is bound by the rules. He does not usually have to sign contracts or swear oaths since he knows what is involved when he asks to join in: once he is in the game he has to obey the rules. There may be penalties for infractions of rules of behaviour in sports, but generally you cannot break the rules without ending your participation, since the game *is* the rules. If a chess player insists on moving a pawn like a rook, the game will cease and he will have no one to play with until he changes his attitude. The specific rules of a particular game are quite arbitrary but the general rule, applicable to all games, that one must obey the rules if one wants to play, is not. People like playing games and since they must obey this general rule in order to make games possible, observance of the rule cannot be separated from the very existence of the game.

We have already used the game analogy in connection with self-preservation. In order to take part in the most important game of all, life, one must first be alive in order to be a player. This requires a certain attention to one's continued survival. The same metaphor applies to human groups from families to clubs to states. The major difference is between those groups that one joins by choice and those into which one is born. But as we noted above, the difference is not as significant as it might seem because it is not a question of *when* one joined the group but whether or not one wants to belong to it *now*. No matter how long I have played chess I may find at the present moment that I have become bored with it and decide to give it up. This does not seem so easy with other groups such as the family or the state. However, it is not impossible. In the case of the state, if I cannot emigrate I do still have the less desirable choice of becoming an outlaw. This option will receive further attention later.

The role of games in the moral development of children is discussed by Jean Piaget in his *Moral Judgment of the Child*.[2] The rationale for his approach is laid out in the following passage:

> Now, most of the moral rules which the child learns to respect he receives from adults, which means that he receives them after they have been fully elaborated, and often elaborated, not in relation to him and as they are needed, but once and for all and through an uninterrupted succession of earlier adult generations.
>
> In the case of the very simplest social games, on the contrary, we are in the presence of rules which have been elaborated by children alone. (13–14)

The game he used for his experiments was marbles, as played by boys in some of the schools of Geneva and Neuchâtel. Observation and questioning led him to postulate various stages in the practice of rules. At first the child plays with the marbles on his own mainly to exercise his motor skills, but between the ages of two and five he moves into the 'egocentric' stage. At this point he has learned that there are rules, and although he imitates the older boys he may play by himself or he may play with others without trying to win. 'In other words, children of this stage, even when they are playing together, play each one on his own (everyone can win at once) and without regard for any codification of rules' (27). During the next stage, that of 'cooperation', which appears between seven and eight, the boys play according to rules but their idea of the rules is vague and shifting. Only when they reach eleven or twelve do they arrive at the final stage which he calls the 'codification of rules'. The rules are now fixed and are known in all their detail to every member of the group.

Piaget found that the consciousness of rules came in stages which overlapped those of their practice.

> During the first stage rules are not yet coercive in character, either because they are purely motor, or else (at the beginning of the egocentric stage) because they are received, as it were, unconsciously, and as interesting examples rather than as obligatory realities.
>
> During the second stage (apogee of egocentric and first half of cooperating stage) rules are regarded as sacred and untouchable, emanating from adults and lasting forever. Every suggested alternative strikes the child as a transgression.
>
> Finally, during the third stage, a rule is looked upon as a law due to mutual consent, which you must respect if you want to

be loyal but which it is permissible to alter on the condition of enlisting general opinion on your side. (28)

This passage lays out for us the major theme of Piaget's book, which is expressed in the title of the last chapter: 'The Two Moralities of the Child'. One of these is the sense of right and wrong that emerges in us as a result of commands and prohibitions emanating from all-powerful adults when we are small. We are too young to understand the reasons for these orders but we learn to obey them on pain of punishment or causing displeasure to someone we love. The relationship that exists between adult and child is one of constraint and unilateral respect. From it flows our ideas of duty, of obligation imposed from without, of authority perceived as something external to us. It is the model of morality as command or imperative and as such it retains a grip on us for the rest of our lives.

The alternative type of morality is that which arises when children engage in activities such as games involving others of their own age group. This requires cooperation rather than constraint, mutual rather than unilateral respect, equality rather than subordination, and autonomy rather than heteronomy. When first learning the game, the young child picks up the idea of rules from the older ones who enjoy the prestige of age, just as adults do. However, when he reaches fourteen or fifteen he loses interest in marbles and moves on to other games. This means that between the ages of eleven and thirteen, children have no seniors. As far as the game of marbles is concerned they are, in effect, adults and are thus able to legislate for themselves. The key to this period, as Piaget emphasizes, is not just that they play according to a particular set of rules, but that they feel free to alter the rules by discussion and agreement. He found many variations in the rules from one school to another and also over time. This continuing creativity leads children a few years older to shake their heads over the fact that the game is no longer played the way it was in their day.

What is significant for our purposes is not so much that rules are being changed but that rules are being *made*. 'In short, law now emanates from the sovereign people and no longer from the tradition laid down by the Elders' (72). All this flows from the child's desire to participate in a game. Playing by himself, he can always win, but he gradually discovers that it is more fun to compete with others, and further, that the more difficult a game is to play, the more interesting it usually is. This calls for rules, and obedience to those rules. The urge to win creates a situation which requires a high degree of collaboration. Ironically, competition thus necessitates cooperation.

There is more to social life than games, of course, but the point is that even in a highly competitive situation like a game, where the goal is to triumph over others, we need a set of rules which has been established beforehand by mutual agreement. And, as Piaget points out, the only basis for that agreement is reciprocity. He also distinguishes between 'constituted' rules – those of a specific game arrived at democratically by the participants – and 'constitutive' rules which are those governing the process whereby this takes place. 'In the same way, so-called moral rules can, generally speaking, be divided into constituted rules dependent upon mutual consent, and constitutive rules or functional principles which render cooperation and reciprocity possible' (98). The latter would be the equivalent of Hobbes's 'laws of nature' and the former would be the actual laws which govern the daily operations of any society.

In the questioning of the children by Piaget and his associates, the following exchange with an eleven-year-old boy called Ross took place:

> Why are there rules in the game of marbles? *So as not to be always quarrelling you must have rules, and then play properly.* – How did these rules begin? – *Some boys came to an agreement amongst themselves and made them.* (66)

Surely, no more succinct statement of what Hobbes is trying to say has ever been made! We have the state of nature, the social contract and the justification of morality, all out of the mouth of a child. It seems strange that what is so clear and so obvious to an eleven-year-old creates problems for many a moral philosopher. I say this not because one has to accept a child's explanation as the last word on the subject but because we are dealing here not just with theory but with actuality as well. Ross is a real person who is telling his interrogators about the social world as he sees himself fitting into it. His insights will govern his behaviour for the rest of his days. And he is not alone; the answers given by his playmates would not differ much from his. Each individual has to work this out for himself when he reaches the age at which he can comprehend what is at stake. The fact that there is substantial agreement indicates that they are saying something very fundamental about human nature, something that cannot be lightly dismissed.

Piaget moves on from the specific case of games to a more general consideration of the two kinds of morality in other contexts, e.g., consequences versus intentions. Since harried parents tend to punish children on the basis of the amount of damage they have done, the younger ones judge culpability by the consequences of their actions. This comes out clearly when they are asked to compare actions in which mischievous behaviour results in minor damage with those in which good intentions lead to more disastrous consequences. They rate the latter as deserving of more severe punishment, since they do not take motivation into consideration. As they grow a little older their attitude changes and they begin to make allowance for good intentions in assessing the moral significance of the actions. This tendency on the part of the younger children to judge behaviour on the basis of punishment is demonstrated clearly in the case of reactions to lying. When asked about lying, they say it is wrong because it is punished; if questioned further they say that it would not be wrong if it were not subject to punishment. The older children (nine or ten), on the other hand, tend to invoke reasons related to reciprocity and mutual respect such as not being able to trust others any more. Summing up this section, Piaget says that taking intentions into account is not as natural as one would think, because the child is more interested in results than his own motivation. 'It is cooperation which leads to the primacy of intentionality, by forcing the individual to be constantly occupied with the point of view of other people so as to compare it with his own' (189–90).

The relevance of this to Hobbes is that he, too, distinguishes between the two types of morality, although this has escaped many of his readers. Despite adoption of the reciprocity model by the older children, this does not mean that they give up the adult constraint model. The latter is retained in later life for the many situations in which the individual is in a dependent position, and it is, of course, the pattern for his relationship to an omnipotent patriarchal God who issues commandments which must be obeyed on pain of eternal punishment. Because Hobbes cannot count on most people to do what they ought to do, he provides for 'some coercive power to compel men equally to the performance of their covenant, by the terror of some punishment, greater than the benefit they expect by the breach of their covenant . . . ' (131, 202). However, it is not the punishment which makes their action wrong but the fact that it violates the covenant. Constraint must be available in case mutual respect is not strong enough. This is true even amongst children playing a game. Expulsion from the game is the method available there, but in a larger society it is not that simple.

The second type of morality is most clearly illustrated in the concept of justice, which Piaget calls 'the most rational of all moral notions' (197). At the beginning of his chapter on this subject, he writes:

> The conclusion which we shall finally reach is that the sense of justice, though naturally capable of being reinforced by the precepts and practical example of the adult, is largely independent of these influences, and requires nothing more for its development than the mutual respect and solidarity which holds among children themselves. It is often at the expense of the adult and not because of him that the notions of just and unjust find their way into the youthful mind. In contrast to a given rule, which from the first has been imposed upon the child from outside and which for many years he has failed to understand, such as the rule for not telling lies, the rule of justice is a sort of immanent condition of social relationships or a law governing their equilibrium. And as the solidarity between children grows we shall find this notion of justice gradually emerging in almost complete autonomy. (198)

It is ironic that a sense of justice should often develop among children at the expense of their moral relationship with adults who have been trying so hard to instill ethical principles in them. For example, what the teacher regards as cheating, the student looks upon as helping a comrade. The solidarity is so strong and the scorn for anyone who betrays that solidarity is so telling that the group may appear like a continuing conspiracy against the values of the adult world. But there is no other way. The adult can, of course, set a good example by practising reciprocity.

> But the most direct effect of adult ascendancy is . . . the feeling of duty, and there is a sort of contradiction between the submission demanded by duty and the complete autonomy required by the development of justice. For, resting as it does on equality and reciprocity, justice can only come into being by free consent. Adult authority, even if it acts in conformity with justice, has

therefore the effect of weakening what constitutes the essence of justice. (319)

Thus, Piaget sees justice as arising by voluntary agreement amongst individuals in a group, as does Hobbes. The difference is due to point of view. The Swiss psychologist is concerned with how we actually develop the idea of justice as children interacting with other children, whereas Hobbes is more interested in the abstract question of why a commitment to justice emerges from, and is required by, the social contract. There is, however, one area of potential disagreement. For Piaget, justice, as fairness and equity, should not be identified with the written law and may, on occasion, conflict with it. This position, which might put one's personal conscience above the law, would not be acceptable to Hobbes. The problem arises from Piaget's sharp distinction between constraint and cooperation in the development of children's morality. In his understandable preference for the latter, he largely ignores the discipline that children impose on themselves. As he says, the older children 'ban lies among themselves, cheating, and everything that compromises solidarity' (320). Since that ban has to be enforced, peer group solidarity achieves a degree of conformity which adults can only marvel at. No matter how much equality and mutual respect may be involved, the group still must enact laws which have to be obeyed and it is precisely this type of law to which Hobbes is referring. If one participates freely in the process which leads to the promulgation of laws, one cannot legitimately go on to call them unjust. Nevertheless, Piaget's distinction is a fruitful one when it comes to understanding the apparently contradictory nature of much moral and political discourse.

6
Morality and Objectivity

Another point at which Piaget's work provides empirical support for Hobbes (and many other thinkers for that matter) is the relationship between ethics and rationality. Here is how he puts it:

> To use an apter comparison, we may say that the child of 7 to 10 plays as he reasons. We have already [in Chapter IV of *Judgment and Reasoning in the Child* (Eng. tr. 1926)] tried to establish the fact that about the age of 7 or 8, precisely, that is to say, at the moment when our third stage appears . . . . discussion and reflection gain an increasing ascendency over unproved affirmation and intellectual egocentrism. Now, these new habits of thought lead to genuine deductions . . . in which the child grapples with a given fact of experience, either present or past. But something is still lacking if deduction is to be generalized and made completely rational: the child must be able to reason formally, *i.e.*, he must have a conscious realization of the rules of reasoning which will enable him to apply them to any case whatsoever, including purely hypothetical cases (mere assumptions). (46)

Thus, about the age of eleven or twelve, the child reaches the point where he or she can comprehend the general principles involved in both logical and moral discourse. These principles emerge in the course of interaction with others.

> Our earlier studies led us to the conclusion that the norms of reason, and in particular the important norm of reciprocity, the source of the logic of relations, can only develop in and through cooperation . . . . (Reason) requires cooperation in so far as being rational consists in 'situating oneself' so as to submit the individual to the universal. Mutual respect therefore appears to us as the necessary condition of autonomy under its double aspect, intellectual and moral. From the intellectual point of view,

it frees the child from the opinions that have been imposed upon him while it favours inner consistency and reciprocal control. From the moral point of view, it replaces the norms of authority by that norm immanent in action and in consciousness themselves, the norm of reciprocity in sympathy. (107)

By noting this parallelism between intellectual and moral development in children, Piaget provides some justification for the position Hobbes takes when he says in *Leviathan*:

> So that *injury* or *injustice*, in the controversies of the world is somewhat like to that, which in the disputations of scholars is called *absurdity*. For as it is then called an absurdity, to contradict what are maintained in the beginning: so in the world, it is called injustice, and injury, voluntarily to undo that, which from the beginning he had voluntarily done. (119, 191)

Piaget sums it up beautifully as follows: 'Logic is the morality of thought just as morality is the logic of action' (398). He assumes that everyone is aware of the truth of this but such is not the case, although C. S. Pierce had written in a letter to a friend that he regarded 'Logic as the Ethics of the Intellect'.[1] Certainly there is not the impassable gulf between them that many modern philosophers claim to find. Any form of human discourse, whether it aims at consensus on what are the correct facts, what is convincing reasoning or what is immoral behaviour, is dependent on rules. Just as competition requires collaboration so the disagreement involved in a meaningful argument requires prior agreement. If there is no concurrence on at least some ground rules, a genuine argument becomes impossible. What occurs instead is people possessing strongly held opinions talking at each other, with no way of ever resolving their disputes.

This is exactly what emotivists, prescriptivists, subjectivists and other non-cognitivists say does occur in moral discourse. They claim that there is no moral knowledge in the same sense that there is scientific knowledge. Emotivists, for example, assert that moral utterances merely express the feelings of those who voice them and therefore cannot be either true or false. The classic expression of this was formulated by A. J. Ayer.

> Thus if I say to someone, 'You acted wrongly in stealing that money', I am not stating anything more than if I had simply

said, 'You stole that money', . . . in a peculiar tone of horror, or written it with the addition of some special exclamation marks.[2]

A prescriptivist pushes this a step further by adding that when I thus express approval or disapproval of an action, I am also commending a similar response to others. There are quite sophisticated variations on this theme but what they all have in common is noted by Marcus G. Singer.[3]

> In general any theory that maintains that there can be no such thing as a good reason for a moral judgment, or that there are no valid moral arguments, or that ultimate moral principles cannot be proved, that morality has no rational basis, or that the difference between right and wrong is merely a matter of taste, opinion, feeling, or convention, is a form of moral skepticism.

Such a theory depends for its credibility on a very sharp distinction being drawn between normative and other forms of discourse, with the purpose of showing that moral statements lack the kind of solidity attributed to factual statements. Or as J. L. Mackie puts it, 'values are not objective, are not part of the fabric of the world'.[4] Like so many moral sceptics he never really makes clear precisely what characteristics are required for something to be part of the fabric of the world. But are moral statements and, say, empirical ones really so different? Mackie himself takes note of an early attempt to show that they are not.

> For example, Richard Price argues that it is not moral knowledge alone that such an empiricism as those of Locke and Hume is unable to account for, but also our knowledge and even our ideas of essence, number, identity, diversity, solidity, inertia, substance, the necessary existence and infinite extension of time and space, necessity and possibility in general, power, and causation.

His response to this is not very convincing: 'I can only state my belief that satisfactory accounts of most of these can be given in empirical terms' (39). He neglects to mention that empiricism itself has been under attack in recent years and no longer elicits the automatic conviction that it once did. Mackie and others like him are victims of what might be called the 'perceptibility fallacy'.

Since morality cannot be seen or touched it somehow lacks genuine reality. This is related to the 'ideal observer' or 'impartial spectator' approach to ethics which treats moral or immoral actions as events which are observed by an outsider while they occur, rather than the result of decisions made by an agent *before* they occur. An earlier example of this tendency is seen in David Hume's *A Treatise of Human Nature*.

> Take an action allow'd to be vicious: Wilful murder for instance. Examine it in all lights, and see if you can find that matter of fact or real existence, which you call *vice*. In which-ever way you take it, you find only certain passions, motives, volitions and thoughts. There is no other matter of fact in the case. The vice entirely escapes you, as long as you consider the object. You never find it, till you turn your reflexion into your own breast, and find a sentiment of disapprobation, which arises in you, towards this action. Here is a matter of fact; but 'tis the object of feeling, not of reason. (III, i, 1)

He goes on to compare virtue and vice to colours or heat and cold which 'are not qualities in objects, but perceptions in the mind'. However he does admit that nothing can be more real 'than our own sentiments of pleasure and uneasiness' as aroused by the action. This type of analysis raises many questions but the most pressing one in my mind is, *why* do I disapprove? If one rejects reason, as Hume does, one is left with the impression that I disapprove of murder the way I do of a bad smell, and as a potential agent I am given no reason for refraining from murder except the anticipation that refined spectators will metaphorically hold their noses.

As Hume himself discovered there is no reason why scepticism has to stop with morality once it is deployed. Renford Bambrough demonstrates exhaustively in *Moral Scepticism and Moral Knowledge* (London, 1979), that there is no argument against the objectivity of morals that cannot be paralleled by an argument against the objectivity of history, physics or any other field of enquiry. Why then do moral sceptics cling to their position despite its inconsistency? The answer seems to be that they have a deep-seated belief that the claims of morality to objectivity are much weaker than those of science – so much weaker that for all practical purposes morality does not qualify as knowledge at all in their eyes.

What persuades many people that this is so is the great variety of moral beliefs and the difficulty in settling disputes among them. However, the particular customs and mores of different societies, to which their members are strongly attached, can be seen as an argument for moral relativism only if one ignores the fact that most of these are not intended to be universal: on the contrary, their purpose is precisely to differentiate one community from another. A Sikh does not believe that it is wrong for a non-Sikh male to cut his hair and refuse to wear a turban and I am sure that the question of circumcision among non-Jews is a matter of indifference to orthodox Jews. We have already noted in our discussion of natural law, that it is to be expected that different societies will have different positive laws; what is of interest is that they all have at least some laws in common. And what all definitely have in common is a conception of right and wrong, so that they understand what it means when they are told that it is wrong to violate their own particular moral code.

However, the moral sceptic can still point to the difficulties that arise within a society. A typical example today is abortion: on what basis can one decide whether it is immoral or not? But as has already been pointed out so often, since both sides agree that innocent human life should not be taken, the argument is not really over morality but over a factual or at least definitional question: whether a foetus is a human being or not, or at what stage it becomes human. A murder trial is a paradigm for all arguments of this kind. Unless it is an open and shut case, the prosecution and defense will produce conflicting versions of what happened, give conflicting interpretations of those events and draw conflicting inferences from the evidence. Not only will ordinary witnesses disagree with each other but experts possessing impeccable credentials will often be found testifying in opposition to one another. Finally, even if the jury is satisfied that the accused is guilty, it has to determine whether what took place was murder or a lesser offense such as manslaughter. The only matter which is never in doubt from the start is that murder is a crime. In the same way, if you break a moral dispute down into its parts, you find it is more difficult to reach agreement on the factual and logical components than the moral ones. This is in direct contradiction to the contentions of the moral sceptics but it make sense, since the argument would not be possible if the disputants did not already agree on the fundamental moral values at stake. This is the high ground that both want to occupy. For example, if the anti-abortionists could produce compelling reasons for regarding a foetus as a human being then abortion could be classified as murder and their case would be won. It is the absence of arguments sufficiently powerful to convince the other side which allows the controversy to continue and encourages the false belief that there is no acceptable method of resolving moral disputes as there is for factual and logical ones.

The success that science has enjoyed is due not to the superiority of the empirical over the normative but to the fact that the fields in which it has been most successful provide more opportunity for verification or falsification procedures than others. If two theories are proposed to explain a phenomenon and they can be subjected to experimental tests which support one over the other, then scientists have an authoritative method for settling disputes. This is the model so much admired by philosophers but it is an ideal not always achieved, even in science. Whenever differing schools of thought exist side by side, it is usually because a definitive test is not available for choosing between them. This is quite common in the social sciences but can also occur in the more traditional sciences, especially where we are dealing with the past. Until recently, for example, dinosaurs were classified as cold-blooded reptiles but there is now a growing belief that they may have been warm-blooded. This illustrates the tentative nature of knowledge, including that which enjoys the prestige of being called 'scientific'. My point here is that certainty is hard to come by even in science, so that the exaggerated distinction made by moral sceptics in order to undermine the cognitive status of morality is unwarranted. Furthermore, if the lack of a recognized method of settling disputes is regarded as fatal to any claim to epistemological respectability, then philosophy itself is extremely vulnerable since the coexistence of opposing theories has characterized it from its beginnings.

Another important reason why moral sceptics hold fast to their position is that they tend to associate objectivity or, as some of them call it, absolutism in morality with tyrannical behaviour of some kind. P. H. Nowell-Smith pictures the objectivist as a man who will not listen to argument and uses force rather than argument to impose his own version of 'the truth' on others: 'It is no accident that religious persecutions are the monopoly of objective theorists'.[5] Nowell-Smith's use of a ruthless religious fanatic as the archetype of moral objectivism is not only unfair but highly misleading, since subjectivism allows one to be at least as dogmatic as objectivism. Furthermore he falls into two significant contradictions here. With respect to argument, a meaningful one, as we have noted before, can only occur between individuals who share some common ground – in this case a belief in objective moral values. It is the sceptic who, if he is to be consistent, cannot engage in a genuine argument. Because he believes that everyone is entitled to construct his own morality (the sub-title of Mackie's book is *Inventing Right and Wrong*) there is nothing on which to base an argument. If I think chocolate is good and you do not, what could I say to convince you that I am right, and further, why should I bother, since you are as entitled to your opinion as I am to mine?

Nowell-Smith's other mistake is to lay the blame for religious persecution on his opponents. This is *moral* condemnation, something a moral sceptic cannot engage in without knocking the props from under his already shaky edifice. Nowell-Smith is not alone in this. The objectivist mentality is blamed for the Inquisition by William James, for the institution of slavery and the subjection of women by R. M. Hare and the impulse to persecution and tyranny by Bertrand Russell. All these instances are discussed by Bamborough (*Moral Scepticism and Moral Knowledge*, chapter 3), who also notes that Hume, a philosopher for whom moral sceptics generally have the greatest respect, condemned this type of argument in his *Treatise of Human Nature* (II, iii, 2), where he said: 'Such topics, therefore, ought entirely to be foreborn, as serving nothing to the discovery of truth, but only to make the person of an antagonist odious'.

In truth, it is very difficult for a moral sceptic not to sound like an objectivist once he gets down to cases. Mackie, for example, when speaking of the right to life says:

> As the world is, wars and revolutions cannot be ruled to be morally out of the question. The death penalty, I believe, can. The prearranged killing of someone at a stated time is a special outrage against the human feelings which are a central part of morality, and this is not outweighed by any extra deterrent effect; in fact the use of the death penalty is likely to increase criminal violence. (195)

Here he manages to beg a number of questions while giving an impression of dogmatic self-righteousness which undermines any claim to impartiality. This is precisely the type of issue, like that of abortion, which can only be argued sensibly if everyone first agrees on a fundamental principle, e.g. that murder is wrong, and then proceeds to discuss whether killing someone during a war or revolution, or executing a criminal can be classified as murder. Both the question of whether the death penalty is a deterrent or whether it encourages further violence are straight factual ones which in theory can be answered by statistical analysis. I say 'in theory' because usually both sides can find studies which support their point of view. But at least these are empirical matters and we know they are susceptible to the same kind of treatment as scientific ones. What *is* unproductive, is to approach a moral problem the way Mackie does, mixing unsupported factual assertions with a strong emotional bias.

There is another very common situation which is thought to lend support to moral scepticism. A frequently cited example is Jean-Paul Sartre's young Frenchman who, during the Second World War faced the choice of going off to fight for freedom or staying home and supporting his mother. This is the existentialist version of the kind of moral problem which leads to scepticism in the Anglo-American philosophical tradition. Because the alternatives are so evenly matched the young man, in effect, creates his own morality when he makes his decision, just as Mackie would have us each invent our own right and wrong. But this dilemma would not exist if moral commitments were not already in place. The young man knows that it is wrong not to participate in the liberation of his country if he is able to do so and he also knows it is wrong to abandon his mother when she needs him. Whatever he does he is bound to feel badly because he is not choosing good over evil but between the lesser of two evils or the greater of two goods. This is a standard dilemma faced by everyone every day and is perfectly compatible with traditional morality. The complexity of life precludes there being easy and obvious answers to all our questions.

Suppose we put Sartre's dilemma in a different light by offering the young man instead a choice between being on the one hand an active member of the resistance and, on the other, a collaborator who is well rewarded for betraying his friends into the hands of Gestapo torturers. If he decided in favour of the latter on the grounds that he is exercising his freedom to erect an authentic morality of his own, on what basis could the moral sceptic criticize him? Whether or not a belief in the objectivity of moral values is likely to lead to religious persecution, it can also provide solid reasons for condemning that persecution, something that a genuine moral sceptic cannot do. He mistakenly thinks that by giving the individual freedom to invent his own morality he is building a better world but, as Hobbes shows, man is freest of all in the state of nature, and it is to escape the horrors of this condition that he allows his freedom to be constrained by morality.

Moral scepticism, as we have seen, draws much of its strength from the variety of apparently irreconcilable beliefs and the blind tenacity with which they are held. But this is a defeatist response as is any form of philosophical scepticism. Many mistaken beliefs are just as firmly held in other areas but we do not give up the possibility of truth in science because some people refuse to believe that the world is round. Nevertheless, the sceptics do have some cause for complaint with the form of objectivism which bothers them the most: intuitionism. Many famous philosophers from Plato to G. E. Moore have been intuitionists and *pace* Nowell-Smith intuitionists are just as likely to be saints as persecutors. But regardless of the personal character of intuitionists there are problems with their form of objectivism.

Intuition, in its modern philosophical usage is defined by the *OED* as 'the immediate apprehension of an object by the mind without the intervention of any reasoning process'. It can also apply to immediate apprehension by the senses. G. E. Moore likens a moral intuition to a sensory one by seeing a similarity between the notion of 'good' and that of 'yellow'.[6] There is no doubt that sense perception is knowledge of the most immediate and compelling kind. Its disadvantage is that by its very nature it is completely private, whereas knowledge in its customary sense is essentially public. If you tell me that you see a ghost in front of us, the fact that I am not able to see it does not allow me to insist that you are mistaken, no matter how much I may think so, any more than a colour-blind person can deny that a person with normal vision is able to see colours. But if you go on to make the statement that there is actually a ghost there, I can disagree, because we have entered the realm of shared knowledge. I can now ask for evidence for your statement. If several other people are called in and they, too, are not able to see a ghost, I can say that you are mistaken or at least, that the onus of proof is on you. To deserve the name of knowledge in this public sense, a belief about the nature of reality must be able to withstand the critical scrutiny of individuals other than the person who holds it. It must at least be inter-subjective even if it cannot be called objective. While an intuition may be perfectly correct, we cannot know, in this social sense, whether it is so, until it has gone public, so to speak, and entered the marketplace where it has to compete with the beliefs and intuitions of others for the status of knowledge. However, even if it passes this test, its truth is not guaranteed; the majority may turn out to be wrong in the end as they often are.

Thus, intuitionists are susceptible to the attacks of sceptics. If you are asked why you believe homosexuality is wrong and you reply: 'I just *know* it is – my intuition tells me so', all I have to say is: 'But *I* know it is *not* wrong', based on *my* intuition and we are both exactly where the sceptics want us. The result is that sceptics and intuitionists share a common problem: neither can give us the kind of knowledge we need. The sceptics do not believe it exists at all, and the intuitionists do not see any need to provide it, since the truth of their moral insights is so obvious it needs no defense. The latter thus end up by admitting what the sceptics claim: that moral disputes cannot be settled by the methods which are applied to empirical and logical ones. Ironically there is further agreement between them since when subjectivists like Mackie offer us their moral prescriptions, as they inevitably do, they have to fall back on intuition since they have excluded other grounds. Thus it turns out that intuitions can still play a respectable part in modern moral philosophy so long as they are so widely held that one questions them only at his peril. An example of this attitude is displayed by T. D. Weldon who would certainly not consider himself an intuitionist.

> I do not therefore, mind saying that some political behaviour is obviously right, or wicked, or silly. 'Obviously' is used here in the way in which it is correctly used of observations made by people with normal eyesight in a good light. In these conditions it is pointless to ask 'How do you know that this pillar-box is red?' It seems to me equally pointless to ask 'How do you know that it is wicked to torture human beings or animals?' But I think it is a mistake to use words like 'intuition' or 'self-evident' in describing such statements since they suggest that there is something odd about them which needs explanation. There is nothing odd about them. They are perfectly clear.[7]

Since neither sceptics nor intuitionists can supply us with moral knowledge, where else can we look for it? One alternative to intuitionism is called naturalism. Like all ethical labels this has to be handled with care since it has been used in a number of ways. What I have in mind here is the claim that ethical knowledge can exist because the 'good' can be identified as some natural property or object, such as what is pleasant or what is desirable for individual or group welfare. The utilitarians and Hobbes himself (except when he is considered to be a non-cognitivist) are offered as examples. Naturalism was put on the defensive early in this century by G. E. Moore, who invented the 'naturalistic fallacy'. This 'fallacy' is actually not confined to naturalism since it concerns *any* attempt to define 'good'; as we have noted already, Moore regarded 'good' as a simple, unanalysable property, like the colour yellow. However, the moral sceptics have found it useful in their assault on objectivism of any kind. Mackie's version of Moore's 'open question' argument, which he finds 'forceful' is as follows:

> Take some proposed analysis of 'good', say 'conducive to pleasure': we can understand the view of someone who says 'I admit that such-and-such is conducive to pleasure, but is it good?' The same move holds if we substitute for 'conducive to pleasure' any other proposed definition, say 'more evolved' or 'socially approved' or 'in tune with the universe' or 'in accordance with God's will'; it is still an open question whether what is described is good, or at least we can understand the view of someone who holds that it is still open. But if the proposed definition had been a correct account of the meaning of 'good', this question could not still be open. (51)

Whether or not this type of argument is convincing (along with many others, I do not find it so) it serves its purpose for the sceptics who, unlike Moore, see it as further evidence that there are no objective moral values. Another argument they utilize, sometimes called Hume's Law, purports to show that an 'ought' cannot be derived from an 'is'. It is not necessary to go into the protracted controversy concerning either of these positions in detail because what they both come down to in the end is quite simple: the firm belief that ethical values cannot be derived from non-ethical facts. Like the intuitionists, the sceptics are convinced ethical statements differ so sharply from empirical ones, that any attempt to link them is doomed to failure.

The reason why they oppose this is clearly exposed by Thomas D.

Perry. He sees naturalism as negating 'personal autonomy in matters of basic principle, leaving the individual with only empirical and deductive questions to answer'. Given the objective standard or standards provided by a naturalistic system, one could in theory, arrive at the correct answer to any moral question.

> Thus . . . if someone were to embrace any other moral opinion besides the current ones it would be possible to demonstrate to him that his opinion is wrong. That is, we could construct a moral argument consisting of true facts, a valid principle and priority, and a valid deductive inference, proving to such a person that his own best judgement is wrong . . . . [8]

This is exactly what I think Hobbes has in mind but Perry finds it unacceptable. 'It is this possibility, jarring so badly as I think it does with the common intuitions about the nature of moral judgement, that has been my chief reason for rejecting ethical naturalism as an account of such judgment.' Given a choice between the two, Perry would reject rational objectivity in favour of personal autonomy. In this he is at one with many recent moral philosophers who, while denying that they are sceptics, cannot bring themselves to limit the freedom of an individual to decide for himself the moral rules he is prepared to follow and those he is not. However, they are also not prepared to give up the possibility of moral reasoning and therefore allow it to survive in a modest way by recognizing as Perry does, 'that moral judgment can be true, i.e. that moral predicates can have fixed non-moral criteria "locally", or within a given way of life' (*Moral Reasoning and Moral Truth*, p. 161). By confining moral truth within a 'way of life', which one can freely adopt or not, as one chooses, he hopes to preserve both personal autonomy and some basis for taking moral arguments seriously.

In a later book, Perry has a passage which reveals how we can have the best of both worlds if we are willing to give a little.

> If [his argument is acceptable], then there can be plenty of good reasoning in morals, and this reasoning can be the basis of a growing critical consensus even if there are no 'moral values existing in the world absolutely', whatever that might mean. Secondly, the conceptual element thus partly sacrificed should begin *to shrink in emotional importance* once we have clarified our thoughts along the lines of the foregoing descriptions and

recommended solution. By this I mean that the *urge to say that our moral principles are true* by reference to 'objective moral facts' *should begin to subside*. For we should then see clearly that there is no rational or institutional basis for it, while there is a basis for rational community without it.⁹ (emphasis added)

The italicized words show how we can escape into the Wittgensteinian world where philosophy is a kind of therapy.

I have quoted from Perry because he clearly and succinctly presents us with the dilemma which is at the heart of modern ethical theory. The so-called 'good reasons' ethicists like Hare, Nowell-Smith, and Toulmin want to maintain the role of reason in ethics without having, at the same time, to swallow what they call objectivism or descriptivism – any position which gives ethical statements a status equivalent to that of non-ethical ones. This is an inherently unstable situation. Hare has been fighting a rearguard action with his critics for years, surrendering ground to the point where he has had to admit there is some plausibility in the charge that he has himself succumbed to the sin of 'descriptivism'.[10]

The concerns raised by the emotivists and their successors, however, are significant and any alternative theory must be prepared to address them. With respect to Ayer's notion that a moral statement is neither true nor false, let us look at one example: 'Murder is wrong'. It is correct to say that this can be seen as an expression of the speaker's abhorrence of murder and therefore satisfies the emotivist criterion. But most utterances have meanings at more than one level. The statement might also be taken as the speaker's injunction to others not to commit murder. This would satisfy the prescriptivist, although not everyone is convinced that all value statements can be converted into imperatives. There is a third meaning which is acceptable to this school despite being empirical in nature. It is what has been called the anthropological interpretation and it arises if we interpret the statement as a description of what is widely believed in the speaker's own society. In that case the statement can be verified by asking people whether or not it is true that murder is considered wrong in their society. Another variant is to interpret the statement as meaning nothing more than the speaker's personal disapproval of murder. In this subjective sense the statement can be considered true or false depending on whether or not the speaker is lying about his feelings.

Neither of the latter two approaches is relevant for the purposes of the moral sceptic. His main concern is to deny that the statement has any more meaning than that contained in the first two interpretations. This leaves out what might be considered the most normal level of communication which is that the speaker is claiming that murder is genuinely wrong – not wrong in his opinion or in his society – but *wrong*, period. He is making a truth claim which he expects to be taken seriously. While it is true that he may, at the same time, be expressing his disapproval of murder, he is, in addition, making what he regards as a factual statement. What he says may be false rather than true. If I disagree with him about the wrongfulness of murder I can say so and provide reasons. He can reject my position and offer his reasons for doing so. In this way we can have a meaningful discussion of the truth or falsity of the statement. Thousands of arguments of this type are waged every day by people in a rational and peaceful manner. The fact that there are thousands of others which degenerate into shouting matches or a scornful refusal to listen to the other side is true also, but non-moral arguments can easily go the same way depending on the temperament of the participants.

This interpretation of a moral statement equates it with any other kind of statement. In traditional logic it is of the same category as 'All men are mortal', i.e., all members of one class are also members of another class. In our example, all acts of murder are members of another class, the class of wrong actions. Just as we have to define the terms 'men' and 'mortal', so we have to define 'murder' and 'wrong'. This exposes in the simplest possible way what the problem that bothers the moral sceptics really amounts to. It is the belief that no satisfactory definition of 'wrong' or other moral terms can ever be arrived at. This is why the naturalistic fallacy is sometimes referred to as the 'definist' fallacy. There is a temptation to use what C. L. Stevenson, one of the fathers of emotivism, called 'persuasive definitions' in an article with that title which appeared in *Mind* in 1938. No matter how one defines the word 'good', it will always retain a strong aura of approval and pro-feelings which it will confer on the definition. Mary Warnock provides a suitable illustration:

> For instance, if I claim to define 'good' as 'more evolved', a supposedly naturalistic or empirical epithet, although I may state that 'good' means *nothing more than* 'more evolved' I shall in so doing be disingenuous. For even if the factual content of

the words were the same, there is more in 'good' than there is in 'more evolved', namely the emotive meaning. My definition is therefore persuasive for I have taken over the emotive content of 'good' . . . . [Stevenson's] insistence that ethics cannot be translated into a non-ethical language, that every attempt to do so is a cheat, is the most fundamental principle of the emotive theory.[11]

There is no doubt some truth to this. But the use of emotionally charged words is not confined to ethics. Because the negative connotation of certain words is so widely recognized, euphemisms flourish today as never before. The urge to sugar coat an unfortunate reality can be seen, for example, in the way economically backward nations have moved from being underdeveloped, to lesser-developed, to developing, to finally, the Third World. The truth is that moral statements are like any other statements: they can do various jobs. By over-emphasizing one aspect of moral language, the sceptics and semi-sceptics have denied cognitive status to all moral propositions and this is, quite simply, unwarranted.

The problem still remains of bringing some order out of the welter of claims and counter-claims concerning morality. I would suggest, as a start, that a distinction be made between what Hobbes calls ethics on the one hand and morality on the other. In a table attached to Chapter 9 of *Leviathan*, 'Of the Several Subjects of Knowledge', he distinguishes between that part of science or knowledge of consequences concerned with 'consequences from the *passions* of men' as ETHICS, and 'consequences from *speech* in *contracting*' as the '*Science* of the JUST and UNJUST' (73, 149), which is what he later called moral philosophy (146, 215). If I may be permitted to adopt his terminology for the moment, it should be clear by now that although I have touched on the virtues and other ethical topics, my attention has been focussed on his morality. In this context, morality is concerned with the rules of right and wrong whereas ethics is about the standards of good and bad. If the words are used in a non-moral sense, the difference is clear to teachers who have to mark both objective tests, where there is only one correct answer for each question, and essay questions which, since they are all different, have to be ranked according to how the paper compares with an ideal standard of some kind. The problem with the latter task is that because it is subjective, the mark might vary from one person to another or even from one time to another, with the same person. If we substitute ethical judgments for marking we are in much the same position. We can certainly say that although both of these people are good, one is better than the other, more courageous, more honest or more of whatever virtue we are discussing. It is in this way that ethics is like aesthetics: there is room for differences of opinion but there will also be much general agreement, especially amongst those most knowledgeable in the field. I may not like a particular piece of music but I would hesitate to call it bad if most competent musicians thought it was very good.

Because of the irreducible element of subjectivity in judging by standards, an emphasis on good and bad or the usual virtues – what I have here called ethics – is not the best point of entry into an examination of moral philosophy as a whole. Adopting an approach which is modelled on aesthetics does not encourage efforts to rationalize the field. This difficulty is demonstrated clearly in the intuitionism of G. E. Moore. If 'good' is an unanalysable quality, like 'yellow', one tends to be reduced to the option taken by Moore, and say that good is something you just 'know' intuitively. The question one then has to ask Moore is what sorts of things does he regard as good. His answer is as follows:

> Once the meaning of the question is clearly understood, the answer to it, in its main outlines, appears to be so obvious, that it runs the risk of seeming to be a platitude. By far the most valuable things which we know or can imagine, are certain states of consciousness which may be roughly described as the pleasures of human intercourse and the enjoyment of beautiful objects. No one probably, who has asked himself the question, has ever doubted that personal affection and the appreciation of what is beautiful in Art or Nature, are good in themselves; nor if we consider strictly what things are worth having *purely for their own sakes*, does it appear probable that anyone will think anything else has *nearly* so great a value as the things which are included under these two heads. (*Principia Ethica*, 188)

What is obvious to Moore may not be so to the rest of us, who will probably have other priorities. But most striking is Moore's emphasis on pleasure, which has led some to call him an ideal utilitarian. That pleasure which he turned away from the front door with his naturalistic fallacy is admitted through the back door, but only in a suitably refined, epicurean form. Another surprising element is the lack of anything we customarily think of as characteristically moral in his short list of intrinsic values. However, he has already discussed the question of what we ought to do in an earlier chapter. 'Our "duty", therefore, can only be defined as that action which will cause more good to exist in the universe than any possible alternative' (142). The morality of an action is thus determined by an assessment of its consequences, as with the utilitarians.

This approach has various problems, which need not detain us, since they have been thoroughly explored in the years since Moore's book appeared. They merely confirm, in my opinion, what was said above about the unsuitability of good and bad as conceptual starting points. Hobbes discusses good and evil in his chapter of *Leviathan* on the passions, which fits in with his definition of ethics. 'But whatsoever is the object of any man's appetite or desire, that is it which he for his part calleth *good*: and the object of his hate or aversion, *evil* . . . ' (41, 120). Good is promised by what is fair or attractive, is reached by what is profitable, and is found in what is delightful. '*Pleasure*, therefore, or *delight*, is the appearance, or sense of good: and *molestation*, or *displeasure*, the appearance or sense of evil' (42, 122). Pleasures can be both of the senses and the mind. Thus Hobbes's definition includes not only those delights of friendship and aesthetic appreciation selected by Moore but many others also. The big difference, however, is that for Hobbes good originates with the individual, each of whom seeks what is good for him or her, and it only takes on a larger meaning, applicable to a group of people when they have agreed among themselves as to a method for deciding what is good for them as a whole. These general goods will be ranked according to the nature and priorities of the society, with courage, perhaps, emphasized in one and holiness in another. Our everyday usage of the words 'good' and 'bad' would appear to support Hobbes here since it indicates that they are deeply rooted in what, either as individuals or communities, we regard as beneficial or detrimental in some way. Thus factual statements can be made about what each person or each society calls good, but statements which attempt to use the word in a sense that is detached from these roots only invite confusion. Much ink has been spilt in an effort to distinguish the meaning of 'good' in, for example, a good knife, from that in, say, a good man. But in both cases the word signifies approval based on benefits received. A sharp knife is good for me because it makes cutting easier; a man is called good by those who know him because his generosity, benevolence, etc. tend to make life better for members of his community. It is difficult, if not impossible, to use the word in a way which does not come back ultimately to human well-being, as Moore's efforts illustrate. Even the quest for the *summum bonum*, the attempt to answer the question, 'How should I live my life?' cannot escape being considered in terms of some form of human satisfaction, no matter how elevated it is made out to be.

Because ethics is a matter of evaluation by standard, it is, as we have seen, quite similar to aesthetics and, for that matter any area in which judgment is involved, such as the marking of term papers. This kind of judgment usually does not have to be made in an instant; the necessary deliberation in fact, requires a certain amount of time and in the case of aesthetics, at least, leisure. This is where ethics differs from what, following Hobbes, I am here calling morality. With respect to the latter, we are not bystanders evaluating the extent to which others measure up to our standards, but participants who have to decide right now whether or not to perform a particular action. There is an urgency attached to morality which is absent from ethics. For this reason, morality is a set of rules which makes the relevant actions either right or wrong and for this reason also it does not function like aesthetics but like a legal system. In fact, the criminal law is set up to provide penalties for the violation of what a society considers the most important moral prohibitions. The golden rule also plays a part in this distinction because its negative version can be used to create rules, and its positive form leads to behaviour which can be judged by a standard, since the amount of good we can do is variable. The virtues of justice and benevolence also reflect the distinction.

Of course, ethics and morality are used interchangeably and I have done so myself for the sake of variety. But there are two different approaches to man's moral life which should be distinguished in some way. They have been referred to as the moralities of aspiration or value on the one hand and duty or obligation on the other. Whatever words are used, this is an important distinction and if it is blurred in the discussion of ethics, as it so often is, unnecessary difficulties ensue. The fact that most books on ethics mix good and bad with right and wrong indiscriminately means that disputes amongst different schools of thought can never be settled, and tend to go round in circles. Let us compare the situation with that of a field containing a number of sheep. If I say that there are 57 sheep there, my statement can be verified or falsified by having the number checked and if I am not exactly right, I am wrong. If, on the other hand, I say that there are quite a few sheep in the field and you say that there aren't all that many, we can argue till doomsday without getting anywhere, because both statements can be correct or incorrect depending on our personal criteria. Much of the discussion of good and bad is in the same category and to this extent, sceptics and subjectivists have a case. However, references to right and wrong must be more specific. Systems of rules are sharply different from standards of evaluation. Once a shoplifter takes goods for which he has not paid through the door leading out of the shop he has committed theft. Inside, he is an innocent customer entitled to pick up and carry with him goods which he may or may not decide to purchase; outside the shop, he is a thief. There is no in-between, although, of course, there may be extenuating circumstances. He has violated a rule – in this case a law – and so must pay the penalty.

It could be pointed out here that a rule is not a law unless it is one of those moral prohibitions which have state-authorized procedures for enforcing them. In the case of games, rules are similar to laws; they are quite specific and a player who violates them can be punished by exclusion from the game. Since neither of these mechanisms applies completely to moral rules, except those incorporated into the law, the question arises as to whether it is profitable to think of morality in terms of rules at all. If something is wrong, it is wrong whether there is a rule against it or not, so why postulate a rule in the first place? This is the view taken by G. J. Warnock: 'If I believe that, say, contraception is morally wrong, I am not in a position to characterize it in any *new* way if I suppose it to be a breach of a "moral rule"; for that is, if anything, just to say again that it is morally wrong'. Bringing in rules adds nothing but the risk of confusion.[12]

In order to answer this type of criticism, one has to distinguish between strongly held opinions and what I am calling rules. In fact, the concept of rules is useful precisely because it allows one to raise a moral dispute from a mere clash of opinions to the level of a discussion based on rationality. Let us take Warnock's example of contraception. If one were to ask a person who believes it to be wrong why it is wrong, he might reply that it is forbidden by the church to which he belongs. What this means, in effect, is that the church has a rule against contraception and that its members are bound, by their membership in the sect, not to violate that rule. To ask him why he should obey this injunction would be like asking a chess player why he feels bound to move his pawns only one square at a time. If one applies the game analogy rather than the legal one, the usefulness of a set of rules in the understanding of morality becomes clearer. Of course rules apply only to those who have accepted them by joining or remaining within a community, whether it is the players of a game, the members of a sect or the citizens of a commonwealth.

That is the reason that a religious answer to the question of why contraception is wrong need not be accepted by those outside that particular church. Although the anti-contraceptionist may believe that it is wrong for anyone to use artificial means for preventing conception, he has not offered the kind of argument which is binding in any way on a non-believer. However, he could put his case in purely secular terms by saying that it is wrong to interfere with natural processes and that since the purpose of sexual intercourse is obviously procreation, it is unnatural to take measures which prevent reproduction. This assumes that what someone believes to be unnatural is wrong. Since much of modern medicine is devoted to going against nature and thereby saving lives and easing pain, this is a very difficult position to defend.

But the Hobbesian would come at this issue from another direction, by asking whether one can derive a prohibition of contraception from his fundamental position, which is the reciprocity rule. This is essentially a requirement that we avoid harming others. Does contraception harm anybody? It is hard to see how, since no other human being is involved. Preventing one of millions of spermatozoa from combining with this month's ovum cannot be seen as wrong in any meaningful sense of the term. From this viewpoint we are not dealing with a moral act at all and there is thus no moral rule to be violated. As a result, instead of causing difficulties, the rule concept helps us to bring some order into moral problems. It forces us to recognize that some moral opinions are based on rules that hold only for a particular group and that other moral opinions cannot be defended because they do not involve the violation of a rule which stems from the basic agreement upon which the society is founded.

Another criticism of moral rules made by Warnock and others is that each moral problem has to be solved on its own merits after an assessment of all aspects of the situation. This arises from the belief that rules are excessively restrictive and in certain cases following them may somehow do more harm than good. Here we have another example of how anything fixed and definite in morality is seen as a limitation on human autonomy. It is very widely held amongst recent moral philosophers, who are able to do so because on the one level they feel that moral options must be kept open as long as possible, but when it is necessary to come to a decision they reach down to another level for the moral principles which will justify that decision. This level contains their most deeply-felt moral convictions, ones which they accept without questioning and which they would be surprised to see questioned by most normal persons. No matter how much autonomy they would like to grant us, most of them cannot really bring themselves to believe that sending millions of Jews to the gas chambers or subjecting one's political opponents to the most painful tortures, can ever be anything but wrong. However, surely that is where the whole enterprise should begin, namely, by asking why these actions are wrong and what we mean when we say they are wrong? If we are not going to be satisfied with the intuitionist answer that we just know they are wrong, we shall have to attempt to create some kind of explanatory structure which will make sense of moral concepts. This is precisely what Hobbes was trying to do.

7

The Nature of Hobbesian Morality

Since morality affects all members of a society regardless of intelligence or education it must rest on a few ideas that are simple enough for nearly everyone to grasp even if he or she cannot explain their logical relationships. The concept most central to Hobbes's moral system is that of personal commitment. If someone else tells me to do something that I am under no obligation to do, I may refuse to do it without any blame attaching to me. I am a free agent in these circumstances and am beholden to no one. However, if *I* tell someone that I will do something, if *I* promise that I will do it if asked, then I am in a different situation. I have placed myself under an obligation by my words and I can no longer refuse to perform the action without being liable to censure. By voluntarily binding myself, I have limited my future freedom of action in the areas specified by the promise.

Let us look at one of the most common examples of this kind of commitment: the making of a loan. Suppose I borrow a sum of money on the understanding that I will pay it back by a certain date. This transaction consists of two parts: my promise to pay the debt and my being handed a sum of money which I would not have received had I not made the promise. The creditor naturally wants and expects his money back and would not have risked it with me if he had any reason to believe that I would not live up to my promise. Whether or not I actually obtain a loan will depend not just on my willingness to make a promise but also on my personal reputation and general credit-worthiness. If I have a history of paying debts promptly I am more likely to be able to borrow successfully than someone who has a habit of delaying repayment or reneging altogether on his financial obligations.

I have emphasized the importance of the lender as well as the borrower because discussions of this kind of transaction by moral philosophers have tended to ignore his role. A good example is the controversy arising from John Searle's article 'How to derive "ought" from "is"'. Searle offers us five statements starting with: '(1) Jones uttered the words, "I hereby promise to pay you, Smith, five dollars" and concluding with: "(5) Jones ought to pay Smith five dollars"'.[1] He then goes on to explain how this sequence demonstrates that one can move successfully from descriptive to evaluative statements. His critics claimed that he has smuggled in an evaluative premise in the form of the 'institution' of promising. Their position is based on the belief that there is both a descriptive and an evaluative meaning of a word like 'promise' and that it is illegitimate to slide from one to the other – from the status of a neutral observer to that of a committed participant – without taking note of the switch that has occurred. Searle's response is to deny that there is a sense in which 'promise' means merely to utter certain words. 'Promise' means to undertake an obligation and anyone in our society who promises is understood to have placed himself under an obligation, since that is the meaning of the word. Communication would be impossible unless we committed ourselves to the accepted meanings of words.

It is certainly possible to look at promising from an anthropological viewpoint and to see it perhaps as a tribal custom like, for example, a rain dance. However this approach is difficult to fit into a real life situation. Does it mean that when Smith comes to collect his five dollars Jones can say, 'True, I uttered certain words but you should not have assumed they implied a serious obligation of some kind.' In order to escape from what is essentially an artificial problem it is necessary to recognize that Smith, the creditor, is involved from the beginning, and that the transaction concerns two people. It is not just the institution of promising which is at stake, it is also the institution of lending and borrowing. If people did not feel that they were placing themselves under a genuine obligation when they promised to repay a debt, those with money would not lend it and business activity, which depends on credit, would grind to a halt. Now, whether Searle, or anyone else, has solved the 'is-ought' problem or whether there actually is such a problem, will doubtless continue to be discussed by professional philosophers. What must concern us is what is in people's minds. As we have noted before, words do not have to be uttered in order for an agreement to have been reached. One can sign an I.O.U., one can shake hands or one can come to an understanding which emerges naturally and obviously from the situation. If someone did me a favour and I later had an opportunity to do something for him, I would gladly do it since I know that one good turn deserves another. But, and this needs to be emphasized again, it is not just in my mind that something is going on; my friend is probably saying to himself, 'Well, after all, he does owe me one'. It is a two-way street and that is what does not emerge clearly enough from the usual philosophical treatment of this question.

As has been noted above, if one is going to engage in any activity which requires advance agreement on what constitutes the set of rules that everyone is to observe, from children's games on up, one must commit one's self to be bound by those rules in the same way that everyone else is. Rationality, itself, is dependent on the acceptance of binding rules and therefore requires commitment. The motivation behind commitment in this broad sense is not a wish to flee from critical rationality but a desire to participate in some human activity which benefits one in some way. A commitment to obey the rules is the entrance fee one pays for this privilege. The kind of obligation that is created by commitment is the same in all spheres; what differentiates them from one another is the special nature of the rules which one has placed oneself under the obligation to observe. The rules of games are different for each game and the rules governing logic are not the same as those peculiar to morality. But as Piaget noted there is a logic to morality as well as a morality in logic. An element of morality appears as soon as the possibility of breaking rules is introduced by the agreement to be bound by them.

The idea of a freely accepted obligation is, of course, central to the notion of going into debt, which I used above as a paradigm of Hobbes's approach to morality. The reason you 'ought' to pay your debt is linguistically as well as morally derivative from the fact that you 'owe' the money, since 'ought' and 'owe' have a common origin. A single word, *devoir*, is used in French to cover both meanings. One should keep this in mind when using 'ought' so that unnecessary confusion is avoided. G. J. Warnock says, for instance: 'As I drive up to London in my comfortable car, you may feel that (out of beneficence) I ought to stop [and pick up a hitchhiker]; but I would not, I think, agree that I have, or am under an *obligation* to do so' (94). This sort of example merely muddies the water, since by 'ought' here he means merely that it would be nice of me to pick someone up. But I would not use 'ought' in such a situation precisely because there is no obligation. One can obviously employ 'ought' in weaker senses like this, and also in non-moral situations where, for instance, your doctor says: 'You ought to take the medicine if you want to get better'. However, the key idea is obligation and as long as 'ought' is considered as a handy brief way of expressing this idea, it serves a useful purpose which can easily be undermined if its meaning is diluted. Jones *ought* to pay Smith because Jones *owes* him the money and has put himself under an *obligation* to repay it.

Moral obligation in general follows the same pattern as it does with the borrowing of money. If we accept Hobbes's model of the social contract as reciprocity, then an obligation to behave in a certain way is undertaken as soon as one enters into a society or acknowledges in any way that one is part of such a group. The major difference is that in the example a sum of money changes hands, whereas with the social contract nothing need happen. There has been some discussion in Hobbesian literature about the problem of the 'first performer'. In the case of a loan, the creditor performs his part of the agreement first and can only hope that the debtor will pay the money back. But this is not a problem in Hobbes's covenant since it is one in which both parties begin performing immediately, by refraining from action which harms the other. These actions might have been necessary for self-preservation in the state of nature but are not so after the agreement has been made. This is why the negative golden rule was emphasized; merely by *not* doing something, one is fulfilling the terms of the compact.

So far then, we have two simple ideas: that of a rule and that of committing oneself to being bound by the rule. The next simple idea is the content of the particular rule to which we agree in the social contract and that is reciprocity or doing nothing to others you would not have them do to you. Gregory Kavka takes the position that the principle summarizing Hobbes's laws of nature cannot be called the golden rule because of the qualifications he makes. Instead Kavka would call it the Copper Rule because it shines less brightly and he would state it as follows: 'Do unto others as they do unto you'.[2] Actually this does not glitter brightly at all; if the action is harmful, it would be better to call it a law of retaliation. It is closer to what occurs in the state of nature especially if we add the phrase, 'but do it first'. This is precisely what Hobbes is trying to get away from and why he realizes that the golden rule in its traditional form is the only way out of the state of nature. However, it is true that reciprocity can be used in several different ways. A third meaning, which is quite common, is the willingness to return favours or *quid pro quo*. This version is passive in that it assumes that the other person acts first. The meaning I have used throughout is the active version in which we treat others in the first instance as we would want to be treated ourselves.

The question remains as to why we should agree to be bound by the golden rule. Hobbes's answer, as we have seen, is given in the form of a story about the state of nature and the means of escaping it. Another way would be to ask the questioner: What better deal can you think of? This approach is discussed in great detail by John Rawls,[3] who postulates a 'veil of ignorance' for his contractors, which denies them the knowledge of what role they will play in the society they create – whether they will be rich or poor, etc. He assumes they will answer in such a way that they will produce a modern liberal welfare state. This result has been disputed by Robert Nozick[4] as well as others. Hobbes does not go out on this particular limb. His contractors are not allowed the luxury of picking and choosing between alternative systems of government. The reason is that their predicament is far too pressing. The state of nature (to use his metaphor) is so menacing that in order to survive they must act immediately and be prepared to accept the minimal terms that serve the purpose. Now if I make you an offer whereby I agree not to do anything to you which I would not want done to me, in return for your promise to do likewise with respect to me, what alternative can you come up with that will provide equally well for your survival? Since you know that I do not want to be harmed any more than you do, you know also that this rule will effectively bind me not to harm you. But it requires that you, in return, do the same, and that is not so easy to swallow. You would prefer that you could do exactly what you want to me without any risk of retaliation. Naturally I would prefer the same. We both want many things which we cannot obtain without trampling on others. Therefore the ideal arrangement would provide for unlimited selfishness on both our parts. But because neither of us will accept this kind of treatment from the other, what would happen in a world of unregulated selfishness would be Hobbes's state of nature. Instead of each of us benefitting from such a situation, both of us would suffer. We want everything but we would get nothing. So, it is not a choice between something and everything but between something and nothing, and as a result it is the best deal either of us can make. It is a trade-off, or to paraphrase Hobbes, you will have to be contented with so much liberty against me, as you would allow me against yourself. This does not sound very generous but in fact it is extremely beneficial to both of us since the alternative is the dangerous uncertainty of the state of nature. Thus the golden rule is based firmly on the desire of each person to best preserve himself in an uncertain world and if he is rational, he will see the logic of it.

Accepting the reasonableness of such an arrangement on the one hand, and agreeing to be bound by it on the other are, however, two different things. There is always the possibility that the other party will break the agreement as soon as it prevents him from obtaining something he really wants. Hobbes realizes it has to be backed up by a coercive power to provide 'some punishment greater than the benefit they expect by the breach of their covenant' (131, 202). In the real world such a system is already in place. If there is no state, with its elaborate apparatus for the apprehension and punishment of wrongdoers, there are the simple but often more effective methods of social control exercised by elders and chiefs in tribal and other smaller communities in which, because there are fewer people, those who engage in anti-social behaviour are easier to detect and to influence.

However, there is, of course, a difference between acts which are immoral and those which are illegal. Certain immoral actions are so serious a threat to public order that they are made illegal, and penalties are laid out for them. But a line has to be drawn at some point or one ends up with a totalitarian police state. Given half a chance many people would have anything of which they disapprove declared a crime. Furthermore, the law creates crimes out of many actions that are not in themselves immoral, such as driving on the wrong side of the road. It is not the law that makes an action immoral; certain immoral acts are considered serious enough to be made illegal. The question remains then: what makes an action immoral?

The answer Hobbes provides in *Leviathan* is quite clear-cut:

> But when a covenant is made, then to break it is *unjust*: and the definition of INJUSTICE, is no other than *the not performance of covenant*. And whatsoever is not unjust, is *just*. (130, 202)

He chooses the word 'unjust' where I have just been using 'immoral' but it is clear when he later calls the 'science' of the laws of nature 'the true and only moral philosophy' (146, 215), that we are talking about the same thing. Now, since the covenant of which he speaks is the social contract and the content of that is the golden rule, an act is unjust if it violates the golden rule. Thus he provides a *definition* of injustice from which a rational system of moral principles can be developed.

Aristotle treated the word 'justice' as having two separate meanings. In the broader sense it was equated with moral uprightness as opposed to law-breaking; in the narrower one it could be subdivided into distributive and reparative justice. Hobbes sometimes talked about the latter but in his definition he is obviously using the broad sense. He also says that moral philosophy is the science of good and evil or of the virtues and vices but these words, because of their varying connotations, are not especially helpful. If we look, however, at the idea which lies behind the word 'injustice' in his context of covenant and reciprocity, we find that there are several other ways of putting it, such as: inequity, unfairness or wrongness. I have preferred the word 'wrong' throughout this discussion because it is the most widely used moral term to emerge from this same notion. Originating as a way of expressing the concept of twisted, bent or crooked, as with tree branches in nature or the shaping of ships' ribs in manufacture, it was borrowed for human behaviour and took on its primary meaning, as given in the *OED*: 'That which is morally unjust, unfair, amiss, or improper; the opposite of right or justice; the negative of equity, goodness or rectitude'. It should be noted that although it is often used to express one's personal disapproval of an action, this is an emotive and subjective application of a word which has acquired that particular unfavourable aura from its core meaning of unfairness and injustice. I am referring here to the moral usage; 'wrong', as in 'wrong answers', also means, of course, incorrect. It is easy to see how that meaning also derived from the idea of twisted or bent. Despite the problems inherent in its broader connotations, the word 'wrong' in its moral sense serves a useful purpose, as it manages to extract out the essence of what is objectionable about unfairness or inequity whilst avoiding the specialized legal implications of 'injustice'. Hobbes, himself, treats 'wrong' as an alternative to 'unjust' when, referring to the state of nature in *Leviathan*, he says: 'The notions of right and wrong, justice and injustice have there no place' (115, 188). Later on he equates wrong with what is contrary to a rule, and right as what is not contrary to it (251, 312). The rule in this case is a civil law, but the principle would apply to any rule – above all the rules established by the social contract. Thus, I think there is little doubt that when Hobbes defined 'injustice' he also provided a definition for 'wrong' as we use it in morality today.

However, something very important is left out of all definitions of wrongness because it, presumably, is felt to be too obvious to mention: Any act which we call wrong carries with it the automatic presumption that it *ought not* to be done. When Hobbes says that to break the covenant is unjust he means, of course, that you ought not to do it, and the same applies even more pointedly to the word 'wrong'. Because this goes without saying, it is not said. Murder *is* wrong, therefore one *ought not* to commit murder. A descriptive statement leads to a prescriptive one. All that is necessary is to link the idea of wrongness with the idea of 'oughtness', something which should be easy since it is already so obvious that nobody mentions it. Once it is recognized that 'wrong' is an action-guiding word, one can then determine what makes an action wrong and which actions are therefore wrong and ought not to be done.

This looks like it might be a solution to the so-called 'is–ought' problem but a true disciple of Hume's Law would not be convinced since the oughtness is already present in the word 'wrong'. However, if the relationship is shifted from grammar to action and the agent has given no indication that he does not subscribe to the institution concerned then it holds. Thus when I agree that I ought to do x, nobody can justifiably claim that I am not under an obligation to do x.

At the heart of both wrongness and injustice lies the idea that is expressed most simply and understandably in English as 'unfairness'. Not to receive fair or equal treatment evokes outrage in human beings from infancy on. It is important to note that unfairness always involves the violation of a rule, explicit or implicit. A soldier in war who is wounded by the enemy or a rugby player hurt in the give and take of the game does not feel any resentment towards the perpetrator of his injuries because the latter was acting within the same context as himself and was exposed to the same risks. However, even a small child knows that something is wrong when another child is not punished for doing exactly the same thing for which he was punished. There was presumably a rule of some kind which specified that a certain type of misbehaviour would be punished in a certain way and when this is not applied equally, there is a natural feeling of discrimination and a sense of injustice. This is a very powerful emotion, and continued exposure to unequal treatment can turn an otherwise peaceable person into a fiery revolutionary.

However, it should be made clear that absolute equality is not required. Just as the same rules cannot be applied to young children as to adults, so there may be different rules for other sub-groups within a society depending on its class structure. This can lead to a generalized discontent with the social and political system itself, depending on the extent to which traditional differences are respected, but it is unequal treatment *within* a group of people, who are otherwise supposed to be equal, which leads to a sense of unfairness and provides the emotional force that animates the mere words used to express moral judgments.

The feeling of unfairness springs not just from the inequitable treatment itself but from the disappointed *expectation* of equal treatment. This raises the question of why one should expect to be treated equally. In the case of a child and his parents this expectation is probably based on his previous experience of their love for him and the resultant belief that they would not intentionally discriminate against him. In the case of children dealing with each other, as well as all normal situations where people are not faced with arbitrary omnipotence, the expectation seems to derive from a feeling that equal treatment is deserved. The only firm ground for this assumption is that we have done something to deserve equity from others. If I have loaned you money, I expect you to pay it back because you agreed to do so. I have handed you something of value on condition that you return it. If you do not, then I have been cheated and, in effect, robbed. The same applies to a situation in which we have agreed to refrain from assaulting each other. Suppose I find your conduct objectionable and, as a result, have the urge to strike you. Feeling bound by the agreement, however, I restrain myself and walk away. You, however, equally indignant, decide to go ahead and hit me now that my back is turned, thus wilfully breaching the agreement. An inequity is created because you have benefited from my restraint but I have not enjoyed the reciprocal benefit of your restraint.

Whatever the circumstances, unfairness arouses in one a feeling which is referred to by the legal scholar, Edmond Cahn, as 'the sense of wrong'.

> Our reaction to an act of moral wrong is a blend of reason that recognizes, of emotion that evaluates, and of glands that pump physical preparations for action. In a single combined response, our muscles tighten and our judgment condemns, anger fills us with heat, or our spirits slide down with sorrow. A wrong is apprehended in one process on every psychic level as equivalent to an assault, that is an assault on the self in its own fleshly body or on the self projected by imaginative drama to some other body.[5]

This is an important reminder that what we are dealing with here is experienced not just as a word or concept, but as something much more intense, a kind of violation.

Unfairness, then must be discouraged even if it cannot be eliminated. Hobbes sees the covenant as a necessary first step. As soon as the agreement is made, all parties stand to benefit by each other's restraint. Obviously more will be required in some situations to fulfil obligations created by the covenant than mere inaction but as I have noted before, the negative aspect of the agreement is the crucial one because of the ease with which humans can be hurt. If we are alerted to danger, as in a state of war, we can take steps to protect ourselves, but once we have entered the civil state we have, in effect, disarmed ourselves and are therefore extremely vulnerable. Anyone who, after having himself enjoyed the security of a peace maintained by the benign behaviour of his fellows, decides to take advantage of their trust by advancing his own interests at their expense, undermines the covenant. People like this have to be deterred by penalties of some kind or the agreement would quickly become unworkable. That is, of course, why Hobbes placed so much emphasis on the necessity for a coercive power. The more serious violations of the covenant are punished by the civil authority but minor infractions are left to public opinion, which can use various forms of ostracism quite effectively. The point is that we do not like being victimized by those who refuse to play by the rules and we show this disapproval in ways that vary with the seriousness of the offense.

Thus when we apply the word 'wrong' to an action which contravenes the covenant, we are not merely noting that it is inequitable, we are also saying that we disapprove of it and that this disapproval may result in sanctions of some kind. These connections are usually made when we learn the meaning of the word as small children.

The Nature of Hobbesian Morality

Parental disapproval and possible punishment are associated with certain behaviour which often also brings forth the question: 'How would you like it if someone did that to you?' The close relationship between moral wrongness and unfairness may not be immediately obvious in some cases but it can be exposed with very little effort. If it cannot be, then there are grounds for arguing that an action so designated is not wrong in any meaningful sense – as I did above with contraception. An interesting parallel relationship can be seen with the words 'inequity' and 'iniquity'. Through the change of one letter the idea acquires a connotation of great wickedness.

This intimate connection between the descriptive and the prescriptive or emotive meanings of moral terms is one that many contemporary philosophers have refused to accept. But they very seldom ask *why* they feel it necessary to prescribe certain actions. When a doctor prescribes a medicine, he usually has reasons, which he can explain to the patient if asked. In the same way, Hobbes can provide an explanation based on his definition of wrongness or injustice as a violation of the social contract-golden rule. One does not have to accept his reasoning but his approach at least provides a foundation on which one can build a solid argument. Modern books on ethics often end with a whimper instead of a bang because all attempts to provide such a footing are rejected by the authors.

For example, Bernard Williams, concludes a recent book in this sort of vein:

> This has been a book about what is rather than about what might be, and the hopes I have expressed are, for now, hopes. They rest on assumptions that some people will think are optimistic. They can be compressed into a belief in three things: in truth, in truthfulness, and in the meaning of an individual life.[6]

Expressions of vague hopes and yearnings like this only seem to confirm what Williams had said on the previous page: 'The resources of most modern moral philosophy are not well adjusted to the modern world'. Williams, of course, is talking about ethics in the broad sense. His book takes as its starting point Socrates' question regarding how one should live, which makes a certain amount of vagueness inevitable. But he refuses the assistance that a narrower focus on what I have called morality could have offered. His chapter on that subject is entitled 'Morality, the Peculiar Institution' (174) and he immediately offers to explain 'why we would be better off without it'. Essentially he objects to its emphasis on moral obligation, duty, the moral law, the categorical imperative, purity and so on. The problem is that he destroys the usefulness of the concept by associating it almost exclusively with the ideas of Sir David Ross and Immanuel Kant. While some of his criticisms may be valid, his desire to jettison 'morality' completely seems to stem from a temperamental aversion to the word due to the connotations it has for him personally. Terms like 'obligation', 'duty', and 'law' are too hard-edged and unyielding for a person who feels that they somehow threaten human freedom and individuality. The only way to counter this attitude is to show, as Hobbes did, that moral concepts are logically derived from the most fundamental human needs and are there to help us, not to hinder us. The fact that authoritarian figures attempt to impose their own rigid beliefs on us by first imposing their own meanings on these words is no reason to abandon morality. They can be defeated by going back to first principles, but in order to do that there must be first principles to which we can return.

If moral philosophers cannot convince themselves that moral knowledge is possible, they are condemned to wander forever the trackless wastes of scepticism, relativism, subjectivism, etc., even though they deny it. Williams, for example, while not accepting completely the usual versions of the naturalistic fallacy or the is-ought problem cannot bring himself to go all the way. He believes that 'science has some chance of being more or less what it seems, a systematized theoretical account of how the *world really is,* while ethical thought has no chance of being everything it seems' (135). On the following page he says: 'In a scientific inquiry there should ideally be convergence on an answer . . . [that] represents *how things are;* in the area of the ethical, at least at a high level of generality, there is no such coherent hope'. Convergence may occur in ethics but not because 'it has been guided by how *things actually are'* (136) since it could not 'meaningfully be said to be a convergence on how *things (anyway) are'* (139 Emphasis added throughout).

Since he insists that ethics must be contrasted with 'the scientific' rather than, say, 'the factual', this definitely puts ethics in its place. However, his belief that science tells us how the world 'actually is' seems, to me, to be naive. First of all there is no such thing as science; what we have in fact are sciences, each with its own methodology for coping with its particular part of the world. A human being, for instance, can be looked at as composed of sub-atomic particles or molecules or cells or organs or as a totality. I, for example, present a very different picture to physicists, chemists, biologists, physiologists and psychologists, and I become nothing more than a statistic to sociologists and political scientists. This seems to preclude any simple response to a request for a description of how the world really is. What characterizes science in general is scientific method and that can be applied to diverse fields of study with varying degrees of success. His aim is a 'conception of the world that is "already" there' (138), one which is to a 'maximum degree independent of our perspective' and 'can be called an "absolute conception" of the world' (139). But no matter how rigorously scientific they may be, a physicist, a biologist and a psychologist approach the world from different perspectives because they are interested in different aspects of a complex phenomenon. His 'absolute conception' of *the* world seems, at least to me, to be a mirage caused by a misunderstanding of what scientists are trying to do and, indeed, are capable of doing.

In any case, why does he insist that 'the contrast with value should be expressed not in terms of knowledge but of science'? (139). Some knowledge is perspectival: 'we can know that grass is green, for instance, though *green*, for certain, and probably *grass* are concepts that would not be available to every competent observer of the world and would not figure in the absolute conception' (139). The reason for this differentiation between knowledge and science is not made clear but it does serve a useful tactical purpose. If, in answer to the critics of ethical scepticism, one admits that some kind of ethical knowledge is possible (as Williams does on p. 155), one can still say that it is merely perspectival knowledge and not science.

This is important for Williams because he believes that 'modern science is what absolute knowledge should be like' (199) and that 'the natural sciences, at least, are capable of objective truth' (198). Ethics obviously fails to meet this exalted standard. But does science provide the ideal model for truth? Scientific theories are always tentative and liable to be falsified in whole or in part by new discoveries. The scientific attitude is the opposite of dogmatic certainty; nothing is, or should be, immune from criticism and questioning. For this reason, truth is much more readily available in everyday life. If I say that it is raining outside, the truth or falsity of my claim can be checked by looking out the window. Thousands of such statements could be made concerning where I am, what I am doing, what is happening around me, etc. and their truth or falsity is easily determined by other observers. One could say that such truths are unimportant compared to those of science but importance is very much in the eye of the beholder. The exact speed of light is very important for scientists who are working in that field but is of no significance to most of us. On the other hand, the knowledge that, say, my house is on fire is of vital importance to me. The essence of the matter is that the distinction between scientific truth and non-scientific truth is an artificial one. The speed of light is a fact and my house being on fire is another fact. All assertions about anything are either true or false, so long as they are worded precisely enough.

I add that proviso because one has to be aware of the often unstated conditions. An example is Williams' claim that we can know that grass is green. If a lawn has not been watered in dry weather the grass is actually brown, and the statement – that grass is green – turns out to be false. However, we can say that under normal circumstances grass is green. My point is that this non-'scientific' statement is no different from the 'scientific' one that, under normal circumstances (at sea-level, etc.), water boils at 100° C, and the moral one that, under normal circumstances, murder is wrong. Once the definitions of the terms are agreed on, all are either true or false, although it is always possible that one does not know which or that one is mistaken. Philosophers too often let themselves be dazzled by the prestige of science and refuse to see that it is merely a highly specialized and disciplined approach to specific parts of a much larger whole. The use of it as the paradigm by which all other areas of life are to be judged and found wanting has no justification whatsoever. Furthermore, the idea that science can tell us 'the way the world really is' has never been less true than it is today. Quantum physics has shattered previous theories without putting anything solid in their place. There are at least eight theories of quantum reality, the most popular of which claims there is *no* deep reality.[7]

The only reason we can have scientific knowledge such as that water boils at 100° C. is that we have previously agreed on what we mean by the word 'water' and what we mean by '100° C'. Similarly, we can only say 'grass is green' if we are agreed on what 'grass' is and what 'green' is. These two examples do not differ in any significant logical way from their moral equivalent: 'murder is wrong'. You have to define 'murder', distinguishing it from other types of killing, and you have, above all, to define 'wrong'. If you refuse to accept that 'wrong' can be defined, as many moral philosophers ultimately do, then of course there will be no such thing as moral knowledge, any more than there would be scientific knowledge if scientists refused for example to agree on one meaning each for the e, m and c in e=mc². Decisions such as these provide the foundation on which one can build in a rational manner. It is the reluctance to seek out such a foundation that gives much of modern moral philosophy an air of futility. Value judgments are made but since they are not anchored to anything, the reader can agree or disagree as he pleases without having to justify himself.

Hobbes put it much better in *Leviathan* where he says:

> Seeing then that truth consisteth in the right ordering of names in our affirmations, a man that seeketh precise truth had need to remember what every name he uses stands for, and to place it accordingly, or else he will find himself entangled in words, as a bird in lime twigs, the more he struggles the more belimed. And therefore in geometry, which is the only science that it hath pleased God hitherto to bestow on mankind, men begin at settling the significations of their words; which settling of significations they call *definitions*, and place them in the beginning of their reckoning. (23, 105)

The importance of definitions is reflected in the confusion which can ensue if they are neglected. The result is that scholars 'spend time in fluttering over their books; as birds that entering by the chimney and finding themselves enclosed in a chamber, flutter at the false light of a glass window, for want of wit to consider which way they came in' (24, 105). Since 'nature itself cannot err' absurdity arises through the misuse of words, which are 'wise men's counters, they do but reckon by them, but they are the money of fools . . . ' (25, 106).

As for science, we have already seen that rational discourse, for Hobbes, originates in that alternation of a chain of opinions he calls doubt.

> No discourse whatsoever, can end in absolute knowledge of fact, past, or to come. For, as for the knowledge of fact, it is originally, sense; and ever after, memory. And for the knowledge of consequence, which I have said before is called science, it is not absolute but conditional. No man can know by discourse, that this, or that, is, has been or will be; which is to know absolutely:

but only, if this be, that is; if this has been, that has been; if this shall be, that shall be: which is to know conditionally . . . But if the first ground of such discourse, be not definitions; or if the definitions be not rightly joined together into syllogisms, then the end or conclusion, is again OPINION . . . (52, 131)

Williams does accept the need for an 'Archimedean Point' but he finds nothing really satisfactory. 'The project of giving to ethical life an objective and determinate grounding in considerations about human nature is not, in my view, very likely to succeed.' However, he admits that it is a comprehensible project which, if it were to succeed, would involve contractualism (153). This was the path chosen by Hobbes and is the one which probably has the best chance of succeeding. As we have seen, it requires a small number of concepts which are simple enough for any moral agent to grasp. If one wants to disagree with Hobbes one at least has something tangible about which to argue.

These basic ideas: contract, commitment, rules, obligations, fairness or reciprocity and its opposite, injustice or wrongness provide the framework for morality. When I say they are simple I do not mean to imply that they lack potential complexity when analyzed in detail; I mean that they are comprehensible enough to ordinary people to be used as a basis for action and judgment in everyday life, as they are, constantly. However, they do not provide the 'Archimedean point' for which we are looking. As normal, selfish human beings trying to avoid the inconvenient and unpleasant we do not really want to undertake obligations, obey rules and treat others fairly. Morality has acquired a bad name because it is constantly telling us to do what we do not want to do and forbidding us from doing what we would like to do. Why should we be expected to slip into what is actually a kind of strait-jacket which places unwelcome limitations on our freedom of action?

What we are asking here is essentially the old question: Why should I be moral? The response of a moral purist would be that the question is out of order. If you have to ask it, you do not understand the true nature of morality. An action which is performed for any reason other than a moral one, cannot be a moral action. Since morality is seen as a closed system, any attempt to seek a foundation outside itself is doomed to failure; to do so would destroy that special character which makes morality what it is. But the question still remains: why should we be moral?

Kant relied on us as rational agents to accept morality in the form of a categorical imperative. However rationality, by itself, is an incomplete explanation of behaviour. Reason is a tool we utilize for other purposes: it is a means to an end. When we say that a particular action is reasonable or rational we mean that it is likely to achieve its objective. We call people irrational when they engage in actions likely to frustrate their goals or what we assume should be their goals. To put it briefly, rational behaviour is that which is best suited to fulfilling our wishes and satisfying our wants. As a result, reason does not exist in a vacuum. It can only be made to appear as if it did by arbitrarily severing its connection with other aspects of the human personality. Kant seems to give us a choice between either acting morally under the guidance of reason or seeking our pleasure like unthinking animals. These alternatives are too extreme and if taken seriously, as they often have been, can lead to unnecessary and sometimes destructive tensions within us.

The idea of morality as a self-sufficient system detached from anything else works only so long as the question: 'Why should we be moral?' is not asked. However, for many people this *is* a silly question. These people have been raised to believe that some actions are right and others are wrong; they have no reason to question these inherited moral values. This is a legitimate position and as long as it promotes peaceful co-existence within the community nothing further need be said. That harming others is bad and helping others, good, seems so obvious to most of us as to be self-evident. It is only when two self-evident moral beliefs come into conflict that one begins to question their self-evidence. In Hobbes's day this was happening: those who regarded loyalty to the monarch as the cornerstone of political ethics saw their values being challenged by opponents who put other loyalties first. His response was to excavate below the surface in order to locate the true foundations of morality with the object of finding rational means for settling the controversies which raged so fiercely at the time.

His conclusion was that the structure of morality was best understood if it could be seen as resting on the strongest of all human drives, that for survival. If we can agree that self-preservation *is* paramount we have a valid starting-point for the enterprise. Rather surprisingly there are some who do not accept this. J. W. N. Watkins claims that the concomitant belief in man's overriding fear of violent death, has been exaggerated. In the volume of Sir James Frazer's *The Golden Bough* entitled *The Dying God*, he finds many examples of men who were willing and even eager to take on the job of king in various primitive societies, where it meant certain death after a period of time. He quotes with approval Frazer's conclusion:

> We shall never understand the long course of history if we persist in measuring mankind . . . by the standard . . . of the modern English middle class with their love of material comfort and their passionate, absorbing, almost bloodthirsty clinging to life.[8]

I hardly think the modern English middle class is unique in its desire to cling to life but, putting that aside, is there any merit in his argument? Does the fact that examples can be found of individuals willing to accept, even welcome death, invalidate the belief, by no means confined to Hobbes but actually extremely widespread, that most people want to avoid death at practically any cost? I see no reason to think so. The fact that a man might volunteer to be king knowing that he would be killed at the end of five years is not hard to understand. He has five years of power, with the possibility that the rules might change before his time is up, as well as the possibility he might die of natural causes before then anyway. It is instructive that in another case quoted by Watkins, where the king was killed on the night of his coronation, there were no volunteers and the throne remained vacant. The truth is that we do not need to delve into Frazer to find examples of willingness to die. People attempt suicide every day. However, other people, just as routinely, try to stop them. Why? Because the latter assume that nobody in his right mind wants to die if he can help it and therefore those who attempt suicide are not in their right minds. The hope is that if they can be saved, they will then have time to get over their troubles and want to go on living. Except where there is serious mental disturbance or extreme physical suffering, this often happens. And it often happens also that the survivors live on to see the day when they are panic-stricken at the possibility of being told by a doctor that they have incurable cancer.

The other type of person who would appear to contradict Hobbes's thesis is the one who is prepared to die for a cause. If the cause is religious then, of course, the Christian martyr or the Moslem warrior is actually trading the remainder of a life in this vale of tears for eternal life in heaven or paradise. In this case death is merely the transition to a better life and would not appear to affect Hobbes's argument as to our preference for life.

Nevertheless, he is talking about life on this earth and if enough people were willing to become martyrs, his generalization would fail. Watkins notes that most of the contemporaries whom Hobbes was addressing did believe in the survival of their souls. However, since a religion in which martyrdom became too popular would soon want for adherents, the Christian church did not encourage it and, of course, severely discouraged suicide. Fortunately, no matter how desirable heaven is made out to be, most believers are just as willing as unbelievers to put off as long as possible the day when, ready or not, they will have to find out for themselves what awaits them on the other side. There is no comfort for Hobbes's critics here.

The only ones yet unaccounted for are those willing to sacrifice their lives for a cause, without having any belief in the hereafter to console them. That there are such individuals is not in doubt; in fact their numbers have been very large, as witnessed by the casualties of two world wars. Not all of those who died were thus motivated but many were. However, Hobbes was aware of this type of motivation as well as of the others we have discussed and I do not think they have the slightest impact on his case. The question we have to answer is not whether every single individual always puts self-preservation first. The obvious reply to that is, of course not. We are all mortal and any decision we make affects only what remains of the limited span available to us. How we allot that, the extent to which we are willing to put it at risk or even the question of whether we want to live on into possible disability or senility – all these are matters which will be weighed and decided differently by each person. The question Hobbes is, in effect, asking is whether or not the desire for self-preservation and its constant companion, the fear of involuntary death, is or is not the strongest drive we have. To admit that it is the strongest, is not to say that it cannot be overcome. Some people have higher priorities than survival in *any* situation. But the evidence is overwhelming that normal human beings want to continue living as long as they can. The fact that some decide to go earlier is not significant. Someone who has attempted or contemplated suicide may, shortly thereafter, fight like a tiger against an attacker. Voluntary death and involuntary death are two very different things and Hobbes was talking about the latter. The urge to survive by fighting back is more instinctive and automatic than reasoned; it is the overcoming of this drive by conscious decision that requires justification. In this case, as in so many others, it is the exception which proves the rule.

A satisfactory theory of morality must be built on as firm a base as we can find in human nature. The most universal and therefore reliable characteristic that Hobbes and, I venture to say, anyone else could find is our desire for self-preservation. There is no doubt that many people are moved by a feeling of altruism, and numerous systems have been erected on this sentiment in the shape of benevolence or a moral sense. But the sorry truth is that many other people are not animated by a concern for others, at least beyond their immediate circle. However, if we were to appeal to their need to survive in a dangerous world we have a lever with which to improve their behaviour. They have to be shown the connection between self-preservation and morality, which is the sum and substance of what Hobbes is trying to demonstrate.

It should be made clear again that narrow self-interest on the one hand and self-preservation on the other, are importantly different. It is in our interest to continue living but that goal is often in conflict with our appetites. We have to sacrifice much immediate gratification in order to improve our chances for long-term survival. This is why Hobbes cannot be called an ethical hedonist. Although he recognizes the significance of pleasure and pain in human motivation, this is not the cornerstone of his system. There is no correlation between a long life and a pleasurable one. The quest for pleasure and the avoidance of pain are powerful forces in human beings but pale in comparison with the fear of death. People will readily put up with considerable pain in the interests of survival. Furthermore, any attempt to found morality exclusively on pleasure and pain faces tremendous obstacles. Morality constantly requires us to abstain from actions which are pleasurable and engage in other actions which may be painful. This innate conflict between morality and hedonism cannot be resolved no matter how sophisticated the attempts may be. Obviously happiness is a worthwhile pursuit in our lives and many people find happiness in making others happy. However there are those, like Luther, who regard suffering as the key to a meaningful life. These are interesting questions and will continue to be discussed in philosophical ethics. But they are of little help in telling me why I should behave morally, in the sense in which that word has been used in this discussion. If it is to be secure, morality must be founded on the one supreme human need which transcends any more immediate and transitory appetite or interest: self-preservation.

This is sometimes regarded as a selfish and unworthy feature of human beings; Watkins and Frazer are not alone in attempting to demean it. But theirs is a superficial attitude which does not take into consideration the full dimensions of what is involved. If we look upon self-preservation as a drive or instinct, there is an involuntary aspect to it which to some degree frees the individual from responsibility for having to justify it. No one, surely would think it reasonable to condemn a starving man who begs for food or a thirsty one for water. We all know that these are essential to life and it is taken for granted that a person should not be denied a chance to go on living. Those who eat too much or devote excessive time and attention to gastronomy are susceptible to criticism but that is because this behaviour can be changed without threatening the life of the person concerned, whereas food is a necessity to the starving, a need over which they have no control. The urge to survive is part of being human and, for that matter, all forms of life. To further this end, nature has instilled in us the emotion of fear, especially the fear of death. I have preferred to emphasize the positive side self-preservation rather than the negative side fear of death because, as an emotion, fear is operative mainly at times of crisis when there is an immediate threat. By goading us into action it can help us escape but if the matter is out of our hands, the raw emotion may be counterproductive. What is more useful is the milder form it can take as the imaginative anticipation of future danger which can provide an impetus for rational decision before the life-threatening situation arises. It is this quiet calculation of risks well ahead of time which is important for Hobbes, not the blind panic that ensues when one's life is actually in danger.

One further word should be said in favour of self-preservation as a reasonable motive for action. Those who attempt to commit suicide are often criticized for being cowards. This seems ironic since cowards typically run away from death, but suicide can be seen as running away from life, an attempt to evade responsibility by opting out. Where the moral drive for self-preservation has been weakened by misfortune, real or imagined, death may be seen as a release. However, there are very few people who do not have either family members who are dependent to some extent on them, or at least friends and relatives who will grieve their passing and miss them greatly. In this case self-preservation is the opposite of Frazer's 'almost bloodthirsty clinging to life'; it is an unselfish and socially beneficent road to take. This is, of course, one reason for the church's attitude towards suicide. My conclusion is that whether actions taken to preserve one's life are looked upon as caused by an instinctive drive, a belief that life, no matter how much tribulation it may involve, is sweet, or a consciousness of one's responsibilities to others, these actions can be justified on the basis of any criterion available to us. Self-preservation is a much more fundamental concept than self-interest and is the most solid foundation for morality that is available to us.

Nevertheless it will only function as such if the individual definitely wants to survive for whatever reason. Hobbes's argument cannot really apply to those who do not. However, the small percentage of people who want to do away with themselves represent a minimal threat to the rest since they quickly vanish from the stage. For those who remain, the next question is how can they best preserve themselves. As was noted before, in the state of nature it is not just a matter of quarrelling over scarce resources: the fear of what others might do leads to preventive action, to violence against innocent but potentially dangerous competitors. This escalation results from the absence of enforced rules of behaviour, and as a result the conflict of interest in this state can be eliminated only by the acceptance of such rules. Submission to them involves limitations on one's own freedom of action as well as that of everyone else, but it is a rational response since by providing protection from the lawless acts of others it enhances one's prospects for survival. However, one, of course, never surrenders the right to defend one's self. In the state of nature one has the right (*ius naturale*) to do *anything* one considers necessary for self-preservation, i.e. to go beyond defense to attack if one perceives a potential threat. Such actions are forbidden in an organized society because they are no longer necessary. They would disturb the peace rather than preserve it. But the ultimate right of self-defense must remain, even to a convicted criminal, because self-preservation was the reason for surrendering the other rights on entering civil society and as a result it could not, itself, be surrendered without destroying the motivational foundation for Hobbes's system.

An individual who has a strong enough desire to survive in a hostile world is thus led to accept the necessity of a covenant as much the lesser of two evils. With his agreement to abide by the terms of the covenant – in essence the golden rule – he becomes a member of a civil society. His commitment leads to an obligation to obey the rules which constitute morality. This move from the hypothetical state of nature does not actually occur but is implicit in the individual's acceptance of the benefits that flow from a settled and regulated society.

In this way Hobbes establishes morality on the solid foundation of the strongest motive exhibited by human beings: the desire to survive. Since any action we take in order to benefit ourselves in some way can be described as prudent, Hobbes would appear to be deriving morality from prudence and that will be seen as unacceptable by those who refuse to allow morality to be derived from anything and still be called morality. They would say that to act from prudential motives and to act from moral motives are two entirely different things, and that even though both acts may have the same beneficent outcome, the prudent man's act is flawed because it does not originate in selflessness, as a moral act should. At the very least, they are vaguely uneasy about the Hobbesian argument and remain unconvinced that morality, as they understand it, can survive on the basis he has in mind.

In order to answer this type of critic, I think that one has to be more specific about the meaning of prudence. Earlier on we treated it as an alternative motivation for acts that had the outward appearance of being moral. The usual example is something like 'honesty is the best policy'. One behaves honestly because it is good business to do so rather than because dishonesty is wrong. The assumption is that if the agent did not have to worry about people finding him out he would be prepared to be dishonest. In this sense, in the context of specific acts, prudence and morality are opposites, and one excludes the other. But if one moves out to a different time scale and operates in a context of long-term well-being, prudence does not contrast so sharply with morality. Hobbes goes even further. For him, self-preservation requires morality; *morality arises precisely because it is necessary for survival*. At this point one cannot make the usual accusations, involved in the prudence argument, that one is acting selfishly. I do not know how wanting to stay alive can be regarded as selfish except in the non-pejorative sense that one is concerned for the preservation of self. Actions taken for this purpose do not, it seems to me, require any defense. One either accepts self-preservation as justifiable or throws in the towel on everything because without life there is nothing.

Our best hope for survival is to live together peacefully and in order to do that a system of morality is necessary. Hobbes, thus, provides an excellent justification for those who ask: why should

I be moral? However, this in no way undermines the integrity of his moral system. Once the individual has opted into the system, his motivation is irrelevant; he is now bound by the rules of that system. To revert to the earlier example of the loan: my reason for borrowing the money is my own affair but once I have accepted the loan and have promised to pay it back, I am under an obligation to do so. The same is true of the individual who has accepted the social contract; he is bound by its provisions. This means that he will constantly have to refrain from acts which might appear to be beneficial to him but are harmful to others. Doing whatever is pleasant or in one's short-term self-interest without regard to the consequences for others is no longer permitted. For this reason Hobbesian morality will not differ in appearance or operation from any other strict, obligation-oriented system.

Of course, we are still left with the question of why I should be moral at the level of individual acts. Hobbes has offered an answer to the larger question of why I should participate in a moral system, but there will still be those who ask, why should I not cheat in this particular situation if I think I can get away with it? As this question has haunted philosophers since before Plato, one is hesitant to claim that it can be answered satisfactorily. However, I believe there are only two possible answers and that Hobbes has provided us with both. The first one is: because it is wrong. As soon as one enters freely into the social contract one has accepted a set of rules, the violation of which is defined as unjust or wrong. Wrong actions are those that one agrees not to do. So at this level, all you have is a word, which is automatically applicable to the kind of behaviour the questioner is contemplating. The truth is that if one had sincerely committed himself to the agreement he would not ask the question. But it is possible to imagine a very simple person or a child who does not necessarily understand the implications of what he has done, asking such a question and being satisfied with the reply that it is wrong. In the case of a loan, eyebrows would be raised, to say the least, if one asked, apparently sincerely, why one should pay it back. To do so would certainly be taken as evidence that one does not understand what is involved in going into debt and raise serious doubts as to whether one is mature or intelligent enough to be engaging in business transactions. Thus this question can be quickly and easily answered within the moral system but to ask it in the first place is, as Hobbes pointed out, absurd. It amounts to saying: Why should I not do what I have just said I would not do?

No sensible person would even ask it within the system because in doing so he would merely expose himself to ridicule.

But in the eyes of Hobbes, to ask it *outside* the system is also a sign of foolishness. He provides his second answer in his argument with the fool, the amoralist who persists in asking it. This argument, in essence, is that because it is difficult, if not impossible to survive without the help of others, anyone who takes the risk of antagonizing his 'confederates' is not acting rationally since he is jeopardizing his continued existence. It would only be reasonable to break the covenant if he knew that the others would remain in ignorance of what was happening. Unfortunately for him, the ring of Gyges remains a myth. As no one can foretell the future, and it is one's life that is on the line, this is a gamble that one cannot afford to take. In other words, for Hobbes *it is never prudent to act immorally*. However, the fact that it is in your long-term interest to be moral does not mean that you have to behave morally only out of self-interest. You can act morally for a variety of reasons. The one that Hobbes offered at the beginning is the best from the conventional viewpoint, which identifies morality with altruism, in opposition to egoism. He suggested, as a practical application of the golden rule, that we imaginatively change places with others by identifying with them in such a way that the preference we tend naturally to give to our own selves is counteracted. By putting ourselves in the shoes of others we can feel their pain as our own; through this process of empathizing, our actions can become as truly selfless as they are ever likely to be.

Whether it is possible for an act to be completely selfless depends on how the word is defined. If it consists in putting someone else's welfare ahead of one's own, it is obviously not only possible but quite common. This is the usual meaning of selfless or unselfish as opposed to selfish or self-regarding. It is a different matter, however, if a moral purist goes further and insists that an action not even be self-referential, in the sense that the agent's self is not involved in the transaction at all. This raises questions about the nature of selfhood which will be considered shortly.

8
Hobbes and Kant

Any discussion of why one should act morally involves two separate questions which are sometimes not clearly distinguished: what is it that makes an act right or wrong and what are the reasons for performing or not performing such an act. An alternative answer to these questions, which many would consider the antithesis of what they regard as the prudentialism of Hobbes, is that offered by Emmanuel Kant. When morality is contrasted with prudence, it is his model of what a moral theory should look like which is followed, although his name is not always invoked. A recent example of this attitude is found in Tom Sorell's book on Hobbes. After quite a spirited defense of Hobbes against many of the usual criticisms Sorell says 'Hobbes's views *are* vulnerable to attack if there is something wrong with appeals in ethics to self-interest, or personal interest of any kind. They are vulnerable if ethical requirements are necessarily universalistic in form or impersonal in content. Since I think both things are true of ethical requirements, I do not think that in the end Hobbes has an acceptable concept of morality'.[1] However, he does add a *caveat*: 'To refute Hobbes one would need no less than a knock-down argument for impersonal morality in the face of claims of self-interest, and such an argument is notoriously difficult to construct' (110). Nevertheless, the attraction of 'impersonal morality' is strong, as he has already indicated in his own case. Since Kant is the best-known proponent of such a position, it might be useful to take a closer look at his work to see whether his approach has more to offer than that of Hobbes. I do this with some trepidation since libraries have shelves full of books explicating, criticizing and defending Kant's ideas on morality. This is a clear indication of how much disagreement there is about what he actually meant.

The *Groundwork of the Metaphysic of Morals* (1785) is the principal source of his ideas on the subject, although it does have to be interpreted in the light of his other works. The reason for its importance is that this is where he develops the theoretical basis for his most famous contribution to ethics, the categorical imperative. However, it should never be forgotten that, in his overall scheme of things, morality is less important in itself than it is as an alternative foundation for freedom, immortality and God, which had apparently been disposed of in his *Critique of Pure Reason*. As he put it in the Preface to the Second Edition of that Critique: 'I have therefore found it necessary to deny *knowledge,* in order to make room for *faith*' (B xxx). He does this by working back from our sense of moral obligation. Naturally, I shall not enter into this aspect of his work but shall concentrate on his derivation of the supreme moral principle in the *Groundwork* utilizing H. J. Paton's edition.

In the Preface Kant asks:

> Do we not think it a matter of the utmost necessity to work out for once a pure moral philosophy completely cleansed of everything that can only be empirical and appropriate to anthropology [psychology]? That there must be such a philosophy is already obvious from the current Idea of duty and from the laws of morality.[2]

He thus makes clear his intention to move beyond the utilitarianism, moral sense theories, and what he later calls the hotch-potch of the 'popular philosophy' of his own day in order to establish a firmer foundation for morality. For support in this quest he appeals, in the first instance, to what is referred to in the title of Chapter I, as 'ordinary rational knowledge of morality'. Despite the high level of abstraction he reaches in his ethical philosophy, it is important to remember that his case ultimately rests, for the average person, on that person's own beliefs about morality. We may disagree about the details, but it would not be difficult to arrive at a consensus that we are all aware of a sense of duty or moral obligation. Kant's aim is 'to seek out and establish *the supreme principle of morality*' (60) using as his starting point, 'the provisional assumption that our ordinary moral judgments may legitimately claim to be true,' as Paton puts it in his 'Analysis of the Argument' (15).

One of these judgments, most people would admit, is that motivation is important. Self-interested motives detract from the moral value of an act no matter how good it may be in its consequences. However, Kant pushes this widely accepted belief beyond the point where many of its supporters would follow him by denying any moral content to an act unless it is done for the sake of duty.

> To help others where one can is a duty, and besides this there are many spirits of so sympathetic a temper that, without any further motive of vanity or self-interest, they find an immense pleasure in spreading happiness around them and can take delight in the contentment of others as their own work. Yet I maintain that in such a case an action of this kind, however right and however amiable it may be, has still no genuinely moral worth. (66)

Such an action because it is done from inclination rather than duty does not deserve our esteem. In order to isolate duty completely from inclination, Kant has to resort to an extreme example. If a man who, with little sympathy in his heart, 'cold in temperament and indifferent to the suffering of others,' and possessing no natural inclination to help them, still does so, out of a sense of duty, then we are seeing an action possessing true moral worth (66). Kant has been subjected to much criticism for implying that unless one is miserable in the performance of one's duty, one is not truly dutiful. This is, of course, not the case. The problem stems from confusing the *motive* for the action, which must be untainted by inclination, with any cheerful emotions which may *accompany* its performance. But the question remains: 'How can I be sure that I am acting purely for duty's sake and not for those pleasant feelings which may be associated with my action?'

This is a legitimate point, given the austere nature of Kant's ethics with its extreme emphasis on the importance of absolute purity of motive. He was, himself, quite aware of the difficulty. At the beginning of Chapter II he says:

> In actual fact it is absolutely impossible for experience to establish with complete certainty a single case in which the maxim of an action in other respects right has rested solely on moral grounds and on the thought of one's duty. . . . Out of love for humanity I am willing to allow that most of our actions may accord with duty; but if we look more closely at our scheming and our striving, we everywhere come across the dear self, which is always turning up; and it is on this that the purpose of our actions is based – not on the strict command of duty, which would often require self-denial. One need not be exactly a foe

to virtue, but merely a dispassionate observer declining to take the liveliest wish for goodness straight away as its realization, in order at certain moments (particularly with advancing years and with a power of judgement at once made shrewder by experience and also more keen in observation) to become doubtful whether any genuine virtue is actually to be encountered in the world. (74–75)

The last sentence reduces the distance between Kant and Hobbes, in that respect, at least, to the infinitesimal. In fact Kant appears the more pessimistic of the two.

No matter how true all this may be, however, Kant's equanimity is not disturbed. The fact that we believe duty *ought* to be the motive for our moral action is sufficient, even if not a single example can be found in practice. Since one of Kant's ultimate concerns is to demonstrate that morality presupposes freedom, that 'ought' implies 'can,' the conviction we have that we ought to act for duty's sake is enough for his purposes. He does not, for one moment, think that a moral system can be grounded on our actual behaviour.

Nevertheless, the ordinary person, on whose consciousness he initially relies, is in danger of being left behind by the philosopher hunting bigger game. For such an individual it is important to know whether it is ever possible to be sure that one's action acquires the moral worth which flows only from having been performed solely from the motive of duty. Aspects of Kant's own philosophy raise grave doubts that such could be the case.

First of all, Kant's attitude towards happiness gives the impression of being ambivalent, although he would probably insist that it was not. We must not act with the attainment of future happiness as our motive but he believes such happiness does await the righteous in a future life. He denies that we could ever know for certain that God does not exist, but if an individual were genuinely convinced that this was so, it is clear that Kant would agree that obedience to the moral law would, in his case, be pointless. 'No man can possibly be righteous without having the hope . . . that righteousness must have its reward.'[3] Thus one may act in this hope but must never let the anticipation of happiness, itself, be the reason for the act. Unless duty alone is the motive, the act is deprived of all moral worth. But in reality, as Kant himself noted, it is for all practical purposes impossible to be certain that the good of an action is not tainted by the hope. To expect someone who believes that God rewards the righteous to blot this from his mind when making a decision to act righteously is to ask a great deal of frail humanity.

There are two further difficulties in the *Groundwork* itself. One is that Kant allows reason 'its own peculiar kind of contentment' (64) when it fulfils its purpose through a good will even though the motive is not inclination. This is a roundabout way of saying that virtue is its own reward; that despite our best efforts we do obtain some kind of enjoyment out of doing what is right. But once we have learned this, how can we undertake to forget it every time we try to act morally?

The second difficulty arises when Kant plants a subversive notion right in the heart of his doctrine. 'To assure one's own happiness is a duty (at least indirectly); for discontent with one's state, in a press of cares and amidst unsatisfied wants, might easily become a great *temptation to the transgression of duty*' (67). Although this makes some sense it is difficult to reconcile with what appears to be the burden of Kant's argument. This puzzle is certainly not solved by the rather strange illustration which he uses – one that has rarely been noted by his commentators. After asserting that although happiness is the satisfaction of all inclinations *in toto*, one definite inclination may have to serve instead of the rather vague general idea (if I understand him correctly), he gives the following example:

> (A) man, for example, a sufferer from gout, may choose to enjoy what he fancies and puts up with what he can – on the ground that on balance he has here at least not killed the enjoyment of the present moment because of some possibly groundless expectations of the good fortune supposed to attach to soundness of health. But in this case also, when the universal inclination towards happiness has failed to determine his will, when good health, at least for him, has not entered into his calculations as so necessary, what remains over, here as in other cases, is a law – the law of furthering his happiness, not from inclination but from duty; and in this for the first time his conduct has a real moral worth. (67)

I think I understand what Kant is driving at but, on the face of it, all this is hard to accommodate to the rigorism which he illustrates again in the next paragraph. 'It is doubtless in this sense that we should understand too the passages from Scripture in which we are commanded to love our neighbour and even our enemy' (67). If we love out of inclination we would not need to be commanded, and kindness done from duty rather than inclination is practical love whereas that which flows from feeling or 'melting compassion' he calls pathological. It is 'this practical love alone which can be an object of command' (67). Although there is something rather distasteful about this, it conforms to what we would expect on the basis of his generally ascetic approach.

The gentleman with gout, to me at least, is not easy to fit into this schema. Here is a person who desperately wants a glass of port. His doctor has warned him that this is bad for his health but he has a strong desire or inclination to satisfy his craving now, and hang the consequences. The last thing one would expect is that Kant would say, as he, in effect, does: 'Go ahead. You have a duty to be happy and there is no guarantee that your health will be adversely affected some time in the future'. The man with gout can reply: 'Right you are. As long as I can convince myself that I am acting from a duty to be happy and not an inclination to satisfy a bodily appetite my conscience is clear. Cheers!'

I may be doing Kant a grave disservice here, but this example of happiness being a duty adds weight to the impression given by the two previous references that it is impossible, on the basis of his own words, to exclude happiness or contentment as a factor in judging the ground of one's actions. My point is not merely that it is difficult, as he admits at the beginning of Chapter II, to be sure if an action is done solely from duty, but that the very nature of his beliefs about happiness is such that he has not succeeded in isolating duty from the contamination of inclination and the desire for happiness. The serpent was in the Garden of Eden from the start. I emphasize this because it seems to support the point I made much earlier on, that there is no satisfactory way to prove that an act is completely free from consideration of self. When Kant holds out the prospect of happiness in another life for the good man who has no hope of receiving his reward in this one, he surrenders the lofty ground from which he has been preaching the rigorism for which he is famous. The high priest of duty in all its stark purity is not successful in his task because he cannot convince even himself that anyone is going to act selflessly without a thought of future reward. What remains is exactly what Kant started with and no more: the widely accepted belief that an action loses moral value if it is done from motives of self-interest. Most people would also agree with Kant that it is extremely difficult, if not impossible, to be sure that one's motives are ever completely pure.

The notion of moral worth, itself, should be subjected to at least a brief look. How significant is it that an act be evaluated in this way? If it is necessary to assess the character of a person for, say, a position of trust, or when choosing a friend, the nature of his or her motivation when performing a moral act will be of great importance. But for the vast majority of people, with whom we have no intimate ties, the reasons they have for acting the way they do are of little interest compared to the consequences of their actions. As long as they behave themselves, the details of their inner lives can be safely ignored. It seems, therefore, that the moral worth of actions is of significance to an outside observer, generally, only if that observer is keeping track of each individual's performance with a view to future reward or punishment. The obvious candidate for such a position is God, and the context is a religious one. Without the religious orientation which pervades Kant's ethics, the question of moral worth sinks into relative insignificance, except for those who are very close to the person concerned.

As for the categorical imperative itself, although it seems clear enough in principle, Kant's handling of the topic makes it far from clear to at least some of his readers. They find anywhere from three to five versions of it and disagree as to whether or not these are more or less equivalent, as Kant says. His examples do not help much, since at least some of them are regarded as unsatisfactory by most commentators. The greatest disagreement has arisen over how the categorical imperative is to be applied in practice, with some critics concluding that it allows for acts of the greatest immorality. Kant's supporters blame this on misunderstanding, but even they have to admit that Kant is easy to misunderstand, since he can be ambiguous, confusing and even, at times, contradictory. For example, he is defended from the charge of excessive rigorism, based on his clearly stated position that one should never tell a lie, even to save a life, by showing that he, himself, was mistaken in believing that his own moral principle required such a hard line. Perhaps one should always keep in mind the penultimate sentence of the *Groundwork*: 'And thus, while we do not comprehend the practical unconditional necessity of the moral imperative, we do comprehend its *incomprehensibility*' (131).

Regardless of Kant's particular applications of it, the categorical imperative is worth examining solely as a concept, to see what its implications are. He distinguishes it from hypothetical imperatives which are conditional because they are a means to some end that one may or may not wish to pursue. Imperatives of skill concern practical ends, such as how to cure a man or alternatively, since they are purely technical, how to kill him. Counsels of prudence, also called assertoric hypothetical imperatives, involve an end that everyone is assumed to have: the advancement of his or her own interests or happiness. The categorical imperative differs from these two because it is unconditional; it takes the form of a command or law of morality which must be obeyed. However, the difference need not be as great as Kant makes out. On the one hand, when the condition of a hypothetical imperative is accepted it becomes categorical and, on the other, the moral imperative can always be seen as a disguised hypothetical imperative with the accepted conditions left unstated. By denying this possibility, Kant frees his morality from inclination of any kind but only at the risk of incoherence. A command must be issued by a commander and if it requires the sacrifices that a moral imperative may very well do, the legitimacy of the commanding authority must be unquestionable. The only imaginable repository of such supreme power is God. The missing condition thus turns out to be something like, 'if I accept God's commandments, then I ought to . . . ' Only by acting on some such basis can I come close to that 'holy' will which Kant holds out as an ideal. Hobbes, as we have seen, allows for this approach by openly offering his laws of nature as commands of God, as well as precepts of practical reason.

However, since the categorical imperative is the cornerstone of Kant's system, we must see what he does with it. The most widely accepted formula is some variation of 'I ought never to act except in such a way *that I can also will that my maxim should become a universal law*' (70). As a principle of universalization, this is regarded by many commentators as quite unexceptionable but it does have its difficulties. First of all, one must come up with a maxim which expresses the policy one would be adopting if one performed a specific action. This is not always easily done since it is usually possible to formulate several maxims for a single action. Then one has to turn the most suitable maxim into a universal law and see if one would be prepared to will such a law. If not, the action is presumably wrong. It is obvious that for such a test to work satisfactorily, the maxim and the law must be worded very carefully so as to capture the exact implications of the action. That even Kant himself has difficulty doing this is illustrated by a criticism of one of his examples made by A. R. C. Duncan.

> The maxim which he rejects when universalised is not the maxim on which the agent is supposed to be acting. He does not call upon the agent to ask himself 'should I be content that everyone else should always make false statements?' but 'should I be content that everyone should lie when in difficulties? While universalisation of the first maxim might destroy all confidence in the written and spoken word, universalisation of the second would merely underline the necessity, familiar to everyone, of exercising caution when called upon to accept a statement or promise made by someone known to be in difficulties.[4]

One of the commonest criticisms of the categorical imperative is that a maxim which is worded in such a way that it would apply to hardly anyone but the agent (people of a specific age, height, weight, hair color, etc.) could be universalized and thus permit him to engage in obviously immoral actions. This approach has been criticized by M. G. Singer as violating his (Singer's) principle of reiterability. After quoting an example in which a student, using such a narrowly defined maxim, decides it is morally permissible not to repay a debt, he says: 'This conclusion is wrong, for the same argument can be reiterated for every maxim of this type, and this would imply that it is morally permissible for everyone to ignore his debts, which is clearly not so'.[5] However, in order to avoid this outcome, the categorical imperative would have to be restated in such a way as to incorporate the principle of reiterability and any other limitations needed to restrict the wording of the maxim so as to make it acceptable. As it stands the imperative does not prohibit maxims of this type. That this problem of wording is not a trivial one is indicated by the necessity of specifying, in the case of Kant's unyielding position on lying that, for example, lying is wrong *except* in certain situations such as when telling the truth might result in an innocent person's death.

However, supposing that a maxim is satisfactory in every way and then cannot be universalized, why does this make the relevant action immoral? The example Kant gives after his first reference to the categorical imperative is that of making a false promise. What happens when I try to make a universal law out of this, one which would permit everybody else to lie when in difficulty?

I then become aware at once that I can indeed will to lie, but I can by no means will a universal law of lying; for by such a law there could properly be no promises at all, since it would be futile to profess a will for future action to others who would not believe my profession or who, if they did so over-hastily, would pay me back in like coin;* and consequently my maxim, as soon as it was made a universal law, would be bound to annul itself. (71)

Paton, always ready to defend Kant from himself, has a footnote where I have used an asterisk: 'This looks like falling back on mere self-interest, but Kant's point is that there could be *no promises at all* if this maxim were universally followed' (136). This is spelled out more clearly in Kant's comments on the similar example in Chapter II:

> For the universality of a law that every one believing himself to be in need can make any promise he pleases with the intention not to keep it would make promising, and the very purpose of promising, itself impossible, since no one would believe he was being promised anything, but would laugh at utterances of this kind as empty shams. (90)

However, the question remains open as to whether self-interest in some form or other is completely excluded by this argument. If my concern is that by universalizing false promising I would eliminate promising as an institution, an institution that I find extremely useful, then my reason for not universalizing it would be that the loss of that practice would be highly detrimental to my interests. In the same way, the universalization of theft would mean the end of the institution of private property, which I would also find inconvenient. Ultimately, the universalization of immoral practices would destroy society along with the benefits it brings to me. Thus self-interest alone would give me an excellent motive for conforming to the categorical imperative.

This would be rejected by many Kantians on the grounds that some promises cannot be made at all on such a basis; the maxim destroys itself, as with the promising example above, before self-interest has a chance to make an appearance. The only problem with this logical type of contradiction is that it does not always apply. If I would like to kill someone I hate, the universal law might be: 'Anyone who hates someone else can kill that person'. There would be no contradiction involved in my going ahead with my act of murder, but it would be very detrimental to my self-interest to will such a law since I could easily become a victim. Some of Kant's own illustrations do not satisfy this criterion, either. Of the man who gives himself up to pleasure rather than cultivating his natural talents, Kant says that he cannot possibly *will* that a maxim based on his proclivities be made a universal law of nature: 'For as a rational being he necessarily wills that all his powers should be developed, since they serve him, and are given him, for all sorts of possible ends' (90). There is no logical contradiction in his going against powers which serve him and other ends as well.

Many commentators feel that Kant is, at times, a very poor exponent of his own theories, often developing out of them conclusions which do not follow, such as his illustrations of the categorical imperative. Almost no one is prepared to accept them all as following from his main principle. But I am inclined to think that the opposite is true. His illustrations, and the specific ethical rules found in his late work, *The Metaphysic of Morals*, represent his real beliefs and the reason they do not flow satisfactorily from the categorical imperative is that the supreme moral principle which he actually uses, is much broader and vaguer than the categorical imperative. He presents the latter initially in such a way that it looks satisfyingly simple and at the same time comprehensive. But almost immediately he begins to blur it. The four examples given in his Chapter II are intended to illustrate the version that uses 'universal law of nature' instead of just 'universal law'. Although Kant seems to think that all his versions are ultimately equivalent, many Kantians regard the 'law of nature' formula as a significant departure. But further complications immediately arise: does he mean a causal law of nature, like the law of gravitation, as some think, or does he mean a teleological law of nature as Paton, for example, holds? Then there are his other variants, the first of which is: '*Act in such a way that you always treat humanity, whether in your own person or in the person of any other, never simply as a means, but always at the same time as an end*' (96). Another one concerned with ends is: 'Accordingly every rational being must so act as if he were through his maxims always a law-making member in the universal kingdom of ends' (106). If we add to these and other slightly different formulations of the categorical imperative, the obligatory ends of happiness and perfection found in *The Metaphysics of Morals*, and other concepts close to his heart such as dignity, autonomy, freedom and so on, we find that the original version of the categorical imperative is completely inadequate as a means of expressing what Kant had in mind. One need only look at the amount of disagreement generated amongst commentators through their attempts to reconcile their interpretations of the categorical imperative with what Kant actually said.

Part of the problem is that in his major critical works, Kant wants to present his ethical ideas in terms of the architectonic of his whole philosophical system. Although this may be necessary for the understanding of the place of ethics in his overall philosophy, his ethical ideas themselves suffer, in my opinion, a loss of clarity. If one wants to see the latter discussed on their own terms, one should turn to his *Lectures in Ethics* which were being given just a few years before the publication of *Groundwork* in 1785. Since the three different sets of notes used in preparing the text differed only in minor details, it must represent quite accurately Kant's ideas as they would be presented in the context of a lecture course.

Here is part of what he has to say about the supreme principle of morality:

> The essence of morality is that our actions are motivated by a general rule, that is, that the reasons for the action are to be found in such a rule . . . Take, for example, the keeping of a promise. To break a promise as it please our sensibility is not moral, for if no man were willing to keep his promise simply in terms of the original proposal promises would in the long run become useless. But I may judge the matter in terms of the understanding, to discover whether it is a universal rule that promises should be kept. I then find that as I wish that all others should keep their promises to me, I must keep my promises to others. My action then conforms to the universal rule of will in general.[6]

This is an earlier version of one of the illustrations which Kant used in the *Groundwork*. The motivation for the rule of promising is stated more clearly here: 'I then find that as I wish that all others should keep their promises to me, I must keep my promises to others'. This is essentially the golden rule and one will find that the more a commentator tries to reduce Kant's complexities to everyday language, the more his moral principle comes to resemble that rule. Furthermore, those versions of the categorical imperative which refer to man as an end rather than a means, are implicit in the golden rule, since it is highly unlikely that you would wish to be treated only as a means, and therefore it is incumbent upon you to refrain from doing so to others.

Kant's repeated use of contradiction as a test of morality is much clearer, also, in the golden rule. If you object to being treated in a certain way then it is plainly contradictory for you to expect to be able to treat others that way. The idea of contradiction can be interpreted in various ways but this seems to be the bottom line in the moral balance sheet. Universalization comes down to the question: 'what would it be like if *everyone* did that?', and this question can only be answered by asking a more personal one: 'How would I like it if someone did that to me?' The answer, 'I wouldn't like it at all', implies the corollary necessary to avoid contradiction: 'Then don't do it to others'.

Kant's contemptuous reference to the rule in its canon law form *'quod tibi non vis fieri,* etc.' (*Groundwork,* 97 fn.) is surprising in light of his respect for the Bible. In his *Lectures in Ethics,* he says: 'The Gospel first presented morality in its purity, and there is nothing in history to compare with it' (128). He repeatedly refers to that other great exhortation: 'Love thy neighbour as thyself,' yet he ignores the golden rule which appears in both Matthew 7,12 and Luke 6,31. E. E. Hirst calls the categorical imperative 'uni-personal,' as opposed to the golden rule which he considers to be 'inter-personal'.[7] By this distinction he means that whereas the golden rule is based on a calculation of the impact of one's actions on other people, the latter were very much in the background as far as the categorical imperative is concerned. The universalization formula and even the means-ends version assume the existence of other persons in a rather remote and abstract way. And this is true only when duties to others are considered; in the case of duties to oneself, they disappear altogether. This lack of interest in morality as a primarily social concern is clearly indicated in the emphasis which Kant gives to duties to oneself. His disdain of the traditional golden rule probably springs as much from the fact that it provides no ground for such duties as from anything else.

In the *Lectures,* he expresses dissatisfaction with previous philosophers who did not recognize the importance of this subject. 'It was taken for granted that a man's duty towards himself consisted, as Wolff in his turn defined it, in promoting his own happiness' (117). In Kant's view self-regarding duties are not related to our well-being 'or earthly happiness'.

> Far from ranking lowest in the scale of precedence, our duties towards ourselves are of primary importance and should have pride of place; for . . . it is obvious that nothing can be expected from a man who dishonours his own person. He who transgresses against himself loses his manliness and becomes incapable of doing his duty towards his fellows. A man who performed his duty to others badly, who lacked generosity, kindness and sympathy, but who nevertheless did his duty to himself by leading a proper life, might yet possess a certain inner worth; but he who has transgressed his duty towards himself, can have no inner worth whatever. (117–18)

It is only when one realizes the extreme weight which he attaches to self-regarding duties, that one can understand why his use of the word 'duty' has led to such varied interpretation of his ethics.

He proceeds to give some examples. 'A drunkard does no harm to another and if he has a strong constitution he does no harm to himself, yet he is an object of contempt.' When a servile man cringes and fawns, 'he degrades his person and loses his manhood'. A liar, even when his lie harms no one also becomes 'an object of contempt'. The faint-hearted who complain and shed tears over their misfortunes 'are despicable in our eyes' (118–19). Suicide is 'abominable' and the mention of it 'makes us shudder' but crimes of the flesh are 'nauseating' and 'loathsome'; 'we are ashamed of them because they degrade us below the level of beasts' (124). Since failure in one's duty to oneself arouses such strong revulsion, it is easy to see why Kant gave it an important place in his ethics. His reaction stems from the elevated position he assigns to humanity as such. We are superior to mere things and to other animals in our possession of freedom, and the surrender of that freedom by committing suicide, demeaning ourselves through servility, selling our sexuality, etc. contradicts the very characteristic which sets us apart. The end we must pursue is to perfect ourselves in every way possible and we can only do this through self-esteem, self-mastery, and honouring the humanity in ourselves. Kant's outlook is best summed up in the last section of the *Lectures*: 'The ultimate destiny of the human race is the greatest moral perfection, provided that it is achieved through human freedom, whereby alone man is capable of the greatest happiness' (252). Man must become worthy of happiness and it is through the fulfilment of his duties to himself that merit and happiness are ultimately combined.

The question remains as to whether one can claim that such duties actually exist. Where an obligation to another person is incurred, as in the case of borrowing money, the obligation can only be extinguished when the loan is either repaid or forgiven by the creditor. On the other hand, if both parties to the obligation are oneself, there is no obstacle to one releasing oneself from it. Kant is aware of this and discusses it in the second part of his *The Metaphysic of Morals*, translated as *The Doctrine of Virtue*, where he points out that 'the obligatory subject (*auctor obligitionis*) could always release the obligated subject (*subiection obligationis*) from the duty (*terminus obligationis*), so that if both are one and the same subject, one would not really be obligated to a duty he imposes on himself'.[8] This would be a contradiction and we know what Kant's opinion of those is. His 'Solution to This Apparent Antimony' falls back on the phenomenal-noumenal distinction. Man, 'considered in terms of his *personality*, i.e. as a being endowed with *inner freedom* (*homo noumenon*), is susceptible of obligation and, indeed, of obligation to himself (to humanity in his own person)' (81). Unfortunately this type of argument has little power to convince those who do not find the presuppositions of his critical philosophy convincing.

Doubtless we do make demands on ourselves and we often do feel shame after we have acted in a servile manner or have engaged in certain types of sexual behaviour, but is duty or obligation to oneself the most useful way of expressing these feelings? The fact that we sometimes say: 'I owe it to myself', adduced by Kant in support of his position, only means that we are borrowing an idea, the real burden of which lies elsewhere. A genuine obligation always involves other people and to apply the word to oneself, except metaphorically, distorts its meaning. Certainly there is no harm in setting high standards for one's personal conduct and one certainly deserves credit for the effort one expends in living up to them. But Kant's list of violations to self-regarding duties illustrates the weakness of this approach. His use of adjectives like 'nauseating', 'revolting', 'loathsome', 'despicable', etc. for masturbation, homosexuality and so on, reflects an attitude towards the body which, while dominant for a long time in our culture, is now considered by many to be not only wrong but even harmful. It is an attitude which resulted in 'immorality' having an almost exclusively sexual connotation until quite recently. By giving excessive significance to 'unnatural' carnal sins against oneself, Kant also risks trivializing the distinction between a socially harmless act like masturbation and a genuine crime like rape.

Leaving aside for the moment the question of whether obligation or duty is the correct terminology, what reasons does Kant give for considering the uni-personal types of behaviour, to which he objects, immoral? Although, he talks in terms of degrading oneself to the animal level (or below) and the frustration of one's capacity for purposeful behaviour, the third reason he gives really encompasses the other two as well: the misuse or perversion of the purposes of nature. The assumption is that, for example, nature intends sex for procreation only and, therefore, any sexual activity which is not for procreation is wrong. By bringing in our duties to others, Kant further limits permissible sex to monogamous marriage.

But how can anyone, including Kant, claim to know what nature's purposes are? We do know that sex is necessary for the survival of the race just as eating is for the survival of the individual. However, why should the physical pleasure which accompanies these activities not have been given to us as a blessing in itself? Hunger alone can drive one to eat, without the additional stimulus of varied and delightful tastes and aromas. Why can we not say that nature intended us to enjoy both food and sex apart from their other purposes? It is very difficult to read nature's intentions and, in fact, it is clear that Kant rests his case ultimately on a belief that his own convictions are self-evident because they were accepted by the respectable people of his own day as they are by some at the present time. It is difficult for many of his readers to realize the extent to which he took his moral ideas without criticism from the environment in which he lived. He would have been astonished if any of his students had questioned the notion that drunkenness was contemptible or that 'carnal self-defilement' was loathsome, as well as the cause of sterility and premature senility, which he claimed in his *Pädagogik*.[9]

Thus we *know* what actions are right and wrong, and we *know* we have a duty to do what is right and do it for duty's sake. We know even more.

> There are certain moral dispositions such that anyone lacking them could have no duty to acquire them. – They are *moral feeling, conscience, love* of one's neighbour, and *reverence for oneself* (*self-esteem*). There is no obligation to have these because they lie at the basis of morality . . . All of them are natural dispositions

of the mind (*praedispositio*) . . . To have them cannot be a duty; every man has them and it is by virtue of them that he can be obligated. (*Doctrine of Virtue*, p. 59)

Men, thus, come equipped with everything that is necessary in order to behave morally. Why, then, do they often not do so? Because they succumb to inclinations. A holy will has no problem since it will automatically act in harmony with the moral law but the human will is determined by reverence (*achtung* when used as the equivalent of *reverentia*) for the law (*Groundwork*, pp. 81 and 68). The words 'holy' and 'reverence' indicate once again how ill-defined the border between philosophy and theology is for Kant, at least with respect to morality. An example can be found in his discussion of conscience in the *Metaphysic of Morals*. When one is brought before the bar of conscience he must imagine someone other than himself as the judge – an individual who may be real or ideal.

Such an ideal person (the authorized judge of conscience) must be a scrutinizer of hearts, since the court of justice is set up *within* man. . . . Now since such a moral being must also have all power (in heaven and on earth) in order to be able to give his law its due effect (a function essential to the office of judge), and since such an omnipotent moral being is called *God*, conscience must be conceived as a subjective principle of responsibility before God for our deeds. (*Doctrine of Virtue*, p. 105)

But once having crossed the theological frontier, Kant quickly scuttles back before being exposed to philosophical fire. 'This is not to say that man is entitled, on the grounds of the Idea to which his conscience inevitably leads him, to *posit* such a Supreme Being as *really existing* outside himself – still less is he *obligated* to do so.' (ibid.) It is only an analogy, a matter of regarding duties *'as if* they were divine commands' (106). But he quickly blurs his position again by adding that 'to have religion is a duty of man to himself'. (ibid.)

There are many passages in his *Lectures* which appear to go further but merely spell out more clearly what is sometimes only implicit in his other works. True religion rests on morality. Ceremonies and observances as well as the subtle questions of speculative theology are as irrelevant for him as they are for Hobbes. To 'enable us to do our duty it does not matter what notions we have of God provided only they are a sufficient ground for pure morality' (79). His natural religion requires only 'a holy lawgiver, a benevolent and a just judge' as the moral attributes of God' (80). Morality, properly understood leads to a belief in God.

> This belief in a God is so deeply ingrained in our moral feeling that no speculative counter-arguments can eradicate it, for the pre-eminent consideration in morality is purity of disposition, and this consideration would lose its force if there existed no being to take notice of it. Without belief in the existence of such a being man could not possibly attain to and be conscious of the highest moral worth. Only God can see that our dispositions are moral and pure, and if there were no God, why ought we to cherish these dispositions? ... More than this, we cannot be moral without believing in God. (80–81)

As he says a few pages later, atheism 'deprives rules of good conduct of their motive power' (86).

> The basis of religion must, therefore, be morality. Morality as such is ideal, but religion imbues it with vigour, beauty, and reality ... [Ethics] tells us in effect to pursue the Idea of morality apart from any hope of being happy. But this is impossible; and as without a Being to give actuality to the Idea, morality would be merely ideal, it follows that there must exist a Being to give vigour and reality to the moral laws, and this Being must be holy, benevolent and righteous. (81–82)

Morality and religion are mutually supportive: the moral law gives us our belief in God, and God, in turn, gives vigour and reality to the moral law.

Kant waffled a bit on this relationship and it has been said that he later rejected the doctrine of the *Lectures*. In a work published in 1793, he says, 'Morality does not need religion at all ... either to know what duty is or to impel the performance of duty'.[10] If interpreted narrowly, however, this does not really contradict his core position as expressed, for example, in the *Groundwork*. Furthermore, *The Metaphysic of Morals* which appeared later than this work (1797) contains a catechism near the end in which, after the pupil has said that 'our happiness always remains a mere wish which cannot become a hope unless some other power is added,' the teacher asks:

> Has reason, in fact, grounds for admitting the reality of such a power, which apportions happiness according to man's merit or guilt – a power ordering the whole of nature and ruling the world in the supreme wisdom? Pupil: Yes. For we see in the works of nature, which we can judge, a wisdom so widespread and profound that we can explain it to ourselves only by the ineffably great act of a creation of the world. And from this we have cause, when we turn to the moral order, which is the highest adornment of the world, to expect there a rule no less wise. In other words, we have cause to hold that if we do not make ourselves *unworthy of happiness* by violating our duty, we can also hope to *share* in happiness'. (*Doctrine of Virtue*, p. 156)

This is close enough to the earlier quotations to indicate that Kant's position remained much the same over the years. His religious ideas differed to a considerable extent from orthodox Christianity but he never seems to have questioned the moral precepts instilled in him by his Pietist parents.

Kant's ethical theory, then, appears to originate with the shame and guilt that society attaches to certain acts which it deems to be wrong. Since not all of these acts involve other people, it follows that one must have duties to oneself as well as duties to others. This complicates the task of the categorical imperative because, as a universalization principle it requires, no matter how indirectly, the involvement of other persons. The problem becomes apparent when Kant provides illustrations of the categorical imperative in Chapter II of the *Groundwork*. The introduction of a teleological concept of nature indicates the importance of ends to Kant and even before they appear in his other versions of the categorical imperative they are mentioned in his third illustration, which concerns the cultivation of talents. A man cannot wilfully neglect his natural gifts 'since they serve him, and are given him, for all sorts of possible ends' (90). Long before the idea is further developed in the *Metaphysic of Morals*, we find Kant using obligatory ends to prop up the categorical imperative which, by itself, cannot produce the conventional morality which Kant seeks to justify. If we look at man as a creature with certain ends or purposes built into his nature, then the shame and guilt that is felt when engaging in immoral acts can be understood as caused by the fact that the latter violate the ends for which man was created. Thus, the disgust which is associated with masturbation makes sense if it is assumed that our sexual organs are given to us for procreation only. Other explanations for such feelings are conceivable but the teleological one is so obvious to Kant that he looks no further.

To recapitulate: if we start with conventional morality and the various emotions aroused by its transgression, we must include duties to oneself and, since these cannot be satisfactorily derived from the categorical imperative, the introduction of teleology is required. Unfortunately, this tactic eliminates the possibility of a secular morality since a Creator must be presupposed, one who provides us with purposes and also judges us on how well we fulfil them. Because life is too short for the attainment of perfection on this earth, God must have made provision for the continuation of our existence in another world where the virtuous will receive that reward, without which the constant struggle they have waged against their inclinations would have been pointless.

One important product of this approach is the heavy emphasis placed by Kant on motivation. The possibility of a future reward for righteousness has to impact on the individual's moral decision-making process and as a result cast doubt upon whether the action is performed for the sake of duty rather than that of inclination. This has been discussed before but my point here is that this uncertainty is a direct outcome of the chain of reasoning that Kant has used. It is no problem for a contract theory like that of Hobbes, which does not depend on such a hope. Furthermore, because motivation is suspect, 'the purity of our disposition and the strictness of our actions,' must be carefully watched and 'self-examination must be constant' (*Lectures*, p. 126). An ethics which requires such continuous self-examination and self-evaluation runs the risk of being self-centred in a way that may not be selfish but is certainly self-absorbed. The golden rule and the rule of love (Love thy neighbour as thyself) are both self-referential but they imagine the effect of an act on oneself in order to use that as a standard for behaviour towards others. Because of his emphasis on duties to oneself and on the need for constant self-evaluation, Kant's use of the self is quite different in orientation. The important thing for him is not the impact of one's action on others but its effect on one's own moral worth and, as a result, there is a narcissistic aspect to Kant's approach which is at odds with the prevailing perception of his ethics. Genuine selflessness is as difficult to achieve as complete purity of motivation. Kant's attempt to deny the self results in a relentless reaffirmation of it.

This is unfortunate since that 'dear self,' which is castigated by Kant, can be used on behalf of morality as well as against it. The Biblical injunction to 'love thy neighbour as thyself' takes for granted, as does modern psychology, that the love of self is the model for the love of others. We now believe that lack of self-love or self-esteem can have a disastrous effect on the mental health of human beings. Altruism or concern for others is possible because I am able to substitute another's self imaginatively for my own through a process of identification. Without this ability to identify with others which is embodied in the golden rule, it is unlikely that morality would be possible. In other words, to seek the impersonality of detachment in ethics is to pursue a will o' the wisp.

9
Contract Theory Today

Given that Kant was influenced by contract theory (through Rousseau) in his political thought, it is surprising that he does not at least consider it in relation to ethics. The closest he comes is his formulation of the categorical imperative which sees the individual as a legislator in the kingdom of ends. But as always for Kant, although the lawmaking obviously involves a relationship with others, it is done by the individual acting on his own, never in conjunction with others. The notion that morality is, and must by its very nature be, *social* as well as personal would doubtless not have been denied by Kant but his vision is focused so intently on the individual, that the community becomes practically invisible in his ethical work. For contract theory a moral rule is arrived at by agreement amongst a group of individuals, whereas for Kant it emerges from a private mental process whereby an individual attempts to determine if a maxim can be universalized in the context of essential ends. This can elicit duty but not what we normally call an obligation. An obligation is created where one individual enters into a particular kind of relationship with another. It can be overtly contractual as with a loan; when I borrow money I place myself under an obligation to repay it. Or, the contract may be implicit: as a parent I am under an obligation to look after my children and as a grownup son or daughter I have an obligation to care for my aged parents. By refusing to look for the basis of obligation in social relationships instead of the abstract realm of practical reason Kant detaches morality from its roots in human experience and sacrifices much of the intelligibility it might have had for the ordinary man. Although he was writing for philosophers rather than the man on the street, it is, after all the conventional morality of the latter which he accepts without question and attempts to justify.

It is significant that a scholar who has spent years studying and teaching Kant's philosophy arrives at much the same position. At the end of his analysis of the *Groundwork*, Robert P. Wolff concludes that Kant has failed 'to find a plausible argument for the validity of substantive moral principles' and confesses that he is 'persuaded that moral obligations, strictly so-called, arise from freely chosen contractual commitments between or among rational agents who have entered into some continuing and organized interaction with one another'. He continues:

> Where such contractual commitments do not exist, cannot plausibly be construed as having been tacitly entered into, and cannot even be supposed to be the sort that *would* be entered into if the persons were to attempt some collective agreement, then no moral obligations bind one person to another.[1]

Aware that such a view would be highly controversial in the eyes of modern liberals, Wolff imagines a situation which would serve as a useful test of one's moral convictions.

> Consider for a moment the familiar case of the Good Samaritan. If I encounter a man by the side of the road, sorely in need of help, my natural response is to think that I have some sort of obligation to help him, particularly if none of the usual countervailing considerations (conflicting obligations, prudential interests) obtain. But suppose that this man looks at me and says, 'I am dying. I desperately need and want your help. I implore you to assist me. But in all honesty I must tell you that if our positions were reversed, I would not lift a finger for you'. My moral intuition tells me that I should then be relieved of my obligation to help him. And that, in turn, suggests that my initial sense of obligation stems from a quasi-contractual understanding or, at least, from an expectation that we would arrive at some contractual agreement if we were in a position to explore the matter of rules governing our interactions. (219–20)

An important qualification to this approach is that there is nothing to stop one from helping such a person for another reason such as, for example, a feeling of compassion. But the attitude of the victim is surely enough to cast grave doubt on the notion that one has an *obligation* or duty to aid him. The Hobbesian type of contractual ethics does not forbid acts of supererogation; in fact, it encourages them but they are not obligatory. Oddly enough, the limits built into contract reciprocity theory are recognized and accepted by Kant himself, although not in the context of that theory.

> Let us take a man who is guided only by justice and not by charity. He may close his heart to all appeal; he may be utterly indifferent to the misery and misfortune around him; but so long as he conscientiously does his duty in giving to every one what is his due, so long as he respects the rights of other men as the most sacred trust given to us by the ruler of the world, his conduct is righteous; let him give to another no trifle in excess of his due, and yet be equally punctilious to keep no jot nor tittle back, and his conduct is righteous. If all of us behaved in this way, if none of us ever did any act of love and charity, but only kept inviolate the rights of every man, there would be no misery in the world except sickness and misfortune and other such sufferings as do not spring from the violation of rights. The most frequent and fertile source of human misery is not misfortune, but the injustice of man. (*Lectures on Ethics*, 194)

This describes perfectly the behaviour of a person bound only by the negative golden rule, interpreted very narrowly. It illustrates how significant for society this simple rule of restraint can be.

The Good Samaritan example, however, is not an ideal one for the purposes of contract theory. It could be argued that even if the victim had not indicated the attitude he would have taken if our situations were reversed, I would still have had no clear obligation to help him. More would have to be known about our prior relationship. If he had been of great help to me in the past, my obligation would be obvious, but what if he were a member of a group dedicated to the extermination of my group? The parable, as written (Luke 10, 30–35), tells us that both a priest and a Levite passed by without feeling any obligation to help the victim, who had to await the compassion of the Samaritan. Because the 'contract' is normally implicit rather than explicit, it is a concept the utility of which is dependent upon the actual circumstances under which it is invoked. The Hobbesian covenant is presented as the outcome of a desire for peaceful relations with the people amongst whom one wishes to live. The preservation of peace requires that I agree not to harm others in return for their agreement not to harm me but it also assumes that all parties involved clearly belong to the same social entity.

Wolff sees no difference between moral and political obligations. 'There is no special sort of commitment, distinct from others, which gives rise to a legitimate state, nor are there obligations whose ultimate source is other than a collective commitment' (224). Given this belief and given also that he is obviously familiar with Hobbes as a political thinker, it is surprising he does not recognize that Hobbes had put forward a contract theory of the type he has in mind, long before the days of Kant and Rawls, who are the only philosophers he believes to have 'even understood the problem correctly and seen what was needed' (221). It is only fair to add that he is not alone. The majority of modern writers on the subject seem unaware of Hobbes's contribution, usually because they see him only as a political philosopher.

In the case of one difficulty raised by Wolff, the approach taken by Hobbes might well offer a way out.

> It is one thing to say that I am obligated to abide by those principles to which I have freely committed myself or even to say that I am *only* obligated insofar as I have freely committed myself. But it is quite something else to claim that I have a standing procedural obligation, as it were, to broaden the scope of my commitments by transforming my interactions with other persons into elements of rational community grounded in collective commitments. The latter claim, if it can be sustained, prohibits a rational agent from taking the position that he will refuse to explore the possibility of collective commitments with other rational agents and (in all consistency) accept whatever evil consequences may redound to him thereby. (226)

If, as it appears, Wolff is referring to dealings with individuals who are outside the community of which he is a member, or else he is still in a state of nature with respect to the others, Hobbes's answer is clear. One does not have a *moral* obligation to enter into a covenant establishing a community founded on mutual commitment since social morality only comes into being for the individual when such a commitment has been undertaken. One is perfectly free not 'to explore the possibility of collective commitment', on the understanding that one must then be prepared to face 'whatever evil consequences may redound to him thereby'. The only obligation, if it can be called that, is a rational one resulting from the desire for self-preservation. This has all been discussed before in connection with Hobbes's laws of nature, but it cannot be emphasized enough. Morality may exist in the state of nature as an ideal or potentiality but it is only realized, insofar as it involves definite obligations to others, when personal commitments are made through the social contract.

In recent years contract theory has been revived, most notably by John Rawls, who offers a version of it as an alternative to utilitarianism as well as intuitionism. His book, *A Theory of Justice*, combines modern game theory and welfare economics with traditional philosophy. However, his approach differs from that of Hobbes and there is considerable doubt as to whether it is genuinely contractarian. Hobbes, like other contract theorists, starts with a state of nature which provides powerful motivation for an agreement, whereas Rawls has a group of rational agents engaged in a bargaining game with no pressure on them to reach a decision. Furthermore, Rawls's theory is largely concerned with distributive justice: how the state would allocate available goods amongst its citizens. Hobbes, on the other hand, is attempting to define justice in the first instance as it applies to relations between individuals: how we should treat each other, rather than how we should be treated by the state. Rawls is essentially trying to justify what he regards as the fairest system by building into the 'Original Position' such assumptions as will make it inevitable that the participants will choose principles favouring such a system. Some of these are extremely controversial, e.g. the parties are granted a great deal of knowledge about the workings of society in general but the 'veil of ignorance' prevents them from knowing their own position in it or even their sex. They also do not suffer from envy. These presuppositions lead to an egalitarian welfare state, but a different set can be used, as they were by Nozick, to justify a more libertarian state.

Hobbes avoided these complications by erecting a more modest structure on much firmer foundations. Recognizing that human beings always have conflicting interests, he looks for something they are likely to have in common, and finds it in their desire for self-preservation. After showing that a state of nature or anarchy represents a serious threat to their individual survival, he then offers them a way out, namely a covenant whereby each allows 'so much liberty against other men, as he would allow other men against himself' (Second Law of Nature). This sounds similar to Rawls's first Principle of Justice which, in its final form, states that 'each person is to have an equal right to the most extensive total system of equal basic liberties compatible with a similar system for all'. Unfortunately, this has drifted away from the simplicity and person-to-person directness of Hobbes's formulation, and its wording raises a number of questions which need answering before its implication can be understood. There is no equivalent in Hobbes to Rawls's second principle of justice, the revised form of which reads:

> Social and economic inequalities are to be arranged so that they are both (a) to the greatest benefit of the least advantaged, and (b) attached to offices and positions open to all under conditions of fair equality of opportunity. (*A Theory of Justice*, p. 83)

This goes beyond anything that could be justified on the basis of Hobbes's approach. He defines justice in his third law of nature as whatever is not unjust, and injustice as the non-performance of covenant. Distributive justice, the giving to every man his own, he felt was more properly referred to as equity (*Leviathan*, 138, 209), which is also his eleventh law of nature (142, 212). Other laws of nature which are relevant to the concerns of Rawls are the ninth which requires 'that every man acknowledge another for his equal by nature' (141, 211) and the twelfth to fourteenth which provide for equitable distribution of goods where possible, and where not, by lot or first possession (142, 212). Having arranged for reciprocity in his earlier laws, Hobbes's emphasis in the later ones is on equity. As he points out at the end of his list, all of his laws of nature are implicit in the golden rule and it is the agreement to be bound by this rule which makes civil society possible. But once it is established it can take a number of forms, which he discusses in Part II of *Leviathan*, entitled 'Of Commonwealth'. Property comes into being only with the social contract and what happens after that cannot be specified in advance. It is clear from his comments elsewhere in the book that economic inequality will be the most likely product of letting people retain the liberty of buying and selling property. In Hobbes's day, the Poor Law provided some relief for the indigent at the parish level but otherwise nothing resembling a modern welfare state was known. However, neither a liberal welfare society nor even communism is precluded by the initial agreement. Historically, each society evolves in its own way under pressure of circumstances and, theoretically at least, nothing is impossible. The purpose of the social contract in Hobbes is not to specify a particular type of state but to justify *any* state or social grouping which protects its members from the perils of anarchy.

Despite the fact that Rawls's critics have collectively refuted practically every aspect of his theory, few of them deny the greatness of his contribution to modern philosophy. This is a bit puzzling to those outside the profession but some of this admiration could be due to a willingness to give credit where it is not really deserved. To quote Wolff again, this time from another book, Rawls starts with 'one of the loveliest ideas in the history of social and political theory'.[2] This was to add to the traditional bargaining game of the contractarians a single constraint, which is essentially that provided by commitment.

> The brilliance of Rawls's idea lies in its promise of a way out of the impasse to which Kant had brought moral theory, an impasse that, as we have already seen, still blocked philosophers almost two centuries later. [That is, the problem of deducing substantive moral principles from purely formal premises]. Through the device of a bargaining game, Rawls hopes to derive substantive principles from premises that, though not purely formal, are not manifestly material, either. The constraint of commitment is a procedural constraint, a quasi-formal premise making no reference to specific ends at which the players in the bargaining game must aim. The constraint merely says, 'You must be willing, once you have arrived at a satisfactory principle, to commit yourselves to it for all time, no matter what.' No limits are placed on *what* principle shall be adopted, nor are the players required to adopt their principle for 'ethical' rather than self-interested reasons. (20)

By now the reader should be aware of the grounds for believing that this programme is essentially that adopted by Hobbes, who may therefore have already succeeded where Wolff and many others conclude that Rawls has failed.

The Rawlsian method has been followed by a number of other writers, including David Gauthier in his book, *Morals by Agreement*.[3] The title would be an excellent way of summarizing much of what I have had to say here, and Gauthier, who wrote an earlier book on Hobbes,[4] is aware of the connection. However, his emphasis on game theory and utility maximization has the same drawbacks as does that of Rawls and this is especially true if one is looking at the contribution of Hobbes. Alan Ryan sums it up nicely.

> The twentieth century obsession with the 'prisoner's dilemma' and with the temptation to be a 'free rider' presupposes a theory of motivation that Hobbes did not believe in. What Hobbes's individuals maximized in the state of nature is *power*. . . . This is because isolated individuals have no other means of security; they are not utility-maximizing but danger-of-death minimizing creatures. . . . The prisoner's dilemma is thus a red herring.[5]

Furthermore, by basing his contract on self-interest alone, Gauthier leaves himself open to criticisms which do not apply to Hobbes, who made the golden rule an essential component right at the start.

Another approach to contractualism has been offered by T. M. Scanlon. He suggests as an account of moral wrongness the following:

> An act is wrong if its performance under the circumstances would be disallowed by any system of rules for the general regulation of behaviour which no one could reasonably reject as a basis for informed, unforced general agreement.[6]

After clarifying his terms, Scanlon notes that his statement is suitably abstract, involving no claim as to what specific principles would be agreed to.

> One way, though not the only way, for a contractualist to arrive at substantive moral claims would be to give a technical definition of the relevant notion of agreement, e.g. by specifying the conditions under which agreement is to be reached, the parties to the agreement and the criteria of reasonableness to be employed. (112)

This is certainly the customary meaning of contractualism and would apply to both Hobbes and Rawls. However, it is not his:

> But contractualism can also be understood as an informal description of the subject matter of morality on the basis of which ordering forms of moral reasoning can be understood and

appraised without proceeding via a technical notice of agreement. (113)

It is his belief that this approach has distinct advantages.

> What an adequate theory should do is to provide a framework within which what seem to be relevant arguments for and against particular interpretations of the moral boundary can be carried out. It is often thought that contractualism can provide no plausible basis for an answer to this question. Critics charge either that contractualism provides no answer at all, because it must begin with some set of contracting parties taken as given, or that contractualism suggests an answer which is obviously too restrictive, since a contract requires parties who are able to make and keep agreements and who are able to offer others some benefit in return for their cooperation. Neither of these objections applies to the version of contractualism that I [am] defending. The general specification of the scope of morality which it implies seems to me to be this: morality applies to a being if the notion of justification to a being of that kind makes sense. (113)

The latter proviso is amplified as follows:

> On the basis of what I have said so far contractualism can explain why the capacity to feel pain should have seemed to many to count in favour of moral status: a being which has this capacity seems also to satisfy the three conditions I have just mentioned as necessary for the idea of justification to it to make sense. If a being can feel pain, then it constitutes a centre of consciousness to which justification can be addressed. Feeling pain is a clear way in which the being can be worse off; having its pain alleviated a way in which it can be benefited; and these are forms of weal and woe which seem directly comparable to our own. (114)

Naturally he does not claim that this settles all possible questions immediately, but the fact that it at least provides a basis for argument is very much in its favour. I have quoted from Scanlon's article at length because he has provided a succinct and helpful summary of the major issues raised by contractualism. The question for us now is how does it compare with the version of contract theory put forward by Hobbes. The latter's definition of wrongness or injustice is shorter and more specific. According to him an act is wrong if it violates the golden rule (as qualified in previous discussions). For the latter part of Scanlon's definition: 'any system of rules of the general regulation of behaviour which no one could reasonably reject as a basis for informed, enforced general agreement', Hobbes would substitute the rule of reciprocity because that is exactly what he has demonstrated that 'no one could reasonably reject'.

Scanlon does mention the golden rule in connection with morality as justification of one's actions to others 'on grounds they could not reasonably reject' (116).

> One rough test of whether you regard a justification as sufficient is whether you would accept that justification if you were in another person's position. This connection between the idea of 'Changing places' and the motivation which underlies morality explains the frequent occurrence of 'Golden Rule' arguments in their different systems of morality and the teachings of various religions. But the thought experiment of changing places is only a rough guide; the fundamental question is what it would be unreasonable to reject as a basis for informed, unforced, general agreement. (117)

But surely the answer to this 'fundamental question' is precisely the golden rule. Something very similar appears as Rawls's first principle of justice and, furthermore, it is an excellent example of the 'maximin' rule which he thinks his contractors would adopt. I would obviously prefer to be treated better by others than I would like to treat them, and they would gladly choose the same arrangement for themselves. But since this is impossible, we could only reach an agreement on the basis of the best minimum deal we can get, which is reciprocity. Scanlon gives no other examples and offers his contractual theory only as a start but I believe that no sooner is the 'fundamental question' asked than an obvious answer immediately presents itself. He implies that there are many possible sets of rules but does not suggest any alternatives to the one he considers and then more or less rejects. The truth is that his definition of 'wrong' is satisfactory as far as it goes, but one then has to decide on what grounds one could reasonably reject a set of rules, and that brings us back to an essential fact of the human condition which he mentioned earlier: we have the capacity to feel pain. Because of this, any agreement we make is going to have to focus on pain avoidance. If we do not want to be hurt by other people then we cannot reasonably reject a rule which minimizes this possibility. The prevalence of the golden rule in the world's religions and philosophies indicates that Hobbes was not alone in finding it a very obvious basis for morality.

The major apparent difference between Scanlon's approach and that of Hobbes seems to be that Scanlon's is contractualism without a contract. He says it can proceed without 'a technical notice of agreement'. However, the difference is more apparent than real. Although Hobbes talks as if there were an actual contract, it must be clear by now that he was usually not speaking about an historical event. The obvious question which constantly dogs this type of theory is thus: why keep talking about a contract when we all agree that there isn't one? The answer, which I have touched on several times already, is simply that it is a useful fiction. Since the hard headed realist is likely to find a fictional contract difficult to distinguish from no contract at all, I would like to take a brief look at the concept.

It is best known in the field of jurisprudence where the legal fiction has a long and often controversial past. Lon L. Fuller describes a fiction variously, as 'an *expedient* but false assumption', a 'false statement recognized as having utility', and as 'frequently a metaphorical way of expressing a truth'.[7] Legal fictions arise as a way of handling new problems in the context of a relatively inflexible system of time-honoured laws and they usually consist of pretending that in a particular case, one thing is really another. Probably the most amazing example of a legal fiction was when an English court once declared that for the purposes of the case at hand the island of Minorca was to be considered part of the City of London (Fuller, pp. 18 and 21). A more familiar example is the treatment of a corporation as a person. However, fictions are not confined to jurisprudence; they are used wherever they are found to be convenient, and may well be an indispensible adjunct to human thought. Mathematicians pretend that nothing is really something, which they then call zero, and find the square root of minus one quite useful. Geometry relies on points without extension and straight lines without depth or breadth.

Adam Smith's 'economic man', driven by nothing but economic self-interest, is not a very admirable sort of human being but he has been of vital importance to economists. 'Hobbesian man', motivated solely by a desire for self-preservation, is a similar construct and can also serve us well. The social contract, itself, is very close to the legal fiction known as a 'quasi-contract' which allows the court to act *as if* a contract existed where none in fact actually did. The purpose of the legal fiction is presumably to see that justice is done in a situation where it otherwise would not have been. The role of the fictional social contract is to explain or make understandable the obligations that men have towards each other when they live together in a community.

For many people who feel an emotional attachment to their tribe or country, for whom obedience to the rules of morality and the laws of the state is ingrained and automatic, no explanation is necessary. Hobbes undertook to provide such an explanation because the old values were being questioned and allegiance to Crown and Church was being challenged. The Age of Reason had begun and many people wanted convincing arguments rather than emotional appeals to traditional loyalties which no longer had the power to move them. Hobbes is not always clear about the exact nature of the covenant upon which he placed so much weight but the only way it makes any sense is as a fiction and he was no stranger to that word. The problem he was trying to address is this: On the one hand we have the world as it is and human nature as we know it in our heart to be – the human condition in other words – and, on the other we have a social structure which keeps us in reasonable order, makes certain demands on us and implants in us emotions of love, duty, guilt, shame, etc. How are they connected; what is the rationale which ties them together? For anyone who asks such questions, the social contract provides a very helpful and quite persuasive answer. Whether or not we ever agreed to such a contract, we behave *as if* we had. Since people act in the same way they would have done if they *had* undertaken such an agreement then, for all practical purposes they have. Because it fills an intellectual gap in this way, the fiction of the social contract, like the point or the straight line in geometry, becomes a valuable aid in making comprensible what is not immediately so. For this reason it is more fruitful than Hume's notion of 'convention'. The latter tells us why we behave the way we do but it is of no help in determining why we *ought* to behave that way. It also satisfies the second part of Hobbes's definition of philosophy as *'the knowledge acquired by reasoning from the manner of the generation of any thing, to the properties: or from the properties, to some possible way of generation of the same* . . . ' (664,682).

As we have already noted, a moral system based on contract has a number of important limitations. Because Hobbes holds that the laws of nature oblige always *in foro interno*, a man is bound in the first instance to practise the golden rule. However, in a state of nature, that would likely lead to his swift destruction by those who do not practise it. As a result, he is usually bound *in foro externo* only if a covenant has been made whereby those among whom he lives also agree to be so bound. The big question is obviously who are and who are not members of the society which has been created by the covenant. One easy answer is all the citizens of the state of which one is a citizen. Because certain moral rules have been made into laws backed by the courts and the police, major crimes are punished by the state. That part of morality which is not enforced by the state remains in the hands of the family, friends, clubs, teams and other smaller groups, all of which use public opinion to discourage rule breaking. Outside of our own borders, we are generally bound by the laws of the other countries we visit or reside in. Thus the rules of good behaviour are generally quite consistent throughout the civilized world.

However, we cannot say that the moral law holds universally, as some theories might claim. It is important to remember that a moral prescription refers to a patient or recipient as well as the agent and the act. Some prescriptions apply only to a specific agent and/or patient. For example, the rules that govern the relationship between spouses or between parents and children do not apply to others outside the family circle. The same is true also within larger groups such as clans, tribes and nations. 'Love thy neighbour' was meant to be applied by Jews to fellow Jews only, not to everyone. Morality is thus generally patient-specific, a fact often ignored by moral philosophers. In the case of social contract morality, as we have seen, the rules hold, strictly speaking, only for those who can be assumed to be part of a contractual relationship. An obvious example of a situation where this is not so is one in which European explorers came into contact with native tribes. Some turned out to be friendly (probably living to regret it) and others hostile, but it was certainly prudent for both sides to exercise caution, not knowing the rules by which the others played. The situation is simpler for the soldier who faces an enemy during a war. He does know the rules and to try to practise morality as he would at home could be fatal.

What should be remembered, however, is that while the Right of Nature allows one to take whatever steps one deems necessary and reasonable to preserve one's life, it does not permit any kind of action whatever. For example, if one takes a prisoner during hostilities, there is nothing in the Hobbesian ethic which would justify subjecting him to torture. This is a clear violation of the golden rule, which is operative in all situations except those where one's life is at risk. A prisoner who is in your power does not constitute any threat, and must be treated accordingly. No imaginable version of the state of nature would make sadistic cruelty permissible. What all this amounts to is that there are very few occasions in the average individual's life where the golden rule has to be suspended because following it would be life-threatening.

It has been noted that the principle of reciprocity brings morality down to the individual level; it involves a person-to-person relationship. However it requires the provision of social and political institutions which, through the use of coercion, will discourage those who want the benefits of peace without its costs. Hobbes assumes that persons who want to live together peacefully will understand the need for such institutions and will be prepared, in general, to obey them, since they have, in effect, undertaken to do so for their own long-term welfare. In his dealings with other people the individual is bound by his commitment to the golden rule, whereas with respect to the commonwealth, his commitment is to the covenant which grants him the security to practise the golden rule safely in return for obedience to the authorities.

This difference has been the cause of much confusion about morality. The relationship between the convicted criminal and the judge, mentioned in Kant's criticism, is not governed by the golden rule, because the judge is not acting as an individual but as a representative of the state, which has delegated certain powers to him. He may feel compassion for the prisoner but this must not be allowed to interfere with his duty, which is to administer justice regardless of his personal feelings. The link between institutions like the state and the individual is impersonal, unlike that between one individual and another. The rule of reciprocity, which requires an imaginative substitution of oneself for another, does not work with institutions, since they lack the human characteristics with which we can empathize, especially the capability of feeling pain. Thus the relationship between an individual and an institution will have to be governed by positive law rather than moral law, always remembering that the individual has a moral obligation, flowing from the original covenant, to obey the positive law.

This brings us to the key question posed by the Hobbesian ethic of contract and reciprocity: what happens when law conflicts with morality? Hobbes's general position is that they cannot come into conflict since the contract binds one to obey the law, including laws one does not like. The best illustration of this is what happens in a democracy when a party for which I did not vote is elected and begins to pass laws of which I disapprove. Can I refuse to obey those laws on grounds of principle? The answer is no, of course, because if everyone did that when they personally objected to a law, or thought it morally wrong, anarchy would quickly replace the order which the body politic was instituted to provide. This answer is not good enough for those who believe immoral law must be opposed by civil disobedience. Some ramifications of this problem will be discussed later. The line between politics and ethics is blurred, especially as politics can, in some of its aspects, be considered a part of ethics. At the moment I would like to remain on the more purely ethical side of the divide, since I believe that many ethical issues are unnecessarily confused by a tendency on the part of theorists to drift back and forth across the boundary.

This is especially noticeable in the discussion of institutions such as slavery. Most people say that slavery is wrong without realizing that they are using 'wrong' in a sense different from that used when they say that murder is wrong. The latter is an action which concerns the welfare of another individual and it is forbidden by the golden rule for the usual reasons. Slavery is quite different. If I live in a slave-holding society and I disapprove of it, I, as an individual can do a number of things. I can lobby to have it done away with, I can free my slaves if I own any, I can buy slaves and free them and I can refuse to treat any slaves I have contact with as inferior beings. These actions reflect my beliefs about the essential equality of mankind, my compassion and my kindness, but if I did not do them I would not be violating the moral code. If slavery is legal, as it was in the Athens of Pericles, this reflects the social and economic realities and beliefs of the age. In many societies slavery was the only alternative to death for a defeated enemy; in fact, if the enemy had been victorious instead, the present slave-owners would themselves have likely ended up as slaves if they had not been killed outright. It is of considerable interest that in none of the great slave revolts of antiquity did the slaves demand an end to slavery. They did not like being slaves themselves but it apparently did not occur to them that slavery as an institution should be eliminated. It came into existence, served a particular purpose and then died out in many places when that purpose was no longer served. In modern times, free wage labour has been found to be more efficient than slave labour and that, rather than high moral principle, unfortunately, is usually why it faded away, perhaps, as in Medieval Europe, after a transitional stage of serfdom.

Is slavery, then, morally acceptable? At a personal level the answer would have to be no. The golden rule obliges me to say: I would not want to be enslaved, therefore I must not enslave others. If everyone applied this rule, there would be no slavery. As we noted earlier in discussing Roman law, under the Law of Nature all men are free, but the jurists nevertheless recognized that slavery did exist and was legal. The point of all this is that in an ideal world slavery would not exist. But it must be remembered that in an ideal world, caste systems would also not exist, women and minorities would not be oppressed, crime would be eliminated, national chauvinism would be muted and war would be banned. There would be one world in which equality and benevolence would prevail everywhere. It would also help if everyone were endowed with equal amounts of good looks, intelligence, charm, and there were no food shortages, disease or natural disasters. This is not meant to ridicule the concept of an ideal world. Its purpose is to remind us that in the real world there are many constraints on us over which, as individuals, we have little control. When Hobbes called life in the state of nature 'poor, nasty, brutish and short', he was not exaggerating, but actually describing accurately the lot of the majority of all human beings ever born. His aim was more limited and therefore, I believe, more realistic than that of many other moralists. If, by means of joining together in a regulated community, we can diminish the misery in the one area where we do have some control, our behaviour towards each other, then it is only sensible for us to do so. But we must not have exaggerated expectations of the moral system which is thus created. Nothing can alter the fact that along with the instinct to survive comes the drive for wealth, status and power. We are competitive creatures and the resulting struggle is responsible for all the triumphs and tragedies that make life interesting as well as dangerous. Hobbes does not share the reluctance of many moralists to give this side of human nature its due. In *The Elements of Law* he sees life as a race. If we accept the game metaphor, his intention is to show us that it is worth putting up with a few rules rather than of letting it degenerate into a free-for-all.

I say 'a few rules' deliberately because as in a game or in law-making, it is better to have a smaller number of rules that are clear and easy to understand, than a large number which are more likely to be confusing and difficult to interpret. The approach taken by Hobbes of limiting morality to the notions of agreement and reciprocity allows us to make a clear distinction between issues of personal ethics and those of social reform. We all have our own opinions about which kind of society is best and the urge to put this on a plane of high morality. But can we decide whether an egalitarian society is superior to a libertarian one, or vice versa, on moral grounds? Rawls tried to do so on the basis of contract theory but the necessary conditions which had to be incorporated into the Original Position, can be easily be replaced by others which are just as convincing. Hobbes's concern was to reconcile restless, quarrelsome, egoistic individuals to the restrictions imposed upon them by *any* type of organization, never mind an ideal one. He did however have a specific kind of government in mind: the one under which we are already living. Comparing monarchy, aristocracy and democracy later in *Leviathan*, Hobbes says:

> And of the three sorts, which is the best is not to be disputed, where one of them is already established; but the present ought always to be preferred, maintained and counted best; because it is against both the law of nature and divine positive law, to do any thing tending to the subversion thereof. (548, 577)

Many contemporary ethical and political theorists labour under the delusion that we have a choice, that we are free to mould our society to conform to our heart's desire. This is a legacy of the exciting early days of the French Revolution, when anything seemed possible. And it continues to charm us despite two hundred years of disillusionment. First of all, situations in which revolutionary change in the structure of society is possible occur very rarely, and secondly, the outcome of such upheavals is seldom a source of much comfort to idealists. Even modest reform programmes undertaken by benevolent governments to improve the lot of the downtrodden often result, after years of effort and expenditure, in a wider disparity than ever between rich and poor. The fact that it is not easy to make changes for the better is no reason, of course, for not trying. But attempting to harness the kind of morality which is necessary in order for communities to exist in the first place, to the objectives favoured by conflicting interest groups, serves only to overload that morality and perhaps lead to its breakdown.

Although contract-reciprocity morality is relatively straightforward, at least two objections can be raised which make it appear not so simple after all. The first of these is the notion of contract. This is regarded by some critics as a sophisticated legal concept which one could hardly expect brutish creatures in the state of nature to comprehend. However, this can quickly be disposed of, since Hobbes's state of nature is hypothetical, an alternative for contemporary individuals with their already existing knowledge of contract to contemplate should they wish to imagine what life would be like if civil society were suddenly dissolved. And, in any case, the reality expressed by the word 'contract' is as old as the human race since the simplest family unit requires a bilateral agreement in order to exist.

The other objection is more serious but not insurmountable. If we start with civil society as it is, rather than with the state of nature, we can determine, at least roughly, who the parties to the contract would be. The members of any group, from children playing marbles to the citizens of a superpower are clearly parties to the contract as long as they regard themselves or are regarded by others as being part of the collectivity. If they cannot be seen as actual fully-fledged participants themselves they can be considered as indirect members through their relationship with others who are, such as husbands, parents, guardians, etc. Since contracting is to be understood as a means of justifying and understanding morality, the details are not necessarily significant since it is usually quite obvious to everyone who is and who is not a member of a particular group.

It is when we move to those who are not recognized as members of the group that potential for trouble arises. How do we treat people outside our group? It is Hobbes's contention that we use the golden rule as our guide at all times except when we put ourselves in danger by so doing. Such occasions are limited to states of war and contact with new peoples on the external side and confrontations with those from within our society who give us reason to believe that they do not consider themselves bound by its rules. An obvious question is how do minorities, inferior castes and slaves fit into this picture? The law may discriminate against such people and it may allow the majority or the aristocracy to exploit them and treat them badly. This is a matter of how a society has developed historically and what status differences have arisen within it. As pointed out above, this is really outside the purview of personal morality. Each individual is required to refrain from doing to others what he would not want done to himself, and therefore no one is entitled to injure anyone who is not a threat to him regardless of what the law and custom say. However, there has probably never been an age in which state-sponsored terrorism has flourished as it has in the present one. Those who engage in torture use the excuse that they were ordered to do it by their superiors. Moral dilemmas do arise and have to be taken into consideration when, for example, the individual's family is being held hostage and threatened with harm unless he cooperates in the persecution. But such cases seem rare. Much more common is the individual who knows that what he is doing is wrong but allows his conscience to be dulled by the fact that those around him are doing the same or that he is acting on behalf of some noble cause such as an independence movement. This region where morality and politics intersect is rife with conditions in which extraordinary situations are used as a justification for the suspension of normal moral rules. It is thus all the more necessary that people have a simple and practically self-evident set of moral rules, such as Hobbes offers, to fall back on when surrounded by doubt and uncertainty.

Ethical philosophers sometimes point to the amount of evil and immorality in the world as evidence that traditional morality is not working and that much more effort on their part is necessary in order to produce a system that will be effective. This attitude rests on a confusion between moral rules themselves, and willingness to obey them. No amount of tinkering with the former is going to affect the latter. The great religious leaders and philosophers we quoted earlier all agree that the simple rule of reciprocity is the foundation for peaceful relations between human beings. But human beings always have the freedom to disobey the rules when it is in their interest to do so. Only the existence of a central authority with power to punish those who are so tempted can provide a suitable setting for peace and security. This is Hobbes's message in a nutshell. He wrote at a time of political breakdown in his own country; today we see it all over the world. It flows from the usual sources: conflict of material interests and hatred of those who are different in any one of a dozen ways. Selfishness, both individual and collective, is as usual responsible for the suffering. But, if you look more closely, you will see that relations between individuals within each group are usually good examples of the golden rule and the social contract at work. The problem lies with the state of nature that exists between different states, tribes and rebellious factions, not with the rules of personal morality. On the contrary, it is actually the individual self-sacrifice required by social morality that provides the idealistic impetus which energizes these units in their struggles with each other. This does not, of course, prevent an individual from striving to change the conditions and attitudes which lead to such enmity. A constant effort to enlarge the group within which one feels obliged to practise reciprocity and can do so safely is the only way to tackle man's continuing inhumanity to man. Although morality is the driving force, the answer generally lies in the realm of politics.

10
Reason and Moral Relativity

I have tried to show that Hobbesian morality is an attempt to answer the questions of someone who wants *reasons* for accepting moral rules. If these questions are not asked then there will be no need to offer a rational justification of ethics. Most people act on the basis of habit or custom and it rarely occurs to them to question the authority of the rules by which they live. For those who do, Hobbes offers a rational basis for morality built on a theory of human motivation and the use of elementary logic. There have, of course, been other attempts to establish a rational foundation for ethics including that of Kant, which was examined above. A recent example of this approach is Alan Gewirth's *Reason and Morality*.[1] It is an exhaustive exposition and defense of his supreme moral principle, the Principle of Generic Consistency or PGC, a topic which he has also discussed in a number of journal articles.[2]

In his essay, 'The Golden Rule Rationalized', Gewirth finds numerous flaws in the traditional golden rule. These he proceeds to correct by demonstrating the superiority of the PGC, which is stated as follows: '*Act in accord with the generic rights of your recipients as well as yourself*'.[3] This is certainly brief enough but his justification of it, especially in *Reason and Morality*, is extremely detailed, since he attempts to answer in advance every criticism that his most sophisticated readers might conceivably make. Before looking at his arguments, I should point out that his criticisms of the golden rule, along with others, were examined above and found wanting. They can all be disposed of by the use of the negative form, the addition of the implicit proviso that one put oneself in the other's place, and the restriction of the rule to the kind of situation for which it was intended. Furthermore, the PGC, although satisfactorily short in itself, requires an elaborate substructure of argument to support it, which diminishes its value as a practical rule.

However, Gewirth's work is of considerable interest insofar as it is an attempt to derive morality from nothing more than what is implicit in the notion of rational agency. Such a derivation, if successful, would doubtless have been of considerable interest to Hobbes since it attempts to do what he did but with an even smaller number of assumptions than he had to make. A short form of Gewirth's argument can be found in *Reason and Morality*.

> By way of brief summary: an agent is a person who initiates or controls his behaviour through his unforced, informed choice with a view to achieving various purposes; since he wants to fulfill his purposes he regards his freedom and well-being, the necessary condition of his successful pursuit of purposes, as necessary goods; hence he holds that he has rights to freedom and well-being; to avoid self-contradiction he must hold that he has these generic rights insofar as he is a prospective purposive agent; hence he must admit that all prospective purposive agents have the generic rights; hence he must acknowledge that he ought at least to refrain from interfering with his recipients' freedom and well-being, so that he ought to act in accord with their generic rights as well as his own. (171)

The first part of the book is devoted to developing and defending this argument and the second part to applying it in ethical and political situations.

The crucial stages of the argument are as follows: from the fact that freedom and well-being are the necessary conditions of my actions and I must have them, he concludes that I have rights to them and as a result all other agents ought to refrain from interfering with them. Obviously if I have genuine rights to freedom and well-being, other people ought to respect them, but what is the basis of my claim to such rights? Gewirth replies that if I do not insist on such rights I am admitting that I do not have them and therefore that others have the right to interfere with my freedom and well-being. To those critics who do not find this convincing he says that his dialectical method requires only that the agent make these claims from within his own viewpoint. At this stage they are prudential rather than moral.

> The prudential aspect pertains to the *agent* and to the 'ought' – judgments he addresses to other persons, because he makes the judgments for his *own* prudential purposes, not for theirs. The prudential aspect does not pertain to the *other persons*, because

it is not for the sake of *their* purposes that the agent makes his 'ought'-judgments. Hence, his 'ought'-judgment . . . is prudential, not moral.[4]

It is clear that Gewirth's intention is to insulate these steps in his argument from any moral contamination so that he can derive morality from prudence by the universalization step of his argument and thus resolve the 'is–ought' problem.[5] Needless to say his critics are still not converted. The difficulty is that words like 'rights' and 'ought' have strong moral connotations which tend to carry over into other usages. 'Rights' is especially tricky since it has often been conscripted for ideological ends. As a result it must be subjected to closer scrutiny.

Earlier on we discussed the historical background of the emergence of rights from the natural law tradition. Some rights are established in law and disputes about them are usually settled in the courts. 'Natural' rights, of course, cannot normally be enforced by law and are thus considered to be moral claims. When people make demands in the form of so-called 'natural' rights, they are appealing to a 'higher' law which can only be conceived of as having moral status of some kind. Great political use was made of this concept in the revolutions of the eighteenth century but after Jeremy Bentham called it 'nonsense on stilts' it fell into disfavour, only to be revived more recently as 'human' rights. The problem however remains the same as it did with natural rights: it is difficult for their proponents to agree on a common list, and also for them to explain satisfactorily exactly what these rights are, or why we should pay any attention to them.

What compounds the problem is that attempts have been made to use what is a legal or at the very most a moral concept in other contexts. Gewirth defends the idea of prudential rights by claiming that there are also intellectual and logical rights. In *Reason and Morality* he quotes a number of examples but they all turn out to be metaphorical extensions of the word. Usages such as '(e) The sceptic may still insist that we have no right to make the assumption that things are known . . . ' or '(h) The right to have one's conjectures taken seriously must be earned by prolonged immersion in the historical sources' imply that others are under some kind of obligation to accept these right claims and although the situations are not what we would normally call moral, they involve the ethical attitude which is required in order to participate in any form of meaningful discourse.

Gewirth's 'prudential' rights are even more problematic. By way of defending them, he notes that 'many of the traditional objections to rights-talk (and hence to the concept of a right) have been based on the view that rights as standardly asserted are egoistic or self-centered', a view which he finds quite acceptable.[6] This is certainly true, but for that very reason, making rights claims is pointless without an attempt to appeal to the interests of others as well as oneself and that brings them into the orbit of morality. If my intended act is murder and I accordingly say I have a right to the freedom necessary to carry it out, Gewirth would not be perturbed because he knows that by the end of the logical sequence I must follow, I shall find that I ought to refrain from interfering with the freedom and well-being of others, which murdering them certainly does, and if I fear the pain of self-contradiction I shall refrain from committing the murder. However that does not alter the fact that each stage of the argument must stand on its own and at that early stage my claim right makes no sense unless I expect it to create corresponding obligations on the part of others. If I am a prudent man I would be unlikely to claim a right to do something which could land me on death row. Since Gewirth says he is using the Hohfeldian claim-right which provides for a correlative duty or obligation on the part of others, his rational agent has two choices: he can make a claim which is nonsensical, detached as it is from its correlative, or he can admit that if he does make such a claim others are under a moral obligation to honour it. In the latter case, however, morality makes an appearance at an early stage of Gewirth's argument and thus nullifies it.

There is one other problem with his derivation which I shall touch on briefly. He says, as quoted above, that the ought-judgments that the agent addresses to others do not pertain to their interests but to his own. This leaves the status of the ought-judgments as viewed from the perspective of the others unclear. Since he denies that it is *their* prudential purposes he is considering, this implies that their motivation would have to be moral, which would undermine his derivation. If, on the other hand, their motives are strictly prudential, this would carry on through his universalization and result in everyone acting for prudential reasons. The final 'ought' would be a prudential one and his derivation would have failed because it did not in the end produce morality.

However, Gewirth's attempt to derive a supreme moral principle is certainly a valiant one. His method is similar to that of Hobbes but he wants to overcome what he sees as a defect in Hobbes.

> The transition from the prudential to the moral and social is thus, in the first instance, not motivational but logical. The reason why the agent must endorse the generic rights of his recipients is not the Hobbesian prudential or contingent one that if he violates or fails to endorse these rights for others he may probably expect them to violate his own rights, but rather the logically necessary one that if there is a sufficient condition that justifies the agent's having the generic rights, then it must justify that these rights are had by all other persons who satisfy that condition. (*Reason and Morality*, p. 146)

Although I believe he misreads Hobbes, there is no doubt that a morality based on logical necessity rather than contingency would be preferable, if it were possible. The advantage of Hobbes's approach is precisely that freedom which Gewirth values so highly. There are logical as well as other necessities in Hobbes but they arise only if the agent agrees to accept the costs associated with them. Rationally he would be a fool not to make the bargain but if he does so freely, his degree of commitment goes beyond that required by Gewirth. The pain of self-contradiction alone is not a very heavy one and is accepted by most people quite regularly, since they find the pain of consistency even more onerous.

Gewirth shies away from anything resembling the social contract precisely because of its contingency. In his 'Obligation: Political, Legal, Moral', he differentiates his own position from 'a pervasive tradition of moral and legal philosophy' which includes as one thesis the belief that moral obligations must be self-imposed.' In a footnote to these words he says that this notion goes back at least to Hobbes and he quotes from *Leviathan*, 'there being no obligation on any man, which ariseth not from some act of his own'. He finds the idea 'highly ambiguous' since it can mean at least three different things. There is no need to list them here since the differences are not significant in the Hobbesian context of the state of nature and the social contract, which he ignores.[7]

As Gewirth notes in several places, contractualism and consent are not free of difficulties but they are at least familiar ideas to the average person. The logical necessities of his argument for the

PGC, on the other hand, are not, and furthermore they have failed to convince many of the academic philosophers at whom they are presumably directed. In this connection there is a revealing sentence in *Reason and Morality*:

> The argument in this section supports the view that rights are necessarily rather than contingently connected with being human, for I have held that the basis of rights must be sought in the *conviction necessarily held* by every human agent that he has rights to the necessary conditions of action by virtue of his having purposes and pursuing goods. (103; emphasis added)

I have always had the impression that however convictions are arrived at, they cannot be imposed on someone by fiat, logical or otherwise. Conviction is missing in my case because I am not convinced that I must *necessarily hold* that I have rights to the necessary conditions of action.

The problem for me is the emphasis in Gewirth's argument on rights. I think they are too insubstantial to provide a solid foundation for morality. To those who have any doubts about the existence of rights they offer no foundation at all. Wesley Hohfeld found the concept confusing because it was used in law to mean four different things: claims, privileges or liberties, immunities and powers.[8] These are legal usages and only the first two, claims (which he takes to be the normal meaning of rights) and liberties, have been carried over into morality or natural law. A liberty-right has no correlative obligation like a claim-right does. Hobbes's Right of Nature is an example of a liberty-right since no blame can be attached to its exercise. Conversely, no one else is under any obligation to honour it since each person possesses the same right. Part of it is given up by the covenant; the rest is retained as the right of self-defense and the right to do what we please so long as we do not harm anyone or break a law.

Gewirth makes it clear throughout that he is using right in the first sense, as a claim-right, the correlative of which is duty or obligation. According to Hobbes, obligations are created by contract and claim-rights arise as a result. If I loan someone $100, he is under an obligation to repay it. If I say I have a right to be paid $100 by him, this will be true if I have, in fact, loaned him the money or have placed myself under some equivalent obligation but false if I have not. Any right I claim will depend on the context. Contrast this with Gewirth's statement in *Reason and Morality*:

> The agent holds that other persons owe him at least noninterference with his freedom and well-being, not because of any specific transaction or agreement they have made with him, but on the basis of his own prudential criteria, because such noninterference is necessary to his being a purposive agent. (66)

As he admits, this is really a demand as well as a claim and is thus in the same category as many political demands, which use rights language to advance the interests of particular individuals or groups. The word 'rights' here is intended to conjure up obligations where none are now admitted by those to whom it is directed. Such attempts often work: a demand for free day-care may result in a recognition by the government of an obligation to establish and fund it. But such examples are only successful because they appeal to moral principles accepted by those who respond.

Thus, it would appear that since claim-rights presuppose moral obligation, they are of little value in establishing morality. It goes without saying that Gewirth would not accept this. At one point, he refers to a suggestion that 'all that can be said in a terminology of such rights can be and indeed is best said in the indispensable terminology of duty', and therefore the concept of a right is redundant. His reply is to insist on the priority of rights. 'Respondents have correlative duties *because* subjects have certain rights, and not conversely; the duties are for the sake of the rights, and not conversely.'[9] His position is obviously deeply-felt but he provides no satisfactory reason for us to accept it.

Gewirth's goal seems to me to be similar to that of Hobbes but his method unnecessarily cumbersome. After having decided on a course of action he wants to undertake, the agent must claim rights to the necessary freedom and well-being which requires that all other agents ought to refrain from interfering with these goods. By the process of universalization, he has to admit that all other agents have the same rights that he does and that he ought therefore to refrain from interfering with their freedom and well-being. In the case of Hobbes, the agent merely has to ask himself if the action violates the golden rule, which he has agreed to observe. Instead of the roundabout method of having first to claim rights against others and then by universalization grant others similar rights against himself, the agent has only to imagine how he would like to be treated and then act accordingly. The idea of interaction as well as action is present from the start.

This is important because any rule which emerges from an individual reasoning with himself, such as the PGC or Categorical Imperative, does not immediately take into account the possible reactions of others. As Hobbes notes, anyone who practises the golden rule without some indication that others will do the same merely places himself at their mercy. For any moral rule to be acceptable there must be at least a tacit agreement amongst the members of the group in which they live, to honour it. Since outsiders may not be prepared to do so, this excludes the possibility of a genuinely universal rule like the PGC, which is intended to apply to all men. People may be prepared to behave altruistically towards those with whom they can identify because of common language, customs, beliefs, etc. but the more different they are from each other, the more likelihood there is of dislike and even hatred. For those who, like Gewirth, want a principle which is universal, categorical and necessary, this irreducible element of contingency is unacceptable, but I do not see any way of avoiding it in the real world. However, the difference is not as great as it might seem. For Hobbes the laws of nature always apply *in foro interno* and for that reason can be considered as immutable. They apply *in foro externo* also, except in situations where the individual has reason to believe he is in danger. This means that he is obliged to observe the golden rule most of the time.

Not only is the Hobbesian contractual golden rule more practical and realistic, it also has other advantages. The PGC and similar principles rely heavily on logical necessity. If we do not accept Gewirth's reasoning we are constantly being threatened with the pain of self-contradiction. As already noted, this kind of suffering is without much deterrent power. The real pain, of course, comes from the adverse judgment of one's peers in the intellectual world. If Gewirth's argument can genuinely be evaded only by self-contradiction (which many critics do not believe is the case), then those who refuse to accept its conclusions expose themselves as unworthy of participating in the debate and are treated as such by the others. This is an example of something I mentioned earlier: that what is to be regarded as convincing in any field of discourse depends on rules which are accepted by the participants. In the case of logic, self-contradiction violates the rules and can only be indulged in by those who are prepared to be ignored by the rest of their peer group. For those who never belonged, the right to play the logical game is of no importance and they can contradict themselves with much greater freedom, although a limit is imposed even by the man on the street.

Hobbes uses the same idea but he places it in the context of action rather than argument. To quote *Leviathan* again:

> So that *injury*, or *injustice*, in the controversies of the world, is somewhat like to that, which in the disputations of scholars is called *absurdity*. For as it is there called an absurdity, to contradict what one has maintained in the beginning: so in the world, it is called injustice, and injury, voluntarily to undo that, which from the beginning he had voluntarily done. (119, 191)

Thus, one motive for observing the contractual golden rule is the avoidance of self-contradiction but this is backed up by at least two others. One flows from the appeal to the agent, implicit in the golden rule, to put himself in the recipient's place. This imaginative exchange is possible because most of us have a capacity for identifying with others such that their pain becomes our pain. Consulting the golden rule before acting is a way of preventing suffering on the part of the agent as well as the recipient.

For those who are less sensitive to the feelings of others, there is always the prudential motive. If I am harmed by someone else my reaction may well take the form of retaliation. If by the same token I harm someone else, his or her response may well be the same, directed at me this time. The golden rule, although not prudential in itself, serves as a useful reminder of this possibility by linking my welfare to that of others in a few appropriate words. These three motives for obeying the rule: logical consistency, empathy, and retaliation-prevention, different as they are, have two things in common. They are all rational in the sense that they represent good reasons for following it, and they all, not just the last one, directly affect the agent's well-being. Self-contradiction can result in the pain associated with loss of respect by persons whose opinions are important to one, and empathy can lead to the pangs of a guilty conscience.

The relationship between prudence and morality has been an uneasy one in western philosophy because of the powerful tradition that an act which does not emphasize the welfare of others as opposed to that of the agent is not truly moral. William Frankena, for example, says that 'prudentialism or living by the principle of enlightened self-interest just is not a kind of ethics'.[10] This oversimplification does an injustice to a moral theory like that of Hobbes. A recurrent theme in my treatment of his contribution has been that there is no necessary conflict between prudence and morality in the outcome and that in any case altruism is perfectly consistent with his position. The other related point I have tried to make is that this tradition, if taken seriously, confines genuine morality to such a narrow spectrum of human behaviour that it is in danger of disappearing from the real world, if it ever has existed, as Kant himself doubted. But it is a conception which lingers on in people's minds and can always be brought out and used as a standard by which to criticize more realistic ethics, without its own weaknesses ever being exposed to thorough scrutiny.

An interesting example of this attitude is provided by John Ladd's book on the morality of the Navaho Indians.[11] The author sets out to provide the theoretical foundations of a moral code before examining in detail the actual morality of the Navaho. His conclusion is that their code is characterized by 'materialistic prudentialism' and 'atomic egoism'. In our society these words are laced with enough negative connotations to make one ask whether this can even be called a morality. William Frankena is referring to Ladd's work when he comments:

> One cannot say that the Navaho have a morality until after one has formed some conception of morality and found that the Navaho have such an institution. The fact that they have some kind of a code which partakes of certain formal properties proves that they have a morality only if these properties suffice to define morality. [If not], it may be a reason for not calling the code a morality at all.[12]

Obviously Ladd would not accept this conclusion since his book is a study of Navaho ethics as an example of a moral code. However, such a reaction is not surprising given western presuppositions about the nature of morality.

How, in fact, does Ladd arrive at the view that he is dealing with 'materialistic prudentialism' and 'atomic egoism'? Navaho society, as described in his study, is at least as caring as our own, if not more so. For example, his informant says that a man with very little food should be prepared to share it with another who is starving, even if the donor may end up risking his own life. Ladd's conclusions, however, are based not on the actions of the Navaho but on the reasons they give for them. These reasons nearly all refer back to the welfare of the agent and the possible harmful effects on himself of not behaving unselfishly. The pain of social disapproval is especially prominent. Even in the case of sharing one's food at the risk of starving, Ladd thinks a concealed fear of the other man's ghost, if he died, would play a part, although his informant was unwilling to say much about ghosts.

There are several problems relating to Ladd's interpretation, as he himself is quite ready to admit. His field work lasted only five weeks and his information was obtained mainly from one man. Admittedly, as an elderly medicine man and singer he would be expected to have a sound knowledge of traditional ways and Ladd is justified in thinking that such a person would be the closest approximation he could find to what we would call a moralist. However, as the informant did not speak English, his replies had to be filtered through an interpreter whose own English was somewhat basic. It is clear that there was considerable scope for misunderstanding on the part of all three of them. In addition, some of the moral dilemmas posed by Ladd seem to have been so alien to the Navaho way of life that they were not really comprehensible to them. He was dealing, after all, with a relatively primitive society. For example, the use of imperatives, so important to western ethics, is impossible because there is no imperative mood in their language. Many concepts that we take for granted just do not seem to exist for them. Ladd is aware of these weaknesses and he does look closely at evidence which might contradict his thesis. However, as he notes:

> The testing of egoism is rendered difficult by the general Navaho presumption that the welfare of others is a necessary condition of one's own welfare. Hence, there are many prescriptions which might appear to be purely altruistic or societarian, but which are ultimately justified on an egoistic basis. (296)

Although the concepts of sympathy, benevolence or disinterestedness were never utilized in justifying morally correct behaviour, there is no reason to believe that these qualities do not exist. When asked why he would give money to a destitute man, the informant replied: 'I don't like for this man to die for food or have no clothes to wear – or could freeze up' (367). I think that the right questions might have brought out sympathetic concern for others. Certainly, Richard Brandt was able to extract such motivation from the Hopi Indians who, although different in some ways, live near the Navaho and share a similar natural environment.[13] My own suspicion is that when asked to justify a moral belief, the informant would naturally look first for reasons which would satisfy an egoist, since an altruist would not be expected to require such justification. If this is so, his mode of reasoning is similar to that of Hobbes, who fashioned his arguments to appeal to a basic need common to all mankind, self-preservation. Ladd compares Navaho ethical ideas with those of three western philosophers whom he regards as egoists: Epicurus, Hobbes and Spinoza. With reference to Hobbes he says:

> The Navaho and Hobbes are both essentially materialists, and consequently they agree in describing their goals in objective or publicly observable terms. In fact, even the lists of goals presented by both are almost identical. Hobbes at one point says that men are motivated by the desires for gain, for safety, and for reputation, and in another place he catalogues the powers sought as including the eminence of mind and body, and 'riches, reputation, friends, and the secret working of God, which men call luck'. (307)

Since these goals are shared by practically all mankind, there is no reason why they should be especially identified with materialists. Nor is there any reason why they should be regarded as reprehensible since there is nothing necessarily antisocial about wanting to enjoy a good reputation, a wide circle of friends, material prosperity, etc. Even ascetics have been known to compete with each other for eminence in self-denial. If this is egoism, then we are all egoists and egoism is inescapably associated with being human.

Ladd's intention is to be descriptive rather than judgmental but by describing the Navaho as egoists he is passing a judgment since the word is often used pejoratively and as he himself notes, 'in the West an egoist is on the defensive' (308). Although Ladd's own personal position is never made explicit, it probably tilts more towards Kant than anyone else. He later translated the first part of the *Metaphysic of Morals* as *The Metaphysical Elements of Justice* (Indianapolis, 1965). At one point he says:

> Perhaps the most extreme antithesis to egoism is found in the Kantian principle that one should 'treat others as ends-in-themselves'. This might be labelled 'pure altruism'. Ethical systems based upon sympathy generally assume some such principle, and it is noteworthy that there is never any appeal to sympathy in Navaho moral discourse. Egoism denies that other people are moral ends-in-themselves. (293)

However, Kant himself denied any moral worth to compassion, a form of sympathy. Furthermore, it is clear that sympathetic behaviour does occur in Navaho society even though Ladd failed to find it in their moral discourse.

The fact is that 'egoism' can be used in two senses. The word can be morally neutral if it is used to describe normal human behaviour as in the quotation about Hobbes above. However, it is usually meant to represent the opposite of altruism. To call Kant the philosopher of altruism and Hobbes the philosopher of egoism is to condemn the latter in the eyes of most westerners. But the situation is not that simple, as Ladd himself notes.

> Western moralists have generally assumed that egoism and altruism are incompatible; and therefore, that one of them must be rejected. . . . According to the Navaho ethical system which I have outlined, it is impossible to be a good egoist without at the same time being a good altruist. Although all the moral prescriptions are ultimately based upon an egoistic premise, in content they are altruistic. . . . The compatibility of egoism and altruism is a consequence of two facts: that there are no egoistically based moral prescriptions of action which could conflict with the interest of others; and there are many egoistic prescriptions which require altruistic action. (303–4)

If this is the case, it means that egoism and altruism in Navaho culture are so intertwined that to insist on calling it 'egoistic' as Ladd does, is to risk being seriously misleading since, as he has already noted, we normally consider egoism and altruism as incompatible. This is precisely the point that I have tried to make with Hobbes: because for him it is never prudent to be immoral, one cannot call him merely a prudentialist without doing him a grave disservice. Just as the Navaho offer egoistic reasons for being altruistic, so Hobbes provides prudential reasons for behaving morally. In both cases, these reasons are offered only to those who ask for them. The rest have no need for such explanations.

What Ladd's study and others like it do tend to show is that there is not as much difference between the moralities of various cultures as we are often led to believe. Ethical relativity of one kind or another has been an extremely important factor in undermining support for a rational ethics like that of Hobbes. How can we talk of rationality when strongly-held moral beliefs are so diverse? The answer is that there are some beliefs peculiar to each culture and others that can be found in all cultures, as we have noted before. The Navaho, for example, believe that a man must not look at his mother-in-law. The reason they give is that he will go blind if he does, whereas anthropologists believe that since the man lives in his mother-in-law's house, it is an attempt to eliminate potential sexual rivalry between mother and daughter. There are many beliefs and customs of this kind which are unique to one particular culture or another. Most of them do not conflict with the universal rational morality which we have been discussing but when they do, they can be judged accordingly. Wife-beating is customary in many societies but the fact that it is not considered culpable does not make it right. The wife does not like being beaten and the husband would not like being beaten, so that according to the golden rule it is wrong for a man to beat his wife, regardless of what the society thinks. The fact that men are used to having their way and women are forced by circumstances to let them have it does not alter the moral status of the act. Thus, moral relativism is correct only if it applies to customs and beliefs as such. In the realm of specific actions, the same rules of morality apply everywhere so long as human beings share the capacity to feel pain.

Moral theories are often divided into two major types: the deontological or duty-driven and the teleological or consequence-driven. It should be clear by now that I agree with those who believe that Hobbesian morality can be considered a strict deontology, based as it is on obligations imposed by the social contract. However, if the individual's motives for honouring this commitment are largely prudential, then it obviously has a teleological aspect as well. This raises the question of the relationship between Hobbesian morality and utilitarianism, the best-known type of consequentialism. Like many others, I do not see how a genuine personal morality can be based on utilitarianism, although it is a useful approach to social policy at the governmental level. For the individual, the golden rule is a much more practical guide; in fact, the best way to achieve the greatest good of the greatest number is for everyone to practise reciprocity. John Stuart Mill seems to admit this himself when he says: 'In the golden rule of Jesus of Nazareth, we read the complete spirit of the ethics of utility'.[14]

In reality, the practical ethics of most modern philosophers do not differ much from that outlined above. A good example is John Mackie. Despite the fact that he presents himself as a moral sceptic and subjectivist when discussing the status of ethics, he does not hesitate to offer his own ethical beliefs in the section of his book called 'The Content of Ethics' and it turns out that they are quite similar to what has been discussed here. He is generally sympathetic to Hobbes although he says that, with his emphasis on 'selfish' motivation, 'Hobbes does not allow for the development of what we might call secondary instinct in favour of morality' (*Ethics*, p. 113). Since Mackie, like so many others, ignores the role of the golden rule in Hobbes's moral theory, he neglects the important part played by empathy in making possible the imaginative exchange which is required in order for reciprocity to work. Although Hobbes has to mobilize the forces of selfishness and coercion on behalf of morality, he knows that without the help of man's innate capacity to identify with others and to make the interests of at least some of them his own, society would not be possible.

However, Mackie does raise an important question in connection with contract theories like that of Hobbes.

> This approach would seem to provide for no duties towards non-participants, and to assign no rights to beings who do not need to be drawn into a quasi-contactual scheme, who have no benefits which they are free either to confer upon others or to withhold, and no powers to do harm. Classes that we ordinarily see as having morally valid claims to consideration, but which seem to be wholly or partly excluded from consideration by this approach, include young children, the unborn, members of future generations, the aged, the sick, the infirm, the insane, the mentally defective, and non-human animals.

He goes on to say that his own approach is not quite the same as the contractual one in that it 'takes general human well-being or the flourishing of human life as the foundation of morality' (193).

A much more economical way would be to use the golden rule

as the content of the contract. By doing this Hobbes automatically provides for the kindly treatment of the weaker members of society, who can also be seen as dependents of those who are capable of understanding the obligations they have undertaken as more fully participating members of the community. This applies also to future generations insofar as we protect the environment, etc. for the immediate benefit of ourselves and our children. Since many human beings can identify with animals, the golden rule for them encompasses the welfare of at least some animals also.

The most controversial topic raised by Mackie, is the status of the unborn. There is already an extensive literature on the subject of abortion which reflects the intensity of feeling it arouses in those taking part in the debate. I shall confine myself to noting that this is a question largely of public policy rather than private morality. Since the pregnant woman and the person who will perform the abortion are the only two individuals directly involved, it is their application of the golden rule which should govern their own actions. If neither can identify with a fertilized ovum any better than an unfertilized one, they will feel little, if any guilt in proceeding. Anyone else who has an interest in the matter can intervene only by attempting to have abortion made illegal if it is legal or vice versa. Both sides agree that murder is immoral and illegal but they differ as to whether abortion can be considered murder, which, in turn, comes down ultimately to the question: Is a foetus to be regarded as a human being eligible for the protection offered to the rest of us?

In practice, one becomes a member of a society by being born. This event is recorded by a birth certificate, or its equivalent, which also bestows a name on the individual. This official recognition means that one is entitled to the rights and privileges associated with belonging to that society. When such a person dies, a death certificate will be issued, thus officially terminating the membership. If there are suspicious circumstances surrounding the death, an inquest may be called to determine if it was a homicide. On the other hand, if a woman has a miscarriage, either voluntary or induced, no official notice is usually taken. In fact, the authorities will normally have no way of knowing that there ever was a foetus. This striking difference in treatment would appear to indicate that for the purposes of the social contract, life begins at birth. The reasons for this are practical, not moral. The state has no way of knowing when conception takes place, and if an abortion pill became widely available, the matter would be removed completely from the hands of doctors, clinics and the state, and would rest solely with the person most immediately concerned, the pregnant woman. Some methods of contraception are essentially very early abortions and the abortion pill would provide a slightly later form of contraception. As a result, the whole debate about abortion would become pointless. Like many other controversial areas such as, for example, homosexuality or pornography, there are limits to what the state can do regardless of the protests of outraged guardians of public morality.

An interesting sidelight on the abortion debate is that here is another case where rights-talk has not been productive. The anti-abortionists make great use of a supposed 'right to life' and their opponents have been forced to wage the battle on unfavourable ground because they, too, believe in such a right. The problem is that if it is interpreted in the strictly biological sense, it obviously begins at conception, and any attempt to suspend or deny it until some later point or to switch to some other criterion such as 'personhood' inevitably gets tangled up in the fate of the newborn, the mentally incapable, etc. Another problem which arises if the question is put in terms of rights is that it becomes a conflict between those of the pregnant woman and those of the foetus. If the right to biological life is recognized, then the woman's rights over her own body and her right not to have to endure the discomforts of pregnancy and the pain of childbirth, while significant, still do not appear to be enough to justify an act of murder. But if the woman is regarded as an already living member of society and as a moral agent with the freedom to choose if and when she wants to bear children, the supposed rights of a fertilized ovum shrink into insignificance.

The only obvious time for life to begin, other than at conception, is at birth. This is when a new human being is welcomed into the community and when it becomes entitled to a genuine right to life in the sense that legal recognition and protection have now been extended to it, and there are people who have undertaken a meaningful obligation with respect to its welfare. I should note, in this connection, that Hobbes's right of nature is not a right to life as such but a right to do what is necessary to preserve one's own life and thus applies only to beings capable of doing so.

When Hobbes said in *De Corpore* (*English Works*, I, ix) that although natural philosophy was young, civil philosophy was much younger, 'being no older than my own book *De Cive*', he was criticized for his conceit. In his *Six Lessons to the Professors of the Mathematics* (ibid.,

VII, 333) he replied that when he made that statement he was not boasting but merely defending himself from his detractors. He then mentions, in support of his claim, that a summary of *De Cive* published in France had been entitled *Ethics Demonstrated*. He obviously felt that although the dream of putting ethics on as sound a basis as Euclid's geometry had been often canvassed, only he himself had succeeded in making it a reality. He, of course, was not able to convert many others to this view but I think he came as close as is possible in a sceptical world. In any case it was a noble goal. A rational morality can only be convincing to people who are prepared to listen to reason and mankind is too often not so inclined. However, this does not alter the fact that the only way to justify a basic morality is on rational grounds. To appeal to reason is just as universal a human characteristic as is the temptation to succumb to passion but only reason has the power to persuade others when they *are* willing to listen and thus make possible a meaningful moral discourse.

How does a sceptic like Mackie, who says that the 'assertion that there are objective values or intrinsically prescriptive entities or features of some kind, which ordinary moral judgements presuppose, is, I hold, not meaningless but false' (40), propose to justify the ethical judgments he offers us later in his book? He is aware of the problem but disposes of it in a few words by evoking John Rawls's doctrine of 'reflective equilibrium'.

> That is, we might start with some *prima facie* acceptable general principles, and with the mass of *prima facie* acceptable detailed moral judgements, and where they do not fully agree adjust either or both until the most satisfactory coherent compromise is reached. . . . This is a legitimate kind of enquiry, but it must not be confused with the superficially similar but in purpose fundamentally different attempt of thinkers like Sidgwick to advance by way of our various 'intuitions' to an objective moral truth, a science of conduct. 'Our sense of justice', whether it is just yours or mine or that of some much larger group, has no authority over those who dissent from its recommendations or even over us if we are inclined to change our minds. But if there is no objective moral truth to be discovered, is there nothing left to do but to describe our sense of justice? (105–6)

His answer is ultimately yes, although he alters the perspective somewhat by adding that our morality is to be made rather than discovered. But since he admits that our 'sense of justice' has no authority over others or over ourselves if we change our minds, he has given no reason for anyone to be more interested in the opinions of John Mackie than in those of the man next door, who has never ventured to publish a book on ethics.

However, the method to which he refers in the first part of the passage, that of 'reflective equilibrium' is close to what the most important moral philosophers engage in. Since people already have strong moral beliefs it might be asked what, if any, is the purpose of ethical theory? One useful answer is that it can provide an hypothesis which attempts to explain why certain behaviour is considered wrong. This theory is then tested against people's actual moral beliefs and if it produces results which do not violate the most significant of these beliefs, it has passed the first test. The next challenge arises in those cases where its prescriptions differ from other beliefs held by at least some segments of the population. If the theory is satisfactory, then those beliefs are mistaken and vice versa. Thus, before a moral theory can be accepted it must pass the first test and before it can be rejected it must clearly fail the second. This pattern is followed, for example, by both Kant and the Utilitarians. They start with the common moral consciousness, develop a theory to explain how it can be validated and from the theory then derive moral principles which can be checked back against that common moral consciousness. Critics have said that both the categorical imperative and the principle of utility produce results which would be considered immoral by most people and therefore both approaches have similar problems.

Hobbes's theory, resting as it does on a supreme moral principle which can be used to generate very specific and definite rules, can easily satisfy the first criterion since the golden rule is used, consciously or unconsciously, by practically everyone, and most of the rules derived from it satisfy the ordinary moral consciousness. We have seen earlier how it can be utilized to evaluate other commonly held beliefs and to offer a reasonable way of dealing with moral disagreements. As I have pointed out several times, it is not designed to offer an easy solution to questions of social policy which occupy so much of the attention of contemporary philosophers but then no theory does, although utilitarianism is more helpful here than it is in personal morality. Scepticism, of course, has no contribution to make in either area since it fails to provide a basis for choosing one theory over another.

One might note, in conclusion, how similar the process described above is to the development of new hypotheses in the traditional sciences. An hypothesis is suggested to explain the relationships of observed facts and if it can do this satisfactorily, inferences will be drawn from it which can be checked against other facts which are not explained as well by current theories. This is a very oversimplified summary of how the Newtonian world view replaced the Ptolemaic and was in turn replaced by the Einsteinian. The parallels are not exact but in both cases it is the explanatory power of the theory which is of paramount importance.

11
Contract and the Commonwealth

In Part II of *Leviathan*, entitled 'Of Commonwealth', Hobbes shifts his focus directly to the realm of politics. The political framework, which was always implicit in his discussion of morality, now emerges into the foreground and itself becomes the subject of analysis. He reiterates the need he had earlier expressed for some kind of constraint on men's natural passions to hold them to their agreement since, in his famous phrase, 'covenants, without the sword, are but words, and of no strength to secure a man at all' (154, 223). His solution is as follows:

> The only way to erect such a common power, as may be able to defend them from the invasion of foreigners, and the injuries of one another . . . is, to confer all their power and strength upon one man, or upon an assembly of men, that they may reduce all their wills, by plurality of voices, unto one will . . . This is more than consent, or concord; it is a real unity of them all, in one and the same person, made by a covenant of every man with every man, in such manner, as if every man should say to every man, *I authorize and give up my right of governing myself, to this man, or to this assembly of men, on this condition that thou give up thy right to him, and authorize all his actions in like manner.* This done, the multitude so united in one person, is called a COMMONWEALTH, in Latin CIVITAS. This is the generation of that great LEVIATHAN, or rather to speak more reverently, of that *mortal god*, to which we owe under the *immortal God*, our peace and defence. (157, 227)

Hobbes's two earlier works differ from *Leviathan* in that they do not provide specific wording for the agreement. Another difference that has attracted considerable attention is that here he has added at the end of Part I a chapter, 'Of Persons, Authors, and Things Personated', which serves to elucidate what he means when he uses the word 'authorize' in the above passage. However, there is no reason to interpret this as a change in his thinking, as some commentators believe, since all he does is to clarify the way in which 'a multitude of men are made *one* person, when they are by one man, or one person, represented' (151, 221). The representative, of course, can be a number of men made one by a plurality of voices. The same idea is expressed by the words 'resign' in *The Elements of Law* (I,19,7) and 'convey' in *De Cive* (V,8) when referring to the transfer of an individual's strength and faculties to whomever he has covenanted to obey. The emphasis in all three books is on the notion of a union which is achieved by subjecting one's will to that of the whole as embodied by the man or council chosen to act on behalf of all.

The content of this agreement is essentially that of the second law of nature – the mutual laying down of the right to all things – to which has been added a provision for the 'coercive force', already mentioned in Part I, as being necessary before the covenant can take effect. The social contract on which morality is based is thus restated in such a way that it simultaneously establishes the political power required to ensure an environment secure enough for one to behave morally without becoming a prey to others. In the first formulation the emphasis is on the establishment of morality by agreement whereas in the second it is on the necessity to submit to a sovereign who has enough power to protect the contractors both from each other and from outsiders.

Although the hypothetical nature of this covenant is clearly indicated by the words 'as if every man should say to every man' which precede it, Hobbes does not isolate it completely from the real world. He justifies his theoretical 'generation' of the commonwealth on the basis of what we know or can surmise about the actual origin of states. He imagines men living in small families disputing with one another and striving to enlarge the extent of their power just as later cities and kingdoms have done. In both situations security cannot be attained just by joining together, but only by doing so in sufficient numbers to be capable of victory in conflicts with other groups. This emphasis on the sheer size of political units reminds us that a commonwealth is sustained as much by the necessity for strength against other commonwealths, occasioned by the belligerence of mankind, as it is by the threat of anarchy from within. The danger posed by the state of nature is transferred from the individual to the political unit. Hobbes sums up both problems neatly when he writes:

> For if we could suppose a great multitude of men to consent in the observation of justice, and other laws of nature, without a common power to keep them all in awe; we might as well suppose all mankind to do the same; and then there neither would be, nor need to be any civil government, or commonwealth at all; because there would be peace without subjection. (155, 225)

This poses an interesting question for those, like Locke and Rousseau, who believe that the state of nature is much less dangerous than Hobbes makes it out to be: why, in such a case, do states feel the necessity to maintain expensive armed forces?

Complex societies actually do exist among certain insects without any visible coercion. In answer to the question as to why what is possible amongst bees and ants is not likewise possible amongst human beings, Hobbes lists the factors which make a firm hand necessary for the latter. These boil down to man's competitive nature and his desire for eminence, which make him reluctant to put public ahead of private good. Furthermore, whereas the agreement amongst social insects is natural, or as we would say, instinctive, that between men is artificial and thus requires a common power to enforce it.

This sovereign power can be arrived at in two ways: by acquisition or by institution. It is the latter method that Hobbes looks at first.

> A *commonwealth* is said to be *instituted*, when a *multitude* of men do agree, and *covenant, every one, with every one*, that to whatsoever *man*, or *assembly of men*, shall be given by the major part, the *right* to *present* the person of them all, that is to say, to be their *representative*; every one, as well he that *voted for it*, as he that *voted against it*, shall *authorize* all the actions and judgments, of that man, or assembly of men, in the same manner, as if they were his own, to the end, to live peaceably amongst themselves, and be protected against other men.
> From this institution of a commonwealth are derived all the *rights*, and *faculties* of him, or them, on whom the sovereign power is conferred by the consent of the people assembled. (159, 228)

This is slightly different from *The Elements*, where unanimity is required at the first meeting because no action can 'be attributed to the multitude . . . unless every man's will (not so much as one excepted) have concurred thereto' (EL,II,1,2). If they decide to be governed 'by the wills of the major part of their whole numbers', they become a democracy. Similarly, if a limited number is chosen they become an aristocracy or oligarchy and if one only, then a monarchy. No matter what their ultimate choice, democracy precedes the other two because it is implicit in the character of their initial meeting. In *Leviathan*, Hobbes requires only a majority, but the difference is of no consequence since by voluntarily joining the congregation, each individual 'tacitly covenanted' to be bound by the majority, and if he refuses to submit to their decision, he is left in the state of nature along with those who did not participate, and may 'without injustice be destroyed by any man whatsoever' (163, 232).

There is an alternative to institution in the origin of states.

> A COMMONWEALTH by *acquisition* is that, where the sovereign power is acquired by force; and it is acquired by force, when men singly, or many together by plurality of voices, for fear of death, or bonds, do authorize all the actions of that man, or assembly, that hath their lives and liberty in his power.
>
> And this kind of dominion, or sovereignty, differeth from sovereignty by institution, only in this, that men who choose their sovereign, do it for fear of one another, and not of him they institute: but, in this case, they subject themselves, to him they are afraid of. In both cases they do it for fear: which is to be noted by them, that hold all such covenants, as proceed from fear of death or violence, void: which if it were true, no man, in any kind of commonwealth, could be obliged to obedience . . .
>
> But the rights, and consequences of sovereignty are the same in both. (185, 251)

This type of dominion is acquired in two ways: by generation, which is called paternal, and by conquest, which is known as despotical. His treatment of the first is unusual in that dominion over the child is based not on generation but on the child's consent, 'either express, or by other sufficient arguments declared' (186, 253). This consent is obviously a fiction but a useful one since both parent and child behave *as if* there were a contractual relationship. He also does not give automatic priority to the father. If there is no contract of matrimony, the child belongs to the mother, or whoever brings it up. Whichever person has dominion over the child also has dominion over his children and so on. In his two earlier works he shows how a monarchy can arise on this basis, one which would have satisfied Sir Robert Filmer, who laid great emphasis on this form of origin in his *Patriarcha* and other writings. But in *Leviathan* Hobbes's treatment is perfunctory, and by introducing consent, which had not appeared before, he seems not to take the idea very seriously. This is understandable to the modern mind which usually fails to see why the idea had so much appeal in the seventeenth century. However, Filmer's works were considered important enough to be attacked by several writers in lengthy works, the best-known of which is the first of Locke's *Two Treatises of Government*.

Dominion by conquest has to be taken much more seriously. For one thing many people, including thinkers such as Hume, believed that most states had originated by force and that to talk of consent was mere wishful thinking. The model for despotical dominion is the master-servant relationship of which slavery was the most extreme example. Hobbes distinguished between the slaves who were kept in chains or otherwise confined and those who were permitted a substantial freedom of movement. In the first case the slave was under no obligation to his master and could, with justice, attempt to escape and even kill him. In the second, Hobbes assumed a covenant whereby the slave was granted his corporal freedom in return for good behaviour. This concept of servitude could be extended more convincingly than that of paternity to the state. Again, Hobbes provides less detail in *Leviathan* than in his earlier works probably because he realized more and more that the question of origin was not of great importance to his theory since, 'In sum, the rights and consequences of both *paternal* and *despotical* dominion, are the very same with those of a sovereign by institution' (190, 256). In all types the ruler's rights are absolute but at the same time, they all have a foundation in consent.

History offers numerous examples of countries conquered by outsiders. Results have varied. In many cases, conquest represents the displacement of one ruling class by another with little change for those members of the lower classes fortunate enough to survive. For example, China was conquered by a succession of invaders but life probably altered little for the average villager, who would doubtless have been very surprised if his opinion on the new rulers had been sought. Closer to home, the English monarchy originated in the success of William the Conqueror who rewarded his followers with land seized from the local population, just as Cromwell was to do in Ireland. There is an interesting contrast with France where the Count of Paris, Hugh Capet, was elected king by the great French nobles in 987 to replace the failed Carolingian line. Since there was no guarantee that his son would be elected on his death, he had him elected soon after his own coronation, a practice known as co-optation, which was continued by his successors until the hereditary principle was firmly established. However, its origins bore some resemblance to dominion by institution.

In both cases, as was typical, only a small percentage of the population participated in the decision-making, namely the warrior aristocracy on whom a feudal monarch was dependent for his success or failure. The Magna Carta imposed on King John by his restive nobles in 1215, was the first of a series of concessions which paved the way for the struggle between King and Parliament and the resultant political writings of Thomas Hobbes. Ironically, the French kings moved in the opposite direction. From a position of weakness, they gradually consolidated their power and enlarged the territory over which they exercised control until the stage was set for the absolutism of Louis XIV, whose long reign began in 1643, one year after the first version of *De Cive* appeared in Paris. However, in a further irony, out of the disorder of the Civil War in England emerged the most absolute ruler it has ever known, Oliver Cromwell, who was for all practical purposes a military dictator. It was under his regime, of course, that Hobbes returned to England and published his *Leviathan* in 1651.

Since some form of consent is required from each individual or, at the very least, adult heads of families, and this requirement is not generally satisfied by real commonwealths, Hobbes would appear to be referring to the kind of hypothetical situation we discussed in connection with the covenant of morality. However, it is not quite that simple. The contract model is not easy to control because one has to talk about the way people actually behave in order to defend the hypothetical version and one can easily get lost switching constantly between the two worlds. We have seen this with Hobbes before and I think it is a problem for all social contract theorists and perhaps with the social contract theory, itself, at least as applied to politics. Did he believe that it had actually taken place? At the end of this chapter he does raise the question. 'The greatest objection is, that of the practice; when men ask, where, and when, such power has by subjects been acknowledged.' But his answer is merely another question.

> But one may ask them again, when, or where has there been a kingdom long free from sedition and civil war. In those nations, whose commonwealths have been long-lived, and not been destroyed but by foreign war, the subjects never did dispute of the sovereign power. But howsoever, an argument from the practice of men, that have not sifted to the bottom, and with exact reason weighed the causes, and nature of commonwealths, and suffer daily those miseries, that proceed from the ignorance thereof, is invalid.

The fact that some people build on sand is no reason for everyone to do so. Commonwealths are constructed soundly on the basis, not of practice but of rules which men, who have had the leisure, have not 'had the curiosity, or the method to find out' (195, 260).

This obviously does not answer our question but it illustrates Hobbes's belief that successful commonwealths *must* be founded on consent and that their subjects must also be aware of this. Later in the book he flirts with the idea that it actually happened.

> The author, or legislator is supposed in every commonwealth to be evident, because he is the sovereign, who having been constituted by the consent of every one, is supposed by every one to be sufficiently known. And though the ignorance and security of men be such, for the most part, as that when the memory of the first constitution of their commonwealth is worn out, they do not consider by whose power they used to be defended against their enemies, and to have their industry protected, and to be righted when injury is done them; yet because no man that considers, can make question of it, no excuse can be derived from the ignorance of where the sovereignty is placed. And it is a dictate of natural reason, and consequently an evident law of nature, that no man ought to weaken that power, the protection whereof he hath himself demanded, or wittingly received against others. (260, 320)

This passage is of interest because Hobbes talks about consent as having actually taken place in the past, perhaps so long ago that remembrance of the event is 'worn out'. This would seem to imply a kind of folk memory of an agreement which still binds us as a people. The image is one of a collectivity composed of generations past, present and future, committed to a sovereign because of a strong sense of continuity. This Burkean notion does not, however, square with his reference to the consent of 'every *one*' which reasserts the individual nature of the original decision. But this apparent contradiction hardly matters since we are immediately given another reason to obey: gratitude based on the practical benefits the sovereign has conferred on us. Furthermore, Hobbes provides an alternative to having demanded this protection – that of having 'wittingly received' it. This seems to reaffirm the idea mentioned earlier in connection with morality, that what we are really dealing with is continuous consent given in the present, if the word 'consent' is to have any meaning. Since we have accepted the benefits offered by the sovereign, we have also consented to his authority and are thus bound to obey him. This is the same reasoning actually used by Socrates in accepting his death sentence by the government of Athens.

Whether this is Hobbes's intent or not, it seems one way of making at least some sense of what he says. What is clear above all, is the moral significance that the consent of each individual has for him. The question is, how meaningful can this idea be in the context of the state, especially if it is assumed to have been given some time in the past. One thing to remember is that for Hobbes, consent does not have to be given verbally. 'Silence in them that will be so taken, is a sign of consent; for so little labour being required to say No, it is to be presumed, that in this he that saith it not, consenteth' (EL,I,13,11). Consent in this sense is often accepted in law and certainly has weight. However, for many people its significance would be affected by the extent to which a genuine choice was available. This is not a problem for Hobbes since he believes that unless one is physically confined, one is free, which means that one can always say no, even if one's life is at stake. Following this reasoning, the subjects of a commonwealth have the option of refusing consent by taking whatever action is needed to dissociate themselves from it, such as refusing to obey the law or leaving the country. If they conclude that any alternative available to them is worse than the status quo and decide to do nothing, then they have effectively given their consent. Of course, there may well be a noticeable difference in the strength of a state inhabited by reluctant consenters and one composed of enthusiastic consenters should an external threat arise, but that is a problem for the sovereign. Hobbes repeatedly says that it is in the sovereign's interest to have a loyal and supportive population, and only he can take the steps necessary to make it so.

What about the question of consent supposedly given at some time in the past, presumably by the subject's ancestors? Oddly enough this has more power to bind than one might think. Christians are familiar with the sin of Adam passed down through successive generations making each man as guilty as if he had committed it himself. In the same way actions taken by our forefathers may be seen as binding on us. Americans, for example, accept without question that a law passed by their duly elected representatives can be declared unconstitutional by the Supreme Court. That constitution which it is judged to have violated was the work of a small number of men in the eighteenth century who had no conception of the sorts of problems which would emerge in a much different future world, yet the product of their deliberations is, subject to interpretation, still held to be binding on contemporary American society. This indicates that even in a country which is accepted as a model of progressive individualism and modernity by most of the world, the notion that one has to play according to the rules laid down by one's predecessors is as strong as ever.

I have used the game metaphor here deliberately because it is as useful as any in understanding the rationale of this sort of behaviour. We have discussed it from the moral point of view earlier but it is, of course, just as applicable to politics. This type of consent involves accepting rules formulated in the past by other people, in the same way that one does when one has decided to take part in a game. The fact that people today actually do feel bound by agreements arrived at many years and even centuries ago is proof enough that we are dealing with a conception of consent which has not lost its persuasiveness.

The American example takes whatever legitimacy it has from the fact that certain events actually did occur 200 years ago, but what of the many other states whose origins were not so clear cut? There is considerable doubt that these differences would have been of much consequence to Hobbes since he seems to be functioning at a different level of reality. In *De Cive* he says: 'Democracy is not framed by contract of particular persons with the people, but by mutual compacts of single men with each other'. The world 'people' is used here to mean the corporate person which results from the agreement as opposed to the multitude of separate individuals. He goes on:

> But hence it appears, in the first place, that the persons contracting must be in being before the contract itself. But the people is not in being before the constitution of government, as not being any person, but a multitude of single persons; wherefore there could then no contract pass between the people and the subjects. Now, if after that government is framed, the subject make any contract with the people, it is in vain; because the people contains within its will, the will of the subject to whom it is supposed to be obliged . . . But, in the second place, that single persons do contract each with other *may be inferred* from hence, that in vain sure would the city have been constituted, if the citizens had been engaged by no contracts to do or omit what the city should command to be done or omitted. Because therefore such compacts *must be understood* to pass as necessary to the making up of a city, but none can be made (as is already shewed) between the subject and the people; it follows, that they *must be made* between single citizens . . . (DC,VII,7; emphasis added)

The italicized words indicate that individuals *had* to contract with each other in this way; logically there was no alternative if we assume as Hobbes did, that a state must rest ultimately on some form of consent. If it does not, then the mortar which is needed to hold it together is missing and it will crumble at the first shock. We seem to be working backward from the fact that strong and united political entities do exist, in an attempt to find out how they can exist. His conclusion is that contract and consent form the only reliable foundation. The question as to when such an agreement was actually made is irrelevant since we are dealing here with logical rather than chronological priority.

That Hobbes does not give actual origins much weight is indicated by a passage near the end of *Leviathan* where, discussing how monarchs try to justify their historical claims to their thrones, he says:

> As if, for example, the rights of the kings of England did depend on the goodness of the cause of William the conqueror, and upon their lineal and remotest descent from him; by which means,

there would perhaps be no tie of the subjects' obedience to their sovereign at this day in all the world: wherein whilst they needlessly think to justify all the successful rebellions that ambition shall at any time rise against them, and their successors. Therefore I put down for one of the most effectual seeds of the death of any state, that the conquerors require not only a submission of men's actions to them for the future, but also an approbation of all their actions past; *when there is scarce a commonwealth in the world, where beginnings can in conscience be justified.* (706, 722; emphasis added)

The italicized words seem to rule out once and for all the possibility that Hobbes believed that an actual contract was a serious factor in the origin of most states.

A critic can easily point to apparent inconsistencies in what Hobbes has to say on this subject but I am trying to determine what was in his mind. As I noted before, the concept of a social contract is extremely difficult to deal with and Hobbes, like both his predecessors and successors, is not as careful in his wording as he might have been. The key to understanding such an idea, it seems to me, is to look for its purpose. That actual social contracts have been made is not in doubt so there is nothing strange or unfamiliar about them; they do not require elaborate justification or explanation. However, what Hobbes and the other contractarians want us to do is to act *as if* there has been a social contract when it is obvious to everyone that there has not, in fact, been one. What is needed is for us to feel obliged in the same manner as if we had actually participated in the kind of covenanting that Hobbes describes as instituting a commonwealth. As we noted in connection with morality, a fictional contract or quasi-contract serves this purpose. It makes meaningful the attitude we have to adopt if our state is to survive and, even more important, it can act as an explanation for the feelings most people actually *do* have towards their homeland. These feelings are usually taken for granted but should someone question them, such an explanation would put his or her relationship with fellow subjects and the sovereign in a rational light. People can say in effect, 'Yes, now I understand. Given the options available that is exactly what I would have had to do'.

If this is what Hobbes has in mind, it must be admitted that he did create confusion for his reader. As we have seen, he sometimes talks as if the covenant is a reality. This shift from fictional to real is hard to avoid when the concept is central to the theory and is subject to so much discussion. For Hobbes, the 'as if' proviso tended to fade in importance as he contemplated the anarchy that can result from not taking one's duties under the covenant seriously enough. However, he does complicate things unnecessarily, in my opinion, when he discusses commonwealth by acquisition. In his anxiety to introduce consent into a situation which displays little evidence of it, he forgets, as he did not in that passage near the end of *Leviathan*, that *how* a state actually originated is not important for his theory. It is true that individuals faced directly with such a situation, as he was with Cromwell's regime, have to make their peace with the new ruler. But a contract of submission made individually with a ruler, as he describes it in the abstract, seldom if ever actually occurs in reaction to an immediate threat on one's life. And this contract is also not equivalent to that which is entered into when instituting a commonwealth even though both can be traced to fear for one's survival. It is fear of other persons which would lead me to contract with them to appoint a sovereign to protect us. My commitment is to them as well as to the ruler. The whole point of the covenant is to create conditions which make it possible to lead a peaceful and therefore moral life. A contract directly with the sovereign to preserve my own life does not provide for the protection of me from the others or them from me. As Hobbes puts it elsewhere, 'the government is upheld by a double obligation from the citizens, first, that which is due to their fellow-citizens, next, that which they owe to their prince' (DC,VI,20).

I think Hobbes has at least two reasons for glossing over this difference. One is that because there were traditionally three ways of establishing a commonwealth (four if one includes foundation by a great legislator, which was popular in the ancient world) he felt he had to deal with paternal and despotical rule as well as commonwealth by institution, but the smaller amount of space he devotes to them in *Leviathan* indicates their declining relevance for him. Any remaining interest, one might add, would have practically disappeared if he had given the matter more thought. The other reason is that, because a sovereign's powers are absolute, no matter how he acquired them, there is no genuine difference between the various types of sovereignty once they are in place. The fact that Cromwell became ruler through the command of an army rather than through hereditary prerogative was of little consequence to the average Englishman.

Since Hobbes was concerned above all with justifying absolute sovereignty his arguments are designed to close any potential loop holes of which his enemies might take advantage. One of the most serious threats arose out of the very concept of contract. Because of its bilateral nature it lends itself readily to being used for the purpose of limiting the sovereign's power. It was the notion that the sovereign could be bound by a contract which made it especially popular with theorists who were opposed to absolute monarchy. This is how it had been utilized in the period before Hobbes, and accounted for most of its appeal in his own day and later. He was very much odd man out in the way he handled it, although there was a long-standing tradition going back at least to the *Lex Regia* that an absolute ruler's power was legitimate because it had been received from the people. By attempting to derive this legitimacy directly from the individual subject, Hobbes was turning his opponents' chief weapon against them. In order to be successful, however, he had to remove all possibility of a bilateral contract between sovereign and subject which would place the sovereign under any kind of obligation.

He was able to do this in a reasonably convincing way in the commonwealth by institution, but his introduction of a contract of submission directly with the sovereign, in the case of acquisition, raised a nagging question. What is supposed to occur is not in doubt: the right of sovereignty by conquest 'is acquired in the people's submission, by which they contract with the victor, promising obedience, for life and liberty' (705, 721). But is this not the thin edge of the wedge for his opponents? The answer is no, since although the sovereign grants the subject his life and liberty at the moment of contract, his later actions are not bound in any meaningful way, given the unlimited nature of Hobbesian sovereignty. Nevertheless, people would be unlikely to enter into such a contract or, in the case of institution, to contract with others to appoint a sovereign, unless they had some reason to believe that their actions were going to have the desired results. In other words, there must be a factor at work here other than the bare minimum specified by Hobbes. And there is. Whenever Hobbes talks about the obligations of sovereigns, as he does in Chapter XIII of *De Cive*, 'Concerning the Duties of Them Who Bear Rule', he obviously believes that rulers will generally do what their subjects expect them to do. The reason is not that they are obliged by contract, since they have made no such commitment, but simply because it is in their own interest to do so.

Hobbes's critics often fail to give sufficient weight to this factor but the truth is that self-interest is a much more reliable motive than any contractual obligation, if it is undertaken by a person who has all the power in his hands. They sometimes exclaim in shock that there is nothing to stop a sovereign from killing all his subjects! In theory there may not be, but such an event is highly unlikely given that a sovereign without subjects is no longer a sovereign. The assumption must be that a sovereign is such because that is what he wants to be. The subjects need a sovereign but it is also true that a sovereign needs his subjects.

This opens up a topic which is not touched on directly by Hobbes, probably because it seemed so self-evident to him. That topic – the motivation of sovereigns – needs, however, to be taken into consideration if one is to make sense of his theory. As I said before, people are unlikely to enter into a contract of submission unless they have adequate grounds for believing that it will give them what they want in return for their surrender of a part of their natural right. The contract that Hobbes offers is silent in that respect, despite the fact that when it comes to the benefits that will flow from the arrangement Hobbes is far from silent. In the above-mentioned Chapter XIII of *De Cive* he says: 'Now all the duties of rulers are contained in this one sentence, the safety of the people is the supreme law'. Further down the page, he adds: 'For the city was not instituted for its own, but for the subject's sake' (DC,XIII,2 and 3). And this includes their happiness, 'that they might as much as their human condition would afford, live delightfully' (Ibid., 4). Previously, in Chapter X, when he is listing the advantages offered by the city as opposed to the state of nature, he concludes:

> Lastly, out of it, there is a dominion of passions, war, fear, poverty, slovenliness, solitude, barbarism, ignorance, cruelty; in it, the dominion of reason, peace, security, riches, decency, society, elegancy, sciences, and benevolence. (DC,X,1)

Of course, the sovereign cannot guarantee all these things, but by providing security, he has established the conditions under which they can flourish.

But, the sceptic asks, where does it say that the sovereign has to do what is necessary for this happy outcome, or that he will even know what is necessary, since the contract makes no mention of this at all? Again, I believe, Hobbes is working back from his contemporary world, seventeenth century Europe, where everyone could see that stable governments were actually doing the job, more or less, that their subjects expected them to do. What then were their motives, or is this an amazing example of pre-established harmony? In a sense it is, since as we have noted, the relationship between ruler and ruled is symbiotic. They need each other in the same way that doctors must have patients as well as vice versa. Rulers are required by natural law to do their duty but it so happens that their duty and their profit coincide with each other and with the profit of their subjects (EL,II,9,1). Thus, if a monarch is governed by rational self-interest he will know that for his kingdom to flourish, his subjects must also flourish and therefore he must give them, at least to some degree, what they expect from him in return for their submission. But what if the ruler acts irrationally and, contrary to his own best interests, brings suffering to his subjects? Hobbes grants that a prince may sometimes act wickedly but it is impossible to guard against such an eventuality, given the nature of power. 'For he that hath strength enough to protect all, wants not sufficiency to oppress all. Here is no difficulty then, but that human affairs cannot be without some inconvenience' (DC,VI,13n.). Since the alternative, a return to the state of nature, is always worse, Hobbes would consider submission a risk worth taking since 'to make men altogether safe from mutual harms, so as they cannot be hurt or injuriously killed, is impossible' (DC,VI,3).

It should be evident by now that the social contract is not without problems, especially the constant temptation to talk about it as if it had actually occurred. This is almost unavoidable since, like most useful fictions, it quickly acquires a degree of reality. An example is the custom of treating a majority as unanimity, and saying 'the people have voted for change' rather than '51 per cent of the people have voted for change'. This, together with the fact that similar types of contracts *have* actually occurred, can lead easily to the kind of confusion that we have encountered in Hobbes and would find in almost any contractarian. Given this uncertainty about the existential status of the social contract, is it really of any value to us? David Hume, of course, said no. However, in his essay, 'Of the Original Contract', he is referring specifically to that version associated with Locke, 'by which the subjects have tacitly reserved the power of resisting their sovereign, whenever they find themselves aggrieved by that authority with which they have, for certain purposes, voluntarily entrusted him'.[1] As we know, this justification for sedition is one of Hobbes's major targets, so that he and Hume do not differ here. Oddly enough, Hume does not deny the likelihood of an original contract early in the history of mankind, due to rough equality in strength and faculties of the individual, but he sees no evidence of it in contemporary states, almost all of which were founded on usurpation or conquest. Hume certainly had commonsense on his side when he attacked Locke's concept of tacit consent by noting how difficult it would be for a poor peasant or artisan to leave his country if its ruler did not meet with his approval. In fact, where the subject 'thinks (as all mankind do who are born under established governments) that by his birth he owes allegiance to a certain prince or certain form of government, it would be absurd to infer a consent or choice which he expressly, in this case, renounces and disclaims' (203). If we compare the civil duty of allegiance with the moral duty of fidelity we are led to ask, with Hume:

> What necessity, therefore, is there to found the duty of *allegiance* or obedience to magistrates on that of *fidelity* or a regard to promises, or to suppose that it is the consent of each individual which subjects him to government, when it appears that both allegiance and fidelity stand precisely on the same foundation .... The obligation to allegiance being of like force or authority with the obligation to fidelity, we gain nothing by resolving the one into the other. The general interests or necessities of society are sufficient to establish both.

Everything rests ultimately on our recognition of the utility of government and our realization that *'society could not otherwise subsist'* (209).

There is nothing here that would be objectionable in principle to Hobbes. Hume is summarizing very briefly what Hobbes was trying to demonstrate at much greater length, as can be seen from this passage which follows Hume's introduction of moral obligation as exemplified in justice or fidelity.

> For as it is evident that every man loves himself better than any other person, he is naturally impelled to extend his acquisitions as much as possible; and nothing can restrain him in this propensity but reflection and experience, by which he learns the pernicious effects of that license and the total dissolution of society which

must ensue from it. His original inclination, therefore, or instinct, is here checked or restrained by a subsequent judgment or observation. (208)

What Hobbes set out to do was to encourage people to engage in that 'reflection' and learn from that 'experience' to which Hume refers, holding forth the danger of that 'total dissolution of society' if their inclinations were not 'checked and restrained'. In other words, the upheavals of the seventeenth century led Hobbes to exhort people to do what in the more placid eighteenth century, Hume merely assumed they had good reason for doing. This did not continue, however, since that century had a big surprise in store as it moved into its last decade and some of the ideas which shaped the French Revolution can be traced back to Rousseau's *Du Contrat Social*, published in 1762, only fourteen years after Hume's essay had appeared.

Even in its Lockean form, as criticized by Hume, contract had already played an extremely useful ideological role in the American Revolution. J. N. Figgis once wrote: 'Theories are taken up, as a rule, to quiet doubts that perplex supporters, rather than to answer opponents'.[2] The leaders of an uprising have to convince large numbers of potential supporters that what they want them to do is not really treasonable, by showing them they will be acting in defense of a legal right: in this case, that George III had broken his contract with them. The rest, who do not accept such arguments, can be taken care of by intimidation. Now it was precisely this sleight of hand, which turned vice into virtue, that Hobbes had attempted to expose over a century before the *Declaration of Independence* was penned.

Unfortunately Hume, whose own work shows evidence of Hobbes's influence both direct and indirect through Locke and Berkeley, apparently shared the unflattering view of many contemporaries. After noting in his *History of England* that Hobbes was much neglected at that time, he says: 'Hobbes's politics are fitted only to promote tyranny, and his ethics to encourage licentiousness'.[3] If he had not succumbed to the prevailing opinion, he might have seen the earlier philosopher as an ally. This is demonstrated in a most interesting paragraph near the end of his essay.

The only passage I meet with in antiquity, where the obligation of obedience to government is ascribed to a promise, is in Plato's

Crito; where Socrates refuses to escape from prison, because he had tacitly promised to obey the laws. Thus he builds a *Tory* consequence of passive obedience on a *Whig* foundation of the original contract. (214)

The last sentence describes exactly what Hobbes did, if one allows for the fact that these party labels were not in use at the time. As has been noted many times, Hobbes turned the idea of consent against his opponents by showing how it could be used to support obedience rather than rebellion. Although he was accused of defending absolutism and tyranny, he was really attempting to justify the status quo, which was precisely what Hume was engaged in doing.

However, since Hume rejects the concept of contract entirely and Hobbes does not, it is necessary to see exactly where the difference lies. The contract that was put forward by Locke and his predecessors, most importantly the monarchomachs of the French Religious Wars, was an agreement between people and ruler. Although often referred to as a contract of government, it is in practice not a true bilateral type of contract at all, but more like a contract of employment, in which the ruler is the employee and can be dismissed if he does not perform to the satisfaction of his employer, the people. The obligation the people have to obey the sovereign is a conditional one, which can be revoked at any time. An example of the sort of ruler implied in this contract is the *podestà*, who was hired by medieval Italian city-states to run their affairs for as long as he could please his paymasters. When it was applied to a seventeenth-century hereditary monarchy, it could only be seen as revolutionary in nature, and a constant threat to public order. Of course, by the same token it had great appeal to those who desired change and needed to clothe that change in the garments of apparent legality. However, its power to convince depended very much on the willingness of its followers to believe what they wanted to believe, regardless of the facts, since, as Hume and, much earlier, Filmer, had shown, the facts were against it. Although Locke was very good at ridiculing Filmer's patriarchalism, he largely ignored the latter's quite effective criticism of consent theory insofar as it applied to a ruler or change of ruler. The truth was that the people were rarely if ever consulted even by those who professed to believe in this theory. As Hume pointed out, the change of monarch in the Glorious Revolution, with which Locke was associated, was decided by about

700 of the 10 million or so inhabitants. This discrepancy is significant because, despite the difficulties and confusions in Locke's thought, there is a pervading emphasis on the overwhelming importance of consent as something freely and expressly given or withdrawn, by each individual. If this requirement were taken literally, there was not one regime of any size in the world which could demonstrate its legitimacy. As it stood, it was a recipe for perpetual revolution. This was doubtless not Locke's intention. But if we do not require the consent of every single person, then whose consent are we talking about? This points to the fatal flaw of Locke's type of contract theory, namely its inability or unwillingness to define 'the people' in a satisfactory way. Exactly who are 'the people' who have the right to depose a sovereign? For many of Locke's associates, if not for Locke himself, it would appear that the Whig magnates who dominated English politics in the eighteenth century were the people; although few in number they could be interpreted as speaking on behalf of all the inhabitants. However, this does make something of a mockery of the notion of consent as a meaningful, individual act of choice. What this contract theory amounted to, in reality, was the defense of the rights of an aristocracy as against a monarchy. The sixteenth-century French writers were quite honest about this: the right of resistance lay in the hands of the 'inferior magistrates' or, in other words, the leading men of the kingdom. The most famous of the Huguenot monarchomach writings, the *Vindiciae Contra Tyrannos* (1579) awarded the right of resistance to persons of accepted status, acting on behalf of the estates and other traditional corporate bodies. Fear of mob rule forbade any resistance on the part of individuals, as such, who were to content themselves with tears and prayers. This made practical sense, since opposition, to be at all effective, had to be led by persons who were already public figures and had a power base on which to build.

Such was certainly the case in England in 1688. However, Locke goes far beyond the *Vindiciae* in the direction of individualism. His statement that 'No one can be . . . subjected to the political power of another, without his own *consent*'[4] is clear enough but exactly how it could be achieved in practice is not. Suppose, for example, that there had been many Englishmen who were no happier being ruled by a Whig oligarchy than a Stuart king. They could certainly claim, with justice, that they had not given their consent to the new system. How would they have gone about freeing themselves from the rule of the great landowners who controlled not only the

House of Lords but indirectly the House of Commons as well? Merely to ask the question is to show how ludicrous the concept of individual consent at this level is, both in theory and in possible practice. Even the American Revolution, which could claim a much broader base of popular participation than that of 1688 resulted in what, to the lower classes, must have appeared largely a change in ruling elites. Those who felt they were free to withdraw their consent *after* the Revolution were in for a rude awakening. When mountaineers in western Pennsylvania objected to the Excise Act of 1791 and talked about another declaration of independence, George Washington called out 15,000 militia and the Whisky Rebellion was quickly crushed.

Returning to the earlier question, what effect does all this have on the credibility of Hobbes's notion of contract? To begin with, of course, his is a social contract which is concerned with the agreement of individuals to participate in a group or community. If human beings were angels and had no conflicting interests, the next step would probably not be necessary, but given human nature as it is, some mechanism needs to be set up to protect those who are prepared to play by the rules against those who are not. For large groups, this is the state, but some form of order needs to be established for smaller groups and even the family needs a final authority to settle disputes that arise within it. The big difference between Hobbes and most of the other contract theorists is that in his case the arrangement between people and sovereign is not conditional. We have to assume that it was intended to be permanent and therefore, there is no legal way of denying obedience to the sovereign power, whether it be an absolute monarchy or a pure democracy. This is due to the nature of sovereignty, which will be examined later.

However, the question has only been partially answered. One of Hume's criticisms is that a contract is superfluous, since there is usually a sense of allegiance based on an awareness that government is both useful and necessary. He was referring, of course, to the contract of government but it could also apply to the social contract. At that level one could again say that belonging to a group is natural as is following the group's customs and mores. However, Hume tells us why people usually do what society expects of them rather than why they *should* do so, except that it is useful to them. Hobbes believes this also, as we pointed out, but at a time of civil war when people were not behaving normally and when both

King and Parliament were competing for their allegiance, another approach was called for. This consisted of going further back, by emphasizing the relationship of individuals with each other as well as their relationship with their government.

It should be evident from the first part of this work that I think the kind of consent implicit in the social contract is a more meaningful and a more realistic notion than that which is required by Locke's contract. In fact, consent is a vital part of Hobbes's moral system, as I have interpreted it, since that is what is required to tie each individual person into the network of moral obligations without which society would not be possible. While, as Hume observes, it is hardly possible for more than a very few to withdraw their consent by physically leaving a territory the ruler of which is not to their taste, we always have the option of withholding consent to the moral agreement by refusing to honour it. In other words we retain the freedom to be immoral or antisocial, if we so decide, and the genuineness of this choice is apparent whenever we look around us at the behaviour of our fellows and, to be honest, at times of ourselves. Of course there is usually a price to be paid but that is part of the arrangement also.

One other point which needs to be touched on is whether, after all, there is not a kind of contract of government in Hobbes. We have downplayed the contract of submission made directly with a conqueror in return for one's life, as not reflecting adequately the various factors at work. But even in the commonwealth by institution, is there not an implicit contract with the ruler? If we choose him to provide us with security then surely he is under an obligation to do so. There is some truth in this but a hypothetical contract may not be the best way to express it. As I mentioned above, it is in the interest of a sovereign to preserve order internally and to protect his territory from foreign invasion. If he does not do this he will fall, and his subjects will be free to seek a new ruler. The situation is one that would not be altered by having a contract and would not be explained by imagining one. With Hobbes, a contract of government would indeed be superfluous.

12
Sovereign and Subject

In Chapter 18 of *Leviathan* Hobbes discussed the rights of sovereigns by institution. There he lists a dozen rights annexed to sovereignty. These are carefully summarized in Chapter 20 which covers commonwealth by acquisition:

> But the rights and consequences of sovereignty, are the same in both. His power cannot, without his consent, be transferred to another: he cannot forfeit it; he cannot be accused by any of his subjects, of injury: he cannot be punished by them; he is judge of what is necessary for peace; and judge of doctrines: he is sole legislator; and supreme judge of controversies; and of the times, and occasions of war, and peace: to him it belongeth to choose magistrates, counsellors, commanders, and all other officers, and ministers; and to determine of rewards, and punishments, honour, and order. (186, 252)

At the end of his original discussion he adds:

> This great authority being indivisible, and inseparably annexed to the sovereignty, there is little ground for the opinion of them, that say of sovereign kings, though they be *singulis majores*, of greater power than every one of their subjects, yet they be *universis minores*, of less power than them all together. For if by *all together*, they mean not the collective body as one person, then *all together*, and *every one*, signify the same; and the speech is absurd. But if by *all together*, they understand them as one person, which person the sovereign bears, then the power of all together, is the same with the sovereign's power; and so again the speech is absurd: which absurdity they see well enough, when the sovereignty is in an assembly of people; but in a monarch they see it not; and yet the power of sovereignty is the same in whomever it be placed. (168,237)

His use of sovereignty in an assembly to prove his point is highly revealing since it not only shows that his sovereign does not have to be a monarch, as some critics still seem to believe, but also that his concept of sovereignty can actually be more convincing when it is not linked to monarchy. In any case, the individual, by authorizing the sovereign to act on his behalf, must regard the sovereign as a kind of alter ego. This is why he cannot complain of injury in a legal sense from his sovereign since he would be accusing himself. The implication of all this is clear:

> So that it appeareth plainly, to my understanding, both from reason, and Scripture, that the sovereign power, whether placed in one man, as in a monarchy, or in one assembly of men, as in popular, and aristocratical commonwealths, is as great, as possibly men can be imagined to make it. And though of so unlimited a power, men may fancy many evil consequences, yet the consequences of the want of it, which is perpetual war of every man against his neighbour, are much worse. (194, 260)

Or, as he puts it in *De Cive*: 'But that power, greater than which cannot by men be conveyed on a man, we call absolute' (DC,VI,13).

In a footnote to this sentence which, like other footnotes in *De Cive*, can be seen as a response to criticisms of the first Latin edition, he is somewhat defensive about monarchy. Referring to a popular state he says: 'For in the gathering together of many men, they acknowledge the face of the city; and even the unskilful understand, that matters there are ruled by a council. Yet monarchy is no less a city than democracy . . . ' He adds shortly thereafter: 'But it appears not to most men how a city is contained in the person of a king; and therefore they object against absolute command . . . ' (DC,VI,13n.). It is clear that he had already been exposed to this type of criticism, which has been repeated ever since. His answer is always the same. In *Leviathan*, after noting that people may object to exposing themselves to 'the lusts, and irregular passions of him, or them that have so unlimited a power in their hands', he adds that by attributing all the inconveniences of being ruled to the kind of government under which they live, they ignore the fact that the power is the same in all cases, if it is enough to protect them. Again, he refuses to make a distinction between monarchy, aristocracy and democracy.

At the end of this paragraph there is an optical metaphor which sums up the attitude that Hobbes is trying to overcome.

> For all men are by nature provided of notable multiplying glasses, that is their passions and self-love, through which, every little payment appeareth a great grievance; but are destitute of those prospective glasses, namely moral and civil science, to see afar off the miseries that hang over them, and cannot without such payments be avoided. (170, 239)

In the next chapter he goes on to discuss the only three kinds of commonwealth. He deliberately excludes any, others.

> There be other names of government, in the histories, and books of policy; as *tyranny*, and *oligarchy*: but they are not the names of other forms of government, but of the same forms misliked. For they that are discontented under *monarchy*, call it *tyranny*; and they that are displeased with *aristocracy*, call it *oligarchy*: so also, they which find themselves grieved under a *democracy*, call it *anarchy*, which signifies want of government; and yet I think no man believes, that want of government, is any new kind of government: nor by the same reason ought they to believe, that the government is of one kind, when they like it, and another, when they mislike it, or are oppressed by the governors. (171, 239)

In doing this he is endeavouring to prevent value judgments from being built into the names. These should be neutral and used merely to inform us whether rule is by one, the few, or the many.

Thus men in 'absolute liberty' may appoint any one of the three to be their representative, including a monarch. However, if a sovereign already exists, they are unable to choose again, because that would create two sovereign powers which would lead back to a state of war. Yet again he uses popular government as the most convincing example:

> And therefore as it is absurd, to think that a sovereign assembly, inviting the people of their dominion, to send up their deputies, with power to make known their advice, or desires, should therefore hold such deputies, rather than themselves, for the absolute representatives of the people: so it is absurd also, to think the same in a monarchy. (172, 240)

The system in place must be accepted and if the sovereign is a monarch he must make sure his subjects understand that he, and not a body such as Parliament which he called on for advice from time to time, was their true representative. Hobbes, thus, blamed the Civil War ultimately on the king for permitting this confusion to arise. He emphasizes that there is no difference in the amount of power possessed by each of the three types of commonwealth but there is in the 'convenience or aptitude to produce the peace, and security of the people; for which end they were instituted' (173, 241). He personally believes that monarchy is the best but in the Preface to *De Cive* he is careful to point out that this is the 'one thing alone I confess in this whole book not to be demonstrated, but only probably stated'. However, he does believe strongly that 'where the public and private interests are most closely united, there is the public most advanced' and since the two are found together in a monarchy, it is preferable to the other two (173, 241). Furthermore, one person has greater freedom of action than a group. Even if he has a weakness for favourites and flatterers, this problem is but multiplied in an assembly.

There are some hybrid versions which Hobbes shows can be reduced to the three principal types. Both elective monarchy and so-called limited monarchy are really either democracies or aristocracies, depending on the assembly which elects or limits the ruler. Similarly a province conquered by a democracy or aristocracy and ruled by a governor or procurator has a monarchical system since its own people have no direct voice in its affairs. This accords with his rejection of divided sovereignty. Because final authority must rest somewhere, any talk of limited monarchy is nonsense. If the king is dependent on an assembly, then it is the latter body which is ultimately sovereign. An example of this, of course, was the dispute between King and Parliament which preoccupied England during the seventeenth century, and which ended only when the monarch accepted the sovereignty of Parliament.

Despite his preference for it, Hobbes admits a possible weakness in monarchy: the question of succession. Where the new ruler is an infant or mentally incapable, a protector or council of regency will normally be appointed. If trouble does arise, 'it is to be attributed, not to the monarchy, but to the ambition, and injustice of the subjects' (176, 244). Furthermore, he believes that commonwealths in which the sovereignty lies with an assembly are no better off. In times of great danger they, too, 'have need of *custodes libertatis*; that is of dictators or protectors of their authority' (177, 245).

However, there remains the larger problem of succession in

general. Inasmuch as all men are mortal, arrangements have to be made for 'an artificial eternity of life' (180, 247). Since members of assemblies can be replaced by election, Hobbes admits that this weakness is confined to monarchies, where it is not always clear who has the right to appoint a successor. The only alternatives seem to be, either that the reigning monarch has that right, or it reverts to the dissolved multitude. As the latter would mean a return to the state of nature which the monarchy was instituted to avoid, Hobbes concludes that the present possessor of the crown has the right to dispose of it as he sees fit. If he has not made his intentions evident in writing or speech, then it will be necessary to fall back on custom or, that failing, his closest relative, on the assumption that natural affection would have governed his choice. On the other hand, what if he has made his wishes known but has chosen a foreigner to succeed him? Hobbes replies that although this might be inconvenient, it is no less lawful than having the crown go to a stranger as a result of a marriage connection with a foreign family.

It is obvious that Hobbes has tried to make the best of a bad business here. Despite the superiority of monarchical rule in some respects, human mortality creates a problem of continuity which is largely absent in the case of rule by an assembly. In attempting to cope with it, he introduces a number of assumptions which are not at all convincing. It is true that if the people agree to submit to an absolute monarch, his right to choose a successor is unquestionable, but if it is not possible to transfer his authority smoothly to a competent heir, capable of taking effective power immediately, practical difficulties arise even within the parameters of Hobbes's model. A reliance on custom, for example, introduces at a crucial moment an uncertainty which undermines the advantages of one man rule. Furthermore, even if the succession is clear enough, a minor heir or a series of short reigns can put a heavy strain on the system. The situation in France following the death of Henry II in the previous century, indicates that even in a country where absolute monarchy was widely accepted, it can by no means guarantee stability. In that example, the throne was occupied by a succession of three weak kings with policy often being made by their mother, Catherine de Medicis, a foreigner. Admittedly religious conflict compounded the difficulties of governing the country but the chief culprit for decades of anarchy and civil war was the failure of hereditary monarchy to produce a strong ruler. It is a better test case than England in Hobbes's time because the principle of absolutism itself was not challenged by a powerful enemy like Parliament. The great advantage possessed by a monarch, his freedom to act quickly and decisively, was nullified by the vagaries of heredity. Others had to fill in the gap and preserve the state but there is no provision for them in the Hobbesian model.

While it is true that Hobbes did not claim to have demonstrated conclusively the superiority of monarchy, the problem of continuity is so serious that it raises the question of whether it has any claim at all to superiority. In an attempt to overcome this handicap, he has to smuggle in assumptions about rules of succession which undermine the straightforward simplicity which is its major attraction. The truth is that his tendency to think of sovereignty as best embodied in absolute monarchy does a serious disservice to his own theory. Since it is his theory we are interested in and not merely his personal preferences, we should be prepared to look more seriously at the other two forms of sovereignty, which he never denies are just as legitimate.

In all fairness, we should also acknowledge that Hobbes's bias in forms of monarchy was quite justified in his own day. As usual he was trying to be realistic. Anyone glancing at a map of Europe in 1648 will see empires, kingdoms, principalities, duchies, etc., whose rulers were more or less absolute. This applied also to lands controlled by princes of the Church, who were elected for life. The rest were city-states governed by oligarchies, but most of these were quite small. The only one which had to be taken seriously was the United Provinces which, although not big in territory, was a major power because of its seaborne empire and lucrative trade. However, it was the exception which proved the rule, since all the other large states were monarchies, in most cases absolute. Where the authority of the ruler was questioned, the country was vulnerable to disorder. France had only recently emerged from civil war, which now engulfed England. The Holy Roman Empire had just been fragmented by the Thirty Years' War, leaving its elected ruler a figurehead, whereas its Hapsburg emperors had few problems in the central European lands which they ruled as absolute hereditary princes. The Polish nobles, who permitted only a weak elected king, were destined to see their homeland dismantled and absorbed by its powerful neighbours. In other words, the alternatives available when Hobbes wrote seemed to be absolute monarchy or anarchy and dissolution. This was only confirmed by what was happening in England while he was writing. Parliament managed to defeat

Charles but, rendered impotent by factionalism, was pushed aside by its military commander, Oliver Cromwell, a man who was to enjoy more unlimited power than most kings. Is it any wonder then, that Hobbes saw absolute monarchy as the only serious contender for the exercise of sovereignty?

This was certainly true in his own day, and it remained true for Europe in general for the next century and a half at least. In fact, the age of absolutism was just dawning for many countries as they emerged from the feudal stage. Unfortunately for Hobbes, however, the one state for which this was not true, was his own. While remaining a monarchy in name, England underwent a constitutional change which gradually shifted real power into the hands of Parliament. His opponents seemed to be right after all; limited monarchy and divided sovereignty now appeared not only preferable but also possible. Already seen by his critics as an atheist, an immoralist, a defender of tyranny and an enemy of freedom, Hobbes was now regarded as the advocate of a political theory which was outmoded and, of course, wrong. This assessment, minus some of the shock and outrage associated with the epithet 'Hobbist', is, rather surprisingly, still accepted by many commentators today.

What is forgotten is that his theory provided for what actually occurred. When James II fled England, he gave up the power to protect his subjects – the essence of sovereignty – and he could quite legitimately be replaced. Although William III became king, real power was now in the hands of Parliament, an assembly dominated by the aristocracy. There was nothing inimical to Hobbesian theory in this. Aristocracy was one of his three forms of sovereignty. What he would not accept was that England had remained a monarchy in the true sense of the word itself. As he said repeatedly, if the king was dependent on an aristocratic council, then sovereignty was held by the aristocracy. The monarch became more and more a ceremonial head of state, retaining the useful function of providing continuity through changes of government, but he or she was not a sovereign as Hobbes defined one.

The same would have been true if England had become, at that time, a democracy as it is now. But such a development was not possible in the seventeenth century; it took more than two centuries of gradual evolution to get there. To think of Hobbes as anti-democratic, as many critics do today, is an exaggeration of his position, which can only be understood if one takes a good look at the word. In its purest form it is an ideal which has rarely, if ever, been fulfilled in practice. The most influential example of an actual democracy, the one that thinkers usually had in mind until recent times, was ancient Athens. As a translator of Thucydides, Hobbes was especially aware of the weaknesses of Athenian democracy. The demagoguery which led to the disasters of the Peloponnesian wars and the condemnation of Socrates left an unfavourable impression of popular rule in the minds of later generations. Despite the obvious greatness of Athens, its citizens were actually a minority, outnumbered by slaves and resident foreigners, and much of the wealth lavished on architecture and sculpture was extracted from an empire ruled with a heavy hand.

But the chief weakness of democracies in the eyes of many of their critics was a practical one: they failed to last. This was the lesson that was drawn from the relatively short-lived Athenian experiment, and the ultimate breakdown of the Roman republic after a century of internal conflict. The latter illustrated another failing: democracy seemed to be feasible only for small states. As Rome acquired an empire the strains of administering such a large area were beyond the capabilities of a popular government. The picture of democracy that remained from the ancient world was one of quarrelling factions swayed this way and that by what Hobbes called 'an aristocracy of orators', one which favoured mediocrity over excellence. An example of the latter was the Athenian institution of ostracism which allowed citizens to exile for ten years anyone considered dangerous to the state. Too often, however, it seemed to be used against outstanding men such as Themistocles, the victor of Salamis and, an example mentioned by Hobbes, Aristides the Just, supposedly because people tired of hearing him called 'the Just'.

The reputation of democracy in the seventeenth century then, was such that it was not considered a practical option. One must remember also that the term usually meant active and continuous participation by the people in their own government, something that was possible only in a territory small enough to allow them to assemble often without the inconvenience of travelling long distances. The problem of size was crucial. Hobbes believed, along with many others, that such small states could exist only until a more powerful neighbour decided to swallow them up. The large modern democratic states are not democracies in that sense of the word and to draw the conclusion that Hobbes would be opposed to them is quite unfair. He can be quoted to the contrary. In *De Cive* he says:

> But if the people in a democracy would bestow the power of deliberating in matters of war and peace, either on one, or some very few, being content with the nomination of magistrates and public ministers, that is to say, with the authority without the ministration, then it must be confessed, that in this particular democracy and monarchy would be equal. (DC,X,15)

If we extend the power of deliberation beyond war and peace, which presents no difficulty, this is a blueprint for the large-scale representative democracy of today.

Much of the misunderstanding about what Hobbes meant is due to the period in which he wrote. The modern centralized state had been gradually emerging from the welter of competing jurisdictions which characterized medieval Christendom. This process moved forward rapidly in the sixteenth century and was being completed in a number of countries in the seventeenth century. In these states more and more power was being concentrated in the hands of the ruler at the expense of the Church and the forces of particularism, especially the feudal nobility. The Reformation, of course, played a part in the wars of the time, but religious differences were often the external garb of political ones. For example, in France, elements hostile to the centralizing forces of the time such as the regional nobility, especially from the south, were well represented among the Huguenots. One of the products of the French Civil Wars was Jean Bodin's theory of sovereignty, which provided a rationale for the unprecedented amount of power which accrued to the ruler of the new all-encompassing state.

The same kind of situation in England prompted a similar response from Hobbes three-quarters of a century after the appearance of Bodin's *Six Livres de la Republique*. However, the situation in England was not as conducive to a defense of sovereignty as that in France had been. In France and elsewhere the representative bodies which had sprung up in the Middle Ages never achieved the stature and independence that Parliament enjoyed in England. As a result, they did not have the authority possessed by Parliament to challenge their kings over who was to control the state. Only in England was this possible, and even there, Parliament failed on its first try in the 1640s. James II's unwillingness to compromise gave it a second opportunity and allowed the parliamentary leaders to import a king who was willing to accept curtailed powers. The way in which the great landowners and their associates achieved effective control of the state under the guise of a limited monarchy was to be a source of confusion about the true nature of sovereignty which continues, at least in Anglo-American political thought, to this very day. The apparent separation of powers, which impressed Montesquieu and influenced the founding fathers in America, was seen as proof that divided sovereignty could exist. Furthermore, since constitutional change in England had taken place as a struggle against the rule of an absolute monarch, it was easy to draw from this the conclusion that absolute sovereignty of any form was objectionable and that anyone who defended it was an enemy of liberty. Thus Hobbes, in a sense, fell victim to the conjunction of two major developments which occurred during the century in which he lived: the emergence of the fully sovereign modern state and the final victory of Parliament over the Crown in England. His attempt to found a science of politics could easily be regarded instead as an apology for an absolutism which had been successfully vanquished by the forces of freedom.

Since so much hangs on the word 'absolute', it is important to learn what limits, if any, Hobbes placed on the sovereign power. He discussed this question in Chapter 21 of *Leviathan*, 'Of the Liberty of Subjects', and Chapter 30, 'Of the Office of the Sovereign Representative'. In the first, he begins by defining liberty or freedom as the absence of opposition, by which he means 'external impediments to motion' (196, 261). This extremely broad definition, when applied to living creatures, means that they lack freedom only when imprisoned by walls or restrained by chains. A freeman, thus, is one who is not hindered from doing those actions of which he is mentally and physically capable. Fear and liberty are not inconsistent. A man who pays his taxes for fear of punishment is acting freely; there is always physical liberty to disobey the law. As for free-will, Hobbes says that we can infer nothing from the use of the word except the liberty of a man to follow his will, desire or inclination without hindrance. It is consistent with necessity, in the sense that if we knew the sequence of cause and effect leading back to God, the first cause, we would see the element of necessity in our actions. To deny it is to deny the liberty of God, without whom we would not have those appetites and passions which motivate our actions. In other words, we are free to operate within the context of our appetites but they themselves are already built in.

Natural liberty must be distinguished from the liberty of subjects. Once men have established a commonwealth, they are bound by 'artificial chains, called *civil laws*', which, although weak, 'may nevertheless be made to hold, by the danger, though not the difficulty of breaking them'. In all activities about which the law is silent, a very large number in most states, men have the liberty of subjects.

> For if we take liberty in the proper sense for corporal liberty; that is to say, freedom from chains and prison; it were very absurd for men to clamour as they do for the liberty they so manifestly enjoy. Again, if we take liberty, for an exemption from laws, it is no less absurd, for men to demand, as they do, that liberty, by which all other men may be masters of their lives. (199, 264)

However, the fact that every subject has authorized every action of the sovereign still means that nothing the sovereign does to a subject can be considered unjust to that subject, even though it may be a violation of a law of nature. Here again he does not draw his example from a monarchy but from Athens – the use of ostracism.

Hobbes goes on to distinguish two other meanings of the word liberty which cause confusion. One refers to the freedom which a commonwealth possesses by not being subject to another one. This liberty is the same as that of a man in the state of nature, i.e. to wage war on others. In this sense all commonwealths are equally free. The other meaning is, in his eyes, a form of deception. This is the idea fostered by Aristotle, Cicero and other Greek and Roman authors, that only the inhabitants of popular commonwealths, like their own, are genuinely free. Hobbes merely repeats what he says many times elsewhere: freedom does not depend on the form of the commonwealth since there is no immunity from the service of any of them.

Before specifying which things commanded by the sovereign a subject may refuse, without injustice, to do, Hobbes refers back to the act of submission in a passage from which we have quoted before.

> For in the act of our *submission*, consisteth both our *obligation*, and our *liberty*; which must therefore be inferred by arguments taken from thence; there being no obligation on any man, which ariseth not from some act of his own; for all men equally, are by nature free. (203, 268)

This really expresses the essence of Hobbes's political philosophy. Liberty and obligation are the two sides of the same coin; you cannot have one without the other. It is the obligation on the part of a subject to obey the sovereign which creates the liberty that can flow only from the security acquired by imposing the same obligation on all the other subjects. This is done either by express words of authorization or 'from the end of the institution of sovereignty, namely the peace of the subjects within themselves, and their defence against a common enemy' (203, 268). In the latter case we are to infer an intention to submit founded on the obvious benefits we derive from the situation.

The principal liberty of the subject is based on the position taken earlier by Hobbes, that agreements not to defend one's own body are void. Therefore, any order to do something that would result in one's own death or maiming can be disobeyed. Self-preservation is, of course, the original motive for the contract and the right to it cannot be surrendered, but Hobbes appears to go much further here by adding the right of refusing to kill another person. This has been seen as a limitation on the power of the sovereign which undermines Hobbes's whole argument. However, Hobbes immediately qualifies this liberty by specifying that the sovereign's command 'to execute any dangerous or dishonourable office' can only be disobeyed if the ends for which the commonwealth was instituted are not thereby frustrated. What he has in mind here is made much clearer by a passage in *De Cive*.

> Nor if he [the sovereign] command to execute a parent, whether he be innocent, or guilty, and condemned by the law, since there are others who, being commanded, will do that, and a son will rather die, than live infamous and hated of all the world. There are many other cases, in which, since the commands are shameful to be done by some, and not by others, obedience may, by right, be performed by these, and refused by those; and this, without breach of that absolute right which was given to the chief ruler. For in no case is the right taken away from him, of slaying those who shall refuse to obey him. But they who thus kill men, although by right, given them from him that hath it, yet if they use that right otherwise than right reason requires, they sin against the laws of nature, that is, against God. (DC,VI,13)

This addresses the issue in dispute quite directly. A man cannot even be imagined to have made a covenant which would require him to do something that he would rather die than do. This is one of the times Hobbes makes clear that while the desire for self-preservation is strong and dependable enough to be utilized as the foundation of the commonwealth, it is not necessary to assume that man has no other values which can, at times, outweigh the fear of death. As we have seen, one is always free to disobey the sovereign's orders but one can only rightfully do so in certain very specific situations such as where, for example, it is a matter of patricide. The sovereign power is not diminished as long as someone else, who has not the excuse of being a son, is available to carry out the order and it would be a very unusual state which could not produce many such persons.

But, the objector will ask, when we let a subject decide whether or not he will obey a command, are we not letting in the right of private judgment which Hobbes has taken some pains to exclude? In order for this question to be answered satisfactorily, it must first be recognized that Hobbes had to walk a fine line between giving the sovereign enough authority to do the job on the one hand, and on the other, giving him so much that there would be no incentive for the individual to submit. If the covenant called for me to be willing to kill a member of my own family or a close friend, I might well prefer the hazards of the state of nature. While it is true that Hobbes was opposed, in general, to allowing conscience to be put ahead of one's duty to the sovereign (311, 365) he was thinking of its use as a pretext for rebellion rather than as a reason for passive disobedience. The right of private judgment has to be retained at that level because the moral law, whether one thinks of it as the law of nature or the law of God, must come first for the individual. The whole purpose of the social contract is to establish an environment where it is safe to act morally. This is confirmed in his summary at the end of Part II of those things he believes he has proved which includes this item: 'that subjects owe to their sovereigns, simple obedience, in all things wherein their obedience is not repugnant to the laws of God' (343, 395). There is, however, one situation in which the right of private judgment can be justifiably disallowed and that, mentioned above, is where it frustrates the end for which the sovereignty was granted, i.e., where it threatens the internal or external security of the commonwealth.

An example of this, of course, is during a war, although even here Hobbes makes exceptions. It is precisely at this crucial moment that he has to be extremely careful because the contract rests, after all, on man's fear of death. If, when ordered to fight, a man's 'natural timorousness' causes him to avoid battle or to run away, he will be acting dishonourably but not unjustly, so long as it is cowardice and not treachery. Hobbes's concern here as before is with maintaining the integrity of his argument. If the individual is assumed to have covenanted because of his fear of death, one cannot then blame him for acting on the basis of this fear in situations of great danger. However, there are two occasions when he cannot rightfully refuse to obey. One is if he has enlisted voluntarily. In this case he has freely undertaken an obligation and has no excuse if he deserts. The other is if the defence of the commonwealth requires the service of all those capable of bearing arms, since the institution of a commonwealth is pointless if those who benefit from it lack the courage to preserve it.

These arguments illustrate the careful distinctions Hobbes has to make in order to support his rationale for the Leviathan. His effort is wasted on some critics who cannot see anything more than self-interest and fear of death in their crudest forms as the basis of his system. It is incomprehensible to them that a man may have to die fighting for a sovereign power, to which he is supposed to have submitted in order to avoid death. As a result Hobbes's theory appears to them contradictory and unconvincing. What they do not seem to recognize is that when a man risks his life defending his commonwealth, he is only doing for a relatively brief period what he would be doing every day of his nasty, brutish and short life in the state of nature. That it is a profitable tradeoff is indicated by the peaceful lives led by inhabitants of most states even in quite strife-ridden times. It is, of course, never in one's short-term interest to have to face enemy fire but that is the risk one must run in return for the long-term benefits. The covenant involves a delicate balance between self-interest and self-sacrifice. Entering into it is somewhat like joining the army: you are in for the duration, not just until the shooting starts.

The liberty to refuse to kill someone under the conditions specified by Hobbes does not extend to protecting others. 'To resist the sword of the commonwealth, in defence of another man, guilty, or innocent, no man hath liberty; because such liberty takes away from the sovereign, the means of protecting us.' However, Hobbes makes an exception which has bothered some of his critics. If a man is one of a number who have rebelled or committed some crime punishable by death, then he can assist his fellows because 'they but defend their lives, which the guilty man may do, as the innocent' (205, 270). Although the original acts were unjust, further acts undertaken to defend themselves are not unjust, unless they have received an offer of pardon. Hobbes's logic can lead him to some strange conclusions but this is merely another example of the right of self-defense, which is a cornerstone of his system.

The broadest liberty of a subject lies in the silence of the law which, of course, may vary from time to time according to the discretion of the sovereign. However, there is one occasion when the subject's rights are clear and definite.

> The obligation of subjects to the sovereign, is understood to last as long, and no longer, than the power lasteth, by which he is able to protect them. For the right men have by nature to defend themselves, when none else can protect them, can by no covenant be relinquished. The sovereignty is the soul of the commonwealth; which once departed from the body, the members do no more receive their motion from it. The object of obedience is protection . . .

In this same passage Hobbes recognizes the harsh reality against which all his political writings are directed but which, nevertheless, must be faced.

> And though sovereignty, in the intention of them that make it, be immortal; yet is it in its own nature, not only subject to violent death, by foreign war; but also through the ignorance, and passions of man, it hath in it, from the very institution, many seeds of a natural mortality, by intestine discord. (208, 272)

Since the latter occurred three times during Hobbes's life, with Charles I, then Parliament, and finally the Commonwealth failing in turn as sovereigns, it is no wonder that he was not concerned about the sovereign's power being excessive.

The other section of *Leviathan* which is mentioned above as being especially relevant to Hobbes's conception of the nature of sovereignty is Chapter 30, 'Of the Office of the Sovereign Representative', which commences with a definition.

> The OFFICE of the sovereign, be it a monarch or an assembly, consisteth in the end, for which he was trusted with the sovereign power, namely the procuration of *the safety of the people*; to which

he is obliged by the law of nature, and to render an account thereof to God, the author of that law, and to none but him. But by safety here, is not meant a bare preservation, but also other contentments of life, which every man by lawful industry, without danger, or hurt to the commonwealth, shall acquire to himself. (322, 376)

Because he cannot do what he should without the necessary power, the sovereign must retain his rights in full and never relinquish or transfer them. Furthermore, it is his duty to inform the people as to the grounds of sovereignty so that they will not easily be led astray. Education is important because sovereign rights 'cannot be maintained by any civil law or terror of legal punishment' (323, 377). A civil law forbidding rebellion is not obligatory as a civil law but only as it reflects the law of nature forbidding breach of faith. If men do not understand the foundation of obedience in the law of nature they will regard punishment as an act of hostility rather than as a corrective. Hobbes makes clear here how the whole apparatus of state power relies for its legitimacy on the *understanding* as well as the *consent* of the people; if they do not realize how their consent binds them by the law of nature, they obviously will not feel bound. Despite his relentless emphasis on the power required by the sovereign, Hobbes is aware that in the end it all rests on an acceptance which can only be achieved by persuasion and education.

To those who say that the vulgar lack the capacity to understand these principles, Hobbes replies that the problem lies not with the intelligence but with the interests of those who are to learn. 'Potent men, digest hardly any thing that setteth up a power to bridle their affections; and learned men, anything that discovereth their errors, and thereby lesseneth their authority' (325, 379). The minds of the common people, on the contrary, are like 'clean paper' which will receive what they are to be taught. Here, as in many other places, Hobbes indicates that it is not the masses, but the privileged classes against whom his arguments are directed. It is they who are likely to lead the ordinary people astray, unless the latter are properly instructed. A policy of providing such instruction is not just the sovereign's duty but it is also in his interest since it provides security from the threat of rebellion.

One of the many specific suggestions Hobbes makes is that people should be taught not to love the form of government of a neighbouring country more than their own. With the United Provinces probably in mind he says:

> For the prosperity of a people ruled by an aristocratical, or democratical assembly, cometh not from aristocracy, nor from democracy, but from the obedience, and concord of the subjects: nor do the people flourish in a monarchy, because one man has the right to rule them, but because they obey him. (326, 380)

Take away the obedience and any kind of commonwealth will dissolve. This emphasis on the significance of obedience points up the practical nature of Hobbes's concept of sovereignty. It is not the right to rule, as such, but the ability to obtain willing obedience that really counts in the end.

In addition to teaching his people about justice, the sovereign must be prepared to administer it fairly to high and low. Above all there should be no partiality towards the great since, 'Impunity maketh insolence; insolence, hatred; and hatred, an endeavour to pull down all oppressing and contumelious greatness, though with the ruin of the commonwealth'. The same applies to taxes but Hobbes would apply equality here not as a tax on wealth but as one on consumption so the commonwealth is not 'defrauded by the luxurious waste of private men' (333, 386). Those who are unable to work should not have to rely on private charity but should be provided for by the commonwealth. However, the able-bodied should be forced to labour, but since this can only be done if jobs are provided for them, Hobbes advocates active encouragement of all branches of the economy. If the poor still increase, they should be 'transplanted into countries not sufficiently inhabited; where nevertheless, they are not to exterminate those they find there'. This is followed by a brisk dose of Hobbesian realism: 'And when all the world is overcharged with inhabitants, then the last remedy of all is war, which provideth for every man, by victory or death' (335, 387).

Above all, the sovereign is responsible for providing good laws which Hobbes describes as 'needful, for the *good of the people*, and withal *perspicuous*', by which he means that they must be drafted so that their intent is clear. Whatever they are, they cannot be just or unjust. He uses the game metaphor again: 'It is in the laws of a commonwealth, as in the laws of gaming: whatsoever the gamesters agree on, is injustice to none of them'. The point of laws is not to limit people's freedom unnecessarily but to prevent them from hurting themselves by their own rashness. He likens them to hedges which are designed not to stop travellers but to keep them on the right path. Hobbes rejects the idea that a law can be good for the sovereign and not for the people. 'For the good of the sovereign and people, cannot be separated. It is a weak sovereign, that has weak subjects; and a weak people, whose sovereign wanteth power to rule them at his will' (335, 388).

The purpose of punishment is not revenge but correction and deterrence. The severest punishments should be for threats to the public well-being. In addition to those directed against the government he includes, 'those that spring from contempt of justice; those which provoke indignation in the multitude; and those, which unpunished, seem authorized, as when they are committed by sons, servants, or favourites of men in authority' (337, 389). On the other hand crimes proceeding from infirmity, great fear, great need, provocation or ignorance, are occasions for leniency. In civil disorders, it is the leaders who should be punished, not the 'poor seduced people'. To treat the latter severely is really to punish their ignorance, for which Hobbes largely blames the sovereign, who should have made sure that they knew better.

In an earlier chapter he had looked into the question of how the right of the sovereign to inflict punishment arose. It was not given to the sovereign by the subjects 'but only in laying down theirs, strengthened him to use his own, as he should think fit, for the preservation of them all' (297, 353). It has been suggested that Hobbes could have provided better justification through the use of authorization. However, he makes it quite clear that he does not want the right founded on any concession or gift because this might involve the surrender of the individual's own fundamental right to defend himself. Again, self-preservation must be given priority because of its importance to the system. This is in line with the real world; we refrain from taking the law into our own hands if the state is able to enforce it satisfactorily, but a plea of self-defense is usually allowable.

Hobbes makes a careful distinction between punishment and acts of hostility. Examples of the latter are when pain is inflicted without a public hearing, by a usurped power, without respect for future good, in excess of the prescribed penalty or where there is no law against the action. Any harm done to a subject in revolt, is also not restricted to punishment laid down by the law since he has put himself outside of the laws altogether. Punishment is for subjects, not enemies. It must never be used against the innocent.

> All punishments of innocent subjects, be they great or little, are against the law of nature; for punishment is only for transgression of the law, and therefore there can be no punishment of the innocent. It is therefore a violation, first of that law of nature, which forbiddeth all men, in their revenges, to look at any thing but some future good: for there can arrive no good to the commonwealth, by punishing the innocent. Secondly, of that, which forbiddeth ingratitude: for seeing all sovereign power, is originally given by the consent of every one of the subjects, to the end they should as long as they are obedient, be protected thereby; the punishment of the innocent, is a rendering of evil for good. And thirdly, of the law that commandeth equity; that is to say, an equal distribution of justice; which in punishing the innocent is not observed. (304, 359)

However, since there is no punishment in this world to deter the sovereign from these violations of natural law, how can such violation be prevented? The answer, of course, is that given the nature of sovereignty, nothing can be done within the judicial system that binds the subjects, but the differentiation that Hobbes has made between punishment and acts of hostility offers another way out, which will be considered later.

Returning to the duties of the sovereign, we find that Hobbes concludes a discussion of the choice of counsellors with the following:

> The best counsel, in those things that concern not other nations, but only the ease and benefit the subjects may enjoy, by laws that look only inward, is to be taken from the general information, and complaints of the people of each province, who are best acquainted with their own wants, and ought therefore, *when they demand nothing in the derogation of the essential rights of sovereignty*, to be diligently taken notice of. For without those essential rights, as I have often before said, the commonwealth cannot at all subsist. (341, 393; emphasis added)

This call for the sovereign to make himself aware of public opinion and to take account of it in his policy indicates Hobbes's awareness of the importance of a contented populace to the stability of a state.

Sovereign and Subject

The italicized words point up something we touched on above concerning passive disobedience. The subject is not expected to be a puppet whose every move is controlled by the sovereign; there are large areas in which he has freedom to act. In others, where he disagrees with the sovereign, there is a clear distinction between those that challenge the sovereignty and those that do not. Parliament itself arose as a channel whereby the people could make their wishes and complaints known to the king; this was very useful and constructive for everyone concerned until Parliament began to assume sovereign powers itself, something that no monarch could accept without a struggle.

In this chapter, as well as in other statements scattered through his writings, Hobbes tells the sovereign what his responsibilities are. Since he has consistently emphasized the enormous power which must be possessed by a sovereign in order for him to do what is required of him, there has been a tendency to underestimate the extent of his obligations. These have been brushed aside by many critics who believe that since people have no power to enforce them they are somewhat irrelevant. This ignores another fact emphasized by Hobbes, that sovereignty is also very fragile, in that it remains ultimately at the mercy of the people, the importance of whose role he not only never denied, but also insisted upon. Writing as he did at a time of civil war, he was obliged to devote more space to the rights of the sovereign than to his duties, and to the duties of the subject than his rights, but he knew only too well that if a sovereign did not act prudently, his days were numbered. Here, Hobbes was doing what Machiavelli had earlier done in much greater detail in *The Prince*: offering advice on how to remain in power. However, he is far less cynical; his recommendations would, in the business world, be called giving value for money. In the realm of politics, the sovereign should earn the support of his subjects by doing what he has been given his power to do, namely to protect the good and punish the wicked. Only by regarding his subjects' interests as his own would he be likely to survive in the long run.

13

Democracy and the Right of Revolution

Since sovereignty is often thought of as incompatible with democracy, I would like to look at this relationship in more detail. The fullest discussion of this subject by Hobbes is in *The Elements of Law*. There he says that of the three sorts of government, 'the first in order of time . . . is democracy, and it must be so of necessity, because an aristocracy and a monarchy, require nominations of persons agreed upon'. A democracy exists 'where the votes of the major part involve the votes of the rest' (EL,II,2,1). When a group of individuals covenant together to be bound by majority decisions, we have the creation of a commonwealth in which the people possess the sovereign power. When Hobbes says that democracy is first in time he means reconstructed time. Working back from our current political system to its genesis, we have to start with a democracy, if we accept Hobbes's assumptions about human motivations and the state of nature. This is the only way an absolute monarchy, for example, can be morally justified in his eyes. But it is also true that the smaller political structures out of which larger ones are built ultimately rest on the willingness of a group of individuals, especially the warriors, to put themselves under a leader and obey his commands. No matter how mighty a conqueror may appear, his strength largely depends on the motivation of his followers. This does not apply to subject peoples but it provides the strength to keep them in subjection, as in the case of the Spartans and their helots. Although he preferred monarchy, Hobbes was never in any doubt about the democratic base upon which it, like aristocracy, had to be built.

How, then, do these other types come into existence? If the people go no further at this stage, they remain a democracy but if, for any reason, they find this unsatisfactory, they can choose a class or an individual to take over the responsibility of ruling them. In the case of an aristocracy, here is what he imagines happening:

> When the particular members of the commonwealth growing weary of attendance at public courts, as dwelling far off, or being attentive to their private businesses, and withal displeased with the government of the people, assemble themselves to make an aristocracy; there is no more required to the making thereof but putting to the question one by one, the names of such men as it shall consist of, and assenting to their election; and by plurality of vote, to transfer that power which before the people had, to the number of men so named and chosen. (EL,II,2,6)

The people cannot then covenant with the aristocracy because as soon as it is erected 'the democracy is annihilated' (EL,II,2,7). The same process gives rise to a monarchy when one man is chosen.

What Hobbes has described probably occurred only rarely. Like all his fictions, it is an attempt to formalize what is involved in order to make clear the ties that bind the subject to the sovereign power and legitimize it in terms of the popular will. To preserve a democracy requires an expenditure of effort on the part of each individual which he is not always willing to give. There is a tendency to let power slip into the hands of those who are willing and able to exercise it. Even in today's democracies, where all that is required is to visit a polling station once every few years, many people do not take the trouble. For example, in the USA, only about 50 per cent of those eligible to vote in a presidential election bother to do so. Another problem is the sheer size of many states. An extensive territory and a numerous population cannot help but limit the participation of the individual even now and this was far more the case in the seventeenth century. The external threat of other large states, in particular, acted to centralize decision-making powers in the hands of a relatively small group of nobles and officials, usually under the leadership of a monarch. However, the forces at work in the Hobbesian model were similar enough to those in real life to make it a convenient generalization.

An important point to note is that if the people have retained no method of making their will felt except through the aristocracy or monarchy, the transfer of sovereignty has to be considered as having been made in perpetuity. Since the purpose of a state is to protect its inhabitants, there must be enough stability to preserve that security.

Any attempt to undermine the existing system merely threatens a return to the insecurity of the state of nature. Thus, if I live under an absolute monarchy, I have to assume that it was meant to continue indefinitely.

Since these other systems rest on the sovereignty of the people, it is necessary to return to the original democracy for a moment in order to determine what that phrase, as used by Hobbes, implies. We are dealing here with a group of people who have covenanted together so that they can live in peace with one another. A multitude has become a people and the members of that multitude have surrendered part of their natural right to the people. At this point he does not describe the mechanism whereby they would function as a democracy. Presumably they would elect officials to rule them on their behalf. This process is not easy to understand, as Rousseau found out. If we start with a number of persons who share a common goal, they must form an association of some kind to forward their interests, but they cannot do it as a mob all talking at once. They have to elect a president or chair who will speak for all of them. By surrendering their right to speak as individuals to their new leader, they have, to use the phraseology in *Leviathan*, authorized this person to act as the voice of each and every one of them. When we say that the Friends of the Earth, for example, want this or that, we are doing what a politician does after an election when he says the People have decided. Hobbes describes a body politic as a 'fictitious' body and that is exactly the case. Whether I personally agree with what my newly elected ruler is saying, does not prevent him from speaking for the People, which includes me. This is the great paradox which lies at the heart of political life and which so disturbed Rousseau: how, even in the most democratic of states, can I still be in charge of my destiny, when I have surrendered my will to a fictitious body called the People? Rousseau felt that, once their elections were over, the English became slaves again; they were only free when casting their votes. Whoever speaks on behalf of the people has all their individual power concentrated in his hands and if, as Acton said, power corrupts and absolute power corrupts absolutely, then the potentiality for corruption comes into existence at the same moment as the original democracy.

It is very important that this be made clear. Hobbes gives no more power or authority to the most despotic of absolute rulers than he does to democracy. This is what is transferred to the aristocracy or the monarchy – no more and no less. If Hobbes had been speaking

Democracy and the Right of Revolution 249

throughout of a democracy instead of a monarchy this would have been more obvious. Take, for instance, the question of injury. When he says the sovereign monarch can do his subject no injury, it may sound like mere sophistry, but when he says that the sovereign people can do no injury to a member of the commonwealth, it is more convincing.

> For first injury [in the sense of an injustice] is breach of covenant; but covenants (as hath been said in the precedent section) there passed none from the people to any private man; and consequently it (viz. the people) can do him no injury. Secondly, how unjust so ever the action be, that this sovereign *demus* shall do, is done by the will of every particular man subject to him, who are therefore guilty of the same. If therefore they style it injury, they but accuse themselves. And it is against reason for the same man, both to do and complain; implying this contradiction, that whereas he first ratified the people's actions in general, he now disalloweth some of them in particular. It is therefore said truly, *volenti non fit injuria* [injury to oneself is no injury]. (EL,II,2,3)

He adds that such actions done by the people may, nevertheless, 'be unjust before God Almighty, as breaches of the law of nature'. Although not unjust by positive law these actions can be seen as unjust if the law of nature is interpreted as a legal system. Any action violating the law of nature which is decreed by a plurality of voices is the act of every man, whether or not he voted for it or was even present. However, only those who voted in favour of such a command can be held responsible for the breach of the law of nature. 'For a body politic, as it is a fictitious body, so are the faculties and will thereof fictitious also.' Only a real person with a real will can act unjustly with respect to the law of nature (EL,II,2,4).

Still thinking of democracy as a great assembly of virtually all the citizens, Hobbes notes that decisions can only be reached after alternative policies are presented for deliberation by various speakers. Those who are most persuasive in swaying their listeners exercise so much influence that a democracy, to him, is really 'an aristocracy of orators, interrupted sometimes with the temporary monarchy of one orator' (EL,II,2,5). This reflects an important characteristic of democracy. In theory, we vote on the basis of our convictions, our perception of our interests and our knowledge of the issues. In practice all of these can be changed, and the manipulation of public opinion has always been an important factor in democracy. What was done by orators in Athens is accomplished by television today. If the democracy has dissolved itself in the process of passing its authority on to an aristocracy or a monarchy, the grant is made for an unlimited time, as mentioned above. Hobbes does not deny that the people may have elected a monarch for his lifetime only. However, if the people have arranged to meet again at the time of his death in order to choose another, they have not actually surrendered their sovereignty. 'For it is to be understood, when a man receiveth any thing from the authority of the people, he receiveth it not from the people his subjects, but the people his sovereign' (EL,II,2,9). Since the people have retained the sovereignty, they can go even further and recall him at any time they see fit. The distance from this to a modern representative democracy is very short. The key to an elective monarchy, as to any system involving popular sovereignty is that the people 'reserve unto themselves the right of assembling at certain times and places limited and made known' (EL,II,2,10).

Hobbes examines next a variation on the theme of elective monarchy which was to have a great future in England.

> There is another kind of limitation of time, to him that shall be elected to use the sovereign power (which whether it hath been practised anywhere or not, I know not, but it may be imagined, and hath been objected against the vigour of sovereign power), and it is this: that the people transfer their sovereignty upon condition. As for example: for so long as he shall observe such and such laws, as they then prescribe him. (EL,II,2,10)

The problem, again, is whether or not they have agreed in advance upon a time and place of assembly to call him to account. If there is such an arrangement, then the people can meet together legally and exercise their sovereign power accordingly. If there is not, then they have no authority to judge him nor to depose him by force. If they try to do so they are then back in the state of war. Hobbes thinks that in such a case the monarch not only has the right but also an obligation under the law of nature 'to compel them to unity and obedience' (EL,II,2,10).

The importance for Hobbes's political theory of the existence or non-existence of a prior arrangement for an assembly of the people cannot be exaggerated. Although one could object to allowing

Democracy and the Right of Revolution

a merely mechanical requirement like this to interfere with the freedom of the people to alter their form of government, there is no legal way out of the impasse because of the nature of sovereignty. If the current system is an absolute monarchy with no formal provision for consulting the popular will, we have to assume that the people covenanted to permit the king and his successors to act on their behalf. When he makes laws and enforces them, he is doing so on their authority. Now, under such conditions, it is impossible for a rebellious subject to be able to claim to speak for the 'people', even if he is able to collect a large group of supporters. The 'people' are already speaking through their sovereign representative, the monarch. To oppose the king is to oppose the people. Anyone who attempts to usurp the authority of the crown automatically puts himself outside the law. This is not just an artificial stumbling-block created by Hobbes to reinforce absolutism, it is a genuine problem which arises every time dissatisfied elements of the population try to undermine the status quo by appealing directly to the populace. No matter how just their cause may be in the eyes of their supporters, there can be no legitimacy in their claims. If every dissatisfied person in the realm could lawfully rebel at any time, no commonwealth would be safe from anarchy.

A critic might react by pointing out that what the people did by covenant, they can also undo, and in the process make a fresh start. However, a genuine state of nature from which a new commonwealth might arise by agreement cannot come about without the complete collapse of the current system. While it is in existence there are nearly always substantial elements of the population which support it. There is no way the revolutionaries can speak on behalf of these persons and therefore the moral legitimacy which grows out of a general covenant is lacking. In *De Cive* Hobbes notes that there is a double obligation: one to the sovereign and, because the covenant was made with them, one to our fellow citizens (DC,VI,20).

This argument is not very convincing to people in twentieth-century democracies, many of which are the result of successful revolutions against despotic monarchies. In order to justify it one must use a contemporary example. There are those who deny the legitimacy of the capitalist 'democratic' state on the grounds that real power lies in the hands of the wealthy few, that the regular appeal to the will of the people through elections is a farce, since it gives the voter a choice between tweedledum and tweedledee, while he is being misled and brainwashed by the capitalist media, and that the whole rotten system must be brought down by force since there is no other way. Most inhabitants of today's democracies would reject this scenario as either untrue or exaggerated. But even if they did not, there is no legitimate way in which the dissatisfied could organize to bring about violent change because the will of the people is already represented by elected assemblies and officials just as it was by the absolute monarch in the earlier example. In both cases, the dissidents could argue that the popular will was not *really* represented by the powers that be and in both cases they could appeal to a higher law. But this does not offer an answer to the question Hobbes always asked: *who* is to decide between conflicting claims? Within the state, the sovereign power is the final authority; outside the state there is no authority. In summary then, one must observe the rules of the commonwealth in which one happens to live, not because they are perfect, but because without them there would be no rules at all except, of course, the laws of nature, which oblige one only in conscience. This is the inexorable logic of sovereignty.

Thus, if they have an established arrangement to meet at a particular time and place, the people retain the sovereignty, and this is the only way they can retain it. Without such a provision they cease to exist as a people except in the person of the monarch or the aristocratic assembly. Of course, any system of government can fall as the result either of conquest from without or collapse of support from within and those are the circumstances under which change has actually taken place historically.

The problem contained in the word 'people' is subjected to a useful analysis in *The Elements*, which is worth quoting at length.

> The controversies that arise concerning the right of the people, proceed from the equivocation of the word. For the word people hath a double signification. In one sense it signifieth only a number of men, distinguished by the place of their habitation; as the *people* of England, or the *people* of France, which is no more but the multitude of those particular persons that inhabit those regions, without consideration of any contracts or covenants among them, by which any of them is obliged to the rest. In another sense, it signifieth a person civil, that is to say either one man, or one council, as the will of every one in particular. As for example, in this latter sense, the lower house of parliament is all the commons, as long as they sit there with authority and right

Democracy and the Right of Revolution 253

thereto; but after they be dissolved, though they remain, they be no more the people, nor the commons, but only the aggregate, or multitude of the particular men there sitting; how well soever they agree, or concur in opinions amongst themselves; whereupon, they that do not distinguish between these two significations, do usually attribute such rights to a dissolved multitude, as belong only to the people virtually contained in the body of the commonwealth or sovereignty. And when a great number of their own authority flock together in any nation, they usually give them the name of the whole nation. In which sense they say the people rebelleth, or the people demandeth, when it is no more than a dissolved multitude, of which though any one man may be said to demand or have right to something, yet the heap or multitude cannot be said to demand or have right to anything. (EL,II,2,11)

As a member of the multitude, a man retains his rights distinct, but when he unites with others to form a body politic then some of his individual rights disappear as they merge into those of the sovereign.

If this distinction had been used in later years, it would have done much to clarify political thought. Unfortunately, those with their own axes to grind have preferred to keep the word vague since this allowed them to utilize the word 'people', with its favourable connotations, while referring, in fact, only to a particular class or segment of the population. However, although Hobbes does refer to this possibility when he talks about a group of inhabitants giving themselves the name of the whole nation, his principal concern in this passage is to distinguish between the people as individuals, each with his or her own particular desires, and the people as a corporate unit making its will felt through a sovereign. The second usage is an abstract concept which is difficult to control because of the ease with which it can slip back into meaning a collection of individual persons. However, it is precisely this ambiguity which allows such a fiction to work. The danger arises when a large number of real people object violently to what is being done by the authorities in the name of the fictional 'people'.

As we know, Hobbes is not impressed by the so-called mixed form of government. He believes the idea that sovereignty can be in more than one place in a commonwealth is founded on confusion about the true nature of sovereignty. This is very true today because of the popularity of the idea of the separation of powers as guarantor of our liberties. Here is how he copes with this apparent division of sovereignty.

> But though the sovereignty be not mixed, but be either simple democracy, or simple aristocracy, or pure monarchy; nevertheless in the administration thereof, all those sorts of government may have place subordinate. For suppose the sovereign power be democracy, as it was sometimes in Rome, yet at the same time they may have a council aristocratical, such as was the senate; and at the same time they may have a subordinate monarch, such as was their dictator, who had, for a time the exercise of the whole sovereignty, and such as are all the generals in war. So also in monarchy there may be a council aristocratical of men, chosen by the monarch; or democratical of men chosen by the consent (the monarch permitting) of all the particular men of the commonwealth. And this mixture is it that imposeth, as if it were the mixture of sovereignty. As if a man should think, because the great council of Venice doth nothing ordinarily but choose magistrates, ministers of state, captains, and governors of towns, ambassadors, counsellors, and the like; that therefore their part of the sovereignty is only choosing of magistrates; and that the making of war, and peace, and laws, were not theirs, but the part of such councillors as they appointed thereto; whereas it is the part of these to do it but subordinately, the supreme authority thereof being in its great council that choose them. (EL,II,1,17)

Thus, a distinction must be made, as Bodin had done earlier, between the sovereignty itself and the different ways in which it may be administered.

For Hobbes, sovereignty always lies with the body which has the final word. It is often said against the concept of sovereignty today that it is difficult if not impossible to locate. In the United States, for example, there is the separation of the executive, legislative and judicial functions, associated with another tripartite division in authority between local, state and federal governments. Furthermore members of the House of Representatives are elected for two years, the President for four years and a Senator for six years. There is a constitution subject to interpretation by a Supreme Court, and a complex procedure for amending that constitution. Where does the sovereignty rest? Hobbes's answer is unequivocal: with the people,

Democracy and the Right of Revolution 255

because, as electors, they are consulted at regular times and places. This would not have satisfied Rousseau, of course, who would probably have seen such an elaborate arrangement as an attempt to paralyze rather than express the General Will. However, given the criteria Hobbes uses for his three forms of sovereignty, the only possible choice for the US would be a democracy.

Does this version of democracy conform with his analysis of the word 'people'? In an absolute monarchy, the king *is* the people in the corporate sense so the distinction between that usage and the multitude is quite clear. Since, in a democracy, popular sovereignty is only involved on election day, where is the embodiment of the people to be found the rest of the time? The most convincing answer is in the state. When Louis XIV said, *'L'état c'est moi'*, he was defining the state in an absolute monarchy. He was the king, the state and the people all rolled into one. If you substitute an aristocracy or a democracy for the monarch, you became more aware of the state as an entity separate from the form of sovereignty. The state, with its constitutional monarchs, presidents, prime ministers, legislative bodies, cabinets and other officials responsible for everything from national defense to grain inspection, is the external manifestation, the public face of that sovereign power which is animated from within by the people. Sovereignty always starts with them but only in democracy does it ultimately remain with them, purely and simply because they have not surrendered it in perpetuity. Although they have entrusted it temporarily to their chosen leaders, the fact that they will be voting again in a few years means that their pressure is felt continuously by those at the top and in a sense they never disband between elections.

The state apparatus is the means whereby the people govern themselves on a day to day basis. Except on a very small scale, it is impossible for them as individuals, to be actively involved. Furthermore, they have to accept the fact that the people as the state, will do many things contrary to the wishes of any one citizen. This is the paradox of popular sovereignty. Rousseau wanted to preserve the complete liberty of each member to do what he or she wished to do, while still retaining the benefits of government. There is only one way in which this happy state of affairs can exist and that is if everyone wants the same thing. Since it is improbable that this will happen naturally, it has to be encouraged by exerting pressure on every one to think alike. Conformity on potentially disruptive issues is easily enforced in small communities, especially ones like religious sects which are defined by their common beliefs. On a larger scale a substantial amount of indoctrination is required and this, of course, brings with it the threat of 1984 style thought control. To the extent that it actually does work in large states, it depends on there being in place a culture which values conformity enough so that everyone tends to cooperate in enforcing it. However, the degree to which this can be achieved is limited and its desirability is questionable. To surrender one's right to be different, to be one's own self, is to enter into voluntary servitude in order to be 'free'. For this reason, modern democracies are all constituted in such a way that the state acts as a buffer between the citizen as ruler and the citizen as subject, thus saving the individual from being absorbed completely by the 'people'. Hobbes contributed to this outcome by constantly emphasizing both the necessity for sovereignty on the one hand and its ultimate source in the people on the other.

It has not been my intention to present Hobbes as a misunderstood champion of democracy; that would certainly be a distortion of his position. What I have tried to show, however, is that although he personally felt that monarchy could provide more efficient and more stable rule than democracy at the time when he was writing, his theory does not in itself discriminate against the other two forms of sovereignty. But that is precisely his sin, in the eyes of many of his critics. He should have given his support to the struggle for greater participation by the people in their own government instead of harping on the absolute nature of sovereignty. He should have favoured liberty of expression, conscience, etc. instead of giving his sovereign so much power in these areas. Above all he should have acknowledged the right of the people to revolt against a tyrannical master. I have perhaps overstated the reservations of his opponents here and I would hope by now that the reader will accept that such an indictment of Hobbes is to a large extent unfair, since it ignores what he was trying to do: establish a science of politics which can provide a justification for the powers required by the emerging national state. However, the question of whether it is not possible to change political systems legitimately is worth pursuing for a moment. It involves Hobbes's theory of revolution.

This word did not then have its current meaning. Hobbes usually describes organized opposition to the government as sedition or rebellion. At the very end of *Leviathan*, after summarizing what he had tried to do, he says: 'And though in the revolution of states, there can be no very good constellation for truth of this nature to be born under . . . ' (713, 728). The word 'revolution' is used here in its astrological sense and by extension as a great change in the affairs of states. It had not yet acquired a specifically political meaning. However, I use it because of the generally favourable connotation it has today and because it better represents what today's critics of Hobbes would have in mind concerning the great events in seventeenth-century England than a word like sedition.

In the *Elements of Law* he discussed the circumstances under which a revolution is likely to occur.

> To dispose men to sedition, three things concur. The first is discontent; for so long as a man thinketh himself well, and that the present government standeth not in his way to hinder his proceeding from well to better; it is impossible for him to desire the change thereof. The second is pretense of right; for though a man be discontent, yet if in his own opinion there be no just cause of striving against, or resisting the government established, nor any pretense to justify his resistance, and to procure aid, he will never show it. The third is hope of success; for it were madness to attempt without hope, when to fail, is to die the death of a traitor. Without these three, discontent, pretense, and hope, there can be no rebellion: and when the same are all together, there wanteth nothing thereto, but a man of credit to set up the standard, and to blow the trumpet. (EL,II,18,1)

Discontent can be due to fear of bodily pain or of want. 'And therefore great exactions, though the right thereof be acknowledged, have caused great sedition' (EL,II,8,3). Another cause is ambition. Men who are otherwise well off can suffer from 'a sense of their want of that power, and that honour and testimony thereof, which they think is due them'. Although in a monarchy such a man can be given a post which satisfies his need for precedence, 'amongst all those that pretend to, or are ambitious of such honour, a few only can be served . . . The rest therefore must be discontent' (EL,II,8,3). Very significantly, he notes that this is not the case in a democracy and thus unwittingly provides another reason for the practical superiority of popular rule.

Turning to the pretense of right, he lists the six most important misconceptions which lead men to believe they can lawfully resist their sovereign: that conscience is above the law, that sovereigns are subject to their own laws, that sovereignty is divisible, that subjects have property right apart from the sovereign, that tyrannicide is lawful, and that the people is a person distinct from the sovereign. These mistaken notions are, of course, precisely the beliefs that his theory of sovereignty was designed to counter.

The third requirement for rebellion, the hope of success, necessitates the following: '1. That the discontented have mutual intelligence; 2. that they have sufficient number; 3. that they have aims; 4. that they agree upon a head' (EL,II,8,11). In addition to being discontented themselves, the leaders must be lacking in prudence since 'for one man that hath thereby advanced himself to honour, twenty have come to a reproachful end', and also wisdom since they are ignorant of what is right and wrong in connection with the state. Referring to Catiline 'who was the author of the greatest sedition that ever was in Rome', Sallust said 'there was *Eloquentia satis, sapientum parum*; eloquence sufficient but little wisdom' (EL,II,8,13). And that brings us to another characteristic necessary for a rebel leader: eloquence. This, of course, is necessary to rouse the passions rather than to stimulate the reason of those who need to be convinced that their discontent is founded on serious injustice, and that their chance of success is good. Hobbes's arguments are designed precisely to combat such appeals by showing that since sovereign power is necessary no matter who holds it, the ordinary people are unlikely to gain by supporting sedition. In *De Cive* he says his book was written for the benefit of his readers so that 'you will no longer suffer ambitious men through the streams of your blood to wade to their own power' (DC, Pref.).

The theory of how revolution originates, summarized here, does not alter the underlying theme of all Hobbes's political writings which is that revolution is never justified. Because of this his position is different from that of practically all other political philosophers. No matter how authoritarian their message, no matter how much power they are willing to grant the ruler, they always tend to leave an escape hatch of some kind. Defiance of natural law or persecution of the true church were two of the most common reasons given for lawful resistance. As any reader of Hobbes knows, he devotes many pages to closing such loopholes. He could not, of course, prevent rebellion from occurring but he adamantly refused to allow it any degree of legitimacy. Does this mean, however, that there are absolutely no conditions which would justify the people in acting against an especially cruel and tyrannical ruler?

It might appear difficult to envisage such conditions within the

Democracy and the Right of Revolution 259

framework of Hobbesian theory but it is not, I think, impossible. The principal stumbling block, which will be quite familiar by now, is that, since the sovereign is the supreme authority, no individual or lesser body is entitled to pass judgment on him. The only time a subject can lawfully cease to obey his sovereign is when the latter is no longer able to provide security. Since this situation can arise as the result of a revolution it might seem that Hobbes is being less than fair when he legitimizes the outcome after declaring the means to it illegitimate, or to put it another way: all revolutions are wrong except successful ones. Actually this is an over-simplification and just as unfair. Hobbes has said there is no theoretical justification of revolution but if one nevertheless does occur and the sovereign cannot defeat the rebels and restore order, then he has lost his *raison d'être* and need not be obeyed any longer. A sovereign's power can crumble for many reasons, from personal ineptitude to the loss of a war. In fact, a glance at the way in which the great revolutions actually unfolded would tend to support the emphasis placed by Hobbes on the collapse of sovereignty rather than revolutionary conspiracies, most of which were, as he noted, doomed to failure. One can blame the loss of their thrones on Charles I, Louis XVI and Nicholas II variously for not being more flexible about religion, not handling their expenditures more prudently or not avoiding disastrous wars, but whatever the cause of their downfall it is the key to what occurred later. Despite the legitimate grievances and genuine idealism of many of those who opposed them initially, the outcome was not usually what the reformers wanted. In England a general took over, in France a king was succeeded a few years later by, of all things, an emperor, and in Russia a Tsar was replaced by a party secretary who exercised power only dreamt of by his imperial predecessors. There was revolutionary change in all three countries but it came about after a period of anarchy, war and vicious power struggles which caused substantial hardship, if not immense suffering, for the people. In all cases, thousands if not millions of lives would have been saved if the monarch had been able to retain sovereignty and adjust gradually to the economic and social developments which made change inevitable. Given the limitations of human nature, this is probably asking too much but it does not alter the fact that Hobbes would have had ample grounds for feeling vindicated. As these great events unfolded there were periods of relative anarchy and periods of strong rule, but, although sovereignty might change hands, it never did change its nature.

Those who possessed it and were able to exercise the enormous power of the modern state made sure of that.

However, twentieth-century totalitarianism, which is often identified with Hobbesian absolute sovereignty is obviously indefensible, and the question we asked earlier about legitimate opposition has yet to be addressed. In order to do so we must clarify concepts such as tyranny and oppression. Like 'fascist' or 'red' in more recent times, they can be used for polemical purposes and often represent the speaker's own attitudes, rather than reality. As Hobbes points out, anyone who objects to something a monarch has done is tempted to call him a tyrant. However, if the oppression affects an individual directly, the situation alters. Any subject always retains the right to resist a threat to his life and liberty. In the normal course of events, the sovereign power will deprive subjects of at least their liberty, if they are convicted of crimes. This is an important part of governing – the protection of subjects from each other by the use of punishment as a deterrent. However, as we noted above, when a sovereign causes suffering to an innocent person, that is an act of hostility, not of punishment. In such a case the sovereign has recreated the state of nature between the subject and himself and treated the subject as an enemy. All the obligations formerly owed by the subject to the ruler now cease, and he is free to take whatever action he deems necessary for his self-preservation, without violating the law of nature. If the ruler alienates large numbers of his subjects in this way, they, being in a state of nature, can presumably covenant amongst themselves and, in effect, create a new body politic with its own leaders and the right to bear arms. Thus an uprising based on a widespread fear of loss of life and liberty, such as might be the case with a particularly oppressive sovereign would have to be considered legitimate under Hobbes's own rules. However, it should be made clear that is so only if there have been killings or imprisonments of people close enough to the rebels to make their fear genuine. The key point for Hobbes is that no theoretical basis is provided which could persuade the rest of the population, who are not personally threatened, that it is lawful to oppose the sovereign power in principle.

In none of the countries where the great revolutions of modern times took place did such conditions exist. Even in Tsarist Russia, repression was relatively mild. In fact, the lives of individuals were far more at risk *after* the breakdown of sovereignty. In France, the Terror became a symbol for the arbitrary killing of people who had not been convicted of any crime, and when a successful revolutionary regime was established in Russia, the ordinary person was at the mercy of the secret police and suffered in large numbers. Unfortunately, it is under such ruthless regimes that a successful revolt is least likely. Stalin remained master of a quiescent USSR until his death of natural causes. Hitler committed suicide while German soldiers were still fighting desperately on his behalf. The dictators of Spain and Portugal both died in bed. In other cases where unrest or foreign pressure resulted in such dictators leaving quietly for exile, usually luxurious, the situation was not much improved. One can think of, amongst others, Uganda, Haiti and above all Iran. None of these follow the pattern of the ideal revolution, which can be seen in retrospect to be more of a myth than a reality.

Movements for the liberation of colonies and other territories living under the domination of foreigners are much more characteristic of the conspiratorial type of revolution. Hobbes was unfamiliar with that kind of revolution because, in his day, nationalism of the modern type was largely unknown. Most sovereigns ruled over more than one ethnic group and even where a common culture was recognizable, regional and local variations of dialect and custom meant that anyone who lived more than a few miles away tended to be regarded as a foreigner. Only as the masses became more and more involved in the political process did the question of who should be included in the people became important. This did not come to a head in Europe until the nineteenth century when the forces of nationalism led to the unification of Italy and Germany and paved the way for the dissolution of multinational empires in the twentieth. Where a number of different nationalities owed allegiance to a distant monarch it was possible for them to live together in peace but once power fell into the hands of a 'people', they often wanted to exercise it at the expense of their neighbours. This led to many ironic situations such as the Hungarians seeking independence from the Hapsburgs in 1848 while refusing to consider it for their own subject peoples, such as the Croatians. National self-determination seemed the only way out and was widely accepted after the First World War as the legitimate solution to these conflicts. Unfortunately significant territorial adjustments are usually possible only after a major war.

Since this problem did not exist to any extent in the seventeenth century, Hobbes felt no need to address it. Sovereignty by institution, of course, assumed that the covenanters could understand one another and therefore commonwealths of this type would be expected to have definite linguistic and cultural boundaries. Sovereignty by acquisition provided for all other combinations but, as we have noted, it is not easy to see how this model works in the real world. Where a conqueror has treated his new subjects well, they have usually rewarded him with their loyalty in bad times as well as good. Where he has not, there will be a sullen acquiescence which lasts as long as he is able to enforce it. In the case of a fairly homogeneous population, such as the English at the time of William the Conqueror, acquisition can work quite well. But when there is a group, usually differentiated from the rest of the people by language, religion or colour, which is treated worse than the others, then its sense of separateness will be reinforced and it will remain a foreign body within the commonwealth.

The situation is far worse if the ruler is a democratic state, unwilling to extend the benefits of citizenship to the conquered. In the modern world where the prevalent norms are democracy and national self-determination such discrimination, accompanied as it usually is by oppression and exploitation, is morally repugnant. Any attempt to use the master-servant covenant to justify the status quo would be inflammatory rather than explanatory. As for the commonwealth by institution, it is difficult to imagine that members of such a group would enter into a covenant under which they and their descendants would be singled out for a permanently inferior status. Although they might enjoy some advantages from their association with the other inhabitants of the state, enough even for them to accept their inequality for a protracted period, it is difficult to see how they could feel bound by any covenant and how therefore, they could have emerged from a state of nature with respect to the sovereign power. This does not mean a state of war: they may not have the leaders or the organization to make an uprising feasible. But unless an attempt is made to ameliorate their condition and make them feel a part of the whole, the threat will always be there and any resistance on their part would have to be considered legitimate, not because their lives are in danger but because they are not bound by covenant.

This is not to say that the Hobbesian model forbids the emergence of economic and social inequality; in fact, much of the dynamic under all three forms of sovereignty is provided by the quest for wealth and higher status. However, where there is a sense of participation in a common culture such differences are usually accepted as natural and even desirable. But members of a group which has been excluded from the start are obviously in a different position.

With these two exceptions, which I believe Hobbes would have had to allow on the basis of his own arguments, no challenge to the power of the sovereign can be legitimate. It is this absoluteness of sovereignty which so many commentators find unacceptable. On the face of it Hobbes's logic seems implausible. However, if it is accepted that the original social contract needs to be enforced, few would deny that no more than one person or body should be given the authority. If there are two or more, it would be like a game with more than one referee. The subject would not know which one to obey and competition between them would lead to conflict. Historically, the problem has usually been raised, as it was in Hobbes's day, when there is one sovereign, but attempts are made to limit his power by another political entity, such as Parliament. Hobbes maintained that in such a case if it has the authority to override the nominal sovereign, it is the real sovereign. A belief that sovereignty can be divided or shared merely indicates ignorance of the purpose of sovereignty, which is to provide one final authority to act in the name of all the people. Since there is no way of limiting it without undoing it, sovereignty must be unlimited. The need for discretionary powers to cope with all the dangers which might arise within or without the state means that the sovereign must possess all the power it is possible to possess and must therefore be absolute.

Hobbes's claim that absolutism is built into the very concept of sovereignty has led to two reactions from those who object. One is to insist that sovereignty can be limited and the other is to deny that sovereignty is a necessary or useful concept. The first position is usually expressed as some form of a right to resistance or revolution. If the ruler becomes tyrannical, the people have the right to rise up and topple him. As we have noted, the individual retains his natural right to self-preservation and if there is a clear threat to his own life by the ruler, he is entitled to resist. With this exception, any right of resistance must be derived from another source. Theories of resistance usually assume a contract of government under which the ruler's power is limited by the terms of the contract and if he violates them he may be lawfully deposed. In the case of Locke, who became the best-known representative of this school, the arrangement was not really a contract but merely a fiduciary trust. The reason it was possible to have a monarch with such limited power was that Locke's state of nature differed from that of Hobbes. The latter's hypothetical one was a world of individuals freed from all the constraints of civil government and therefore from all the security it offered them. Their conflicting needs and desires forced them to compete with one another under conditions best described as a state of war. However, Hobbes also referred to something like a real state of nature where 'confederacies' were formed for mutual protection. This seems to be what Locke had in mind but one is never certain since his discussion is so confused.

His clearest exposition occurs in Chapter 9 of the *Second Treatise*, which Laslett considers to be a restatement of his whole position probably inserted in 1689. He begins by asking why anyone would want to give up the freedom of the state of nature. 'To which 'tis obvious to Answer, that though in the state of Nature he hath such a right, yet the enjoyment of it is very uncertain, and constantly exposed to the Invasion of others' (368). Although 'the Law of Nature be plain and intelligible to all rational Creatures', men are biassed by their interests and need a *'known and indifferent Judge'*, with the power to punish offences (369). For this reason, despite the privileges of the state of nature, mankind 'are quickly driven into society'. In fact, they seldom live together very long in the state of nature before taking sanctuary 'under the establish'd Laws of Government, and therein seek *the preservation of their Property'*, which includes life and liberties as well as estates. This requires that the individual give up the two powers he enjoys in the state of nature: 'to do whatsoever he thinks fit for the preservation of himself and others within the permission of the *Law of Nature'*, and 'to punish the crimes committed against that Law'. The limitations on the first power make his state of nature appear more civilized than that of Hobbes but the right to punish as well as his references to 'the corruption, and vitiousness of degenerate Men' restores some of the atmosphere associated with his predecessor's version (370). The outcome would not be as different from Hobbes's hypothetical state of nature as is commonly believed.

Although he talks about government here, Locke generally makes the community an intermediate stage, to which power returns if, for any reason, government is dissolved. It is possible nonetheless for society itself to dissolve and the people to 'become a confused Multitude, without Order or Connexion' (429). This return to a state of nature might occur as a result of war but the quotation comes from a section which seems to be a late insertion referring to the circumstances of 1689. The more usual situation, however, is for power to revert to the community or the people. The closest Hobbesian equivalent would be the initial democratic stage before a move to aristocracy or monarchy took place. The big difference is that this community is already a commonwealth, equipped for self-government. Locke is never specific about his community, except that it is the body which apparently entrusted the ruler with his authority which it could remove if he betrays that trust. Exactly how it would do this is not discussed. All we know is that if the ruler becomes a tyrant, the people can appeal to heaven or, in other words, wage war on him. However, for this to happen as Locke describes it, the people must be an organized entity of some kind capable of taking such action. If it can remove a king at will, it would, in the eyes of Hobbes, be the true sovereign. But is it?

Locke never really faces the question of sovereignty because he seems unwilling to do what must come first, and that is to define the community, as it appears in his theory. If it is taken to be all the people, then it would have to be the traditional organic model in which the community is seen as a tightly-knit body willing to be represented by its natural leaders. This is the most charitable interpretation of the Glorious Revolution, since, although very few persons were involved in the decision to invite William to be king, there was probably substantial support for this action amongst the general populace. That is certainly how the Whigs would have interpreted these events.

However, Locke also clings stubbornly to the idea that each individual must give his personal consent. If one then thinks of the community as a collection of individuals rather than a mystical union, who would these be? George Lawson, who anticipated Locke in many ways, published his *Politica Sacra et Civilis* in 1660 and in it he was prepared to be specific as to who is excluded.

> The lowest rank is of such as are not . . . free and in their own power. To this form are reduced women, children, servants, strangers, whether sojourning, or inhabiting and of their own commonwealth; some kinds of tenants or vassals do so much depend upon others that they are not competent members; all these are virtually included in others on whom they depend.[1]

Such people do not participate in the original agreement. Those who do, the freemen, are equal but there are some, more eminent, who 'by reason of their descent, estates, parts, noble acts, are not only members, but somewhat more, as being fit for honour, offices and places of power, if once a commonwealth be constructed' (25). Later on, he discusses the importance of the rational judicious part (*sanior pars*) of the population and its weightier part (*pars valentior*).

> When I mention the people of England as the primary subject of power and the heir of real majesty, I mean the rational judicious party; for no consent of people, that is not rational and agreeable to the laws of God, is of any force. And I exclude not only such as are barely members virtually, but all rebels, traytors and malignant persons ... And when many members of a community are insufficient of themselves to judge what is just and good, and many of them perverted, the power remains in *parte sanior aut in parte hujus partis valentiore*; and in those who upon right information shall consent with them. (382–83)

It was Lawson's opinion that when king and parliament each issued writs on the militia in 1642, the subject could not lawfully choose one over the other and he was therefore freed from his allegiance and what Lawson called the 'personal majesty' was dissolved. Power then reverted to the 'real majesty' of the general community.

> For if the constitution was dissolved, and the personal majesty forfeited, it must devolve unto the people, and no Parliament, nor part of a Parliament, or any other person but the people could either alter the former government or model a new one: For according to the general principles of government, the right of constitution, alteration, abolition, reformation is the right of real majesty; if it be not their right, then the people may be bound to subjection without their consent. (382)

Ideally a convention should have been called, with an important role allotted to the courts of the forty counties or shires of England on which the national community was based.

Lawson, who is given credit for being the first publicist to break away from the belief that Parliament always represented the people, and to provide a doctrine of resistance to a mixed monarchy, is refreshing in his willingness to offer us his idea of who the 'people' were for practical purposes, and giving at least some indication of how they could be consulted in a crisis. This is missing from Locke and all we can do is speculate as to what his own position might have been. Given his socio-economic background, one would tend to assume that it was similar to that of Lawson as far as his definition of the 'people' is concerned and if this is so, any revolutionary movement would have had to be instigated by the 'weightier' part of society, as it was in 1688. However, Richard Ashcraft has made a good case that Locke was more radical in his political outlook and would have supported a wider franchise than did most Whigs.[2] Unfortunately, Locke gives us little guidance in his published work as to what he had in mind. This vagueness is very important since it allowed Locke to be all things to all men: a respectable defender of the Revolution Settlement to the more conservative and a justifier of violent revolution to the more radical. One thing is confirmed in great detail by Ashcraft and that is Locke's active participation in the Rye House Plot and the Duke of Monmouth's attempt to seize the throne. Since the first was intended to capture and probably kill the king, and the second resulted in the futile death of hundreds of ordinary people, Locke was a perfect example of the kind of plotter against whom Hobbes directed his bitterest attacks.

By refusing to tackle the question of sovereignty head on, Locke gave tremendous aid and comfort to those who believed in constitutionalism, the separation of powers, and freedom from excessive government of any kind. This is, of course, an extremely popular position today, and is one of the principal reasons why there is still so much antipathy towards Hobbes. If people in the prepolitical state are basically decent and cooperative, the hand of authority can rest rather lightly on them when they do decide to place themselves under it. There is no need for strong centralized government in the Hobbesian mode. Power is seen by liberal individualism as so diffused amongst various offices and corporate bodies, that it seems bereft of its menace. It is especially easy to adopt this position in the Anglo-Saxon world because of its political evolution, which took the form of a struggle between a king and a representative body. However, the result is misleading because it serves to conceal the realities of power. Sovereignty was still there but it was now possessed by the leaders of what was really an aristocratic republic and in their hands it was exercised just as firmly as it was by the king of France. This was disguised by the widespread belief that Britain was a mixed monarchy in which there was a balance between the monarchic, aristocratic and democratic principles. Unlike Locke, who was writing on behalf of a political movement originally organized by the Earl of Shaftesbury, Hobbes was trying, at least, to develop a science of politics which would apply equally to all systems of government.This is difficult to do in politics since it is all about adjudicating conflicting interests and using rhetoric to gain support for policies that will benefit one faction rather than another. Hobbes recognized the dangers involved, by attempting to adopt a value-free terminology. For example, no one would deny that Charles I was a monarch, because that is a technical word for rule by one person. However, if I call him a tyrant, I am saying that I think he is cruel and oppressive and you can disagree because you do not think he is. All we have done is to express our approval or disapproval. Such emotive use of language does not advance the cause of science. Tyrant was originally a technical term in ancient Greece just as fascist was in Mussolini's Italy but today 'fascist' is usually used as a term of opprobrium. Hobbes would be the first to admit that there are oppressive monarchs as well as benevolent ones but this says nothing more about the institution of monarchy than the fact that some democracies oppress minorities reflects on democracy in general.

An example we have used repeatedly is 'people'. As the quotation from Lawson indicates, there is often far less in it than meets the eye. A good illustration of this is the French Revolution of 1830 when many of those who risked their lives on the barricades were excluded from a share in power by the limited franchise of the July Monarchy. In its general sense it means *all* of the adult population, not just forty shilling freeholders or those with a white skin. If the people are considered as individual persons gathered in an unorganized group, Hobbes usually refers to them as a multitude. Since they cannot all speak at once or even necessarily agree on any common action, they must have a spokesman of some kind. In politics, their leaders speak and act on their behalf. In this technical sense a monarchy or assembly is the people if, as individuals, they have authorized it to represent them. If the people have retained the right to elect their representatives by arranging to meet at a certain place and time for that purpose, then at that moment those who have the right to vote will constitute the people and will be exercising their sovereignty. The point is that even in the most democratic of

Democracy and the Right of Revolution 269

states, a mob assembling for some reason between elections has no right to call itself the 'people', no matter how worthy the cause. The same rule applies equally to an aristocracy or a monarchy. When Wat Tyler marched on London in 1351, his followers had many justified grievances but they could not claim to be the people of England any more than could the landowners, clergy and lawyers they had killed along the way. In the absence of a constitution which said otherwise, only the king who rode out to meet them, Richard II, was in a position to speak for the nation as a whole.

This is the problem posed by the theory of revolution as discussed above. Lawson suggests the local bodies which might be consulted as representing the people but Locke is content to speak of the community without further definition. In any case, the question is ultimately who, or what members of society, make the actual arrangements. There seems to be an assumption shared by writers both of that time and today, that the community or people is an easily identified entity animated by common feelings of outrage at the obvious tyranny of the ruler. The whole thing seems self-evident to them because they see the people as both individuals and community at the same time – as if a difference of opinion amongst them were most unlikely. In actual uprisings, however, there is rarely anything approaching such a consensus. The rebellion is not only illegal and treasonable in the eyes of the sovereign but highly risky for the participants. Furthermore violence is rarely confined to the revolutionaries and the army or police, but is usually inflicted on innocent bystanders. Both sides routinely resort to intimidation when persuasion fails, and the result is that those who do not want to become involved are often themselves the first victims. Not only is unanimity amongst the population usually rare but often there is not even a majority in favour of the rebellion. It was admitted by leading radicals afterwards, that when the American Revolution began, only about one-third of the population supported the break, with about the same number opposed, and the rest neutral. In other words, revolutions are complex events which rarely, if ever, follow the model of a general uprising caused by an apprehension of tyranny.

What about the *right* to revolution as opposed to the question of who decides and participates? Obviously there can be no legal right since that defies the whole purpose of the state and could never be accepted by a sovereign of any kind. It must, therefore, depend on an appeal to natural or divine law. In Hobbesian theory, as we have seen, there is a right of nature which allows one to act in self-defense and there is the law of nature, which essentially amounts to practising the golden rule. We have already noted the legitimacy of resistance under direct threat to one's life and, since revolutionaries have to start breaking the law of nature as soon as they resort to force, there is clearly nothing here which would justify the kind of rebellion the monarchomachs and Lockeans had in mind. Religious beliefs, on the other hand, motivated many of the participants in 1642 and 1688. A fear of Catholicizing tendencies in the Anglican church or of Catholicism itself, played an important emotional role in both cases and in the former one, a desire to alter the organizational structure of the state church was important in the case of the Puritans. Religious liberty was the battle cry but for most of the sects a wish to impose their own beliefs on others was more significant than a genuine interest in toleration. Even Locke, famous for his works on toleration, was not prepared to grant it to Catholics or atheists. Hobbes has been criticized for allowing his sovereign too much power in ecclesiastical affairs but whenever people are prepared to persecute others over religion differences, it is essential that the state intervene and impose conformity in the interests of peace. Furthermore, he insisted that 'no human law is intended to oblige the conscience of a man, but the actions only' (EL,II,6,3). By 'actions' here he meant those which threatened to disturb the peace. He was quite prepared to allow toleration if it were possible. In *Leviathan*, referring to the situation in Cromwell's England, he noted that since the Presbyterians had lost power after having taken it from the episcopacy, 'we are reduced to the independency of the primitive Christian, to follow Paul, or Cephas, or Apollos, every man as he liketh best: which if it be without contention ... is perhaps the best' (696, 711). His own position was that the essential and necessary truths of Christianity were few in number, and that if people resisted the temptation to seek out and quarrel over subtle distinctions in doctrine, much unnecessary strife would be avoided. However, if the different sects were inclined to use violence instead of persuasion to advance their version of the truth, then it was necessary for the state to enforce conformity to one church.

In sum it can be said that a legal right to revolution is a contradiction in terms, and a moral right is itself open to grave moral objections. Moreover, the theoretical right to revolution is too unspecific to be practical. It relies on vague undefined concepts like 'people' and 'tyranny', and provides no real guidance as to the precise circumstances which would activate it. It is a useful rallying cry in partisan politics but has very little place in a science of politics. The concept's distance from reality becomes apparent as soon as one looks at actual revolutions. In none of the major ones did the 'people' rise up, and in none of them could the label 'tyrant' honestly be applied to the ruler concerned. In most cases they were fairly ordinary men trying to do a difficult job at a time when events were slipping out of their control. Reincarnations of Nero and Caligula existed only in the fevered imaginations of some of the revolutionaries. The right of resistance or revolution, thus, does not appear to be a significant threat to Hobbes's theory of absolute sovereignty and is therefore of little legitimate use to liberal constitutionalism.

14
The Nature of Sovereignty

What I have called liberal constitutionalism is based on the belief that safeguards against absolutism can be built into a political system through the adoption of a written constitution or fundamental laws of some kind. Before going further we must address one source of confusion which had dogged Hobbes since his own time and, despite numerous attempts to clear it up, still does today. Despite his personal preference for monarchy, which made a great deal of sense when he was writing, he not only stated repeatedly that his theory applied equally to aristocracy and democracy, but he also occasionally used illustrations drawn from them. Yet many commentators still believe he was defending absolute monarchy rather than absolute sovereignty, whatever the form. Deborah Baumgold, after noting that in the Preface to the 1647 edition of *De Cive*, Hobbes admits that although he believes that monarchy is the most commodious form of government, it is the one thing in the book that he has not demonstrated, goes on to say that, 'in view of its date, too much should not be made of the remark'. She feels that it may be nothing more than 'a passing opinion mirroring the current political climate'.[1] However, since Hobbes claims to have demonstrated everything else in the book *except* the superiority of monarchy, if he had changed his mind later, he would have had either to admit that he had not demonstrated everything else in the book or to insist that he had after all demonstrated its truth. Since he did neither I do not see that this was a 'passing opinion'. She probably interprets the statement to mean that he did not support monarchy as strongly in 1647 as he did both before and after that date but there is no evidence that his position on this matter changed. In all three books he argued the advantages of monarchy at length while still accepting that it was only one of three types of sovereignty. The quotations above come from a chapter called 'Hobbesian absolutism' and it is clear that she sees no difference between his defense of monarchy and of sovereignty in general.

The Nature of Sovereignty

She has made an important point, however. The passage in *De Cive* is significant because it is evidence that Hobbes is quite conscious of the distinction between opinion and logical proof, and that he is being scrupulously honest when he refuses to confuse the two.

Jean Hampton rejects absolute sovereignty altogether. 'Of course, in one sense, most of us in the twentieth century are already confident that the argument fails in some way, for we believe that there is no successful argument for a polity as distasteful as was absolute sovereignty.' However, she feels that an 'investigation of Hobbes's argument and an appreciation of its failure can help us to explain our rejection of this type of government and thus make more sophisticated our own political beliefs'.[2] As I understand her, there are two major problems. Unlike Baumgold, she accepts what Hobbes says in that passage from *De Cive* as representing his view that monarchy, no matter how much better it seems to him, is only one of three legitimate forms of sovereignty. However, she denies, on the basis of his own theory, that absolute sovereignty can be invested in some or all of the people; absolute monarchy 'is not only the preferable but also the necessary form of government for a commonwealth'. She intends to show 'that the reasons Hobbes gives for rejecting governments with sovereignty divided between different branches of government are also reasons for rejecting governments with sovereignty divided between two or more people' (105). She compares divided sovereignty in which two or more powers compete with each other for dominance with an aristocracy or democracy, in which the same kind of competition would occur between individuals, given the nature of Hobbesian man. This sort of criticism can only arise from a fundamental misunderstanding of Hobbes's theory, which is illustrated when she asks: 'If they could not cooperate outside of government, how could we expect them to cooperate inside a government?' (106). The answer is that they have covenanted to do so. Her problem clearly is that she does not really think that persons motivated only by short-term self-interest, which is how she sees Hobbesian man, ever could agree to submit themselves to a regulating authority of any kind. This is a good example of how Hobbes's theories of morality and sovereignty are related; one's conception of the latter will obviously be dependent on one's conception of the former.

The other problem Hampton has with Hobbes's theory is concerned with the absolute rather than the individual aspect of sovereignty. Having shown that absolute sovereignty is only possible if it is possessed by one person, she goes on to demolish even that possibility. Quoting conservative seventeenth-century critics such as Filmer, Clarendon and Bramhall for support, she notes how many rights Hobbes's subjects actually held against their sovereign, to the extent that Bramhall referred to *Leviathan* as a 'Rebell's Catechism' (189). 'Indeed, as long as the subjects retain the right to preserve themselves in a commonwealth, they cannot be said to have surrendered *anything* to the sovereign' (202). Since they have the right to decide what is necessary for their self-preservation, their submission is highly conditional and is certainly not complete enough to support any claim that the ruler's power is absolute. Hobbesian man ends up looking more like Lockean man.

The key is the right of private judgment which certainly appears to have been retained, yet is declared by Hobbes in *Leviathan* to be one 'Of those things that weaken, or tend to the dissolution of a commonwealth' (title of Chapter 29). This apparent contradiction has been discussed above. As we noted there, Hobbes does allow the subject a right of refusal which goes beyond physical self-preservation to encompass what might be called psychic self-preservation. A subject does not have to perform a 'dishonourable' office, presumably because he would not have covenanted to do something that to him would be worse than death itself, but there is no right to refuse if the fate of the commonwealth itself is at risk. Hampton would say that since he is the one who decides this, the sovereign's power is not absolute. However, such situations are usually easy to discern and whether they exist or not is apparent to his fellow subjects who would doubtless let him know what they think of his actions. Such a liberty is only allowed if it is clearly based on deeply felt beliefs for which the subject is prepared to die, and not as an excuse to avoid responsibilities he undertook when he entered into the covenant. Hampton would doubtless not accept this, since she does not believe Hobbes has a genuine morality but the question of whether to disobey the orders of a superior when they conflict with one's personal values is very common and occurs in democracies such as the United States, as well as in more authoritarian countries.

This discussion of two contemporary writers was intended mainly to demonstrate that Hobbes's theory of absolute sovereignty is still controversial to this very day. The same can be said of the concept of sovereignty itself. It is often remarked that because the idea has many meanings it must therefore either be very carefully defined

The Nature of Sovereignty

when used or else should be dispensed with altogether. The latter is difficult because despite its amorphous nature it is in some areas quite necessary. One of these is the arena of international relations. The world is divided up into political units which, despite enormous differences in size and power, have one thing in common: they are all sovereign states. This means that each one claims exclusive jurisdiction within its own boundaries, is independent of any other state and will admit of no superior. Sovereignty in this context is the external manifestation of the internal political unity of the modern state. In its dealings with other states it must speak with a single voice on behalf of its inhabitants. Its status within the community of nations will be indicated by diplomatic recognition and usually an exchange of ambassadors. Thus, in order to be a member of the United Nations and other international bodies, participate in international conferences, negotiate the settlement of disputes, and make treaties which are supposed to bind it regardless of changes in government, a state must possess the power and authority which can only be derived from sovereignty. Since sovereignty thus faces outward as well as inward, those who question its legitimacy in its latter manifestation are not able so easily to do the same with the former because it concerns something they cannot but regard as vital to themselves, namely the continued existence of their own country.

The other area in which the concept is difficult to do without is the law. The legal order is a hierarchical system, in which the validity of a particular law is derived from the level above it. Ultimately this regression must terminate in a first cause or supreme norm, the validity of which is not open to challenge. Without such an ultimate authority, beyond which no appeal is possible, the legal system could not function and government would be unworkable. This is sovereignty in its legal aspect, and although there is much argument as to where it lies, there is also little doubt concerning the need for it. That it is ultimately connected to external sovereignty, as discussed above, can be seen from the fact that the laws of one country only apply within its own frontiers.

This leaves us still with the problem of political sovereignty: does it exist and, if so, where is it located? If it appears to be necessary to support both our legal system and our relations with the inhabitants of other states, we are hardly in a position to dispense with it. There is no doubt that it is a very difficult concept to pin down but that alone is not a sufficient reason for abandoning it. The more common opposition to sovereignty came from its early association with absolute monarchy. It is regarded by many as inherently anti-democratic and as a result is considered both immoral and irrelevant, given the popular nature of most western governments. What is certainly true is that it is easier to understand when it is embodied in one person, who can make the laws and enforce them as well as decide on policy and execute it. The rise of modern democracy has had the effect of dispersing these powers and making them problematic. Many constitutionalists try to evade the difficulties by insisting that sovereignty can be divided and thus made less threatening. In many ways they are the counterparts of the moral subjectivists and relativists discussed earlier, who do not want to be bound by a fixed objective morality and feel that freedom is only possible where they can choose their own moral system. The arguments against both positions are bound to have much in common.

Let us begin again, using the regress argument of the jurists but broadening it to cover the state as a whole. Is there any answer to the argument that if there is an authority over and above what is considered the final authority, it is the true final authority and therefore the sovereign? The only escape from such a closed system is to move outside it into another system with different criteria. This we did with morality, following Hobbes in seeing a moral system as something one would enter for prudential reasons. If one adopts it for moral reasons, one is merely substituting a higher morality for a lower one. In the same way, a Hobbesian would join a closed political system, because it is preferable to remaining in the state of nature which is the available alternative. Thus it would appear the regress argument is unanswerable unless one can find a satisfactory way of escaping the sovereign state while retaining its benefits.

Hampton thinks she had done this by postulating an agency type of contract in which the people retain the right of dismissing their sovereign if he or she becomes tyrannical. This is the medieval *concessio* as opposed to the *translatio* as adopted by Hobbes. We have already looked at this and found it unsatisfactory but it is so much part of our tradition that it keeps springing back. She uses as an analogy a baseball game. The players choose the umpires and obey their rulings unless these are considered unfair, in which case, they fire the umpires. However, this merely emphasizes that sovereignty remains with the players as, in the equivalent political situation, it would with the people. Furthermore, it does nothing to illuminate the problems we have been discussing. She seems

The Nature of Sovereignty

to assume that the players would rise in a unified group, like the Lockean community, to depose the umpires. But in real life games, as many players may approve of the umpires' decisions as disapprove of them. Any kind of arbitration will usually disappoint one side. So who gets to fire the umpires? The game metaphor is a very useful one but the wrong conclusions are often drawn from it. One goes into a game only if one is prepared to follow its rules and be bound by the umpires or referees. If one is unhappy with the way the game is being conducted, one can stop playing. The difference between participating in a game and being a member of a political society is that in the latter case one's commitments have to be more permanent.

The reason for the confusion here is the tendency of so many critics of sovereignty, who live in democracies where elections are held regularly, not to discriminate between a system in which rulers can be replaced by the ballot, and the adoption of such a system in the first place. For explanatory purposes Hobbes imagines a group of individuals contracting together to give up part of their natural freedom of action in return for others doing the same. However, in order to provide genuine security, such an arrangement must be policed and therefore one of the three forms of sovereignty must be introduced. The social contract creates the community out of isolated individuals and it, in turn, adopts a political system which is either a democracy, an aristocracy or a form of monarchy. If anyone doubts that a group of people would ever voluntarily submit to one-man rule, for example, they need look no further than recent history. Hitler was immensely popular with the German people and most of them were quite prepared to accept him as their dictator. Both Napoleon I and Napoleon III held plebiscites and despite their ability to influence the results, it is generally conceded that the vast majority of Frenchmen were happy to hand imperial powers over to them. There is nothing farfetched about popular approval for one-man rule under certain conditions. The fall of all three of those rulers, incidentally, was caused by defeat in war, rather than by revolution from within.

The purpose of Hobbes's scheme was to attempt to show how the political system a person lived under, whatever it was, could be justified and legitimated. He works back from a given present to provide us with good reasons for accepting it; while admitting that it might not be the best of all possible worlds, he tries to show it is not the worst that is conceivable either. Enslavement is a word bandied about by constitutionalists when discussing sovereignty but they forget that if there is such a thing, it arises at the moment when the community comes into being, not when it submits to a sovereign. An individual has to surrender much of his freedom of action when he joins a group or when he recognizes the significance of his membership in a group. In the case of a democracy, the die is cast not when one goes to the polling booth every few years but when one submitted to the rules providing for these elections and much else, by becoming part of the community. In the case of the United States, taking the oath of allegiance makes the relationship quite specific, because one agrees to be bound in future by the actions of the government whether one approves of them or not. One can disagree with them, lobby against them and so on but one has made a commitment which is morally binding in all circumstances except where conscience decrees otherwise, and then only if the fate of the country is not at stake. The result of all this is that where the community can dismiss a ruler, as with Locke, the community is the sovereign. If the community can act in this way, it is clear that it must already be a body politic with recognized leaders it is prepared to follow. Thus the problems raised by sovereignty merely regress one step to a new level where they continue to exist.

What differentiates the state or political community from a football club or any other voluntary organization is that it possesses much greater power over its members, specifically the power of life or death. Whether this is exercised internally for law enforcement or externally by engaging in wars with other states, it is obviously on a different plane from other types of power. When Hobbes talked about sovereignty being absolute, this is what he meant. The various other powers he grants to the sovereign, objectionable as they may seem to some people, are merely by-products of this great authority which animates the Leviathan. To quibble over them while admitting the other is absurd. If I, as an individual in the state of nature, have the capacity to kill, it is surely obvious that the political entity to which I submit for protection must have that capacity multiplied a thousandfold. Since a commonwealth is created to do for me what I am unable to do as an isolated individual, it must have the right to do at least what I was prepared to do on my own behalf. For internal security, the sovereign must wield the sword of justice and for external the sword of war and the two cannot be separated.

Thus, in order to do the job entrusted to it by the people, it must

The Nature of Sovereignty

have the necessary authority and this will have to be in the end, unlimited. No matter how its critics may twist and turn to avoid this consequence, there is no way to limit such an authority without regressing eventually to one which is unlimited, and this is the sovereign power. The only appeal from sovereignty possessed by a national state which can be imagined is to a supra-national or world commonwealth which would exercise unlimited power over the whole planet.

When I have said occasionally that Hobbes grants the sovereign certain powers, I was speaking from the viewpoint of theory construction. In fact, the ruler must, by the nature of sovereignty, actually *have* these powers. When Hobbes says he should have these powers, he is not really prescribing a particular content for the idea. He is merely informing rulers and people alike that if he does not have these powers, he is not a sovereign and that it is necessary that they understand this, since if he is not a genuine sovereign he cannot perform the functions which they have assigned him. His prescription is like that of a doctor who says: 'Take this medicine now or face unpleasant consequences'. And it is not the sort of medicine which is effective in half doses. It is an all or nothing remedy. This means that Hobbes both defines and prescribes sovereignty at the same time.

What all this amounts to is that the theoretical power of the sovereign is unlimited because there is no way in which it can be limited without destroying its efficacy. As Hobbes points out repeatedly, any attempt to limit sovereignty is contrary to the purpose for which it was established. However, and this is an extremely important point which should help to dispel some of the concerns of those who have a quite legitimate fear of such a concentration of power, while there are no *theoretical* limits, there certainly are *practical* limits to the power of the sovereign. His capacity to act is dependent ultimately on the willingness of his subjects to do his bidding and that, in turn, is dependent on his success in making his interest also theirs. As we have noted earlier, the importance of this factor too, is repeatedly emphasized by Hobbes. Recent scholarship has tended to show that the revolutions of 1642 and 1688 were by no means inevitable, and that a little less stubbornness and a little more courage at the crucial moment might have saved the Stuarts their thrones and altered the constitutional history of England. However, knowing when to stand firm and when to yield is the essence of statesmanship, a talent that does not always come with a crown. As W. A. Speck writes in connection with the Glorious Revolution:

> Both Charles II and James II worked for the most part within the letter of the law. The notion that there were legal limitations on their authority imposed by an ancient constitution, requiring for them to account for their actions was a Whig myth. Provided they did not violate statutes or common-law precedents their prerogative powers were still formidable. Moreover, they were backed by powerful sections of the political nation who regarded the Crown as the essential ally of the Church of England. As long as the later Stuarts kept up the alliance of Crown and Church they bade fair to make the monarchy as absolute in the 1680s as it had ever been since their accession to the English throne. It was not as if the civil wars had never happened. On the contrary, it was precisely because they had occurred that the bulk of the political nation rallied to the Crown when it seemed there was the awful possibility that 'forty-one' would happen again.[3]

When James antagonized the Anglicans in his quest for toleration of the Catholics, he alienated his most devoted supporters. They did not engage in resistance but did little to help in 1688 as compared with 1685, when their opposition to the Duke of Monmouth's rising was overwhelming.

Thus, although Hobbes does not allow any theoretical limitations in his concept of sovereignty, he would be the first to admit that a sovereign, unlike God, is not omnipotent. There is an art to ruling and if a king cannot master it, he may very well fall. Being completely unsentimental, Hobbes, unlike the divine right theorists, had no difficulty in making his peace with Cromwell. It really does not matter in his theory who rules, as long as there is a ruler. But whatever personal weaknesses they may have, rulers must be prepared to *rule*, in other words, lay down the law and see that it is obeyed. If they cannot, in practice, obtain the necessary obedience, then they may have to go. We live in a harsh and unforgiving world, and sovereigns are no more immune from its tribulations than are their subjects. They are especially vulnerable to the belief held by the more ruthless amongst us that there is no better time to kick a man than when he is down. Take the case of Nicholas II. The 1905 revolution occurred after his defeat in the Russo-Japanese War and that of 1917 was occasioned by military collapse during the First World World. When his soldiers began deserting *en masse*, his power and his authority evaporated – as good an example as one can find of how sovereignty is dependent on popular support, and how it comes to an end. The frontispiece of *Leviathan*, which shows the figure of the sovereign composed of a mass of little figures representing the people, illustrates the ultimate fragility of the sovereignty. Hume sums it up nicely in an oft-quoted passage.

> Nothing is more surprising to those, who consider human affairs with a philosophical eye, than to see the easiness with which the many are governed by the few; and to observe the explicit submission with which men resign their own sentiments and passions to those of their rulers. When we enquire by what means this wonder is brought about, we shall find, that as force is always on the side of the governed, the governors have nothing to support them but opinion. 'Tis therefore on opinion only that government is founded; and this maxim extends to the most despotic and most military governments, as well as the most free and popular.[4]

Or, as Hobbes put it more briefly a century earlier: 'For the power of the mighty hath no foundation but in the opinion and belief of the people'.[5]

We have usually referred to the sovereign as a monarch of some kind, since it is easier to comprehend when it is focused on one person. The fact that we are no longer ruled by kings but by much more complicated political structures has often been put forward as a reason for dispensing with the concept of sovereignty. However, even a monarchy is not as simple as it might seem. For example, Louis XIV had to contend with the occasional refusal of the *Parlement* of Paris to register an edict. This was one of the few traditional limitations on his power and he could overcome such opposition easily by appearing before them on the *lit de justice* and commanding them to register the law, which was also a traditional procedure. I mention this situation only to indicate that even the Sun-king did not get his way all the time, at least not without some inconvenience. Monarchical societies, by their hierarchical nature, often become very tradition-bound. An example is the tendency for offices to become hereditary and to be regarded as property which could be bought and sold. Given this survival of feudalism it was very often difficult for the king to control his servants with as much freedom as he would have liked. Getting the bureaucracy to do what he wants has remained a problem for rulers as disparate as Louis himself, Lenin, and American presidents. What this means is that every ruler has to work through layers of functionaries, official inertia, vested interests, and in many cases considerable corruption. Thus, absolute power is much less absolute than it appears on the surface. In fact a monarch like Louis XVI was not absolute enough, since he lacked the power to make badly needed reforms in his creaking administrative machinery, reforms which would probably have forestalled the French Revolution. His efforts to appease the aristocracy and other groups opposed to change, were what ultimately cost Louis his head. It was not excessive power but excessive inefficiency and inequity at the administrative level which led to the collapse of the *ancien régime*.

Another important fact is that the average subject or citizen's contact with authority is at a level considerably lower than that of the ruler(s) and it is at that level where discontent is usually manifested. The officialdom one has to deal with on a day to day basis is the face of the state for most people. The reason we have to obey these functionaries is that they have been granted the power to enforce the laws by a higher authority. That authority must be accepted as legitimate in order for its orders to be binding, but whether it is a king or a Parliament or a Chamber of Deputies makes very little immediate difference to the person who has to do what he is told. If I am being drafted to be shipped off to the jungles of Viet Nam, it is little comfort to know that it is by order of the people instead of a king. In other words, there is always something distant and intangible in the nature of sovereignty no matter what form it takes.

As we have noted, the possibility of absolute sovereignty only makes sense to many commentators if it is associated with the rule of one. How, they ask, can a number of people ever exercise power in the same focussed way that an individual is able to? This problem can be addressed by separating out the various roles which may be combined in the person of the monarch. He may or may not act in an executive capacity for reasons of personality or age. Thus Louis XIII relied heavily on Cardinal Richelieu to run France for him because of his own lack of interest, and Louis XIV needed Cardinal Mazarin because of his youth and inexperience. When Mazarin died, Louis became his own first minister. In both cases executive power was delegated, but sovereignty rested firmly in the possession of the Crown, regardless of the personal characteristics of its wearer. He might be a talented administrator or he might leave administration entirely up to others. However, he remained the court of final appeal in all decision-making and his advisors and officials could act only by his leave.

Thus, if we detach the attribute of sovereignty from the other attributes of the monarch, we find that monarchy is similar to sovereignty in its other manifestations. A Cardinal Richelieu and a President of the United States have this in common: although they both wield enormous power they are both at the same time, subject to dismissal by the sovereign power of the state, in the form of the king in one case or the electorate in the other. Regardless of any moral advantage possessed by a democracy, it has the great practical advantage that regular elections make resort to violent uprisings largely unnecessary. Absolute monarchy usually exists where a more responsive representative system has not evolved for various historical reasons, and the only way in which the nation can act as a political unit is through an unelected ruler who has some claim to speak for all. Unsuccessful efforts to transplant western style democracy to other lands indicate that religious, cultural and other differences are such that it may not be feasible everywhere. That is why it is wrong to treat someone like Hobbes, who defends the status quo, as an apologist for despotism. The welcome given to Charles II in 1660 indicates that the English were still a nation of monarchists and that Hobbes was closer to the ordinary man's thinking at that time than are his modern critics.

The approach taken by Hobbes to the location of sovereignty has the virtue of simplicity. If there is a means of appeal from the one or the few to the many, then the people, in a practical and not just in a nominal sense, is sovereign. This does not mean that all or even a majority of them, must approve the action of the legislature but, essentially, that there is an accepted mechanism for consulting them regularly. This is as far as he goes and, I think, there is merit in this position. Trying to be more precise only leads to the confusion which has bedevilled the theory of sovereignty in recent times. Attempts to pinpoint it in a democratic state, especially a federal one, tend to lose themselves in the complex details of the actual workings of government and eventually to arouse a scepticism about whether it exists at all. In the case of the United States, if one works back from the relationships between the state and federal governments, and the Presidency, Congress and Supreme Court, one arrives at the Constitution, but since that can be amended, we end up with a two-thirds majority of both Houses of Congress acting in conjunction with three-fourths of the States. The problem here, as W. J. Rees notes is that 'since this body has acted as a body only on twenty-one occasions in a hundred and sixty years, and since both Houses of Congress, in any case derive their own legal existence from the constitution, this is even less plausible'.[6] But Rees and many others complicate the matter unnecessarily. Since the people were responsible, through their representatives, for approving the original constitution and, since they also, by the same means, approved the amendments and, since they also participate in the multitude of elections called for by the constitution, why not just conclude, as Hobbes would, that sovereignty is located in the people?

One reason for the reluctance of recent theorists to do this may be that the 'people' seems too vague and amorphous to be the seat of sovereignty. Power is exercised by individuals or tightly-knit groups, whereas the people is split into numerous conflicting factions led this way and that by those with the ability to influence them. For Hobbes, as we have seen, democracy tended to be an aristocracy of orators. However, a quest for the real wellsprings of power is doomed to failure because there are too many of them and the question of who is really running the country is so difficult to determine that many find it preferable to abandon the whole notion of sovereignty. As S. I. Benn says: 'In the light of this analysis it would appear to be a mistake to treat "sovereignty" as denoting a genus of which the species can be distinguished by suitable adjectives, and there would seem to be a strong case for giving up so protean a word'.[7]

However, this is due to a misunderstanding of what the word is intended to signify, at least in the theory of Hobbes. In Chapter 23 of *Leviathan*, 'Of the Public Ministers of Sovereign Power', he discusses the public ministers who actually administer the commonwealth. They are ministers, 'in that they do it not by their own authority, but by another's; and public, because they do it, or should do it, by no authority but that of the sovereign' (228, 291). Included are those in charge of the general administration of the whole or part of the country, or of specific areas such as finance, military affairs, political education, the judicature, foreign affairs, etc. 'And this kind of public ministers resembleth the nerves, and tendons

The Nature of Sovereignty

that move the several limbs of a body natural' (227, 290). Those who are servants to the monarch, or members of the assembly in their capacity as natural men and not as sovereigns, are not public ministers. The latter act on behalf of the sovereign as sovereign, not as a man or men. Hobbes is careful here as elsewhere to treat as sovereigns not just monarchs but also popular assemblies.

These public ministers, together with their assistants, are in charge of the day-to-day operation of the state, whether it is a monarchy or a democracy. Their power, however, lasts only so long as they are authorized to act in the name of the sovereign. When their actions prove unsatisfactory they can be dismissed by the grantor of that authority whether it be a monarch or the people. In the latter case, this usually results from an election, in which the leader who appointed them is turned out and replaced by another. Since it is impossible for the people, or even a king, to have meaningful control over all facets of government, officials have to be given a great deal of discretion and as a result may engage in unjust and oppressive acts. The process by which their victims can have these wrongs righted is often long and labourious, whether it is the monarch or the elected rulers to whom an appeal must be directed. The responsiveness of the rulers is a measure not of the form of government but of the care they have for the welfare of their people. No system of government can completely eliminate sloth and insensitivity on the part of its servants.

What this means to the theory of sovereignty is that it should not be associated too closely with the exercise of power in any given sphere or space of time. It must be regarded as the final court of appeal, whether it is an absolute monarch or the voters in a democratic election. It may be dormant for long periods because the administration of the realm has been successful in keeping everyone reasonably content. But when things are going wrong, it will not be long before the king will seek out more competent advisors or the voters will shift to a party which promises to do better. This is when the sovereign power is easy to identify because it is being called upon to perform its function. To identify it too closely with the exercise of power in the multifaceted activities of the modern state is to mistake both what it can do and what it ought to do. Much of the available power has to be delegated. Even the most potent of autocrats must do this, because one person cannot possibly oversee all the activities of a medium-sized business corporation, never mind a large state.

When those with such delegated power are in charge of the armed forces and foreign policy, they represent sovereignty of the state in relation to other states; when they supervise the administration of justice, they represent it in the legal sphere, and when they make policy in general, they represent it in a political sense. The one thing which is absolutely necessary is that the sovereign power must have no superior or even equal, and therefore it must not be divided or limited. This has been another source of difficulty for modern critics. For them, not only is sovereignty hard to find but they do not really want to find it. As defined by Bodin and Hobbes, it represents a threat to the freedom of the individual and they would rather see it break down into the fragments of power held by the many different organs of the state and ultimately disappear. It does not dawn on them how disastrous this would be if it were true. The state would become a battlefield for competing warlords, much as Lebanon has been in the latter part of the twentieth century or China was in the 1920s and '30s – easy prey to outsiders who *do* have the power which comes from unity. It should be especially difficult for Americans to support this position since it was in their country that divided sovereignty was put to the acid test not much more than a century ago.

One of the dogmas which dominated political theory in the newly-created United States of America was that of double sovereignty. This idea was advanced by the *Federalist* before the adoption of the Constitution and supported afterwards by many decisions of the courts. That sovereignty was divided between the state and federal governments was regarded by Madison and even by Tocqueville as one of the distinguishing features of the new nation. Since this was widely believed and appeared to work, it seemed one more piece of evidence which contradicted the strictures of Bodin and Hobbes, although many did admit that it was probably unique to the United States. Tocqueville pointed to a general and potentially fatal weakness in the theory when he said: 'A people which should divide its sovereignty into fractional parts in the presence of the great military monarchies of Europe would in my opinion, by that very act abdicate its power and perhaps its existence and name'.[8]

Sovereignty of the people is possible only where the issues which divide the people into factions are not regarded as matters of life and death. Differences in language or religion can eventually result in an unwillingness to compromise anymore and a readiness to resort to arms. The American population was relatively homogeneous and prepared to seek accommodation on most issues except one, as it turned out: slavery. The southern planters were not only not prepared to give it up but wanted to extend it to some, at least, of the new western states, in order to preserve their relative strength in the Union. Much of American politics in the first half of the nineteenth century was governed by a desire on the part of both sides to paper over the cracks, but a breach was probably inevitable. It was even foreseen by a Loyalist pamphleteer who, eighty-five years earlier, wrote that there would be a split between north and south over the western lands and that the ensuing war would be won by the 'cunning Yankees'.[9]

However, the Civil War was not fought over slavery as such but over the issue of sovereignty. The compromise on which the country had been built gradually failed as the crisis approached. John C. Calhoun, the political philosopher of the southern states, rejected double sovereignty in favour of sovereignty of the states, insisting that they had never surrendered it. He believed that sovereignty could not be divided without being destroyed. 'It is the supreme power in a State, and we might just as well speak of half a square, or half a triangle as of half a sovereignty.'[10] Interestingly, he also opposed the social contract theory on the grounds that men are not created equal, thus recognizing the implicit egalitarianism of the social contract. This theory was also rejected by those who supported the central government rather than the states. Beginning with Francis Lieber, the author of the *Manual of Political Ethics*, published in 1838–39, they placed sovereignty with the nation rather than the people. Following Hegel and other influential German writers, they tended to elevate the nation, a culturally homogeneous group of people occupying a clearly-defined territory, into an organic entity to which sovereignty was attached. The argument of the unionists was thus based on a strong sense of nationalism which could provide a satisfactory alternative to the local patriotism of the secessionists and it became the dominant theme after the North won the Civil War.

By then, of course, the doctrine of double sovereignty was dead. It is the type of theory that works beautifully until it is actually put to the test. President Lincoln never seems to have doubted for a moment that sovereignty lay with the nation as a whole. In his message to Congress on July 4, 1861, he defined sovereignty as: 'A political community without a political superior', and on this basis he denied that any of the states except Texas, which had surrendered its claim upon entering the union, ever was a sovereignty. Many Americans, even in the North, might not have agreed with him on this matter. Tocqueville certainly came away with a different impression of American attitudes. He was so impressed with the hold of the states over their citizens that he said: 'If the sovereignty of the Union were to engage in a struggle with that of the states at the present day, its defeat may be confidently predicted; and it is not probable that such a struggle would be seriously undertaken' (I, 403). Admittedly, his visit to America took place in 1831–32 and much had changed during the intervening thirty years. However, a case could certainly be made on democratic grounds for allowing dissatisfied states to leave the union. Nullification and secession had been, after all, precisely the measures adapted against the British Empire in 1776, and Lincoln's arguments bear an ironic resemblance to those of American Loyalists opposed to the breach. To quote Tocqueville again:

> However strong a government may be, it cannot easily escape from the emergence of a principle which it has once admitted as the foundation of its constitution. The Union was formed by the voluntary agreement of the states; and these, in uniting together, have not forfeited their sovereignty, nor have they been reduced to the condition of one and the same people. If one of the states chose to withdraw its name from the contract, it would be difficult to disprove its right of doing so.

However, he adds a proviso which covers what actually occurred.

> In order to enable the Federal government easily to conquer the resistance that may be offered to it by any of its subjects [the states], it would be necessary that one or more of them should be specially interested in the existence of the Union, as has frequently been the case in the history of confederations. (I, 403)

Lincoln's actions in the situation which confronted him would certainly have been supported by Hobbes, not only because no ruler has the authority to allow his state to be dismembered or its sovereignty divided or surrendered but also because the larger a state is the more secure it is likely to be. Given the alternative of allowing the United States to break up into smaller units, which could become a prey to outside intervention, or of maintaining the

The Nature of Sovereignty

territorial integrity of a great power obviously destined to become much greater, Lincoln really had no choice. The tragedy is that so many Americans had to die before the issue was settled.

There is a tendency on the part of those who regard sovereignty as an outmoded concept, to look upon the Civil War as just another war between two belligerents, and therefore of little relevance to the issue. However, it was known originally, in the North at least, as the War of the Rebellion and it is difficult to see it only as a contest about territory rather than principle. In fact, there were supporters of state-sovereignty in the north as well as unionists in the south, but once hostilities commenced, theoretical differences came to be matters of life or death and the time for discussion was finished. After the war was over, however, sovereignty became a matter of considerable interest to writers on politics. Probably the most scholarly treatment of the subject was that of by John W. Burgess. After defining the state as all-comprehensive, exclusive, permanent, and, most essentially, sovereign, he goes on:

> An organization may be conceived which would include every member of a given population, or every inhabitant of a given territory, and which might continue with great permanence, and yet it might not be a state. If, however, it possesses the sovereignty over the population, then it is a state. What now do we mean by this all-important term and principle, the sovereignty. I understand by it original, absolute, unlimited, universal power over the individual subject and over all associations of subjects. This is a proposition from which most of the publicists, down to the most modern period, have labored hard to escape. It has appeared to them to contain the destruction of individual liberty and individual right. The principle cannot, however, be logically or practically avoided, and it is not only not inimical to individual liberty and individual rights, but it is their only solid foundation and guaranty. A little earnest reflection will manifest the truth of this double statement.
>
> First, power cannot be sovereign if it be limited; that which imposes the limitation is sovereign; and not until we reach the power which is unlimited, or only self-limited, have we attained the sovereignty. Those who hold to the idea of a limited sovereignty (which, I contend, is a *contradictis in adjecto*) do not, indeed, assert a real legal limitation, but a limitation by the laws of God, the laws of nature, the laws of reason, the laws

between nations. But who is to interpret, in last instance, these principles . . . when they are involved by anybody in justification of disobedience to a command of the state, or of the powers which the state authorizes? . . . But, it may be objected, if sovereignty must have this character of infallibility, it should be denied to the state altogether. That would mean, at once and from the start, the annihilation of the state. The state must have the power to compel the subject against his will: otherwise it is no state; it is only an anarchic society. Now the power to compel obedience and to punish disobedience, is, or originates in sovereignty. This condition can, therefore, offer no loophole of escape from the proposition. In the second place, the unlimited sovereignty of the state is not hostile to individual liberty, but is its source and support. Deprive the state, either wholly or in part, of the power to determine the elements and the scope of individual liberty, and the result must be that each individual will make such determination, wholly or in part, for himself; that the determination of different individuals will come into conflict with each other; and that those individuals who have power to help themselves will remain free, reducing the rest to personal subjection.[11]

I have quoted Burgess at some length because, without once invoking the name of Hobbes, he has presented a late nineteenth-century view of sovereignty – and an American one at that – which is strikingly similar to the Hobbesian version of two and a half centuries earlier. I interpret this as convincing evidence that the arguments used by Hobbes are as applicable to a modern democracy as they are to a seventeenth-century absolute monarchy and represent, therefore, something more than special pleading. Burgess, in fact, with the advantage of having those 250 years behind him, is able to see a connection between sovereignty and the historical advance of freedom.

Now the modern national popular state is the most perfectly and undisputedly sovereign organization of the state which the world has yet attained. It exempts no class or person from its law, and no matter from its jurisdiction. . . . This fact surely indicates that the more completely and really sovereign the state is, the truer and securer is the liberty of the individual. If we go back an era in the history of political civilization, we shall find this

The Nature of Sovereignty

view confirmed without dispute. The absolute monarchies of the fifteenth, sixteenth and seventeenth centuries were, no one will gainsay, far more sovereign organizations of the state than the feudal system which they displaced; and yet they gave liberty to the common man at the same time that they subjected the nobles to the law of the state. In fact they gave liberty to the common man by subjecting the nobles to the law of the state. (55–56)

In other words, the more perfect the sovereignty, the more potentiality there is for protecting the liberty of the subject. Why then is there so much resistance to the concept?

I think the difficulty which lies in the way of the general acceptance by publicists of the principle of the sovereignty of the state is the fact that they do not sufficiently distinguish the state from the government. They see the danger to individual liberty of recognizing an unlimited power in the government; and they immediately conclude the same danger exists if the sovereignty of the state be recognized.

The Germans, especially, are prone to this because the government and the state have been closely identified in their experience.

In America we share a great advantage in regard to this subject. With us the government is not the sovereign organization of the state. Back of the government lies the constitution; and back of the constitution the original sovereign state, which ordains the constitution both of government and of liberty. (57)

Since he has referred to his own country as a 'modern national popular state' he obviously means here the state as the political manifestation of the nation or community.

I add this because Burgess is perhaps too optimistic in his identification of sovereignty and liberty. There is probably a better chance of maximizing human liberty in such a state than in any other, but the hard reality, as noted by Hobbes, always remains with us. This is referred to in a later work by Hymen Ezra Cohen. 'When the legal formula is enunciated that "sovereignty resides in the nation and can only reside there", it has a meaning and significance which reaches into and through almost all the relations of man and his government'.[12] Cohen goes on to show how the government is subject to and limited by the will of individuals in a democratic state. These rights flow from the fact that sovereignty is located not in the government but in the nation:

> As against the nation itself, however, the individual stands in a less advantageous position. As against the nation itself, once its will is expressed and determined and certified, the formula recognizes no appeal, for there is no appeal against the supreme power. Resistance against the government there may be – active, defensive, or passive. But against the nation there is no such possibility. Resistance against the constitutionally formulated, legal dictation of the nation can find no legal justification. From the point of view of the state and its jurists, no other way is possible. The state cannot permit itself to be frustrated. Minorities, recalcitrant individuals, cannot obstruct sovereign power, once it expresses itself through legally recognized channels. What limitation there is on the sovereign power, be it the nation or society, is one of extra-legal considerations – expediency, morality, economy – but there is no legally recognized source within the state to which the individual can appeal successfully against the state. There is an appeal to heaven, but it is not lawful.... For a *state* cannot commit or permit suicide; since the act has consequences for the *nation*. (132–33)

This is a position which Cohen presents to the reader but does not, himself, support. He sees it as a defense of the status quo, and only convincing if its logic is not questioned. His thinking is an example of how difficult it is to grasp the essence of sovereignty, without extending it into something it is not. He asks: 'And can we not have, even within the recognition of this fact, a constitutionalism, a liberalism, a respect for the individual and for minorities fully as great as that which the theory of national sovereignty actually achieves?' (134). Of course we can, and do. The nation can take any political form it wants and it can alter that structure if its members and circumstance so decide. Gradual change is not only possible but probably inevitable. However, this does not affect the nature of sovereignty itself, which remains the same throughout. Whether there is a written constitution as with the United States or an unwritten one, as with Great Britain, matters not since sovereignty lies ultimately with the people or nation. Whether the state is a democracy or not is irrelevant. If Scotland wants to

The Nature of Sovereignty

separate from Great Britain or Quebec from Canada, both central governments will be in exactly the same position as was the government of the United States in 1861. They can either recognize the claim for independence as reasonable and let part of the state secede, or they can refuse and retain their sovereignty by force, as did the United States.

15
Sovereignty and Constitutional Rights

A country can have a constitution which its inhabitants regard as a marvellous, even sacred, document but it is of little use if a really serious disagreement arises. Being a democracy does not help; it can actually make the conflict worse. The American Civil War was such a long, destructive bloody affair precisely because both the commitment of the populace to their cause on both sides was so strong. In the south especially, the government was able to count on the willingness of the white population to make almost unlimited sacrifices in the desperate struggle to maintain their way of life. However, democracy alone is, of course, not always the critical factor, since governments have a tendency to act in a similar way in similar situations regardless of the source of their authority. Because of this, the presence or absence of a constitution, bill of rights, or other guarantees of personal liberty has little to do with the nature of sovereignty. There is no doubt that constitutional guarantees are highly desirable, but their existence and effectiveness depend entirely on the attitudes and beliefs of the community and also, to a disheartening extent, on its uniformity. If the population is not homogeneous, then they depend on the toleration of the majority or dominant minority.

War is usually the test. During the Second World War, citizens of Japanese extraction were rounded up and moved to inland camps from the Pacific coast in both the United States and Canada, despite the protection of constitutional guarantees in one case, and that of traditional British liberties in the other. But the US Civil War can, again, be used to illustrate what happens to fundamental law in situations of stress. Even before it began, of course, slavery was recognized in the constitution, so that blacks were already excluded from the 'people' of the United States. With the commencement of hostilities, the constitution itself came under attack. Lincoln

Sovereignty and Constitutional Rights 295

declared a blockade of the Cotton States, which was an act of war, before the meeting of Congress and also exceeded his constitutional powers by enlarging the armed forces. 'Whether legal or not', these actions 'were ventured upon under what appeared to be popular demand and public necessity', he said in his message to congress of July 4, 1861. He was right: Congress was quite prepared to see legality abandoned. As reported by William Archibald Dunning, 'Howe, of Wisconsin, proclaimed in the Senate that he approved it in exact proportion to the extent to which it was a violation of existing law'.[1]

The Confiscation Act was the next challenge. From the beginning the question was whether the southerners were to be treated as belligerents, with all the usual rights recognized by international law, or as traitors. Generally an attempt was made to do either or both as convenient.

> A man's property may be seized by virtue of the war power, but at the same time the man himself may be tried and hung for treason under the regular civil procedure. 'We may treat them [the rebels] as traitors, and we may treat them as enemies', said Senator Trumbull, 'and we have the right of both belligerent and sovereign, so far as they are concerned'. (34)

The Confiscation Act provided for the seizure of property belonging to rebels and the proceeds of its sale to be used for the support of the war effort.

> This act assumed the power in Congress to deprive several millions of persons of all their property, and this by a simple legislative act. By the theory of our constitution, such power must be granted by the organic law, or be inferable from some clearly granted power.

It involved the violation of clauses concerning bills of attainder and due process. The fact of a state of war and the provisions of international law were used as a justification. 'But in the modern practice of civilized nations the general confiscation of enemies' private property is unknown. It is as obsolete as the poisoning of wells in an enemy's country' (31–32). Despite the fact that it violated both the Constitution and international law, it went ahead. 'In the struggle between those who upheld the restraints of the constitution and those who considered only the limits of international law, the government practically escaped all restrictions whatsoever' (36-37).

At least the people concerned here were rebels. More serious was what happened to the civil rights of citizens in loyal states. After Lincoln had suspended the writ of *habeas corpus* in 1861, Chief Justice Taney gave an opinion against his right to do so on his own initiative.

> [However] the impotence of the judiciary as against the executive, and the neglect of congress to take any action in the matter, had left the administration in a position to realize its own idea of its powers. Arrests of disaffected persons and Southern sympathizers under secret orders from Washington had gone on without ceasing, and in no case was the service of the great writ allowed. Not only in Maryland, and the regions near the seat of war, but in the most distant parts of the land, from Maine to California, men were seized without any information as to the charges against them, and were confined in forts and prison camps. (37-38)

Dissatisfaction with the administration of the war led to defeat for the ruling party in the elections of 1862. Congress eventually got to the matter of *habeas corpus* and passed the somewhat ambiguous act of March 3, 1863, more or less authorizing what the President had done. 'To check the torrent of prosecutions for malicious imprisonment that was threatening United States officers everywhere, it was enacted that the order of the President should be a sufficient defence in such action' (42). The President followed with a general suspension of the writ later that year. It was limited to 'aiders and abettors of the enemy' but the wording of this was so broad that 'the boundary line between political opponents to the President and treason became extremely hazy in the eyes of the President's agents'. Trials were usually held before military commissions, which were outside the ordinary courts. 'The whole process of arresting, trying, convicting and executing a man could be carried through without any recourse to the constitutional judiciary, and with no security whatever against the arbitrary will of the military commander' (44). It should be noted, however, that the great majority of those arbitrarily arrested were just as arbitrarily released shortly thereafter, without ever being charged or tried.

The impact of the war on the constitution in general is dealt with at the end of Dunning's chapter on the subject:

> Leaving out of account the dogma of state sovereignty, it had been a matter of faith with most of the people of the United States that the federal constitution embodied a peculiarly effective solution of the problem of liberty *versus* authority. Many rights of the citizen were guaranteed by direct and unequivocal prohibitions upon the government. But in addition to these the eternal tendency of government to encroach upon the individual was held to be counteracted by three principles: first, that no department of the government should exercise any power not delegated to it in the constitution; second, that through the clear separation of the three departments – executive, legislative and judicial – each should act as a restraint upon the others; and third, that the two most aggressive departments, executive and legislative, should be subject to frequent judgement by the people in the elections. (56–57)

When the war began, the prohibitions of the constitution fell by the wayside, the first being those connected with the rights of life and liberty. As for the separation of powers, the judiciary was treated as an 'unconsidered trifle' and military necessity was used as an excuse for placing themselves above the law by the other two branches. 'Hence while Congress was endowed with authority to legislate at its discretion, the President was privileged to disregard all this legislation' (59). However, it was different with the third principle.

> In the practice of war-time the only principle working efficiently in limitation of the government was that of frequent elections. Public opinion, in short, and not the elaborate devices of the constitution, played the decisive role in the United States just as it had played it in earlier centuries and presumably less favoured lands. American chauvinists had boasted long and loudly of the superior stability of the written constitution; a great natural crisis revealed that it was no more secure against the forces of popular passion than the less artificial structures with which it had been so favourably compared. (Ibid.)

Thus, if we use the American Civil War as a test case, and there is no more valid one than a crisis involving the democratic state with the oldest written constitution, our conclusion has to be that a democracy is governed ultimately by public opinion and that no mere document can stand in the way of this powerful force. And, so long as the popular will can express itself formally at regular intervals, it remains a democracy as defined by Hobbes, regardless of whether it has a written constitution or not. If the objection is raised that it is unfair to judge constitutional guarantees in rare and unusual situations such as a war or rebellion, my reply would be that there you have the exact moment at which they must be judged. A bank has sometimes been defined as an organization which loans you an umbrella when the weather is fine and wants it back as soon as rain begins to fall. If a constitution is only a fair weather document then its guarantees are not worth much, as experience has repeatedly demonstrated.

My point is not that constitutions are unimportant. There must be a set of rules on the basis of which a commonwealth functions. Even absolute monarchies require customs governing succession and a legal system of some kind for settling disputes. But constitutionalism, as it is used by critics of Hobbes, is something of a mirage. A written constitution is convenient because it sets down in black and white the rules governing a political community and a bill or charter of rights may serve to enhance the degree of fairness in the day-to-day management of affairs. But the assumption that the power of the sovereign people can be limited in this way, is simply false. Lincoln and others holding power during the civil war were able to act illegally or unconstitutionally, when it seemed necessary, because they knew they had popular support. And that is what counts in the end. As we said earlier, it is the attitudes, beliefs and expectations of the majority of the public which are the key factors. A bill of rights represents the aspirations and the hopes of the people at their best but it is effective only as long as they are prepared to honour it. And to that extent it is of limited value, at least as a legal document. John Austin understood this when, in his discussion of sovereignty in the early nineteenth century, he refused constitutional law the character of true law; he considered it to be essentially ethical in nature. The sovereign, especially if it is the people, cannot allow itself to be hampered, in the last instance, by any restriction, even those self-imposed at an earlier time.

Furthermore, fundamental law, when accepted for what it is

intended to be, can also act as a straitjacket on the popular will. The amending procedure built into the American constitution is such that the thirteen least populous states could block an amendment supported by states representing about twenty-four times their population. This is a highly unlikely event but it is certainly true that strict construction has been used in the past as a means of protecting special interests at the expense of the rest of the people. At the present time, proponents of gun control in the US, a majority of Americans according to polls, seem to be rendered impotent by the Second Amendment, which guarantees the right to keep and bear arms. Written constitutions are usually necessary in the case of federal states and there is much to be said for them but they are not the political panacea they are made out to be, the impenetrable shield which will always protect the rights of individuals, minorities, or even majorities. The only genuine protection is the unwritten bill of rights embodied in the minds and hearts of the members of the political community. To the extent that we are not prepared to extend to others the rights we want for ourselves – the old rule of reciprocity – to that extent we and our fellow citizens are always at risk.

If the above is accepted, then it will tend to confirm Hobbes's claim that sovereignty cannot be limited. I have interpreted this to mean that no limits can be placed on it by means of written constitutions or fundamental laws. In the case of democracies such documents can provide limitations on the actions of governments but if popular support is strong enough such restrictions can always be overridden, especially in a crisis. On the other hand, when guarantees which protect the individual or minority from the majority as represented by the government, are written out and given the kind of authority associated with constitutional law, this may act as a deterrent to rash and unfair acts. Creating a mechanism which provides the possibility of a remedy for the injured party through judicial process can be very useful in advancing the cause of justice. But it must always be remembered that any constitutional guarantee of rights is the result of what is essentially a self-denying ordinance on the part of the sovereign people. Although a constitutional amendment is more difficult to repeal than an ordinary act of the legislature, it is not impossible. In the US, the twenty-first amendment ended prohibition by repealing the eighteenth. There is no way that such changes can be placed beyond the reach of the sovereign.

Even more important is the fact that, like all law, constitutional law is subject to judicial interpretation. Much has been said in favour of a government of laws rather than one of men but the decisive role is always played by men. The Constitution of the United States is, as Charles Evans Hughes put it, 'what the Supreme Court says it is'. Since only a bare majority is necessary, many important decisions have been handed down as the result of a 5–4 vote. Obviously there are strong differences of opinion among the Justices and just as obviously these are due as much to differences of social and economic philosophy as they are to conflicting interpretations of the Constitution and previous decisions. If a President is given the opportunity to fill vacancies, he will naturally choose jurists with an outlook similar to his own, and the court may reflect his predilections for many years after his term is over. The confirmation hearings in Congress make it quite clear that no one is in doubt about the importance for future decisions of whether the candidate is regarded as a liberal or a conservative on key issues.

The power of interpretation has in the past, often run contrary to the clear intention of the law. The most notorious example is that of the fourteenth amendment. After the emancipation of the slaves by the thirteenth amendment, some southern states passed black codes which bore a suspicious resemblance to the earlier slave codes, and indicated a desire to severely restrict the new-found freedom of the blacks. This led the northerners to secure the passage of a constitutional amendment intended to rectify this situation. Section I of the Fourteenth amendment includes the following:

> No State shall make or enforce any law which shall abridge the privileges or immunities of citizens of the United States; nor shall any state deprive any person of life, liberty, or property, without due process of law; nor deny to any person within its jurisdiction the equal protection of the laws.

The first ruling on this amendment was made in the *Slaughterhouse Cases* of 1873 and by a 5–4 decision the Court interpreted this section so narrowly that any protection it might offer to blacks was practically nullified . The Civil War had effectively disposed of state sovereignty but states' rights were still very much alive, and the Court drew back at any suggestion that federal protection be offered to citizens of the states as such. This precedent was used to uphold laws discriminating against blacks and to deny them

Sovereignty and Constitutional Rights

federal protection when attacked by whites. By a supreme irony, however, this same fourteenth amendment, which allowed states alone complete discretion in withholding civil rights from blacks, was, by the 1890s being used to strike down state regulation of big business.

This came about because the rapid industrial growth of the US had produced large corporations, especially railroads, which were able in many areas to practise monopolistic pricing. When state legislatures intervened to shield their citizens, corporation lawyers began to appeal to the Supreme Court by asking that a corporation be treated as a person under the due process section of the Fourteenth Amendment. The Court gradually came around to their way of thinking (some of the new appointees were former corporation lawyers themselves) and finally in 1898, it disallowed a Nebraska statute which set intrastate freight rates, on the grounds that the rates were 'unreasonably' low and represented a deprivation of property without due process of law. Although this appeared to be a reversal of the *Slaughterhouse Cases* decision, there was no relief for the blacks; that same year the Supreme Court ruled that state laws which segregated the races were constitutional. It was not until the 1950s that the tide began to turn with the Warren Court's ruling in *Brown vs. Board of Education* (1954) that school segregation was unconstitutional.

The Court's use of due process in protecting large corporations from government regulation is an interesting example of the continuing influence of ideas from the seventeenth and eighteenth centuries, especially those of John Locke and Adam Smith. Property rights, so emphasized by Locke in the *Two Treatises*, and *laissez-faire*, Smith's contribution in the *Wealth of Nations* combined to form a very powerful ideology which was accepted to some extent by most Americans. However, the ordinary people, especially, also believed strongly in popular sovereignty, and there was always the possibility of conflict between the two. Since the days of Athens, the propertied classes in democracies have always had to live with the fear that the have-nots, being more numerous, could deprive them of their possessions by majority vote. In the case of the US, the founding fathers, most of whom were at least reasonably prosperous, tried to build safeguards into the Constitution. All that is really necessary for a democracy is one elected body in which the majority and its leaders exercise power. The presence of a bicameral legislature, in which the Senators were at the time selected by the state legislatures, a separately elected president, a powerful Supreme Court and a constitution that was difficult to amend, together with the decentralization provided by a federal system all helped to cushion the impact of direct democracy. At the beginning there were also property qualifications for office and the franchise in most states. However, these were gradually swept away and popular sovereignty became more widely accepted during the Jacksonian period. What prevented serious class conflict from arising was the opportunity offered by millions of fertile land acres to the west for any ambitious American to improve his condition in life. It was only when these were occupied and when large-scale industry and huge inequalities of wealth appeared towards the end of the century that class differences became a potential problem.

In the discussion prior to adoption of the Constitution it was widely believed that a bill of rights was not necessary since natural rights were so fundamental that they were obvious to anyone and they were also embedded in English common law. However, there were others who wanted them to be specified, as they were in some state constitutions. It was eventually agreed that a bill of rights would be added after the adoption of the Constitution, in the form of amendments. The danger, of course, was that any rights that were not enumerated might have no status, although an attempt was made to forestall this in Article IX: 'The enumeration in the Constitution, of certain rights, shall not be construed to deny or disparage others retained by the people'. Despite this amendment and despite the fact that the Court relied on vested rights, as natural rights were called, in some of the decisions where specific constitutional authority was lacking, it was obviously preferable to have the support of such authority. One possibility was Article I, Section 10, which prohibited states from, among other things, passing any law impairing the obligation of contracts. This, incidentally, was used in the early twentieth century in striking down laws regulating hours and conditions of labour, etc. Another was the original due process section which appeared in the Fifth amendment and applied to federal rather than state powers. The most famous example of its use prior to the Civil war was the Dred Scott case, in which slaveowners were assured of the secure possession of their property, namely slaves.

However, the due process clause of the Fourteenth amendment which concerned state powers, became the chosen instrument for the protection of vested rights from the late nineteenth century to the end of the 1930s. What was interesting about these interpretations was their lack of historical authority. Due process of law has traditionally had a procedural meaning. It was the protection afforded to the accused in criminal cases, guaranteeing him the right to counsel, to hear the evidence against him, to trial by jury, etc. What the Supreme Court gradually did was to give it a substantive meaning. Before this change took place the right of legislatures to regulate private property in the interests of the public good had rarely been questioned. Now the due process clause was invoked to stop them from doing this if the Supreme Court thought it was an unreasonable interference with vested property rights. The Supreme Court, in substituting its own criteria of reasonableness for those of the legislature, was thus acting as a quasi-legislative body. It was the strong belief in *laissez-faire* held by most of the Justices rather than strictly juristic considerations which lay behind these decisions.

Since the states were unable to do what seemed necessary, the Federal government stepped in with the Interstate Commerce Act of 1887 and the Sherman Anti-trust Act of 1890. The Supreme Court soon emasculated them, using grounds other than the Fourteenth Amendment, with the ludicrous result that important areas of economic policy lay outside the control of either state *or* federal governments. By the Progressive era of the early twentieth century dissatisfaction with the Supreme Court led an attack on the whole concept of judicial review. The arguments are summarized by Kelly and Harbison as follows:

(1) Under the doctrine of the separation of powers, there is no more reason for the judiciary to have the final right of constitutional interpretation than for the President or Congress to exercise the power . . . (2) Most decisions holding laws unconstitutional are not in reality interpretations of the Constitution. Almost never does an act of Congress or of a state legislature violate specifically some provision of the written Constitution. Instead the law is found to violate some precept of social or economic philosophy held by the judges. This practice the Progressives denounced as in effect judicial legislation. (3) Five-to-four decisions on crucial constitutional questions are particularly obnoxious. Laws are not supposed to be declared invalid unless they are unconstitutional beyond a reasonable doubt. (4) Judicial review is an utterly undemocratic method of settling constitutional questions. Its result is that a few men, removed from

popular control, formulate the supreme law. (5) Judges are not fitted to interpret the Constitution in the light of modern social needs. Their training is legal, not economic or social . . . Most judges do not understand modern society, and are incapable of formulating constitutional and legal precepts to meet modern conditions.[2]

However, although nothing came of proposals for reform, the Supreme Court did become more responsive, particularly during the period of Wilson's New Freedom. Then in the business-oriented 1920s, it settled back in its old ways, choosing from whichever of two streams of precedents favoured the welfare of corporations as opposed to that of the workers. When Roosevelt tried to cope with the Great Depression through various legislative initiatives, the Supreme Court began to strike them down. Roosevelt's landslide victory of 1936 and his threat to pack the Court, together with some new appointees, led to a change in the Court's rulings, which eventually restored needed power to the other two branches. Nevertheless, if we turn from matters of social and economic policy to civil liberties, we find the Court's record was less than satisfactory. It heard cases involving the detention and relocation of Japanese-Americans during the Second World War in both 1943 and 1944 and defended the government's action on the grounds of military necessity. To quote Kelly and Harbison again:

> In future wars, no person belonging to a racial, religious, cultural, or political minority can be assured that community prejudice and bigotry will not express itself in a program of suppression justified as 'military necessity', with resulting destruction of his basic rights as a member of a free society. Bills of rights are written in large part to protect society against precisely such a possibility, and insofar as they fail to do so, they lose their meaning. (861)

Furthermore, the Constitution offered no protection to Americans who were victims of character-assassination by the House Un-American Activities Committee and the Senate Permanent Sub-Committee on Investigation under Senator McCarthy. These committees acted like courts, without offering the protection of normal legal proceedings, and could be accused of violating the First Amendment, the guarantee of due process in the Fifth amendment, the Sixth amendment's provision for allowing witnesses counsel, and the Constitution's prohibition of what amounted to bills of attainder. The Supreme Court was of no help at that time as it seemed unwilling to interfere with the congressional power of investigation.

I have explored the American experience at some length because if constitutionalism is going to work anywhere, it has had its best chance in the United States. There was already a centuries' old tradition of local self-government when the colonies achieved their independence and this was reinforced repeatedly as Americans moved westward and set up new communities. The result has been a people imbued with a strong belief in the values of democracy and the rule of law. No more favourable conditions for the successful operation of government based on a written constitution have ever existed. If any weaknesses are apparent in the American example one can, therefore, assume that they are inherent in the system and are not due to other factors such as a lack of political sophistication on the part of the populace.

As we have seen, there are numerous defects in the way the constitution works in the United States. These flow from the fact that it has to be interpreted by fallible human beings. The Supreme Court's decisions have often been so perverse that the logic behind them has baffled even the dissenting Justices. Too often they have been completely opposed to the declared will of the people and have made attempts to deal with pressing social and economic problems excessively difficult. For example, the Court struck down the provision for a federal income tax which was part of the Wilson-Gorman Tariff Act of 1894. Because this was another 5–4 decision, it meant that one Justice delayed the adoption of the income tax until 1913 when it was made constitutional by the Sixteenth Amendment. Furthermore, the system has not worked well at doing what most constitutionalists claim is its *raison d'être*: the protection of the rights of individuals and minorities. Too often the only minority it has defended with any zeal has been the captains of industry. In all fairness, one has to admit that over the long haul, the Court has ultimately been responsive to public opinion and has even run ahead of it at times. However a political system with a written constitution seems, in practice, to offer no obvious advantages over a system without one.

As we have noted before, the moral standards of the populace are the true measure and the only guarantee of whatever degree of liberty and equality is granted to citizens and no mere document can alter this. The striking fact is that the raising of standards in this area cannot usually be legislated; the legislation tends to follow a change in public values rather than vice versa. This change is most often the result of efforts made by those members of the society whose standards are already higher, to influence the country at large, and this is most effectively done by persuasion rather than force. The Supreme Court's decision in 1873 not to interfere on behalf of the blacks reflected the unwillingness of the other states to maintain an army in the south after the failure of radical reconstruction. Furthermore, any ideals generated by the Civil War had begun to fade, aided by the fact that most northerners were just as convinced of black inferiority as were the southerners. It was only when white public opinion began to change after the Second World War that the civil rights movement became effective. In the same way attitudes towards women and sex in general have undergone a peaceful revolution in recent years. Laws are enacted and the constitution reinterpreted, of course, but the pressure for these legal initiatives comes from changing values amongst the people at large, the people whose judgment is final, and whose sovereignty, as always, remains absolute.

Nevertheless, the failure of constitutionalism to alter this is no more willingly recognized than it was in the days of Bodin and Hobbes. Sir William Holdsworth, author of the great seventeen volume *History of English Law* once wrote that Hobbes was the only Englishman in the seventeenth century who really grasped the theory of sovereignty. However, he 'failed to influence his contemporaries, because his theories were detested by statesmen like Clarendon, lawyers like Hale, and of course by all theologians, for the sufficient reason that his political philosophy attacked the practice and theories of all'.[3] Unfortunately, this failure has continued down to the present day. One of the reasons for this is the Lockean doctrine that the primary role of society is to protect the individual's natural rights. Referring to the confusion found in Blackstone's *Commentaries*, Holdsworth says:

> In fact, the division of the sovereign power in England, to which Blackstone, following Montesquieu, was inclined to ascribe much of the excellence of the English constitution, tended in England, or later in America, to prevent the sovereign from acting frequently and regularly. It tended to relegate the theory of

sovereignty to the background, and to put the rights of the subject in the foreground of the picture, because it was for their sake that political society existed. (130)

The discussion above has shown how this worked in the case of the United States, where the courts often deflected the popular will and also often failed to protect the rights supposedly guaranteed by this approach. The Industrial Revolution and accompanying developments in Great Britain made clear earlier there than elsewhere the necessity for a greater degree of legislative intervention than was usual in the past, and when Jeremy Bentham put forward utility as the desirable basis for change, a different attitude towards sovereignty had to be adopted. Bentham's disciple, John Austin, responded by founding what is known as the school of analytical jurisprudence, which emphasized the need for the legislature to exercise the kind of power possessed by Hobbes's sovereign. This led to a revival of interest in Hobbes and eventually to the publication of the Molesworth edition of his collected works in the middle of the nineteenth century. It also paved the way for such pioneering legislation as the Factory Act of 1833, which began the regulation of the working hours of children and the Factory Act of 1847 which limited the working day to ten hours for women and children in the textile industry. Later acts extended such restrictions to other categories of workers. In the United States, by contrast, the Supreme Court struck down a New York Statute providing for a ten-hour day in bakeries in 1905 and, as late as 1922, declared a federal act regulating child labour to be unconstitutional.

Regardless of all this, many people are still reluctant to accept a theory which seems to violate long held beliefs about the limitation of governmental power. Even proponents such as Holdsworth sometimes appear to have reservations, displayed in his case by an approving reference to statesmen 'who refused to become its slaves' (ibid.). He had in mind the policy of the British government when dealing with the American colonies, as opposed to its later enlightened treatment of the self-governing members of the Commonwealth. However, sovereignty was gradually surrendered to the latter voluntarily by the mother country as they undertook the responsibility of their own defence and internal policing. Such was not possible with the American colonies due to divisions amongst them. If they had united first and then negotiated with the British, as Franklin suggested at the Albany Conference of 1754 or Galloway at the First Continental Congress in 1774, something like dominion status might have emerged much earlier. However, the colonies really required the emergency created by war to bring them together and even then they were unwilling to surrender enough power to Congress to make their joint efforts as effective as they might have been. Only bitter experience under the Articles of Confederation taught them that a stronger union was necessary and, as we have seen, it finally took a civil war to make the lesson stick. Thus Britain did not have the same options available in the 1770s that she did later. Her response then had to be the same as Lincoln's was in 1861: to maintain existing sovereignty, by force if necessary.

These various examples have indicated some of the problems raised by the concept of sovereignty and, hopefully, how they can be resolved without having to surrender its essence. Nothing has occurred since the days of Hobbes either in theory or in practical politics to invalidate his analysis, which has been threatened more by confusion and misunderstanding than by convincing argument. The problem is not that the concept is difficult to comprehend in itself; it is that in a peaceful, relatively well-ordered country, it seems somewhat irrelevant to the most pressing concerns of the inhabitants. They feel no urge to contemplate the potentially depressing subject of the immense power available to their governments when it is not being exercised to their detriment. The modern notion of sovereignty, which emerged out of the French Religious Wars of the sixteenth century and the English Civil War of the seventeenth century, is a product of crisis, and it only comes to the fore when the status quo is seriously challenged. Such situations are not new, however. In Matthew 12, 25, one can find the well-known words of Jesus: 'Every kingdom divided against itself is brought to desolation; and every city or house divided against itself shall not stand', and when he adds in verse 30, 'he who is not with me, is against me', he has summed up about all there is to say concerning civil war and its unpleasantness. Even earlier, Odysseus had said, 'Lordship for many is no good thing. Let there be one ruler, one king . . . to watch over his people' (*Iliad*,2.204).

Living in such a time, and with his own ideas about the origins of civil strife, Hobbes put forward his solution: a theory of sovereignty which legitimized the power necessary to maintain the peace, and a theory of morality which provided subjects and citizens with good reason for supporting that authority. Unfortunately, his work was not seen for what it was: an attempt to give ethics and politics a solid scientific foundation. With a few honourable exceptions, commentators have failed to grasp the importance of the golden rule in his moral theory and the impressive logic supporting his theory of sovereignty. I shall leave the last word on this matter to R. G. Collingwood, who wrote in the Preface to his wartime book, *The New Leviathan* (Oxford, 1942), p. iv:

> It is only now, towards the middle of the twentieth century, that men here and there are for the first time becoming able to appreciate Hobbes's *Leviathan* at its true worth, as the world's greatest store of political wisdom. I say this is only now beginning to happen. From the time of its publication, when it impressed every reader with a force directly proportional to his own intelligence as the greatest work of political science the world had ever seen, but pleased nobody because there was no class of readers whose corns it left untrodden upon or whose withers it left unwrung, it fell more and more deeply into disfavour beneath a rising tide of ethical and political sentimentalism. Hardly a single political writer from the seventeenth century to the present day has been able so to clear his mind of that sentimentalism as to look Hobbes in the face and see behind those repellently grim features what manner of man he was; or to see behind the savage irony of his style how deeply he understood himself and his fellow men.

Notes

CHAPTER 1: HUMAN NATURE

1. Alasdair MacIntyre, *A Short History of Ethics* (London, 1966), pp. 135–36.
2. C. B. Macpherson, *The Political Theory of Possessive Individualism: Hobbes to Locke* (Oxford, 1962), p. 37.

CHAPTER 2: THE OF STATE NATURE AND NATURAL LAW

1. Sir John Salmond, *Jurisprudence*, seventh edition (London, 1924), p. 504.
2. A. J. and R. W. Carlyle, *A History of Medieval Political Theory and the West*, 6 vols (London, 1928), I, 35.
3. Francisco Suarez, *Selections from Three Works*, Vol. II. The translation. Classics of International Law. Edited by James Brom Scott (New York and London, 1939).
4. Hugo Grotius, *The Law of War and Peace*. Trans. by Francis W. Kelsey (Oxford and London, 1925).
5. Hugo Grotius, *De Iure Belli ac Pacis Libri Tres* (Carnegie Institute of Washington, 1913), p. 6.
6. This is the translation favoured by Richard Tuck in his *Natural Rights Theories* (Cambridge, 1979). The importance of whether the emphasis is placed on rights or laws can be seen by comparing Tuck's book with another which was published the same year: John Finnis, *Natural Law and Natural Rights* (Oxford, 1979).
7. Alexander Passerin d'Entrèves, *Natural Law: An Introduction to Legal Philosophy*, Second edition (London, 1970), p. 61.
8. It has been pointed out by several commentators that the quotation, which first appears in *Leviticus* 19, 18, is based on an incorrect translation from the Hebrew into the Greek and should be amended to read something like 'as he is like yourself' or 'as he is one of your own.' However, the meaning is similar enough and since the phrase has long been embedded in our discourse, I shall use it in the well-known version.
9. Samuel I. Mintz, *The Hunting of Leviathan* (Cambridge, 1962), pp. 26–27.
10. As quoted in Paul Sigmund, *Natural Law in Political Thought* (Cambridge, Mass., 1971), p. 48.
11. Grotius, *War and Peace*, p. 38.

Notes to pp. 43–91   311

CHAPTER 3: THE LAWS OF NATURE AND MORALITY

1. Howard Warrender, *The Political Philosophy of Hobbes: His Theory of Obligation* (Oxford, 1957).
2. Cicero, *De Officiis/On Duties*, Translated, with an introduction and note by Harry G. Edinger (Indianapolis, 1974), p. 137, n. 28.
3. Frederick Albert Lange, *The History of Materialism and Criticism of its Present Importance*, Trans. E. C. Thomas, Third Edition with an Introduction by Bertrand Russell (London, 1925). First Book, pp. 283–85.

CHAPTER 4: MORALITY AS RECIPROCITY

1. Thomas Nagel, 'Hobbes's Concept of Obligation,' *Phil. Rev.*, LXVIII, 1959, p. 69.
2. H. J. Paton, *The Moral Law. Kant's Groundwork of the Metaphysic of Morals*. (Third edition. London, 1961), p. 97 note.
3. George Bernard Shaw, *Man and Superman*, app., 'Maxims for Revolutionists' in *Collected Works of Bernard Shaw* X, 217 (New York, 1930), p. 217.
4. G. W. Leibniz, *New Essays on Human Understanding*, Tr. and ed. by Peter Remnant and Jonathan Bennett (Cambridge, 1981), pp. 91–2.
5. Alan Gewirth, 'The Golden Rule Rationalized,' *Midwest Studies in Philosophy*, III (1978), p. 134.
6. Henry Sidgwick, *The Methods of Ethics*, 7th edition (London, 1907), p. 380.
7. Hans Kelsen, 'What is Justice?' in *What is Justice? Justice, Law and Politics in the Mirror of Science* (Berkeley, 1957), p. 16.
8. C. D. Broad, 'Reply to My Critics' in *Broad's Critical Essays in Moral Philosophy*, ed. David R. Cheney (London, 1971), p. 313. This article originally appeared in Paul A. Schilpp, ed., *The Philosophy of C. D. Broad* (New York, 1959).
9. Brian Barry, *A Treatise on Social Justice*, Volume I, *Theories of Justice* (Berkeley and Los Angeles, 1989), p. 334.

CHAPTER 5: THE SOCIAL CONTRACT AND THE GOLDEN RULE IN PRACTICE

1. Gregory S. Kavka, *Hobbesian Moral and Political Theory* (Princeton, N.J., 1986), p. 399.
2. Jean Piaget, *The Moral Judgement of the Child* (New York, 1965). This work was first published in French in 1932 and the translation into English by Marjorie Cabain first appeared the following year. This was Piaget's only book on the subject and it was not until the 1960s that Laurence Kohlberg followed up on its ideas in the field

of education. There has been some controversy over the nature of the stages through which a child passes and their number, which is irrelevant here since they are not essential to the argument.

CHAPTER 6: MORALITY AND OBJECTIVITY

1. C. S. Pierce, *Values in a Universe of Chance*, ed. and intro. by Philip R. Wiener (Stanford, 1958), p. 415.
2. A. J. Ayer, *Language, Truth and Logic*, second edition (London, 1948), p. 107.
3. Marcus G. Singer, 'Moral Skepticism' in Curtis L. Carter, ed., *Skepticism and Moral Principles* (Evanston, 1973), p. 78.
4. J. L. Mackie, *Ethics: Inventing Right and Wrong* (Harmondsworth, 1977), p. 15.
5. P. H. Nowell-Smith, *Ethics* (Harmondsworth, 1954), p. 47.
6. G. E. Moore, *Principia Ethica* (Cambridge, 1903), p. 7.
7. T. D. Weldon, *The Vocabulary of Politics* (Harmondsworth, 1953), p. 16.
8. Thomas D. Perry, *Moral Reasoning and Moral Truth* (Oxford, 1976), p. 160.
9. Thomas D. Perry, *Professional Philosophy, What it is and Why it Matters* (Dordrecht, 1986), p. 175.
10. R. M. Hare, *Moral Thinking* (Oxford, 1981), pp. 218 and 227.
11. Mary Warnock, *Ethics Since 1900* (London, 1960), pp. 105–6.
12. G. J. Warnock, *The Object of Morality* (London, 1971), p. 61.

CHAPTER 7: THE NATURE OF HOBBESIAN MORALITY

1. John R. Searle, 'How to derive "Ought" from "is".' *The Philosophical Review*, LXXIII (1964) reprinted together with replies in W. D. Hudson, ed., *The Is–Ought Question* (London, 1969), p. 121.
2. Gregory Kavka, *Hobbesian Moral and Political Theory* (Princeton, 1986), p. 347.
3. John Rawls, *A Theory of Justice* (Cambridge, Mass., 1971).
4. Robert Nozick, *Anarchy, State and Utopia* (New York, 1974).
5. Edmond Cahn, *The Moral Decision* (Bloomington, Ind., 1955), p. 18. In an earlier book, the author discussed the same reaction in terms of injustice: Edmond N. Cahn, *The Sense of Injustice: An Anthropocentric View of Law* (New York and London, 1949).
6. Bernard Williams, *Ethics and the Limits of Philosophy* (London, 1985), p. 198.
7. For a summary of these, see Chapter 2 of Nick Herbert, *Quantum Reality* (New York, 1985), which is entitled, appropriately, 'Physicists Losing Their Grip.'
8. J. W. N. Watkins, *Hobbes's System of Ideas*, 2nd edition (London, 1973), p. 123.

CHAPTER 8: HOBBES AND KANT

1. Tom Sorell, *Hobbes* (London, 1986), pp. 109–10.
2. H. J. Paton, *The Moral Law. Kant's Groundwork of the Metaphysic of Morals*, third edition (London, 1961), p. 57.
3. Emmanuel Kant, *Lectures on Ethics*, tr. L. Infield (London, 1930), p. 54.
4. A. R. C. Duncan, *Practical Reason and Morality* (London, 1957), pp. 162–63.
5. Marcus G. Singer, *Generalization in Ethics* (New York, 1961), pp. 297–98.
6. Emmanuel Kant, *Lectures in Ethics*, tr. L. Infield (London, 1930), p. 42.
7. E. E. Hirst, 'The Categorical Imperative and the Golden Rule,' *Philosophy*, IX, 1939, pp. 328–35.
8. Emmanuel Kant, *The Doctrine of Virtue*, Tr. Mary G. Gregor (New York, 1964), p. 79.
9. *The Educational Theory of Immanuel Kant*, Tr. and ed. by Edward Franklin Buchner (Philadelphia and London, 1904), p. 219.
10. Emmanuel Kant, *Religion within the Limits of Reason Alone*, tr. T. M. Greene and H. H. Hudson (New York, 1960), p. 3.

CHAPTER 9: CONTRACT THEORY TODAY

1. Robert P. Wolff, *The Anatomy of Reason* (New York, 1973), p. 219.
2. Robert P. Wolff, *Understanding Rawls* (Princeton, 1977), p. 16.
3. David P. Gauthier, *Morals by Agreement* (Oxford, 1986).
4. David P. Gauthier, *The Logic of Leviathan* (Oxford, 1969).
5. Alan Ryan, 'Hobbes and Individualism' in *Perspectives on Thomas Hobbes*, ed. G. A. J. Rogers and Alan Ryan (Oxford, 1988), pp. 92–3.
6. T. M. Scanlon, 'Contractualism and Utilitarianism,' in Amartya Sen and Bernard Williams, ed., *Utilitarianism and Beyond* (Cambridge, 1982), p. 110.
7. Lon L. Fuller, *Legal Fictions* (Stanford, 1967), pp. 9–10.

CHAPTER 10: REASON AND MORAL RELATIVITY

1. Alan Gewirth, *Reason and Morality* (Chicago, 1978).
2. Some of them can be found in Alan Gewirth, *Human Rights* (Chicago, 1982). Edward Regis Jr., ed., *Gewirth, Ethical Rationalism* (Chicago, 1984) is a collection of critical essays by other philosophers with Replies by Gewirth.
3. Alan Gewirth, 'The Golden Rule Rationalized,' *Midwest Studies in Philosophy*, Vol. III (Minneapolis, 1980), p. 140. Reprinted in *Human Rights*.

4. 'Replies to my Critics' in Regis, ed., *Gewirth's Ethical Rationalism*, pp. 208-9.
5. 'The "Is-Ought" Problem Resolved' in Gewirth, *Human Rights*, pp. 100-27.
6. 'The Basics and Content of Human Rights, Addendum: Replies to Some Criticisms' in Gewirth, *Human Rights*, pp. 69-70.
7. In Gewirth, *Human Rights*, p. 270.
8. Wesley N. Hohfeld, *Fundamental Legal Conceptions* (New Haven, 1964, originally published 1919).
9. Gewirth, *Human Rights*, p. 14. The first quotation is from H. L. A. Hart, 'Bentham on Legal Rights,' *Oxford Essays in Jurisprudence*, 2d. ser. ed., A. W. B. Simpson (Oxford, 1973), p. 190.
10. William K. Frankena, *Ethics* (Englewood Cliffs, N.J., 1963), p. 18.
11. John Ladd, *The Structure of a Moral Code* (Cambridge, Mass., 1957).
12. William K. Frankena, 'Recent Conceptions of Morality' in Hector-Neri Castaneda and George Nakhuikian, ed., *Morality and the Language of Conduct* (Detroit, 1963), p. 17.
13. Richard Brandt, *Hopi Ethics* (Chicago, 1954).
14. John Stuart Mill, *Utilitarianism*, ed. Oskar Piest (Indianapolis, 1957), p. 22.

CHAPTER 11: CONTRACT AND THE COMMONWEALTH

1. David Hume, *Theory of Politics*, ed. Frederick Watkins (Edinburgh, 1951), p. 194.
2. J. N. Figgis, *Studies of Political Thought from Gerson to Grotius 1414-1625*, second edition (Cambridge, 1916), p. 131.
3. David Hume, *The History of England* (Oxford, 1826), VII, 306.
4. John Locke, *Two Treatises of Government*, ed. Peter Laslett, Second edition (Cambridge, 1967), p. 348.

CHAPTER 13: DEMOCRACY AND THE RIGHT OF REVOLUTION

1. George Lawson, *Politica Sacra et Civilis*, second edition (London, 1689), pp. 24-25.
2. Richard Ashcraft, *Revolutionary Politics and Locke's Two Treatises of Government* (Princeton, N.J., 1986).

CHAPTER 14: THE NATURE OF SOVEREIGNTY

1. Deborah Baumgold, *Hobbes's Political Theory* (Cambridge, 1988), p. 75.
2. Jean Hampton, *Hobbes and the Social Contract Tradition* (Cambridge, 1986), p. 3.

3. W. A. Speck, *Reluctant Revolutionaries: Englishmen in the Revolution of 1688* (Oxford, 1988), pp. 242–43.
4. 'Of the First Principles of Government' in *Hume: Theory of Politics*, ed. Frederick Wilkins (Edinburgh 1951), p. 148.
5. Thomas Hobbes, *Behemoth or The Long Parliament*, second edition (London, 1969), p. 16.
6. 'The Theory of Sovereignty Restated' in *In Defense of Sovereignty*, ed. W. J. Stankiewicz (New York, 1969), p. 235).
7. 'The Uses of Sovereignty', in ibid., p. 85.
8. Alexis de Tocqueville, *Democracy in America* (New York, 1945), I, 179.
9. [Joseph Galloway], *A Candid Examination of the Mutual Claims of Great Britain and the Colonies* (New York, 1775), 59.
10. John C. Calhoun, *Works*, 6 vols (New York, 1851–6) II, 232.
11. John W. Burgess, *Political Science and Comparative Constitutional Law*, 2 vols (Boston, 1890), I, pp. 52–55.
12. Hymen Ezra Cohen, *Recent Theories of Sovereignty* (Chicago, 1937), pp. 232–33.

CHAPTER 15: SOVEREIGNTY AND CONSTITUTIONAL RIGHTS

1. William Archibald Dunning, *Essays on the Civil War and Reconstruction* (New York, 1965. Originally published 1897), p. 18.
2. Alfred H. Kelly and Winfred B. Harbison, *The American Constitution* (revised edition, New York, 1955), pp. 623–24.
3. Sir William Holdsworth, *Some Lessons from our Legal History* (New York, 1928), p. 127.

Index

abortion, 102–4, 200
absurdity, 50, 70, 142
aesthetics, 113–15
agency, rational, 166, 186, 188
agreement, 52, 58, 85–6, 88–90, 94, 97, 99, 117, 122–3, 127–8, 140, 166, 174–5, 205, 206
Albany Conference, 308
altruism, 75, 138, 143, 164, 194–6
American Revolution, 31, 224, 269
Americans, 213, 286
anarchy, 51, 86, 206, 216, 251
Anglicans (Church of England), 270, 280
animals, 200, 207
anthropology, 77, 110, 120, 128
appetite, 5, 9, 13
Archimedean point, 134
Aristides the Just, 233
aristocracy, 181, 183, 208, 227, 247, 250
  of orators, 233, 249, 284
Aristotle, 4, 64, 125, 236
Articles of Confederation, 308
Ashcraft, Richard, 267
assault, 82, 127
Athens, 212, 233, 301
Aubrey, John, 6
Austen, Jane, 17
Austin, John, 298, 307
authorization, 206, 237, 243
autonomy, 93, 109, 118, 154
aversion, 5, 63
Ayer, A. J., 99, 110
Azo, 78

Bambrough, Renford, 101, 104
Barry, Brian, 83, 84
Baumgold, Deborah, 272–3
behaviourism, 3
beliefs, moral, 102, 116–17, 198, 203
benevolence, 74, 82, 114, 115, 195
Benn, S. I., 284

Bentham, Jeremy, 187, 307
Berkeley, George, 2, 221
Bible, 34, 44, 77
birth, 200, 201
Blacks, 79, 294
Blackstone, Sir William, 306
Bodin, Jean, 234, 286
Bracton, Henry de, 31
Bramhall, John, 8, 274
Brandt, Richard, 196
British Empire and Commonwealth, 288, 307
Broad, C. D., 83
Brown vs Board of Education, 301
bureaucracy, 282, 285
Burgess, John W., 289–91
Butler, Joseph, 6

Cahn, Edmond, 127
Calhoun, John C., 287
Canada, 293, 294
Capet, Hugh, Count of Paris, 211
Carlyle, A. J., 26
categorical imperative, 81, 130, 145, 150–5, 162, 165, 192, 203
Catherine de Medicis, 230
Catholicism, 270, 280
certainty, 103, 131
Charles I, King, 240, 259, 268
Charles II, King, 283
cheating, 96, 97, 127
China, 209, 286
Christianity, 34, 162, 220
Cicero, 25–7, 30, 39, 59, 236
citizens, 68, 117, 177
Civil War,
  American, 287, 289, 294, 298, 306, 308
  English, 1, 55, 229
claim-right, 188, 190, 191
Clarendon, Earl of, 274
coercion, 54, 56, 58, 95, 178, 206
Cohen, Hymen Ezra, 291–2

Index 317

Collingwood, R. G., 309
command, 71, 93, 95, 149, 151, 160
commitment, 70, 87, 89, 105, 119, 121, 134, 140, 165, 169, 171, 216
commonwealth, 13, 15, 21, 23, 53–5, 58, 67, 85–6, 178, 207, 211, 226, 236
Communism, 170
community, 58, 74, 85, 88, 176, 201, 255–6, 264–5, 278
comparison, 6, 52, 149, 166
competition, 19, 90, 180, 207
Confiscation Act, The, 295
conformity, 97, 255
Confucius, 77
Congress, The U.S., 284, 295–7
conquest, 209, 220
conscience, 63, 72, 160, 183
consequences, 95, 114, 150, 168
consent, 38, 87, 289, 208, 210–14, 220, 223
constitution, 32, 213, 286, 292, 294, 298–9
Constitution (U.S.), 284, 295–305
Continental Congress, First, 308
contraception, 116–17
contract, 15, 52, 55, 70–1, 88, 90, 134, 182, 189, 214, 217, 225–6
   social, 67, 85, 88, 97, 125–6, 129, 176–7, 200, 206, 210, 215
contractualism, 165–6, 172–3, 174–5, 199
contradiction, 50, 70, 153, 154, 158, 188, 192
Contrat Social, Du, 221
conventions, 176
cooperation, 68, 93, 95, 98
Corpus Iuris, Civilis, 26
covenant (pact), 51–60, 70–1, 85–7, 90, 95–6, 122, 125, 128, 140, 169, 239
crime, 83, 102, 105, 140, 177
Critique of Pure Reason, 145
Croatians, 261
crocodile (leviathan), 46–7
Cromwell, Oliver, 210, 216, 232, 270, 280

death, 14, 25, 104, 135, 136, 137, 200

debt, 119–21, 142
De Cive, 1, 18–20, 22, 38, 43, 61, 67, 75–6, 201–2, 206, 210, 213–14, 217–18, 227, 229, 233, 251, 258, 272–3
Declaration of Independence, 221
De Corpore, 1, 2, 21, 201
De Corpore Politico, 2
'definist' fallacy, 111
definitions, 133, 228
De Homine, 1, 4, 6, 10, 52
De Legibus, Ac Deo, Legislatore, 29
deliberation, 8–9
democracy, 179, 208, 213, 227, 232–4, 246–56, 277, 284, 301
Democritus, 2
deontology, 198
Descartes, René, 2
descriptivism, 110
determinism, 8
deterrence, 192, 243
dictator, 210
Digest, 26, 27
dilemmas, moral, 105, 183, 195
disapproval, 128, 195
disarmament, unilateral, 48, 49
discourse, 10, 97, 133, 192
Doctrine of Virtue, 158, 160, 162
dominion, despotical, 208–9
doubt, 10, 133
Dred Scott case, 302
drive, 69, 137
drunkenness, 157, 159
due process, 301–3, 304
duelling, 13
Duncan, A. R. C., 152
Dunning, William Archibald, 295
duty, 115, 130, 145, 147–9, 156–61, 163, 165

education, need for, 241
egoism, 72, 75, 143, 188, 194–7
elections, 247, 251
Elements of Law, The, 2, 5, 7, 8, 11, 33, 38, 41, 43, 52–3, 67, 75–6, 180, 206, 208–9, 246, 252, 257
emotivism, 99, 110, 111, 129
empathy, 76, 143, 193
empirical, 103, 109, 110

empiricism, 2, 100
ends, 154–5, 162, 165
England, 58, 234–5, 248, 279
Epicurean, 59, 60
Epicurus, 196
equality, 18, 37, 127, 262
equity, 62, 63, 97, 127, 170
ethics, 16, 34, 82–3, 98, 112–14, 129–30, 155, 179
Ethics Demonstrated, 202
euphemisms, 112
Existentialism, 105

Factory Acts, 307
fairness, 97, 125–8, 134
fear, 15, 18, 19, 54, 139, 235, 238
Federalist, The, 286
fiction, 125–6, 208, 216, 219, 249
Figgis, J. N., 221
Filmer, Sir Robert, 209, 222, 274
foetus, 102, 103, 200
fool, the, 56, 57, 59–61, 71, 85, 86, 143
Fortescue, Sir John, 31
France, 58, 282
Frankena, William, 194
Franklin, Benjamin, 308
Frazer, Sir James, 135–6, 139
free will, 8, 235
freedom, 29, 33, 68, 70, 119, 134, 154, 157, 235
French Religious Wars, 222, 231, 234
French Revolution, 31, 181, 221, 268, 282
Fuller, Lon F., 175

Gaius, 26
Galileo, 21
Galloway, Joseph, 308
game, 15, 69, 90–3, 96, 116–17, 121, 171, 213
gang, ghetto, 87, 88
Gauthier, David, 84, 171
geometry, 16, 202
George III, King, 221
Gewirth, Alan, 80, 185–92
Glaucon, 59
Glorious Revolution, 222, 265, 280

God, 27, 34, 36, 40–7, 64, 66, 71, 147, 150, 160, 161, 163, 196, 235
Golden Bough, The, 135
golden mean, 64
golden rule, 6, 49, 62, 69, 75–8, 80–5, 88, 115, 122, 124–5, 129, 140, 143, 156, 164, 172, 174, 177–9, 182, 184–5, 191–3, 199, 203
  negative form of, 78–9, 82–3, 115, 122, 167
good (and evil), 4–5, 7, 12, 17, 45, 63, 73, 105–6, 108, 111, 113–14, 118, 135
Gratian, 37
gratitude, 212
Great Britain, 292–3
Great Depression, 304
Greece, 268
Grotius, Hugo, 24, 29–31, 37, 38, 39, 41, 44, 68
Groundwork of the Metaphysic of Morals, 144, 148, 150, 155, 156, 160, 161, 165
group, 58, 88, 90, 91, 182
Gyges, ring of, 59, 143

habeus corpus, writ of, 296
Hampton, Jean, 273–4, 276
happiness, 138, 147, 149, 156–7, 161–2
Hapsburgs, 231, 261
Hare, R. M., 83, 104, 110
harm, 118, 123, 135
hedonism, ethical, 138
Hegel, G. W. F., 287
Henry II, King (of France), 230
Henry VIII, King, 45
heteronomy, 93
Hillel, Rabbi, 77
hippopotamus, (behemoth), 46
Hirst, E. E., 156
History of England, 221
History of English Law, 306
Hitler, Adolf, 261, 277
Hobbes, Thomas, comments on, by Brian Barry, 83
  by Deborah Baumgold, 272
  by R. G. Collingwood, 309

by Alan Gewirth, 189
by Jean Hampton, 273–4, 276
by Sir William Holdsworth, 306–7
by David Hume, 221
by Gregory Kavka, 122
by John Ladd, 196
by F. A. Lange, 65
by Alastair MacIntyre, 6
by C. B. MacPherson, 13
by Samuel Mintz, 35–6, 40
by Thomas Nagel, 72
by Tom Sorell, 144
Hohfeld, Wesley, 189, 190
Holdsworth, Sir William 306
Holy Roman Empire, 231
holy will, 151, 160
Homer, 13
homosexuality, 37, 107, 158
Hood, F. C., 64
hostility, 243, 260
House of Commons, 224
House of Lords, 224
House of Representatives, 254, 304
Hughes, Chief Justice Charles Evans, 300
human nature, 1, 2, 16, 70, 102–3, 157–8
Human Nature, 2, 67
Hume, David, 2, 101, 104, 176, 209, 219–22, 224, 225, 281
Hume's Law, 108, 126
Hungarians, 261
hypothetical imperative, 151

Iliad, 308
impersonality, 144, 178
inclinations, 146, 149, 160, 163, 164
individualism, 17, 68
Industrial Revolution, 307
in foro interno or *externo*, 63, 72, 177, 192
iniquity, 129
instinct, 87, 140
Institutes, 26
institution, 120, 126, 178
intentions, 76, 95
interests, 169, 188
Interstate Commerce Act, 303

inter-subjectivity, 106
intuition, 106, 107, 113
intuitionism, 107, 108
is-ought problem, 120, 126, 130, 187
Italy, 222, 268
ius (jus), 25, 27–9, 69
ius gentium, 26, 29, 37, 38
ius naturale, 24, 26, 28, 32, 41, 140

James II, King, 232, 234, 280
James, William, 104
Japanese-Americans, 294, 304
Japanese-Canadians, 304
Jews, 49, 79, 102, 118, 177
Job, 46–7
John, King, 210
jurisprudence, 28, 36, 175
justice and injustice, 23, 56–7, 61, 71, 85–6, 96, 112, 115, 124–5, 127, 129, 203
Justinian, 26

Kant, Emmanuel, 76, 77, 78, 80, 81, 130, 135, 144–68, 196, 197, 203
Kavka, Gregory, 86, 87, 122
Kelsen, Hans, 81
killing, 37, 105, 132, 153
King and Parliament, 210, 225, 229
knowledge, 103, 106, 107, 131
    moral, 207, 130–1, 133

Ladd, John, 194–97
Lange, F. A., 65
law, 42, 43, 45, 53, 72–3, 97, 102, 116, 130, 151–2, 178, 235, 242
    civil, 28
    divine, 36, 38, 43
    international, 27, 296
    natural, 18, 27, 35–7, 40, 43–3, 50, 54, 63, 102, 187, 244
    Roman, 25
Law(s) of Nature, Hobbes's, 24, 31, 36, 39, 41, 48–9, 53, 55, 62–4, 66, 72–3, 75, 94, 125, 154, 169–70
Law of War and Peace, The, 29
Lawson, George, 265–7, 269
Lebanon, 286

Lectures on Ethics, 155, 156, 160, 161, 163, 167
legal system, 68, 80
Leibniz, G. W., 78
Lenin, Vladimir, 282
Leviathan, viii, 2–4, 15, 19, 22, 24, 38, 48, 54, 67, 71, 75–6, 99, 112, 114, 125, 133, 170, 181, 189, 193, 205, 208–10, 214, 216, 226, 227, 235, 240, 248, 256, 270, 274, 281, 284
lex, 25, 27, 28, 30, 44
lex naturalis, 24, 27–9
Lex Regia, 217
liberty, 55, 69, 76, 85, 235–6
liberty, blameless, 33, 34, 41, 47
liberty-right, 33, 190
Lieber, Francis W., 287
Lincoln, Abraham, 287–9, 295–308
loan, 119, 127, 158, 165, 190
Locke, John, 2, 24, 55, 68, 207, 209, 219–23, 263–5, 267–70, 274, 277–8, 301
logic, 50, 90, 99, 111, 121, 193
Louis XIII, King, 282
Louis XIV, King, 255, 281–2
Louis XVI, King, 259, 281–2
Loyalists, American, 287–8
Luke, 156, 157
Luther, Martin, 138
lying, 150, 152, 159

Machiavelli, Nicolo, 245
MacIntyre, Alasdair, 6
Mackie, J. L., 100, 104, 105, 107, 108, 199, 200, 202
Macpherson, C. B., 13
Madison, James, 286
Magna Carta, 210
Mahabharata, 77
majority, 183, 208
Manual of Political Ethics, 287
marriage, 89, 159
martyrdom, 136–7
masturbation, 158, 159, 163
materialism, 2, 3, 196
Matthew, 77, 78, 156, 308
maxim, 151–3
'maximin' rule, 174

Mazarin, Cardinal, 282
membership, 88, 200
Metaphysic of Morals, 254, 258, 160, 161, 162, 196
Metaphysical Elements of Justice, The, 196
Mill, John Stuart, 199
ministers, public, 284–5
minorities, 182
Mintz, Samuel, 35–7, 40, 41, 42
miscarriage, 200
monarch, 45, 60, 135
monarchomach, 223, 270
monarchy, 208, 210, 227, 229–30, 251
Monmouth, Duke of, 267, 280
Montesquieu, Baron de, 235
Moore, G. E., 106, 108, 113, 114, 115
moral code, 79, 194
Moral Judgment of the Child, The, 91
Moral Scepticism and Moral Knowledge, 101
moral system, 80, 142
moral worth, 146–8, 150, 163
morality, 1, 11, 14, 27, 39, 50, 55, 60, 64, 67, 69, 70–4, 89, 93–4, 97, 99, 105, 112, 114–16, 156, 160–5, 183–4, 188, 194, 200
Morals by Agreement, 171
Moses, 36
motivation, 19, 47–8, 51, 58, 61–3, 74, 137, 139, 141, 145, 150, 161, 163, 188, 218
murder, 25, 82, 101–5, 110, 126, 132, 179, 188, 200
mushrooms, 21
Mussolini, Benito, 268

Nagel, Thomas, 72
Napoleon I, Emperor, 277
Napoleon III, Emperor, 277
nationalism, 261–2
natural and unnatural, 117, 158, 159
naturalism, 108–9
naturalistic fallacy, 108, 113, 130
Navaho Indians, 194–7
New Leviathan, The, 309
Nicholas II, Tsar, 259, 280
non-cognitivism, 99, 108

Index 321

Nowell-Smith, P. H., 103, 104, 106, 110
Nozick, Robert, 123, 169

Oakeshott, Michael, 36, 48
objectivism, moral, 103, 104
objectivity, 101, 106, 109
obligation, moral, 21, 23, 34, 36, 48, 51–4, 57, 63, 70, 72, 80, 89, 90, 115, 119–22, 126, 128, 130, 134, 140, 145, 158–9, 165, 190, 216–17, 236, 239, 251
rational, 268, 188–9
Ockham, William of, 36, 45
oligarchy, 208, 221
'open-question' argument, 108
'original position', 169, 181
ought judgments, 108, 121–2, 126, 147, 187–8
ovum, 117, 200, 201

Pädagogik, 159
pain, 173, 175, 178
Parlement of Paris, 281
Parliament, 210, 225, 229, 232, 234–5, 240, 245, 263, 266
Passerin d'Entrèves, Alexander, 31–2
passions, 4, 9, 12
paternal dominion, 208–9
Paton, H. J., 145, 153
Patriarcha, 209
peace, 48, 49, 55, 63, 69, 128, 135, 140, 167
Peloponnesian Wars, 233
people, the, 93, 214, 217, 241, 248, 252–3, 255, 258, 266–7, 284
'perceptibility fallacy', 100
Perry, Thomas D., 108–10
Philosophical Rudiments concerning Government and Society (De Cive), 2
philosophy
  moral, 63–4, 125
  Western, 193, 195–6
Piaget, Jean, 91–99, 121
Pierce, C. S., 99
Plato, 57, 59, 106, 142

pleasure, 2, 5, 73, 83–4, 108, 113, 114, 135, 138, 159
policy, public or social, 200, 203
Politica Sacra et Civilis, 265
Poor Law, 120
power, 12, 55, 64, 124, 128, 180, 235, 248, 254, 278
prescriptivism, 99, 100, 129
President of U.S., 254, 282–4
Principle of Generic Consistency (PGC), 185, 190, 192
principle, supreme moral, 154, 203
procreation, 117
prohibitions, 25, 79, 93, 115
promising, 71, 119, 120, 152–4
property, 55, 86, 170
prudence, 11, 48–50, 55, 57, 59–62, 70–3, 75, 141, 144, 151, 187–8, 193–4, 197
punishment, 56, 62, 66, 71–2, 95–6, 124, 127–8, 183, 243–4
Pufendorf, Samuel, 29
public opinion, 59, 67, 128, 244, 298

Quebec, 293

rape, 159
rationality, 47, 96, 98, 121, 135
Rawls, John, 123, 168–71, 174, 181, 202
reason, 9, 10, 39, 44, 49, 57, 98, 101, 135, 176
Reason and Morality, 185–7, 189–91
rebellion, 57, 60, 238, 258
reciprocity, 49, 50, 77, 80, 84, 89, 94–6, 117, 122–3, 125, 134, 167, 174, 178, 299
Rees, W. J., 284
Reformation, 234
relativism, 81, 130, 198
Republic, 57, 59
reputation, 19, 70, 119
respect, 95, 97, 98, 193
retaliation, 122, 123, 193
revolution, 256–9, 269
reward, 147, 149, 150, 160
Richard II, King, 269
Richelieu, Cardinal, 282–3
right and wrong, 16, 23, 44, 78, 83,

86, 93, 107, 110, 112, 116–17, 132, 142, 159
right(s), 14, 22, 28–9, 31, 33, 48, 50–2, 67, 69, 86, 89, 186–8, 190
  of man, 31
  of private judgment, 234, 274
  of revolution, 257
  of self-defence, 52, 140, 240, 260
Right of Nature, Hobbes's, 24, 32, 48, 52, 177
rigorism, 148, 150
Robinson Crusoe, 21
Roman republic, 233
Roosevelt, Franklin D., 304
Ross, Sir David, 130
Rousseau, Jean-Jacques, 68, 165, 207, 221, 248, 255
rules, 43, 68–9, 77, 86, 91–4, 112, 115–17, 121–2, 126, 128, 134, 142, 161, 165, 174, 177, 181, 183, 213
Russell, Bertrand, 104
Russian Revolutions, 280
Ryan, Alan, 172
Rye House Plot, 267

St Ambrose, 27
St Augustine, 27, 37, 78
St Paul, 27
St Thomas Aquinas, 27, 34, 36, 37
Salmond, Sir John, 25
Samaritan, Good, 166, 167
sanctions, 72, 128
Sartre, Jean-Paul, 105
Scanlon, T. M., 172–5
scepticism, 2, 60, 196, 202, 203
  moral, 100–12, 116, 130–1
science, 101, 103, 131, 133, 204
Scotland, 292
Searle, John, 120
security, 69, 75, 87, 128
self, 83, 143, 149, 163
self-denial, 74, 157, 196
self-interest, 36, 51, 56, 60, 72–3, 75, 83, 89, 138, 142, 144–5, 149, 153–4, 172, 194, 217–18, 239
self-love, 34, 71, 157, 164
self-preservation, 15, 33–4, 42, 51, 60, 69, 70, 73, 91,
122, 135, 137–40, 168, 176, 274
self-regarding, 143, 163
self-sacrifice, 16, 74
selfishness, 74, 84, 141
selflessness, 75, 83, 123, 149, 164, 183
Senate, U.S., 254
Senate Permanent Sub-Committee on Investigation, 304
sex, 117, 158, 159
Shaftesbury, First Earl of, 268
shame, 162
Shaw, George Bernard, 77
Sherman Anti-Trust Act, 303
Sidgwick, Henry, 80, 202
Singer, M. G., 100, 152
Six Lessons to the Professors of Mathematics, 201
Six Livres de la République, 234
signs, 51, 70, 88
Slaughterhouse Cases, 300, 301
slavery, 26, 37, 79, 104, 179, 180, 182, 209, 248
Smith, Adam, 175, 301
societies, 67, 68, 102
society, 81, 85, 86, 167, 181–2
Socrates, 129, 212, 222, 233
solidarity, 96–7
Sorell, Tom, 144
sovereign, 20, 45, 71–2, 212, 216, 218–19, 228, 238, 247, 279
sovereignty, 55, 216–17, 227, 240, 255, 263, 275, 273, 278, 283–93
Spain, 261
Spartans, 246
Speck, W. A., 280
sperm, 117
Spinoza, Benedict, 196
Stalin, Joseph, 261
standards, valuation by, 115–16
state of nature, 19–23, 48–51, 53–4, 58, 68, 70, 72, 86–7, 94, 106, 122–4, 140, 169, 184, 251
  hypothetical, 20–1, 53, 55, 72, 85–7, 141
state(s), 23, 53, 67–8, 85–6, 91, 123–4, 171, 177, 206, 219, 247
states (U.S.), 284, 287

statements, 108, 110, 114, 116, 132
status, 180
Stevenson, C. L., 111
Stuarts, 223, 279
Suarez, Francisco, 28–9, 36, 45
subjectivism, 99, 103, 107, 116, 130
subjects, 68, 217
submission, 217, 236, 274
succession, problem of, 229
suicide, 24, 136, 137, 139, 157
Summa Theologica, 27, 34
summum bonum, 14, 115
supererogation, 166
Supreme Court, U.S., 213, 254, 284, 300–7
survival, 33–4, 47, 51–2, 57, 69, 73, 91, 123, 137–8, 141
sympathy, 195, 196

Taney, Chief Justice Roger B., 296
taxes, 55
teleology, 162, 163, 198
Ten Commandments, 36, 45
Terror, the, 260
terrorism, 183
Texas, 287
Thales, 77
theft, 37, 82, 116
Themistocles, 233
theorems, 42–3
Theory of Justice, A, 169, 170
Third World, 82, 112
Thomasius, Christian, 29
Thrasymachus, 57
Thucydides, 233
Tocqueville, Alexis de, 286, 288
tolerance, 81, 82
torture, 118, 178
totalitarianism, 124, 260
Tory, 222
Toulmin, Stephen, 110
Treatise of Human Nature, 101
Treatise on Laws and God the Lawgiver, 28
tribes, 58, 184
truth, 111, 131
Tryphoninus, 26
Two Treatises of Government, 209, 264, 301

Tyler, Wat, 269
tyranny, 104, 268–9

Ulpian, 26, 28
Un-American Activities Committee, 304
unanimity requirement, 208
unborn, 200
understanding, an, 90, 120
United Provinces, 231, 242
United States of America, 247, 254, 283, 286, 288, 292–3, 305
universality, 102, 144, 177
universalization, principle of, 151–3, 191
usury, 37
utilitarianism, 108, 113, 114, 145, 198, 203
utility, 171, 220
utterances, 110, 120

values, moral, 102, 135, 145
Viet Nam, 282
Vindiciae Contra Tyrannos, 223
virtue and vice, 11, 61, 63, 74, 101, 113, 125
voluntarism, 36, 45
voting, 247, 249

war, 48, 49, 126, 128, 177, 182
 state of, 18, 22, 33, 57, 72
Warnock, G. J., 116, 117, 121
Warnock, Mary, 111
Warrender, Howard, 36, 43, 64, 71
Washington, George,
Watkins, J. W. N., 135–7, 139
Wealth of Nations, The, 301
Weldon, T. D., 107
welfare, 170, 193
Whig, 222, 223
Whiskey Rebellion, 224
William the Conqueror, 262
William III, King, 232, 265
Williams, Bernard, 129–32, 134
Wilson, Woodrow, 304
Wilson-Gorman Tariff Act, 305
Wittgenstein, Ludwig, 110
Wolff, J. C., 29
Wolff, Robert P., 165–6, 168, 171

women, 104, 201
words, 51, 53, 70, 72, 88, 89, 119, 120
world views, 204
World War
  First, 261, 281
  Second, 105, 294, 304
wrong, 125, 126, 133, 174
  sense of, 128
wrongfulness, 111, 118, 125, 129

Zoroastrians, 77